Love Me,
Love Me Not

5

IO SAKISAKA

Contents

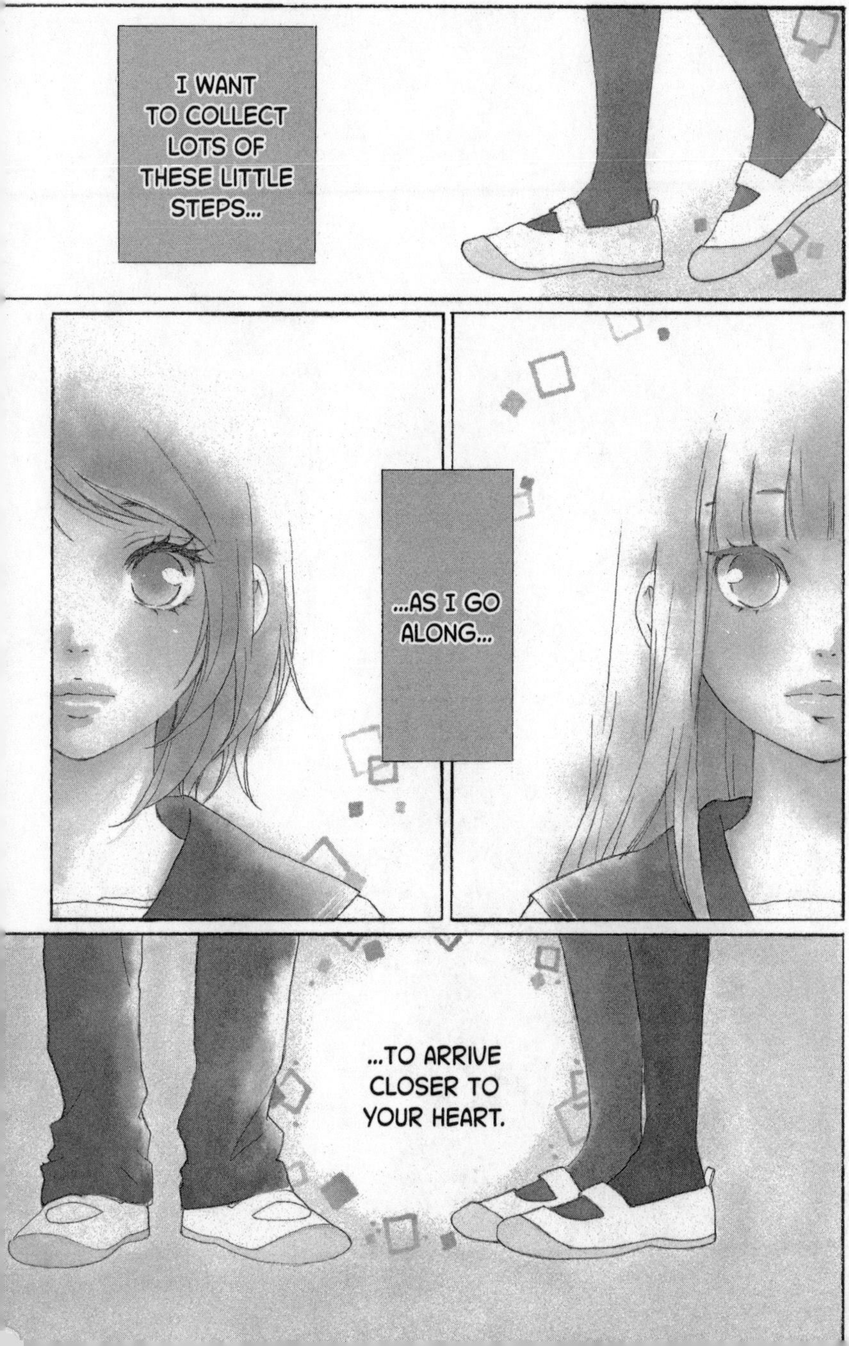
I WANT TO COLLECT LOTS OF THESE LITTLE STEPS...
...AS I GO ALONG...
...TO ARRIVE CLOSER TO YOUR HEART.

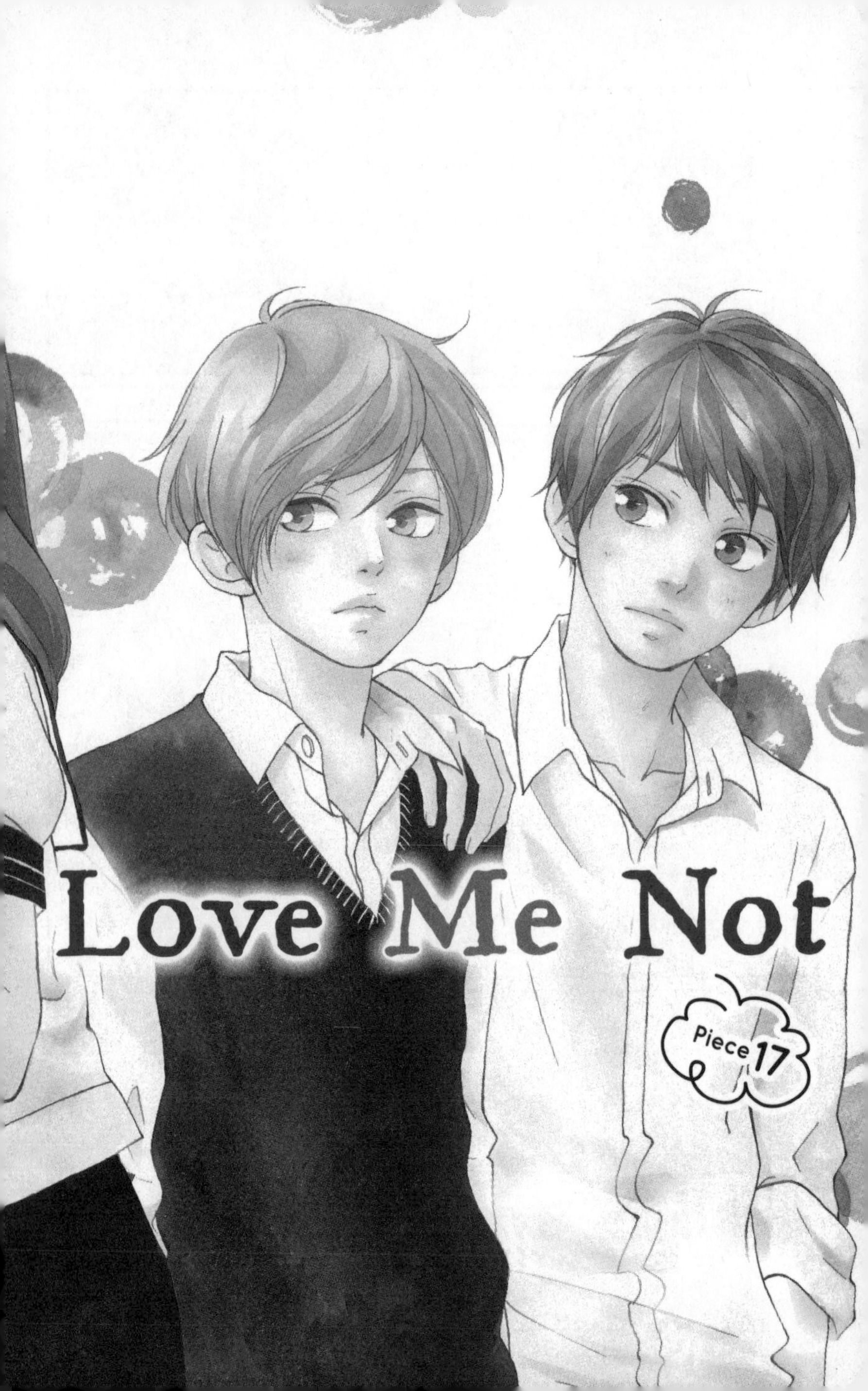
Love Me Not
Piece 17

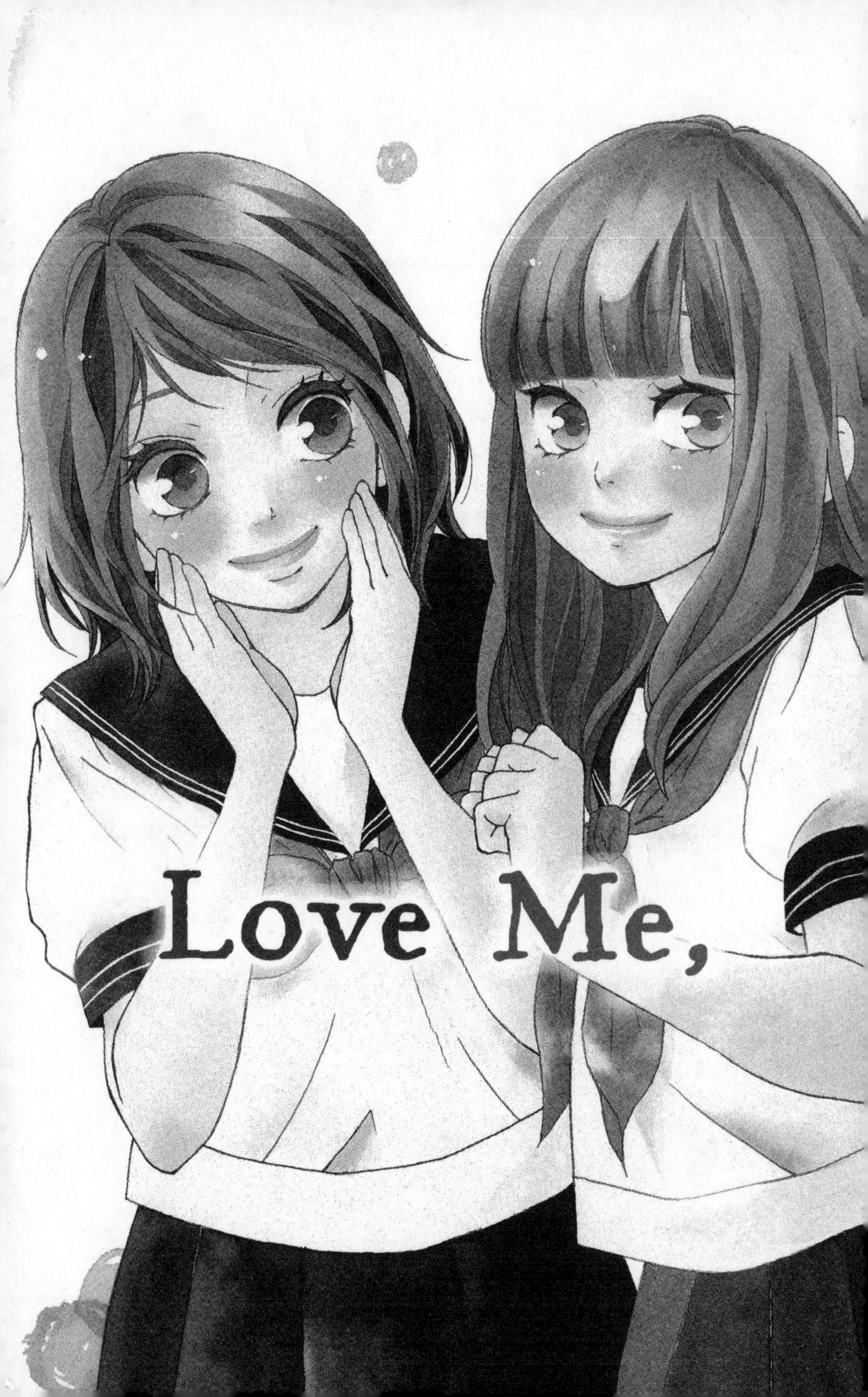
Love Me,

GREETINGS

Hello. I'm Io Sakisaka. Thank you very much for picking up
volume 5 of *Love Me, Love Me Not*.

Starting with this volume, I've changed up the cover
illustrations a little. It used to be two people on the cover,
but the pairs that were left didn't seem to have that much to
do with the story, so I decided to start using a single character
instead. (In all honesty, I did think of doing a Rio and Kazuomi
cover, but it didn't turn out very well, so I scrapped it...) (*laugh*)

Yuna is the first of our one-character covers. ⇒KLAP KLAP KLAP⇐
I tried to achieve a greater contrast with the pen strokes. I tried
changing the paper. Then I messed up and had to start all over...
I enjoy the feeling of doing something new.

I would be so happy if everyone likes this cover too. Of course I'm
wishing that you'll enjoy the actual volume much more.
I hope you'll read through to the end of volume 5!

Io Sakisaka

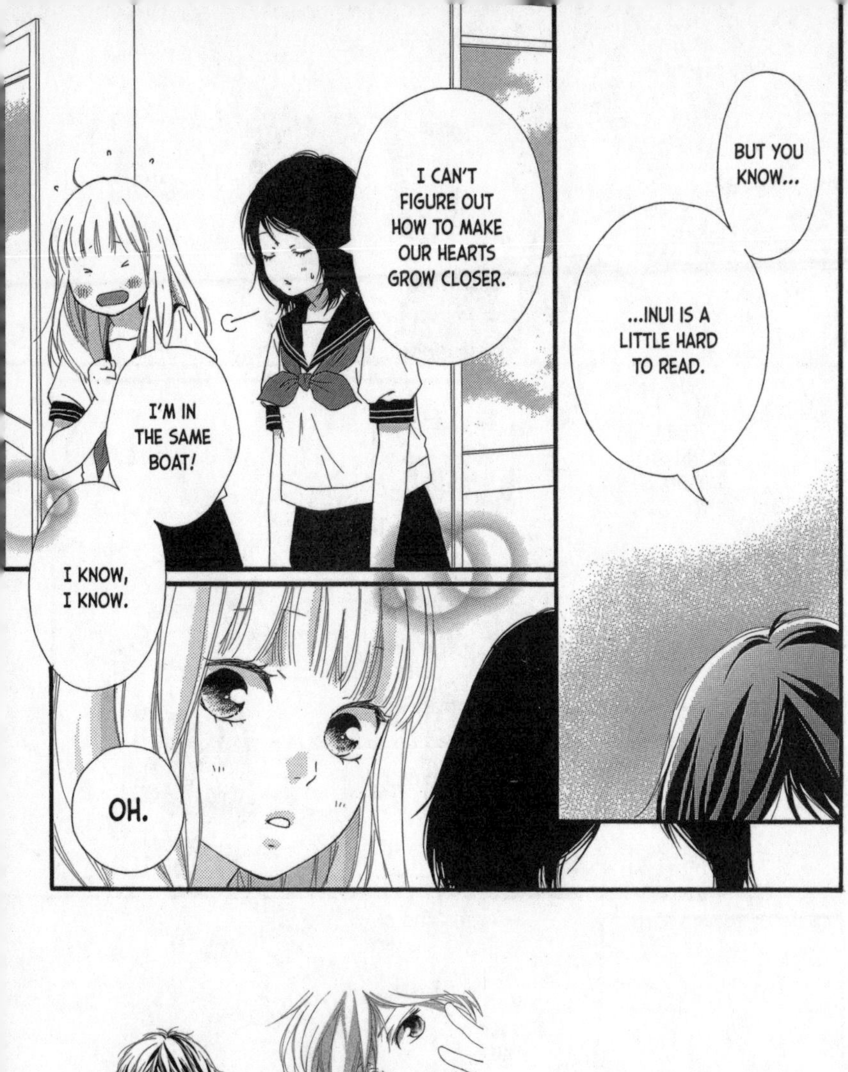
BUT YOU KNOW...
...INUI IS A LITTLE HARD TO READ.
I CAN'T FIGURE OUT HOW TO MAKE OUR HEARTS GROW CLOSER.
I'M IN THE SAME BOAT!
I KNOW, I KNOW.
OH.

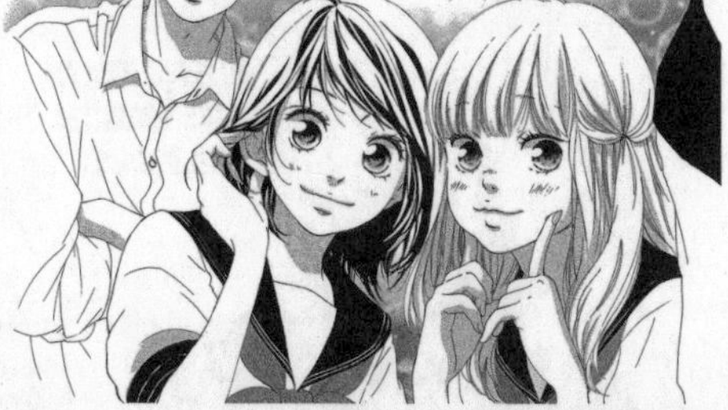

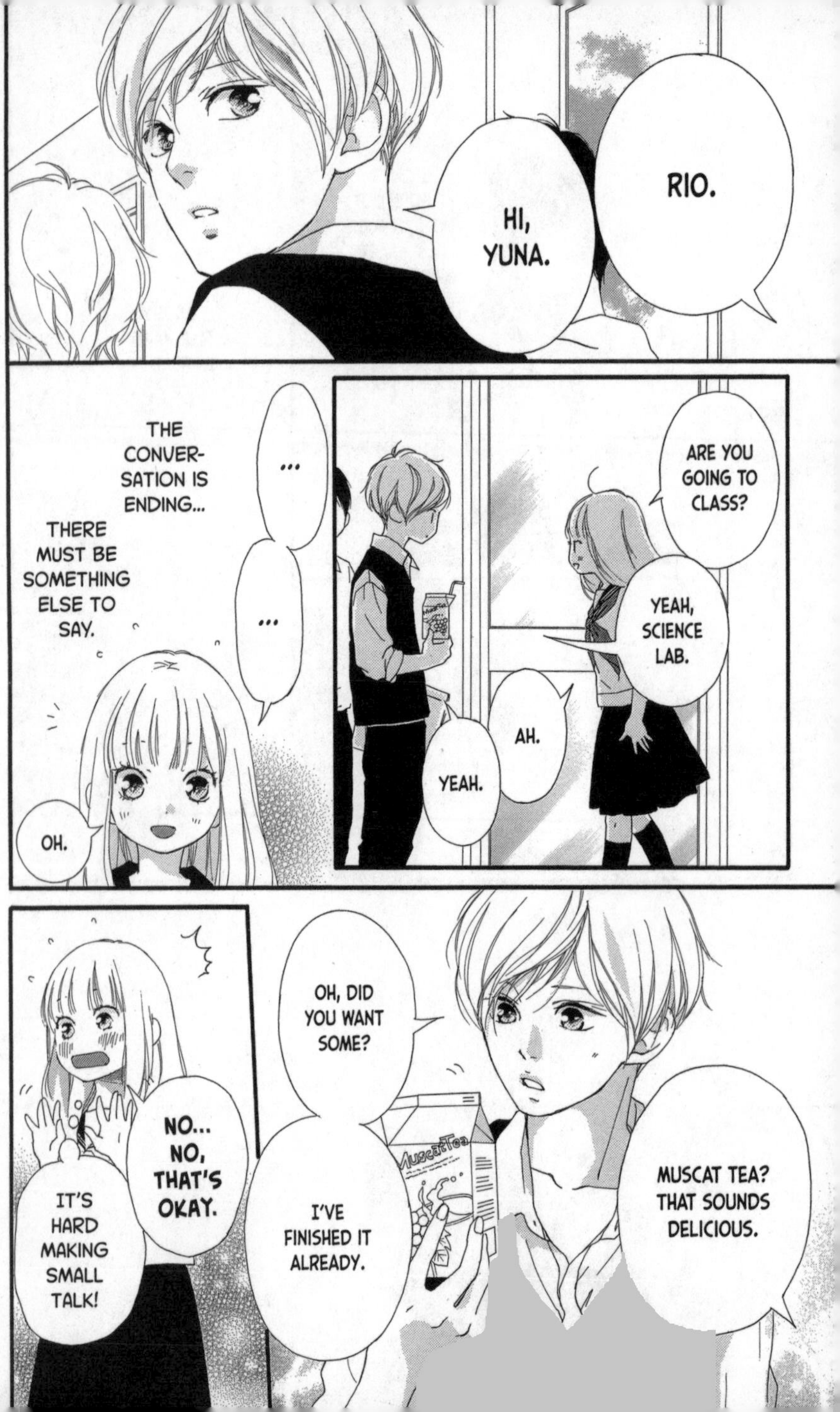
RIO.
HI, YUNA.
ARE YOU GOING TO CLASS?
YEAH, SCIENCE LAB.
AH.
YEAH.
...
THE CONVERSATION IS ENDING...
...
THERE MUST BE SOMETHING ELSE TO SAY.
OH.
MUSCAT TEA? THAT SOUNDS DELICIOUS.
OH, DID YOU WANT SOME?
I'VE FINISHED IT ALREADY.
NO... NO, THAT'S OKAY.
IT'S HARD MAKING SMALL TALK!

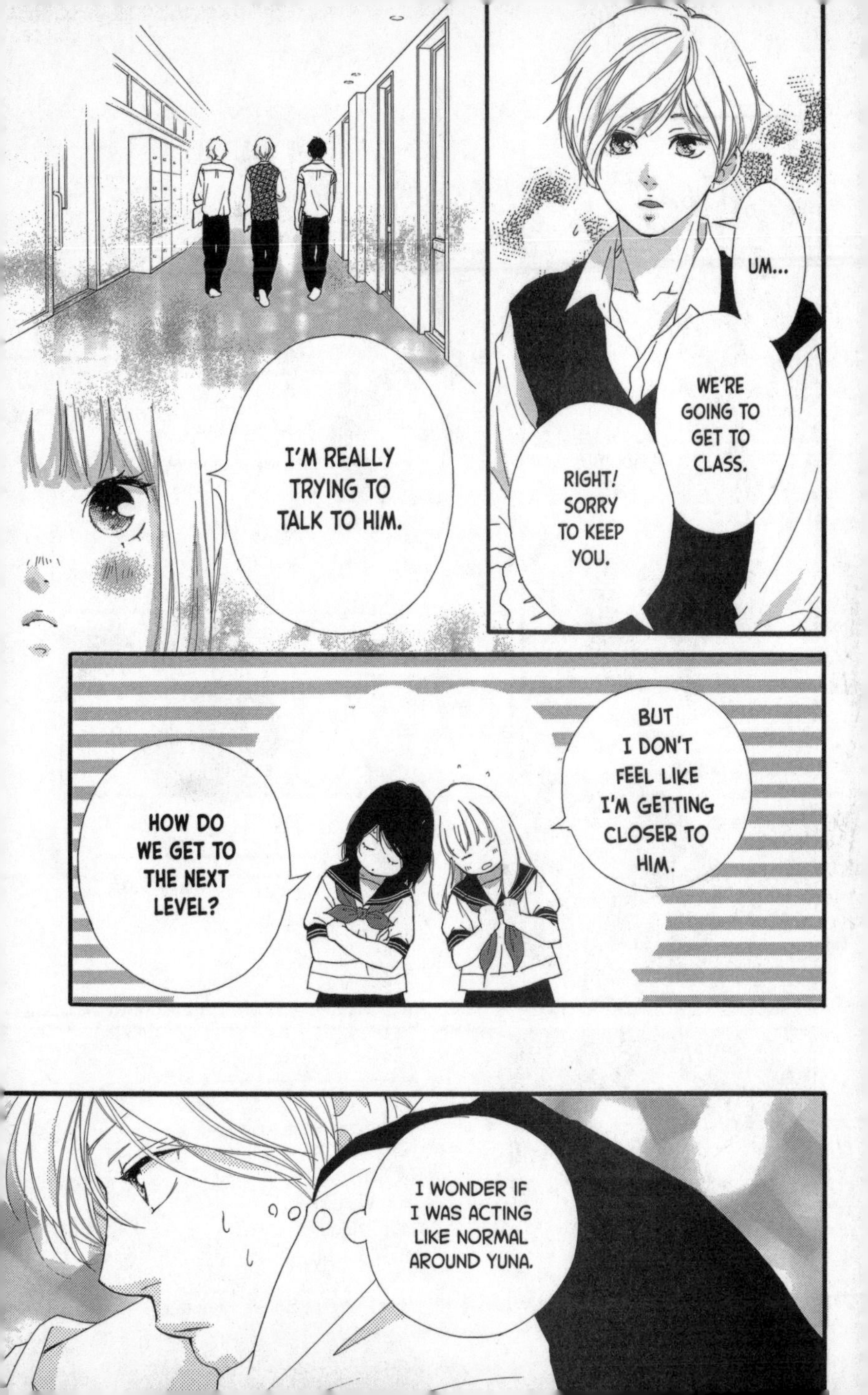
UM...
WE'RE GOING TO GET TO CLASS.
RIGHT! SORRY TO KEEP YOU.
I'M REALLY TRYING TO TALK TO HIM.
BUT I DON'T FEEL LIKE I'M GETTING CLOSER TO HIM.
HOW DO WE GET TO THE NEXT LEVEL?
I WONDER IF I WAS ACTING LIKE NORMAL AROUND YUNA.

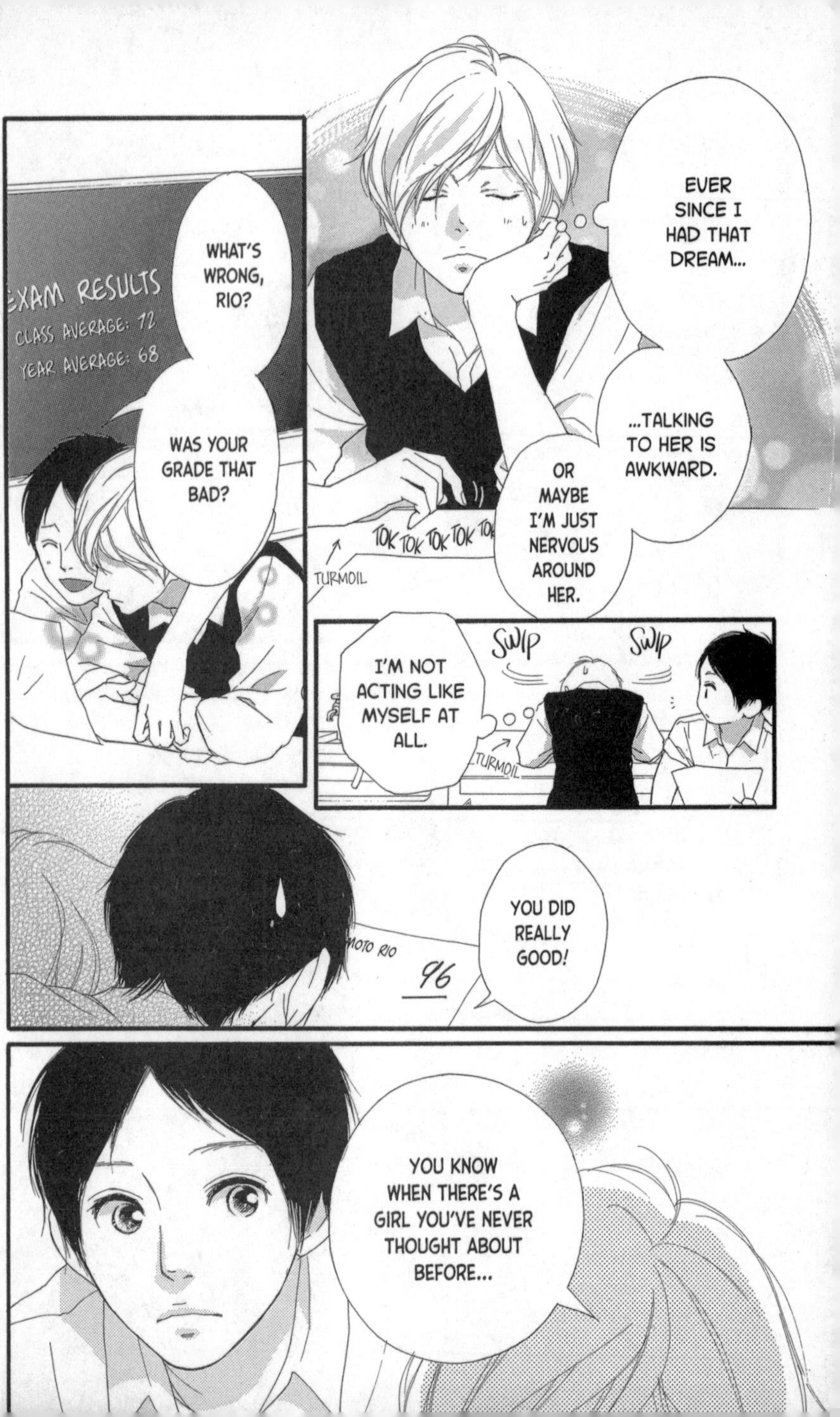
EVER SINCE I HAD THAT DREAM...
...TALKING TO HER IS AWKWARD.
OR MAYBE I'M JUST NERVOUS AROUND HER.
TOK TOK TOK TOK TOK
TURMOIL
SWIP SWIP
I'M NOT ACTING LIKE MYSELF AT ALL.
TURMOIL
EXAM RESULTS
CLASS AVERAGE: 72
YEAR AVERAGE: 68
WHAT'S WRONG, RIO?
WAS YOUR GRADE THAT BAD?
YOU DID REALLY GOOD!
MOTO RIO
96
YOU KNOW WHEN THERE'S A GIRL YOU'VE NEVER THOUGHT ABOUT BEFORE...

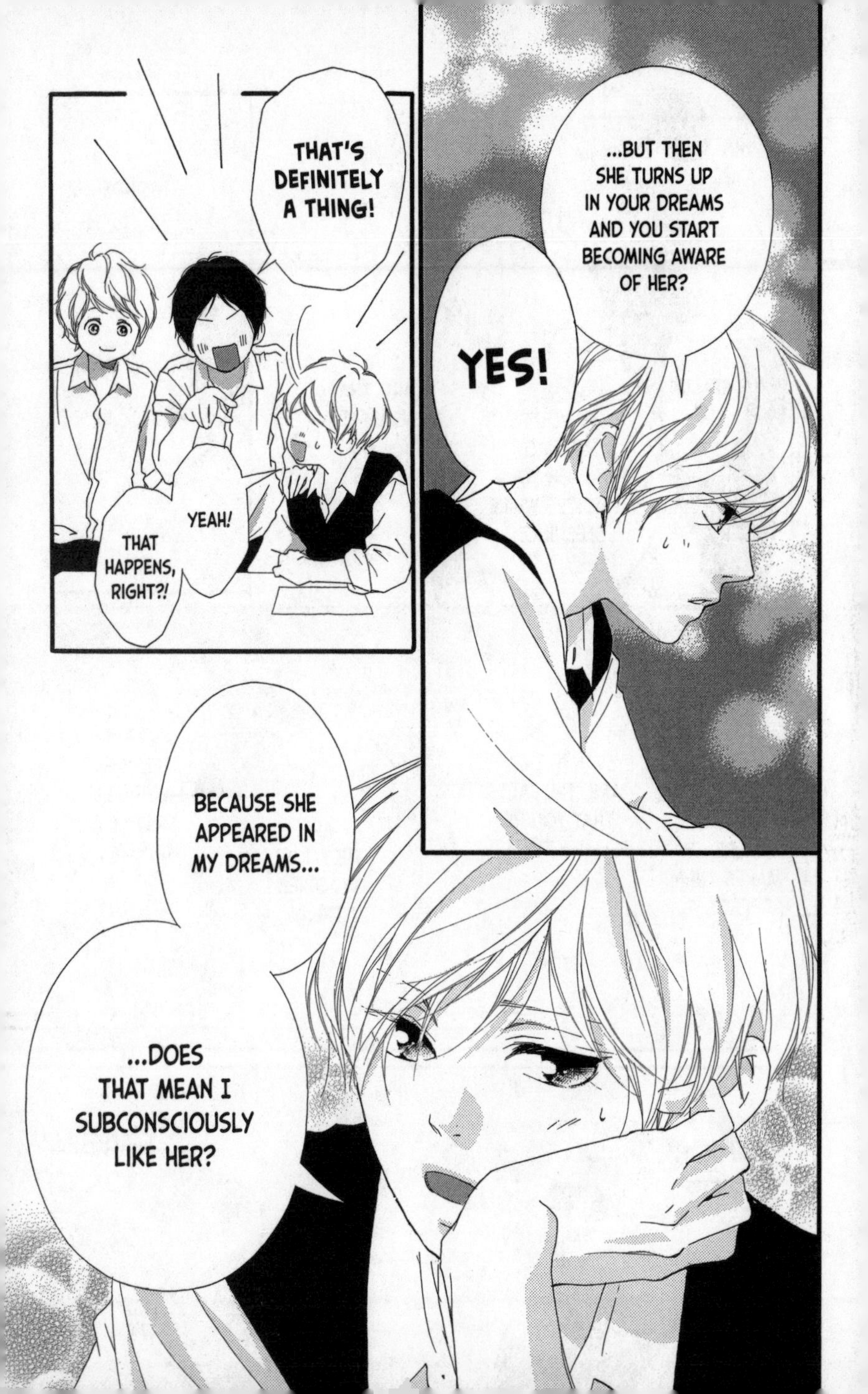
...BUT THEN SHE TURNS UP IN YOUR DREAMS AND YOU START BECOMING AWARE OF HER?
YES!
THAT'S DEFINITELY A THING!
YEAH!
THAT HAPPENS, RIGHT?!
BECAUSE SHE APPEARED IN MY DREAMS...
...DOES THAT MEAN I SUBCONSCIOUSLY LIKE HER?

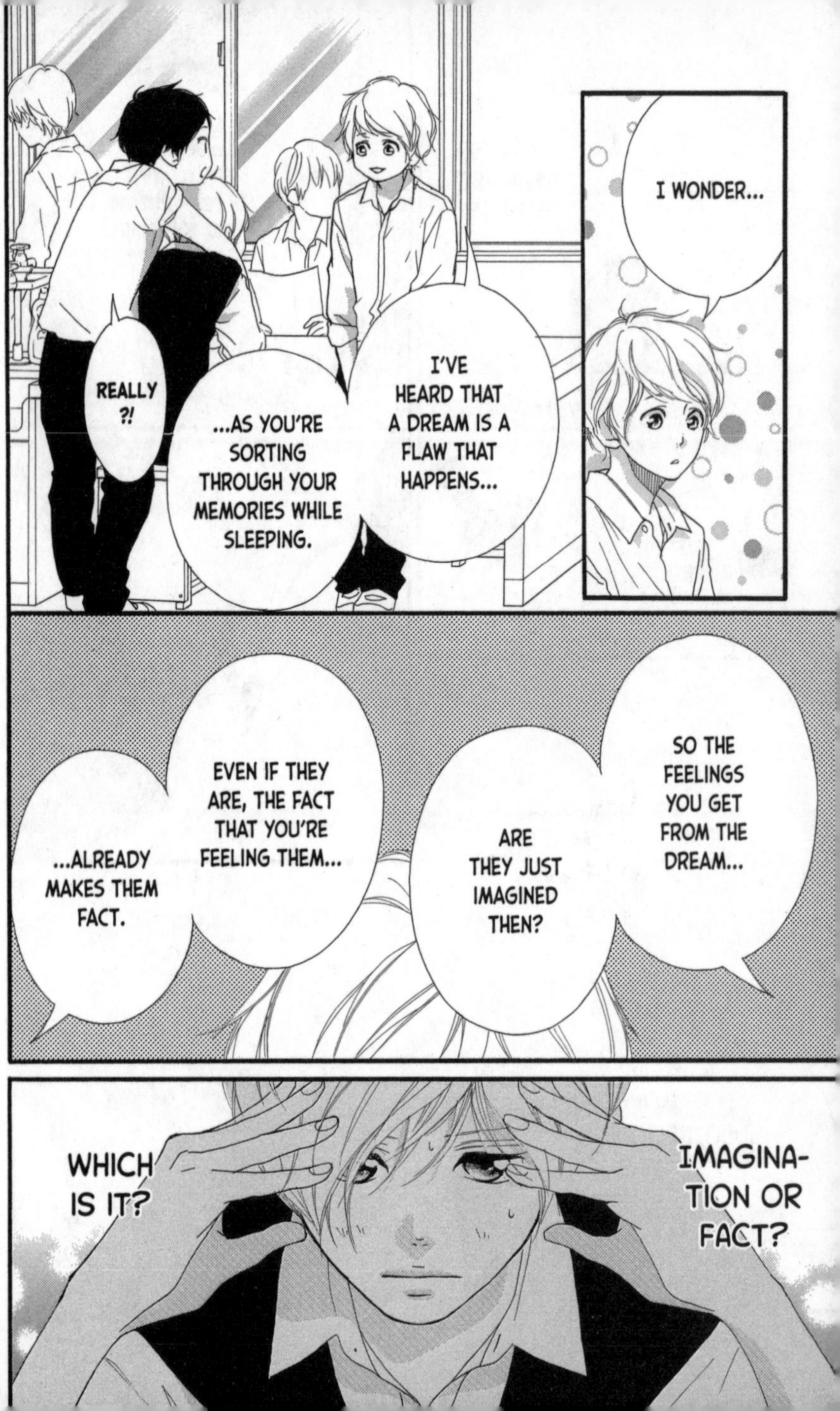
I WONDER...
I'VE HEARD THAT A DREAM IS A FLAW THAT HAPPENS...
...AS YOU'RE SORTING THROUGH YOUR MEMORIES WHILE SLEEPING.
REALLY?!
SO THE FEELINGS YOU GET FROM THE DREAM...
ARE THEY JUST IMAGINED THEN?
EVEN IF THEY ARE, THE FACT THAT YOU'RE FEELING THEM...
...ALREADY MAKES THEM FACT.
IMAGINA-TION OR FACT?
WHICH IS IT?

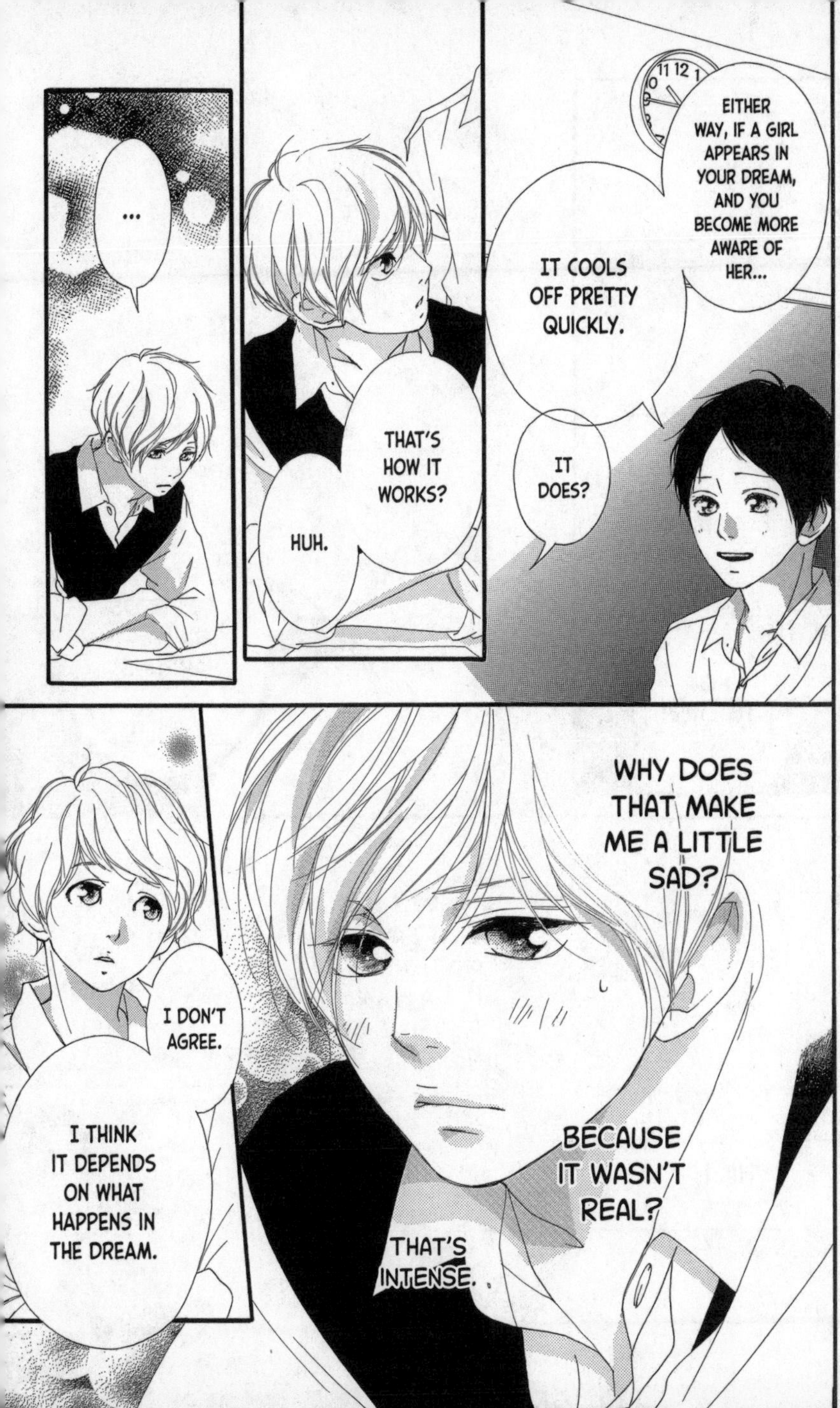
EITHER WAY, IF A GIRL APPEARS IN YOUR DREAM, AND YOU BECOME MORE AWARE OF HER...
IT COOLS OFF PRETTY QUICKLY.
IT DOES?
THAT'S HOW IT WORKS?
HUH.
...
WHY DOES THAT MAKE ME A LITTLE SAD?
BECAUSE IT WASN'T REAL?
THAT'S INTENSE.
I DON'T AGREE.
I THINK IT DEPENDS ON WHAT HAPPENS IN THE DREAM.

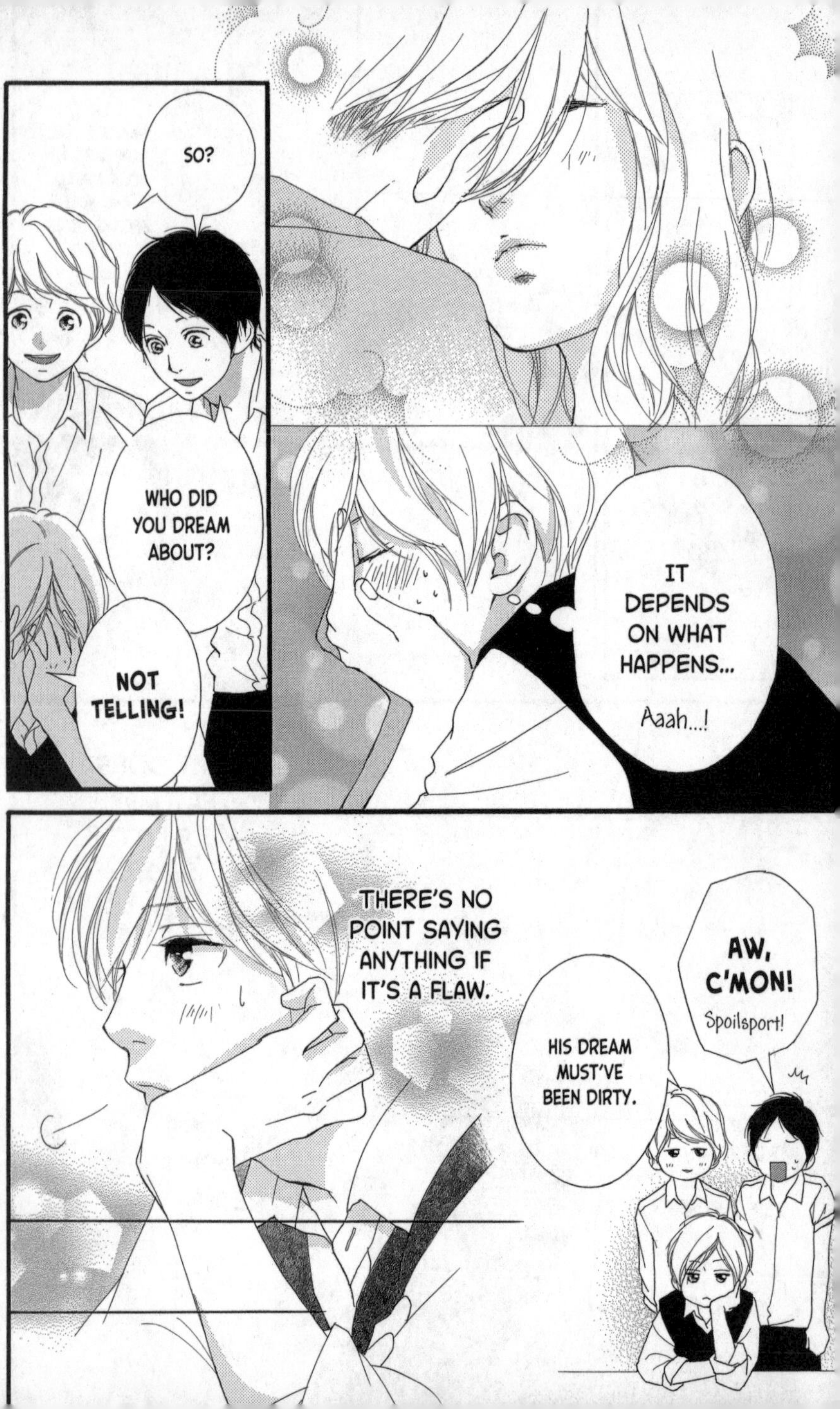
IT DEPENDS ON WHAT HAPPENS...
Aaah...!
SO?
WHO DID YOU DREAM ABOUT?
NOT TELLING!
AW, C'MON!
Spoilsport!
HIS DREAM MUST'VE BEEN DIRTY.
THERE'S NO POINT SAYING ANYTHING IF IT'S A FLAW.

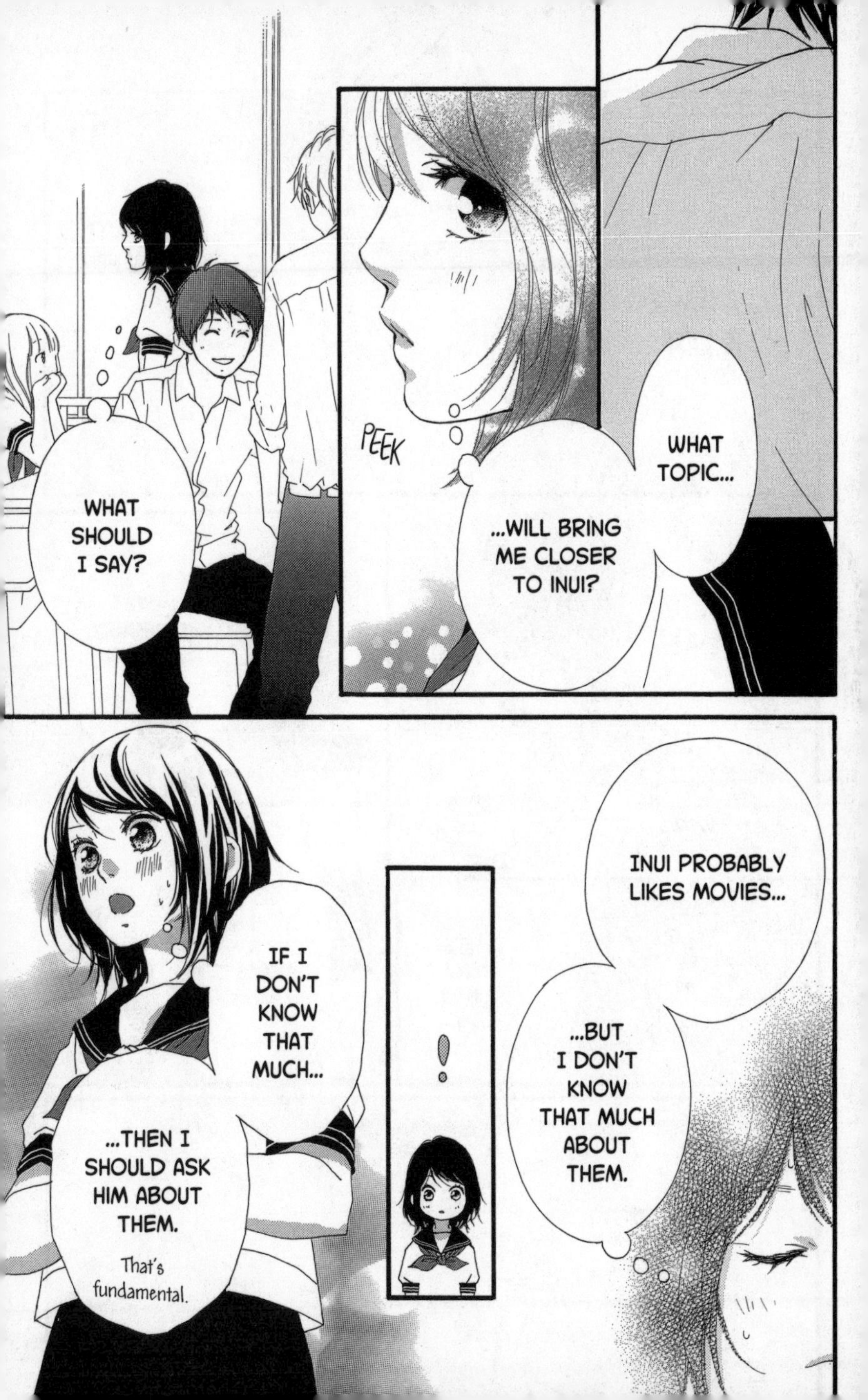
WHAT TOPIC...
...WILL BRING ME CLOSER TO INUI?
PEEK
WHAT SHOULD I SAY?
INUI PROBABLY LIKES MOVIES...
...BUT I DON'T KNOW THAT MUCH ABOUT THEM.
!
IF I DON'T KNOW THAT MUCH...
...THEN I SHOULD ASK HIM ABOUT THEM.
That's fundamental.

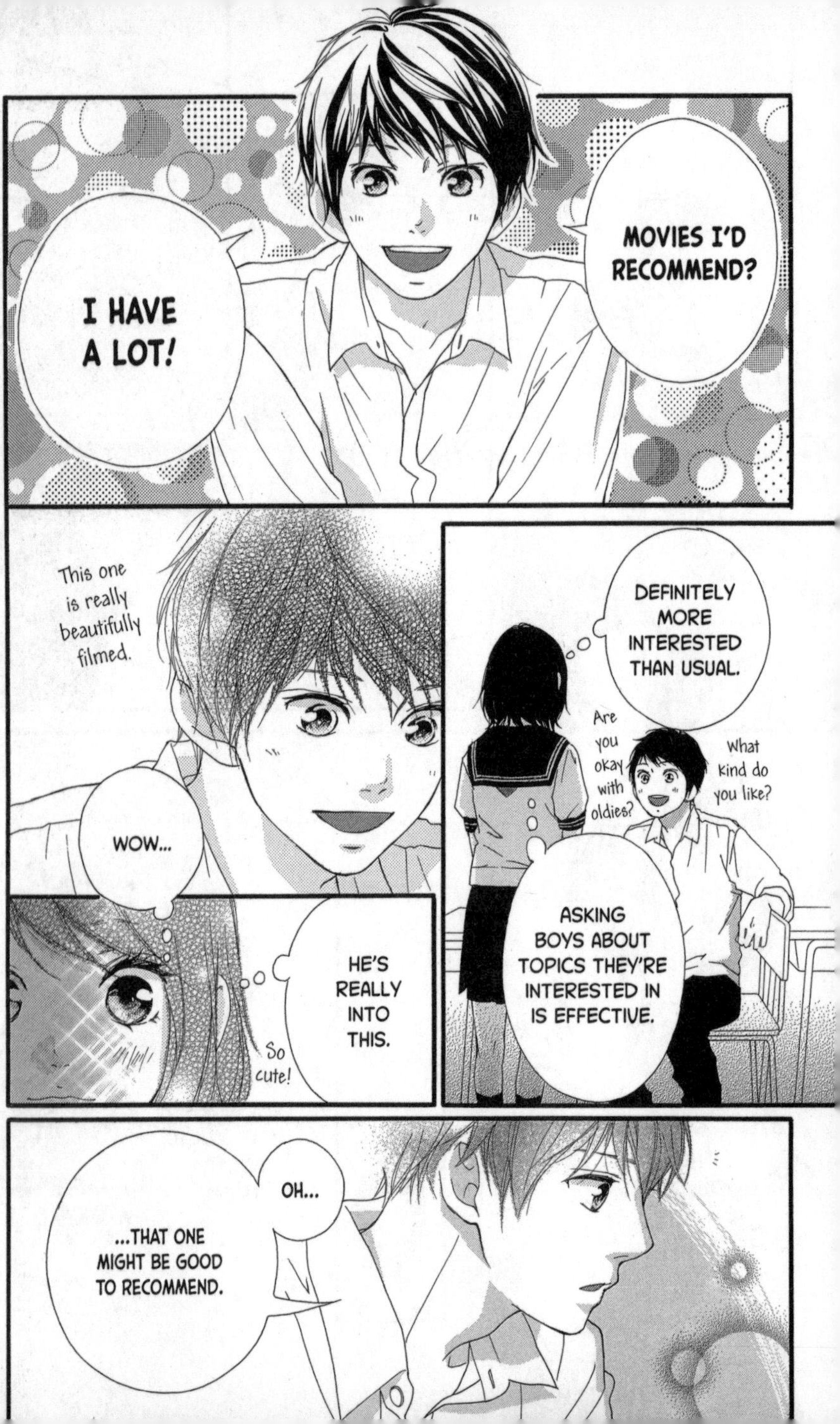
MOVIES I'D RECOMMEND?
I HAVE A LOT!
DEFINITELY MORE INTERESTED THAN USUAL.
What kind do you like?
Are you okay with oldies?
ASKING BOYS ABOUT TOPICS THEY'RE INTERESTED IN IS EFFECTIVE.
This one is really beautifully filmed.
WOW...
HE'S REALLY INTO THIS.
So cute!
OH...
...THAT ONE MIGHT BE GOOD TO RECOMMEND.

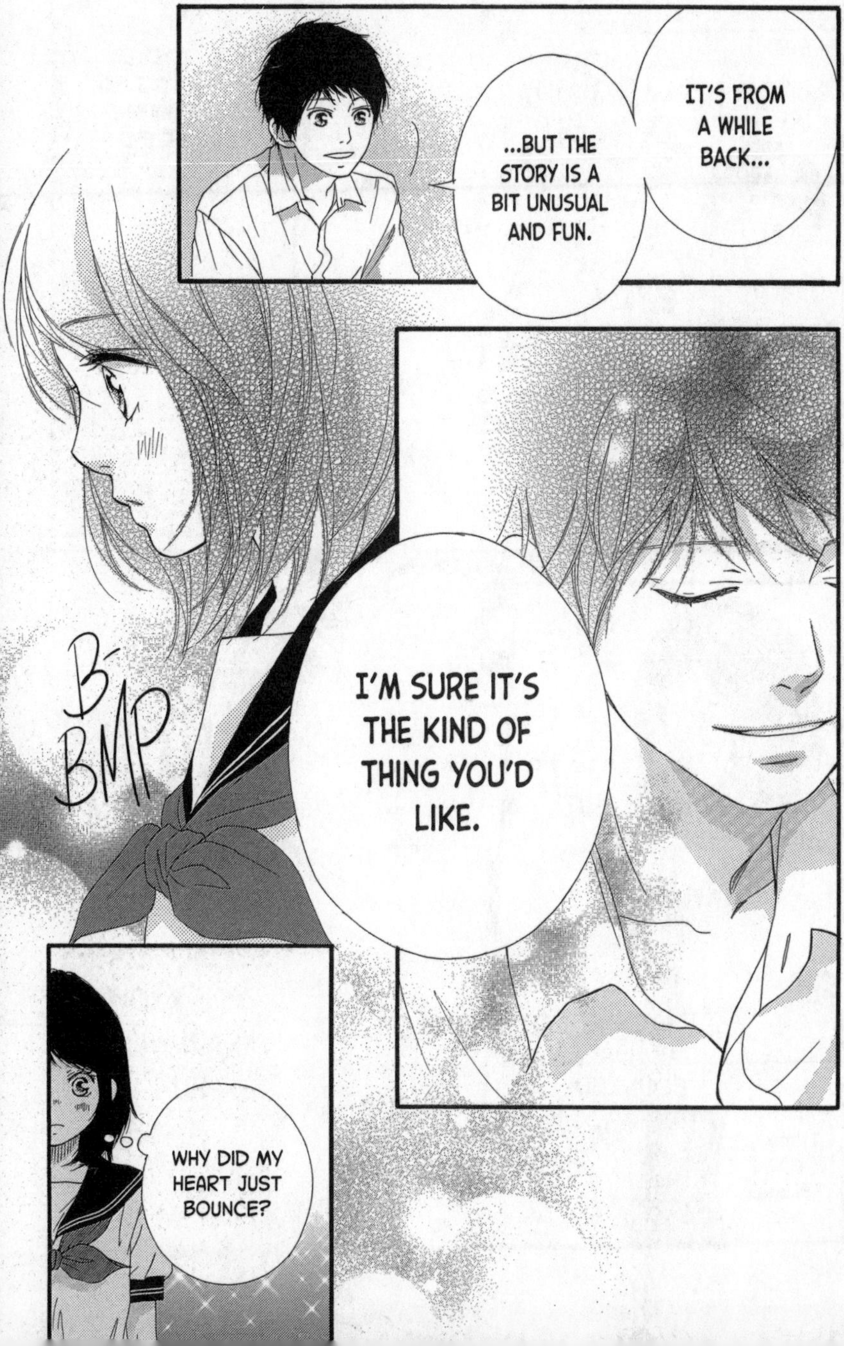
IT'S FROM A WHILE BACK...
...BUT THE STORY IS A BIT UNUSUAL AND FUN.
I'M SURE IT'S THE KIND OF THING YOU'D LIKE.
B-BMP
WHY DID MY HEART JUST BOUNCE?

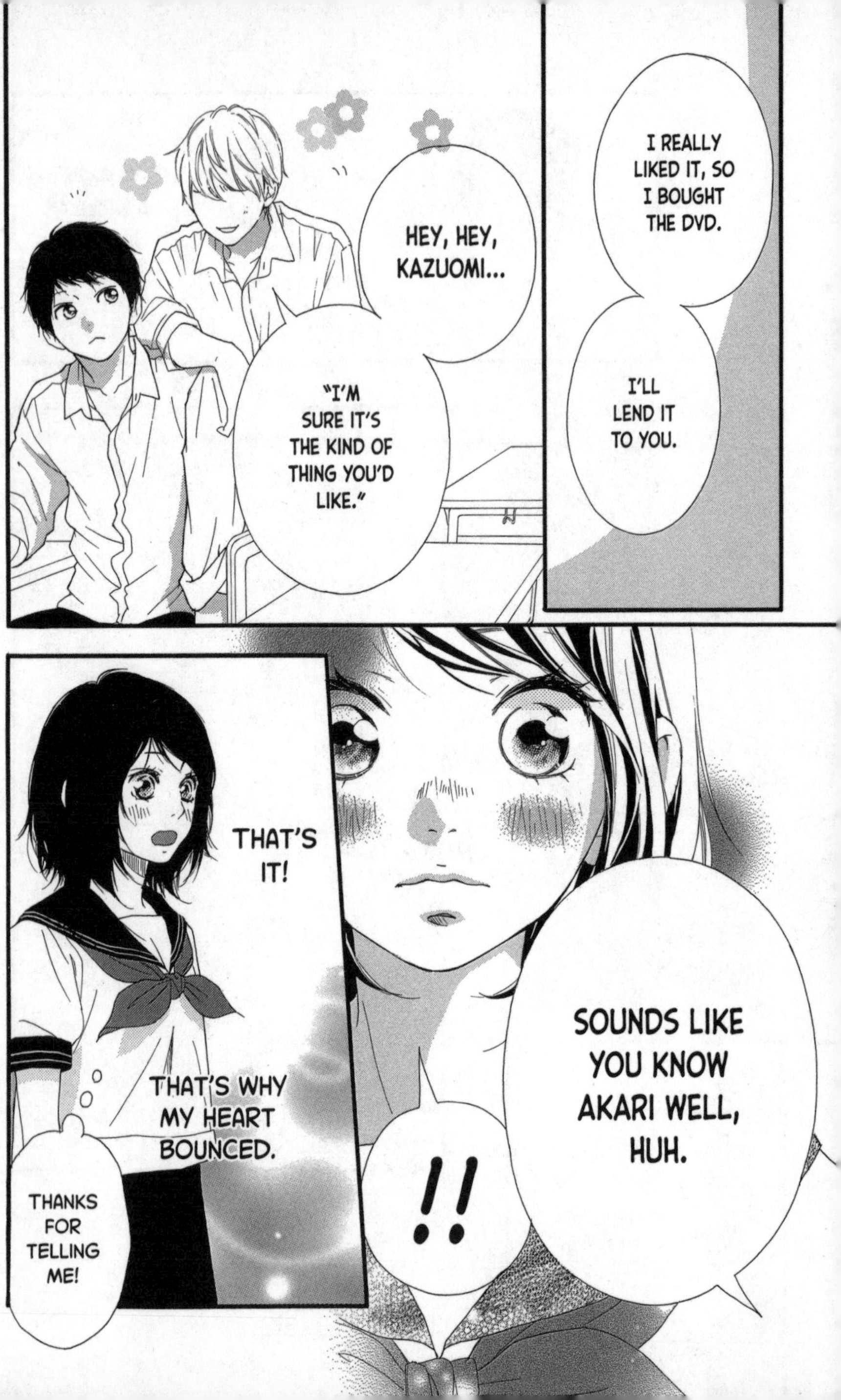
I REALLY LIKED IT, SO I BOUGHT THE DVD.
I'LL LEND IT TO YOU.
HEY, HEY, KAZUOMI...
"I'M SURE IT'S THE KIND OF THING YOU'D LIKE."
SOUNDS LIKE YOU KNOW AKARI WELL, HUH.
!!
THAT'S IT!
THAT'S WHY MY HEART BOUNCED.
THANKS FOR TELLING ME!

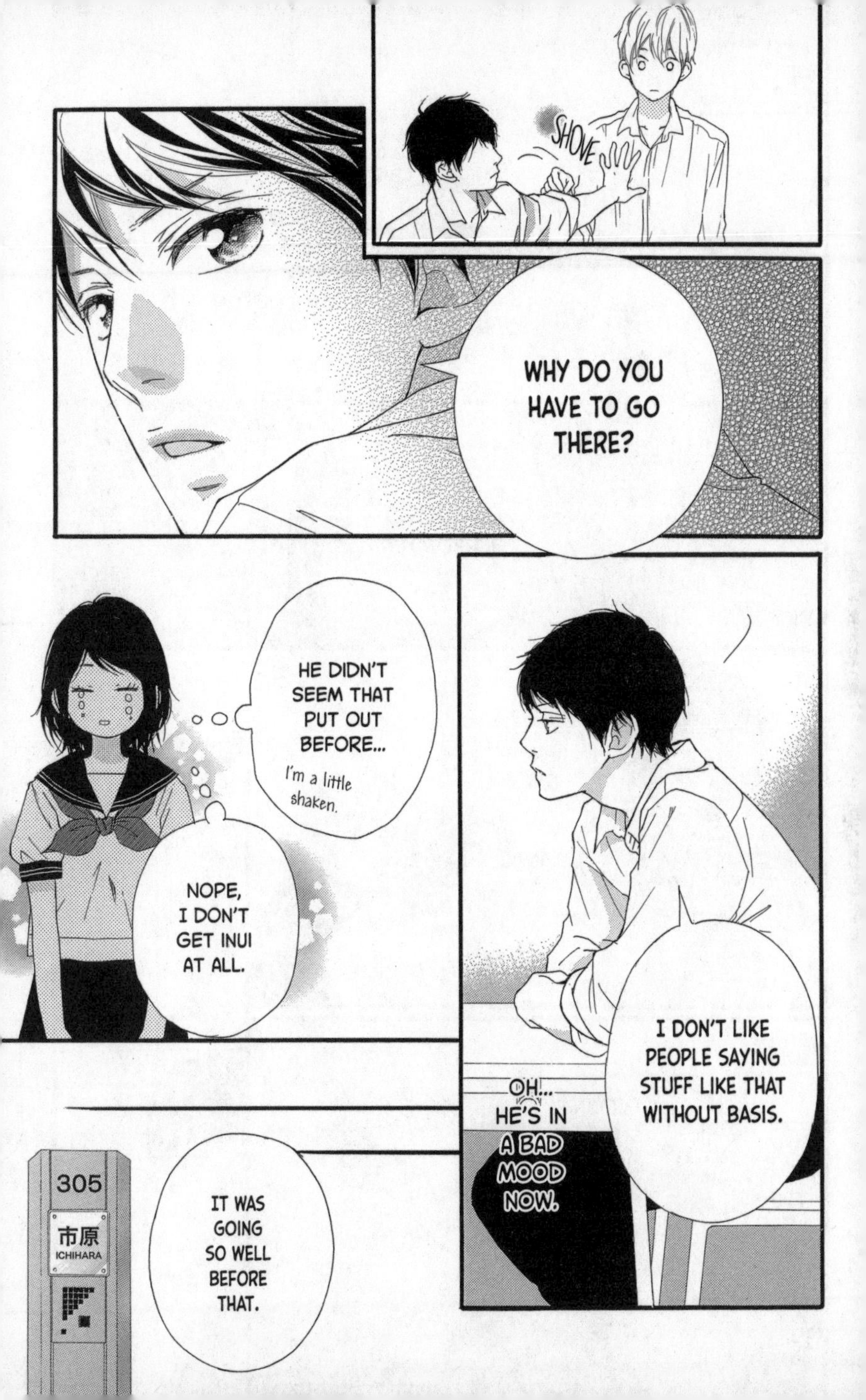
SHOVE
WHY DO YOU HAVE TO GO THERE?
I DON'T LIKE PEOPLE SAYING STUFF LIKE THAT WITHOUT BASIS.
OH... HE'S IN A BAD MOOD NOW.
HE DIDN'T SEEM THAT PUT OUT BEFORE...
I'm a little shaken.
NOPE, I DON'T GET INUI AT ALL.
305
市原
ICHIHARA
IT WAS GOING SO WELL BEFORE THAT.

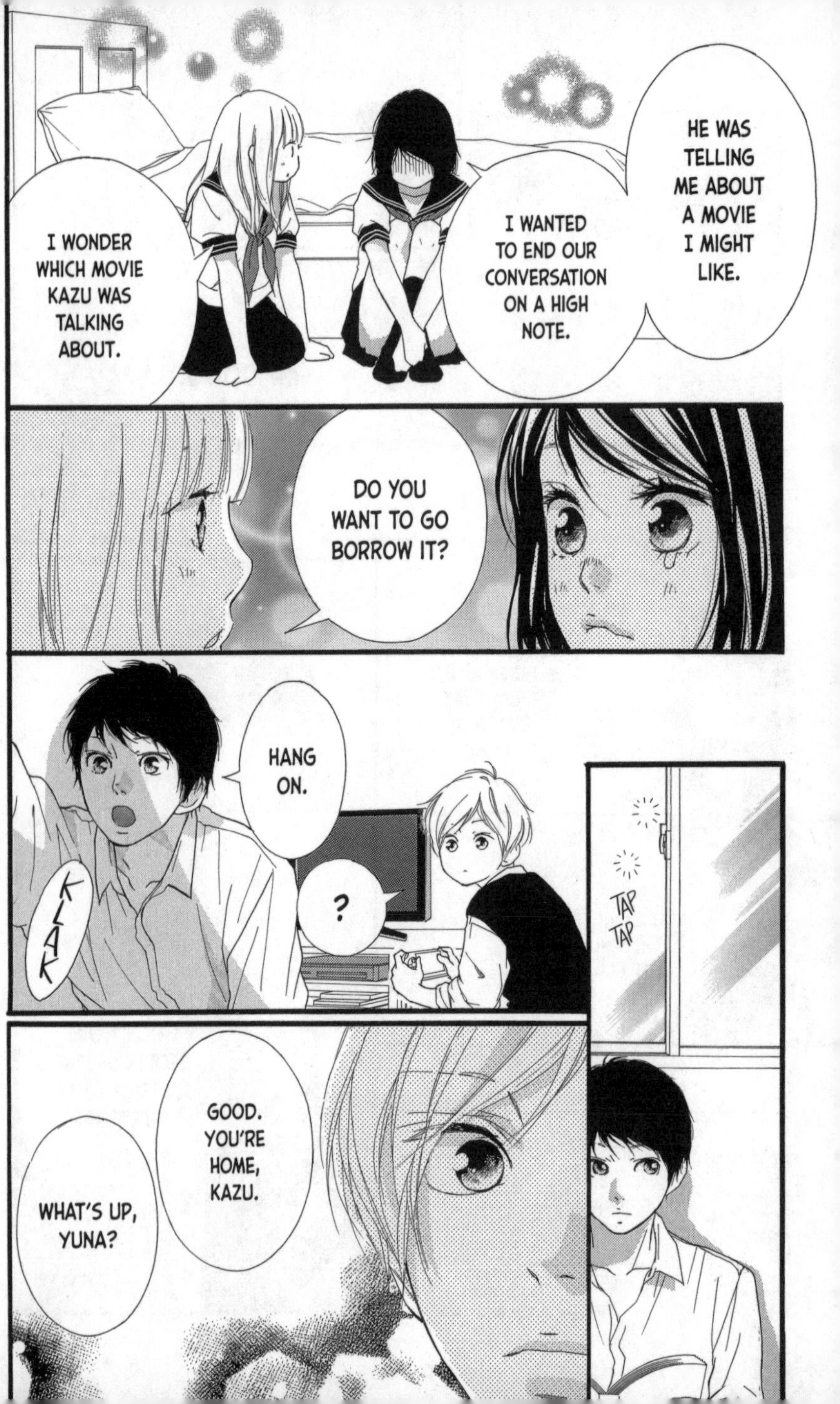
HE WAS TELLING ME ABOUT A MOVIE I MIGHT LIKE.
I WANTED TO END OUR CONVERSATION ON A HIGH NOTE.
I WONDER WHICH MOVIE KAZU WAS TALKING ABOUT.
DO YOU WANT TO GO BORROW IT?
TAP TAP
HANG ON.
?
KLAK
GOOD. YOU'RE HOME, KAZU.
WHAT'S UP, YUNA?

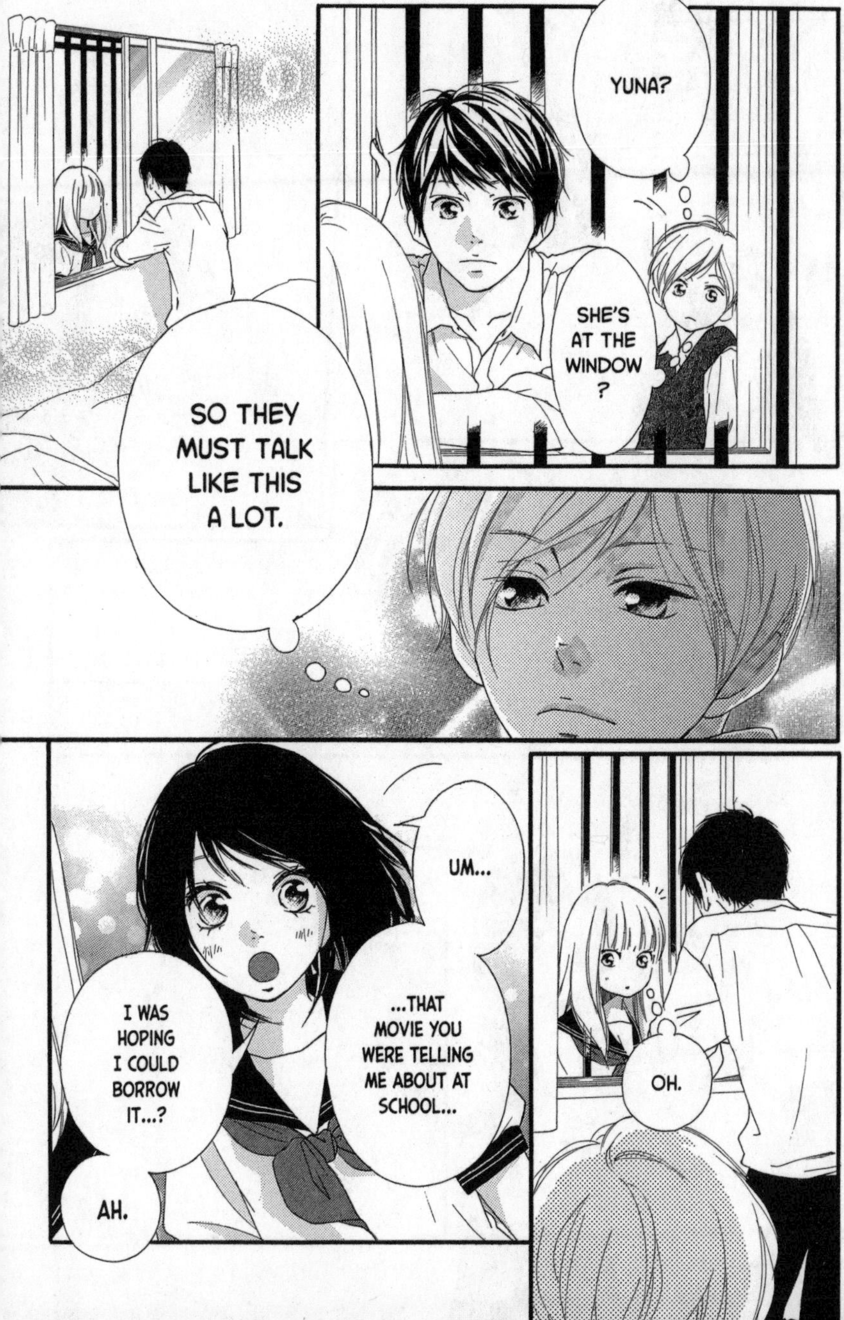
YUNA?
SHE'S AT THE WINDOW?
SO THEY MUST TALK LIKE THIS A LOT.
OH.
UM...
...THAT MOVIE YOU WERE TELLING ME ABOUT AT SCHOOL...
I WAS HOPING I COULD BORROW IT...?
AH.

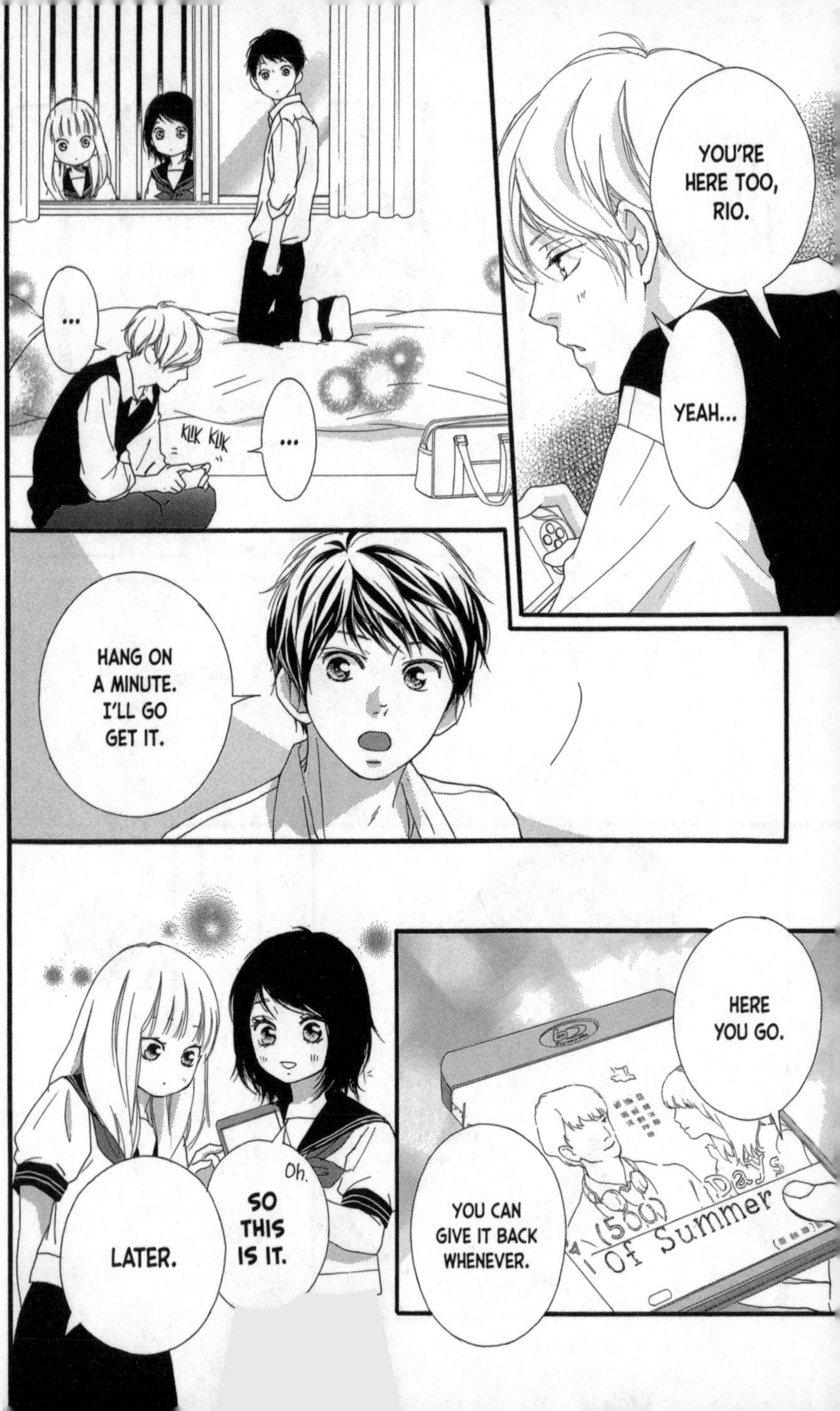
YOU'RE HERE TOO, RIO.
YEAH...
...
KLIK KLIK
...
HANG ON A MINUTE. I'LL GO GET IT.
HERE YOU GO.
(500) Days of Summer
YOU CAN GIVE IT BACK WHENEVER.
Oh.
SO THIS IS IT.
LATER.

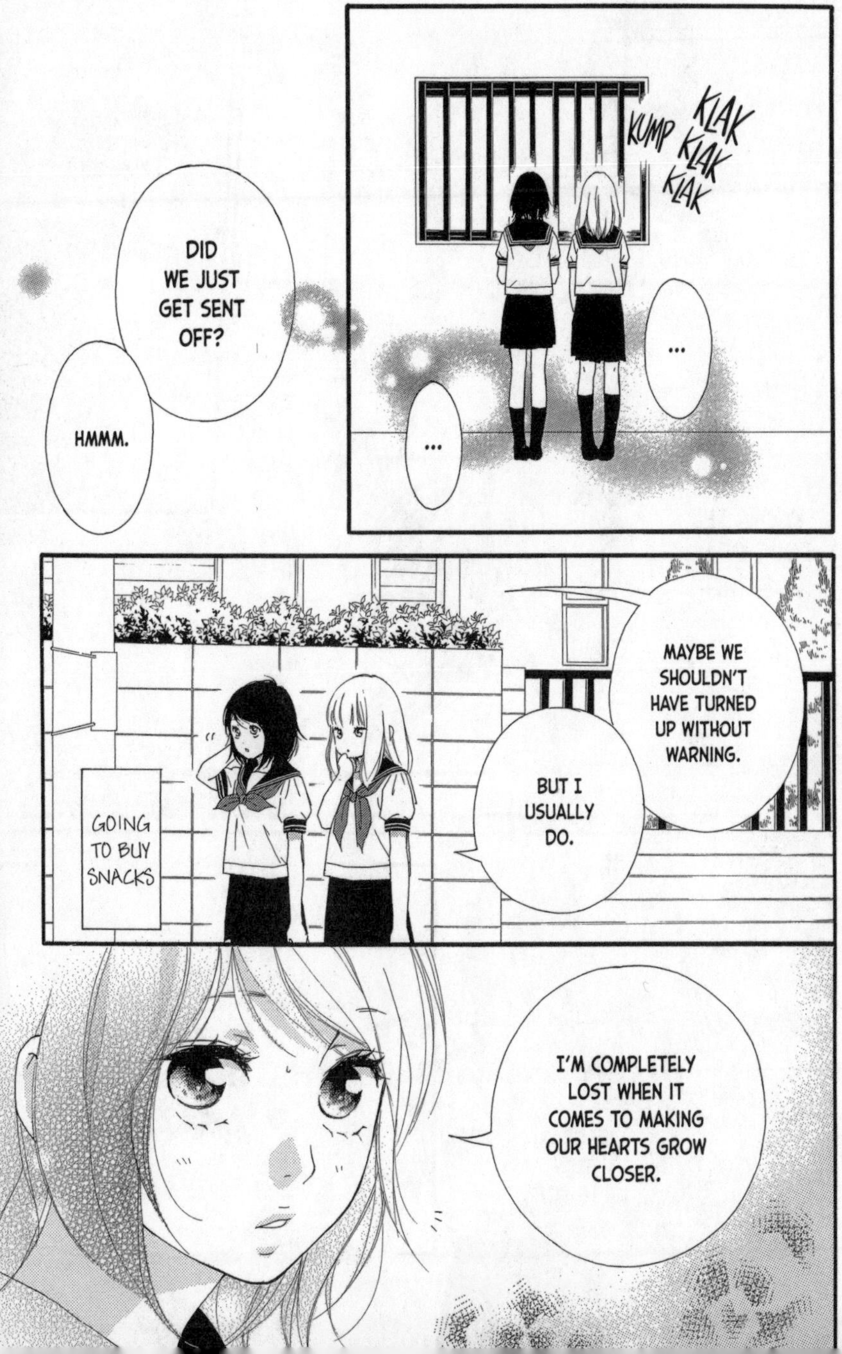
KUMP
KLAK KLAK KLAK
...
...
DID WE JUST GET SENT OFF?
HMMM.
MAYBE WE SHOULDN'T HAVE TURNED UP WITHOUT WARNING.
BUT I USUALLY DO.
GOING TO BUY SNACKS
I'M COMPLETELY LOST WHEN IT COMES TO MAKING OUR HEARTS GROW CLOSER.

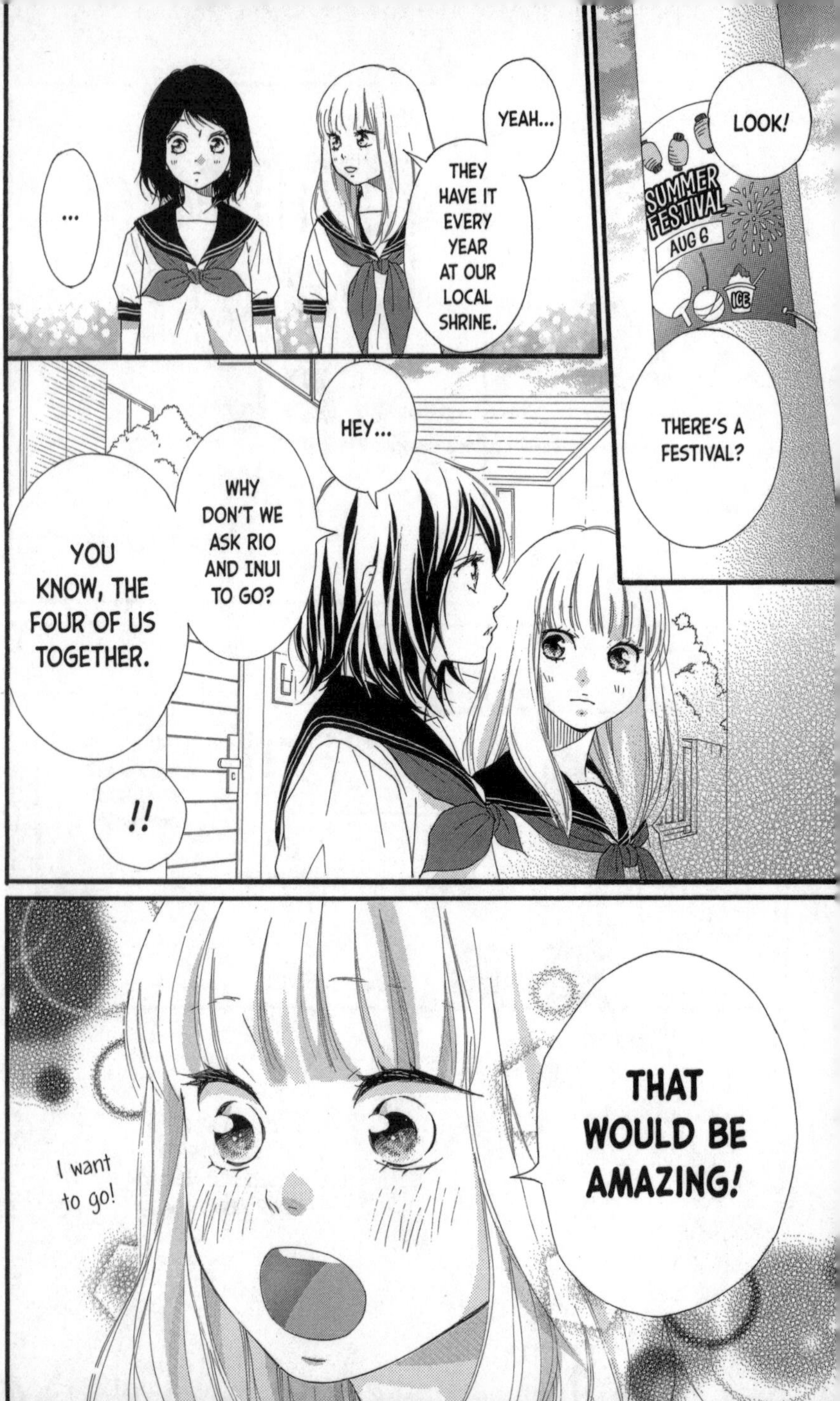
LOOK!
SUMMER FESTIVAL
AUG 6
ICE
THERE'S A FESTIVAL?
YEAH...
THEY HAVE IT EVERY YEAR AT OUR LOCAL SHRINE.
...
HEY...
WHY DON'T WE ASK RIO AND INUI TO GO?
YOU KNOW, THE FOUR OF US TOGETHER.
!!
THAT WOULD BE AMAZING!
I want to go!

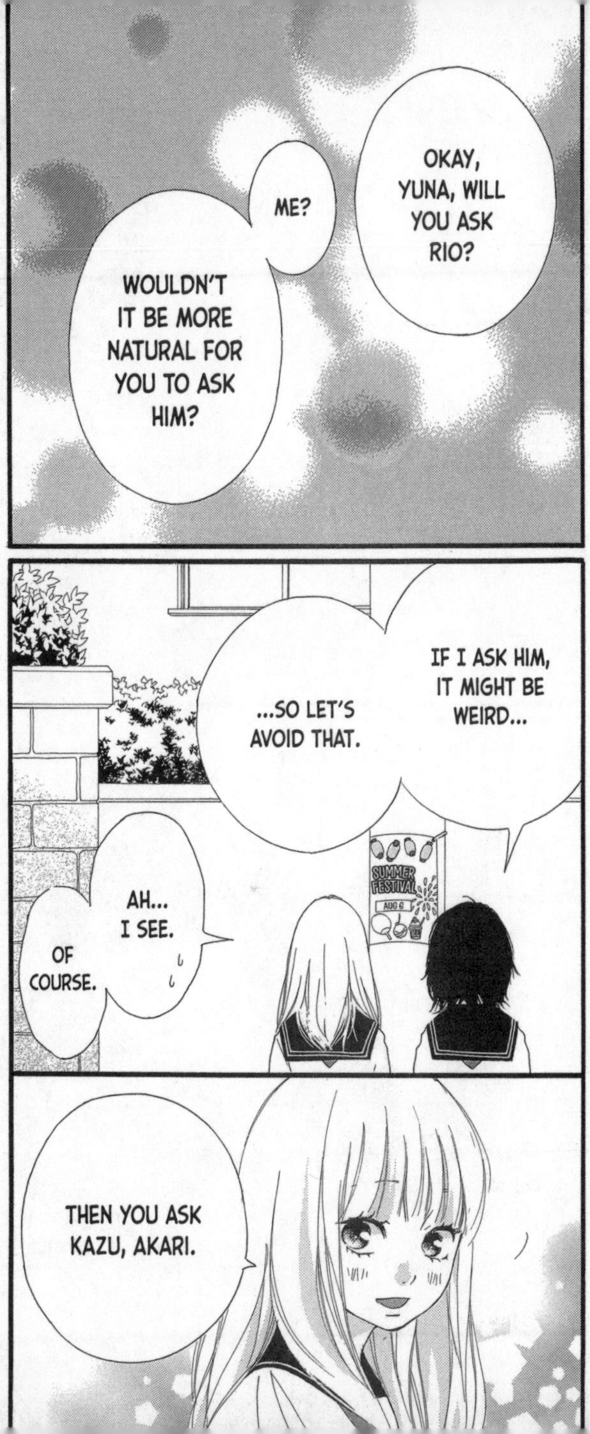
OKAY, YUNA, WILL YOU ASK RIO?
ME?
WOULDN'T IT BE MORE NATURAL FOR YOU TO ASK HIM?
IF I ASK HIM, IT MIGHT BE WEIRD...
...SO LET'S AVOID THAT.
SUMMER FESTIVAL
AUG 6
AH... I SEE.
OF COURSE.
THEN YOU ASK KAZU, AKARI.

Rio Yamamoto
Profile

Birthday: February 9
Sign: Aquarius
Blood type: A
Height: 5'7" still growing (hopeful)
Weight: 125 lbs

Favorite colors:
Black, white

Favorite subjects:
Math, English

Least favorite subject:
Nothing in particular

Favorite food:
Meat

Least favorite food:
Pickled plum

Hobby:
Shogi

Favorite thing about himself:
Voice

Favorite movie:
Mad Max: Fury Road

Favorite magazine:
Men's FUDGE

Favorite band:
Tofubeats

Favorite celebrity:
Masakiyo Maezono

Place he wants to visit:
Machu Picchu

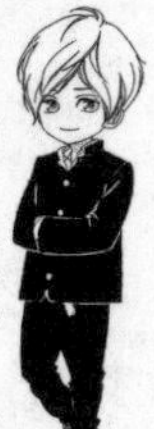

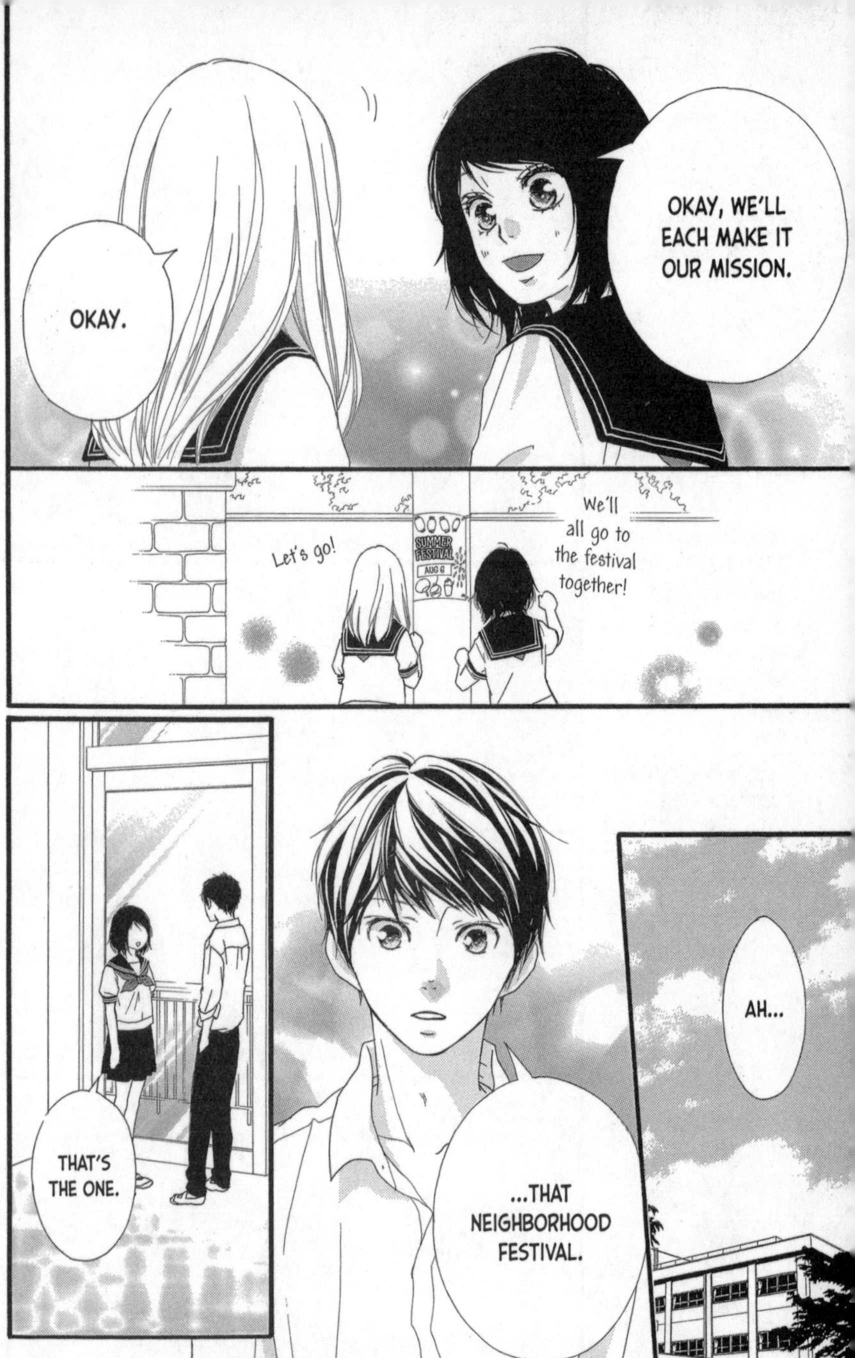
OKAY, WE'LL EACH MAKE IT OUR MISSION.
OKAY.
We'll all go to the festival together!
SUMMER FESTIVAL
AUG 6
Let's go!
AH...
...THAT NEIGHBORHOOD FESTIVAL.
THAT'S THE ONE.

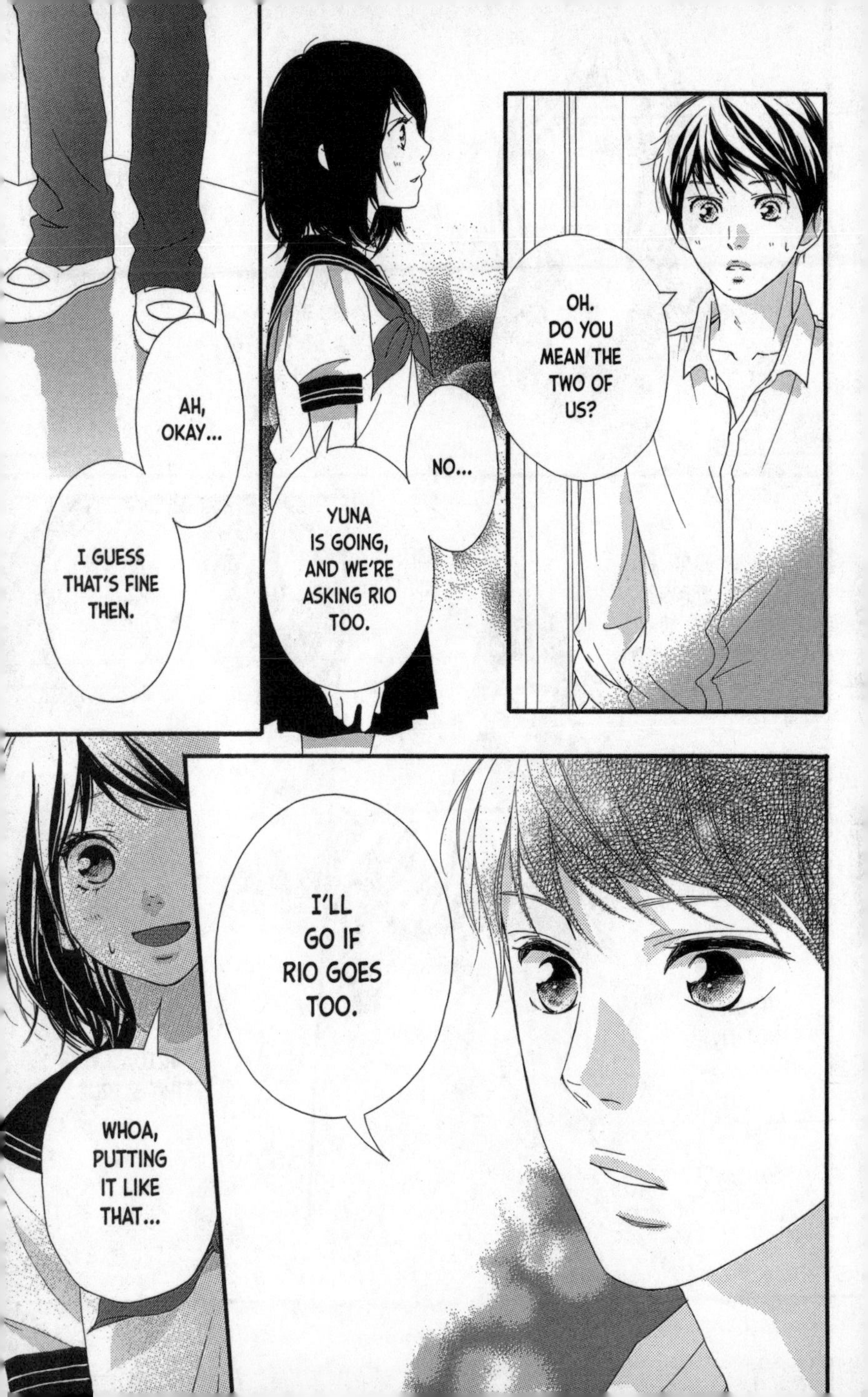
OH. DO YOU MEAN THE TWO OF US?
NO...
YUNA IS GOING, AND WE'RE ASKING RIO TOO.
AH, OKAY...
I GUESS THAT'S FINE THEN.
I'LL GO IF RIO GOES TOO.
WHOA, PUTTING IT LIKE THAT...

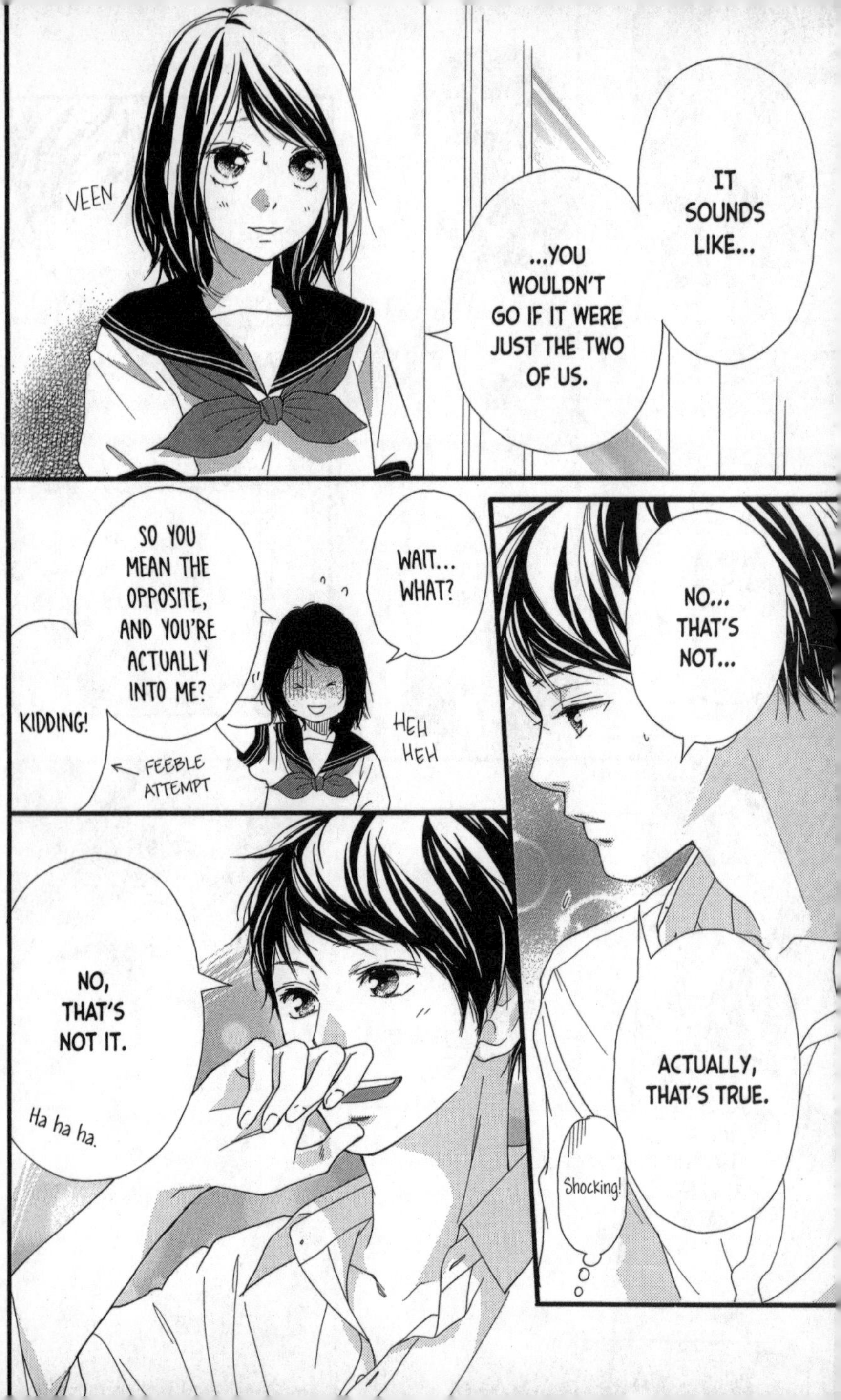
IT SOUNDS LIKE...
...YOU WOULDN'T GO IF IT WERE JUST THE TWO OF US.
VEEN
NO... THAT'S NOT...
ACTUALLY, THAT'S TRUE.
Shocking!
WAIT... WHAT?
SO YOU MEAN THE OPPOSITE, AND YOU'RE ACTUALLY INTO ME?
KIDDING!
HEH HEH
FEEBLE ATTEMPT
NO, THAT'S NOT IT.
Ha ha ha.

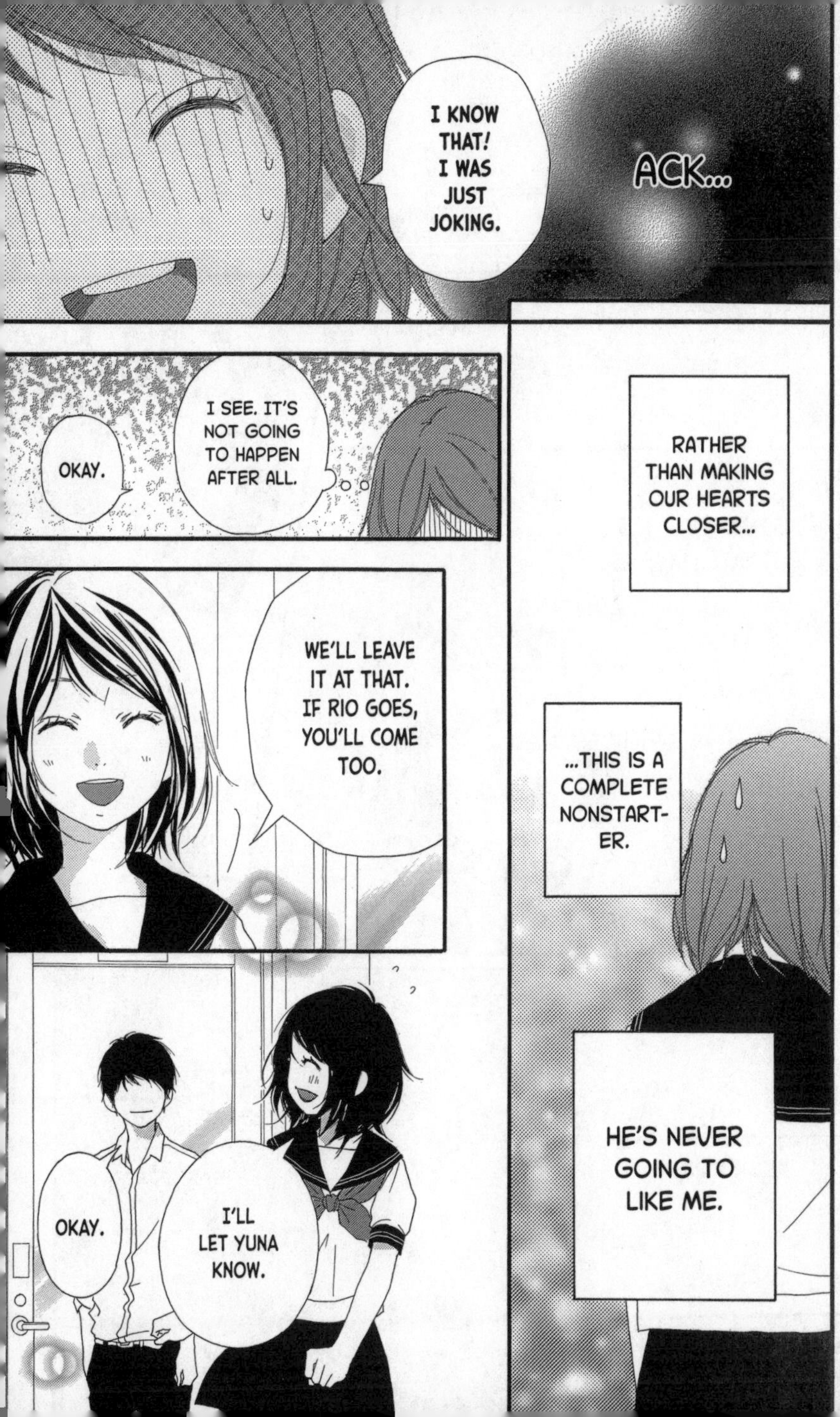
I KNOW THAT! I WAS JUST JOKING.
ACK...
RATHER THAN MAKING OUR HEARTS CLOSER...
...THIS IS A COMPLETE NONSTART-ER.
HE'S NEVER GOING TO LIKE ME.
I SEE. IT'S NOT GOING TO HAPPEN AFTER ALL.
OKAY.
WE'LL LEAVE IT AT THAT. IF RIO GOES, YOU'LL COME TOO.
I'LL LET YUNA KNOW.
OKAY.

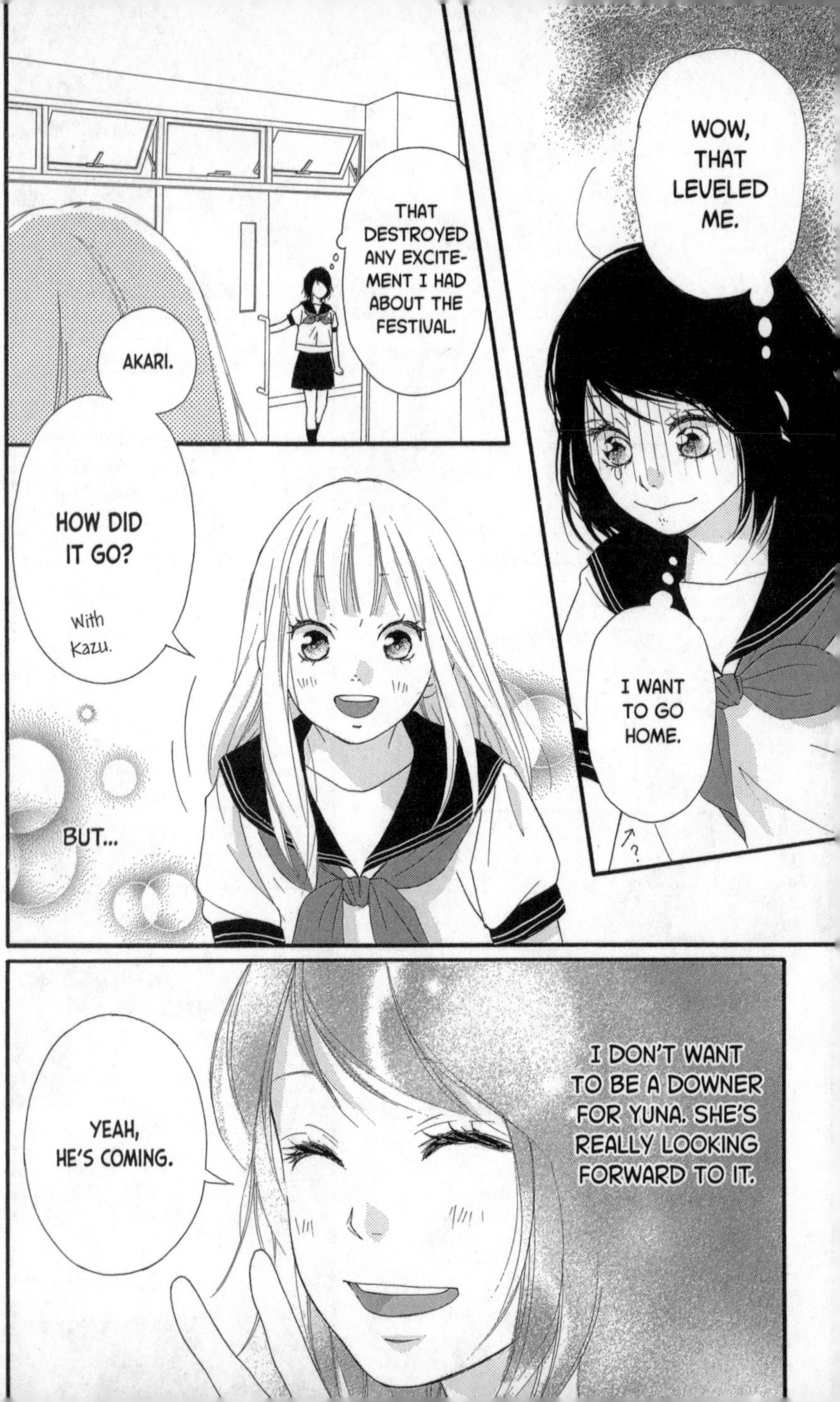
WOW, THAT LEVELED ME.
I WANT TO GO HOME.
THAT DESTROYED ANY EXCITEMENT I HAD ABOUT THE FESTIVAL.
AKARI.
HOW DID IT GO?
With Kazu.
BUT...
I DON'T WANT TO BE A DOWNER FOR YUNA. SHE'S REALLY LOOKING FORWARD TO IT.
YEAH, HE'S COMING.

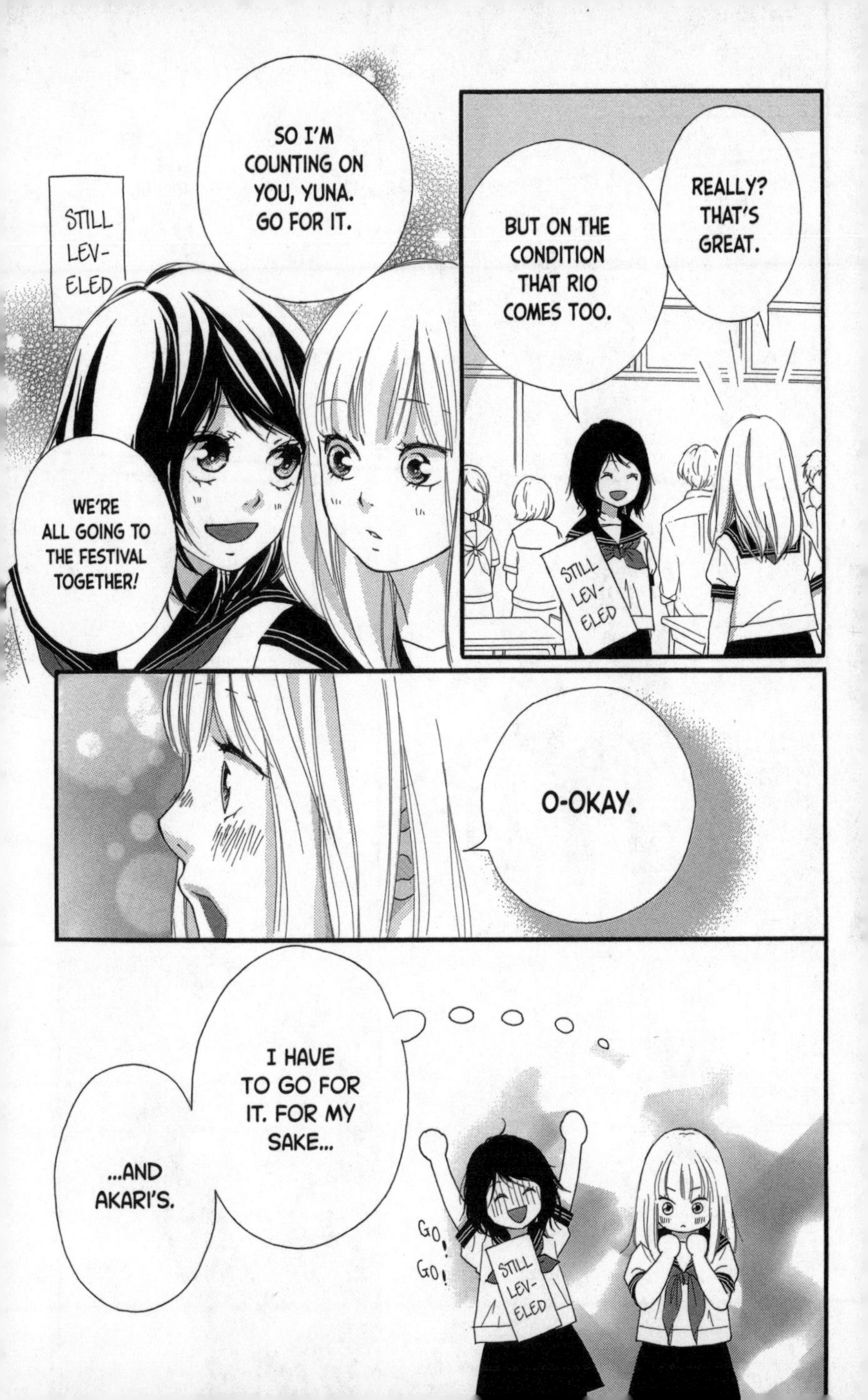
REALLY? THAT'S GREAT.
BUT ON THE CONDITION THAT RIO COMES TOO.
STILL LEV-ELED
SO I'M COUNTING ON YOU, YUNA. GO FOR IT.
STILL LEV-ELED
WE'RE ALL GOING TO THE FESTIVAL TOGETHER!
O-OKAY.
I HAVE TO GO FOR IT. FOR MY SAKE...
...AND AKARI'S.
GO! GO!
STILL LEV-ELED

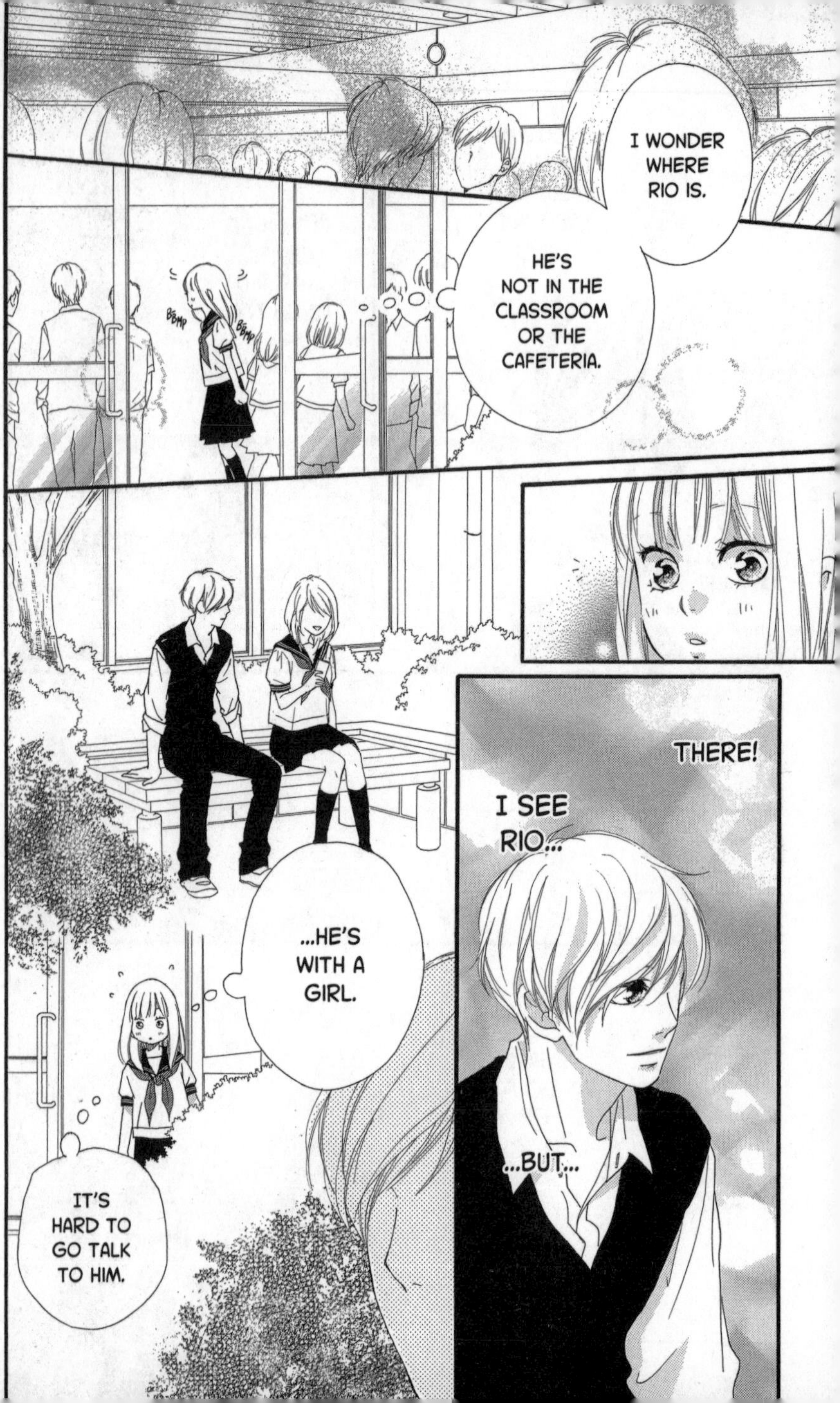
I WONDER WHERE RIO IS.
HE'S NOT IN THE CLASSROOM OR THE CAFETERIA.
THERE!
I SEE RIO...
...BUT...
...HE'S WITH A GIRL.
IT'S HARD TO GO TALK TO HIM.

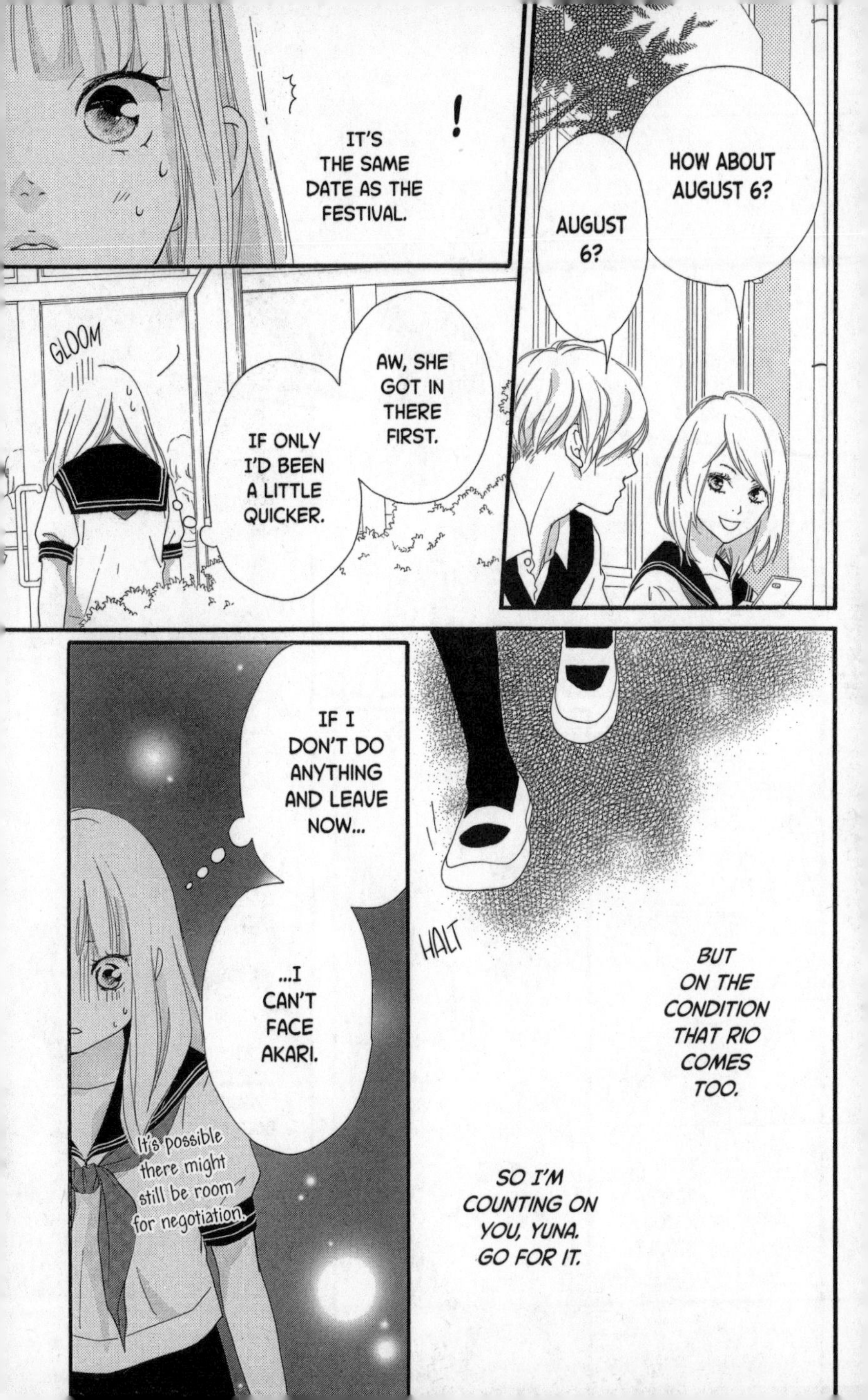
HOW ABOUT AUGUST 6?
AUGUST 6?
!
IT'S THE SAME DATE AS THE FESTIVAL.
GLOOM
AW, SHE GOT IN THERE FIRST.
IF ONLY I'D BEEN A LITTLE QUICKER.
HALT
BUT ON THE CONDITION THAT RIO COMES TOO.
SO I'M COUNTING ON YOU, YUNA. GO FOR IT.
IF I DON'T DO ANYTHING AND LEAVE NOW...
...I CAN'T FACE AKARI.
It's possible there might still be room for negotiation.

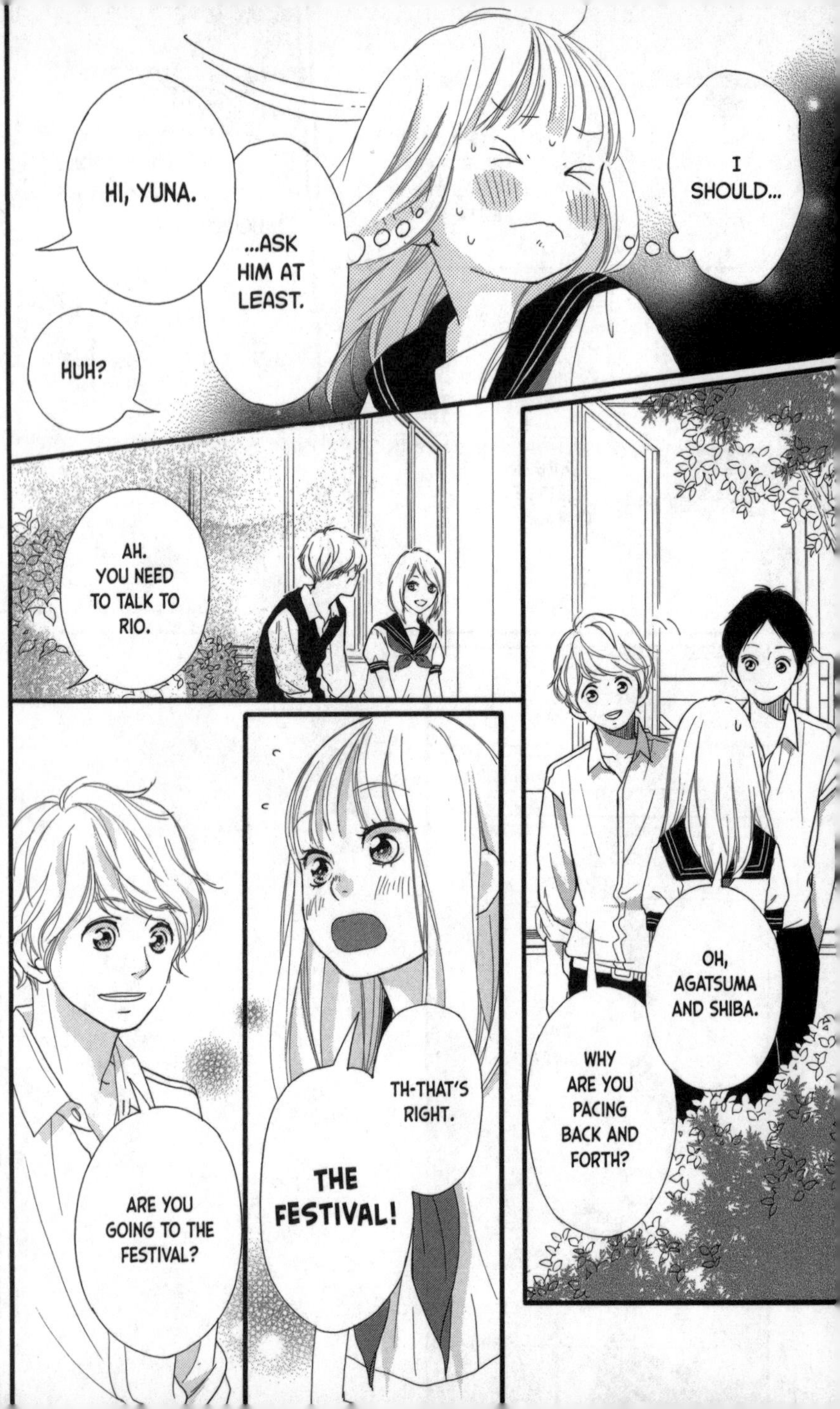
I SHOULD...
...ASK HIM AT LEAST.
HI, YUNA.
HUH?
OH, AGATSUMA AND SHIBA.
WHY ARE YOU PACING BACK AND FORTH?
AH. YOU NEED TO TALK TO RIO.
TH-THAT'S RIGHT.
THE FESTIVAL!
ARE YOU GOING TO THE FESTIVAL?

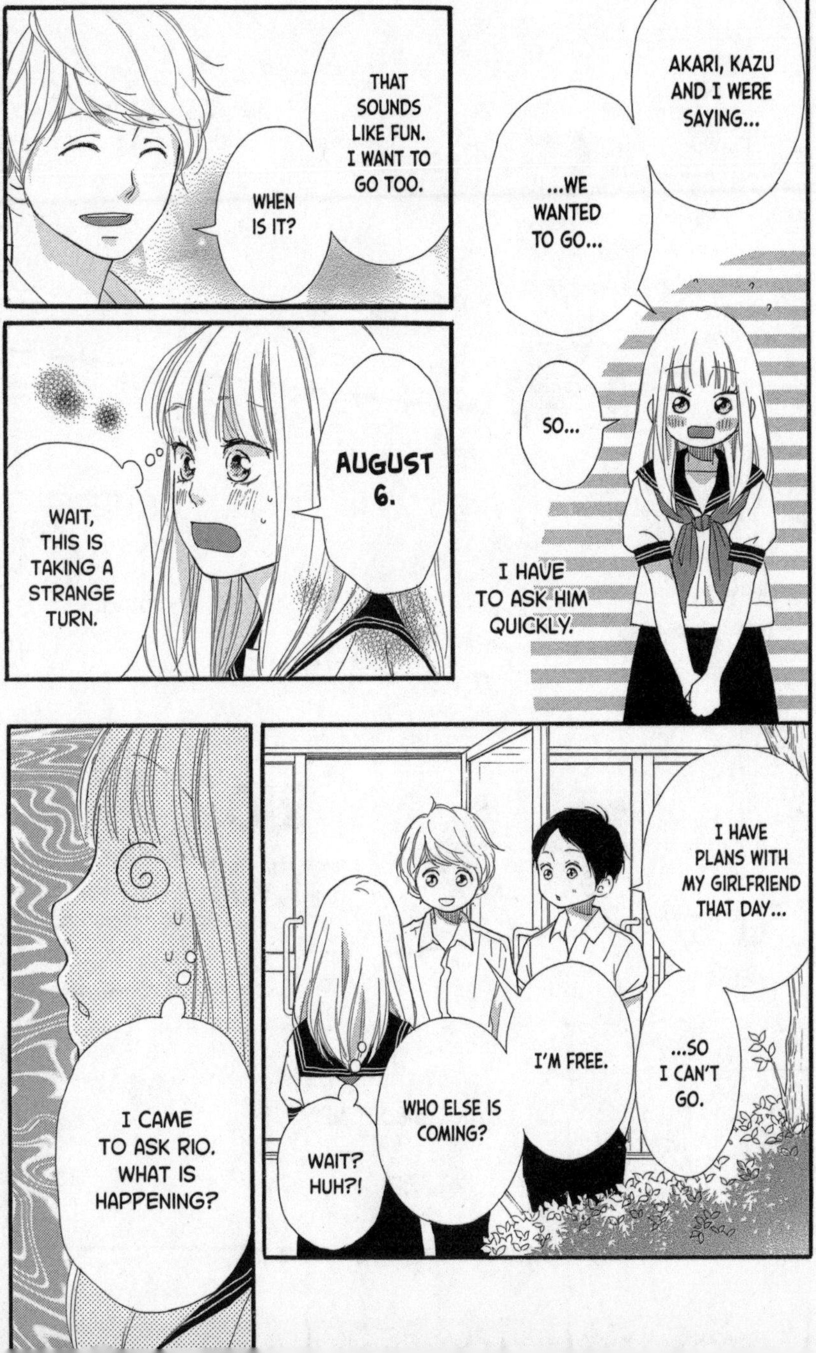
AKARI, KAZU AND I WERE SAYING...
...WE WANTED TO GO...
SO...
I HAVE TO ASK HIM QUICKLY.
THAT SOUNDS LIKE FUN. I WANT TO GO TOO.
WHEN IS IT?
AUGUST 6.
WAIT, THIS IS TAKING A STRANGE TURN.
I HAVE PLANS WITH MY GIRLFRIEND THAT DAY...
...SO I CAN'T GO.
I'M FREE.
WHO ELSE IS COMING?
WAIT? HUH?!
I CAME TO ASK RIO. WHAT IS HAPPENING?

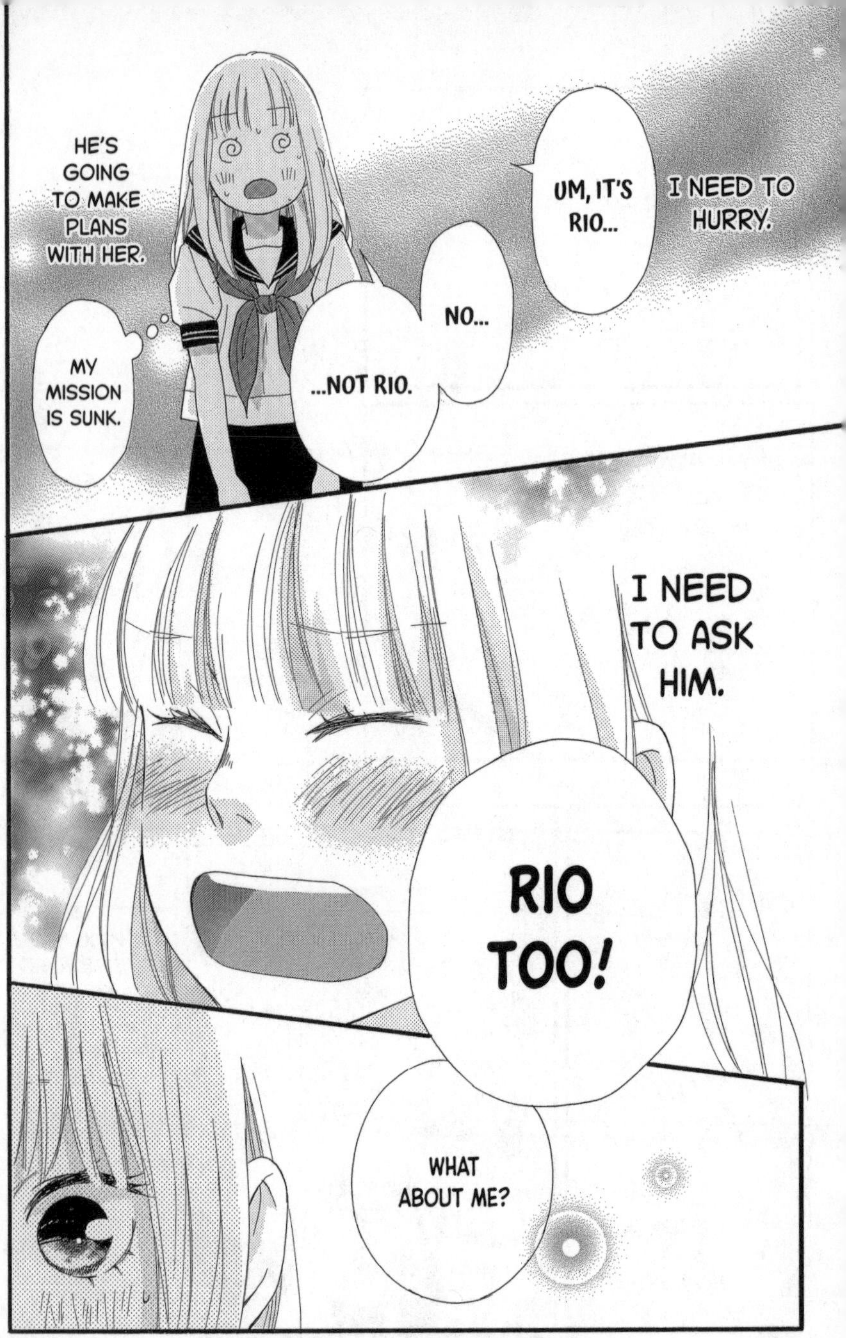
I NEED TO HURRY.
UM, IT'S RIO...
NO...
...NOT RIO.
HE'S GOING TO MAKE PLANS WITH HER.
MY MISSION IS SUNK.
I NEED TO ASK HIM.
RIO TOO!
WHAT ABOUT ME?

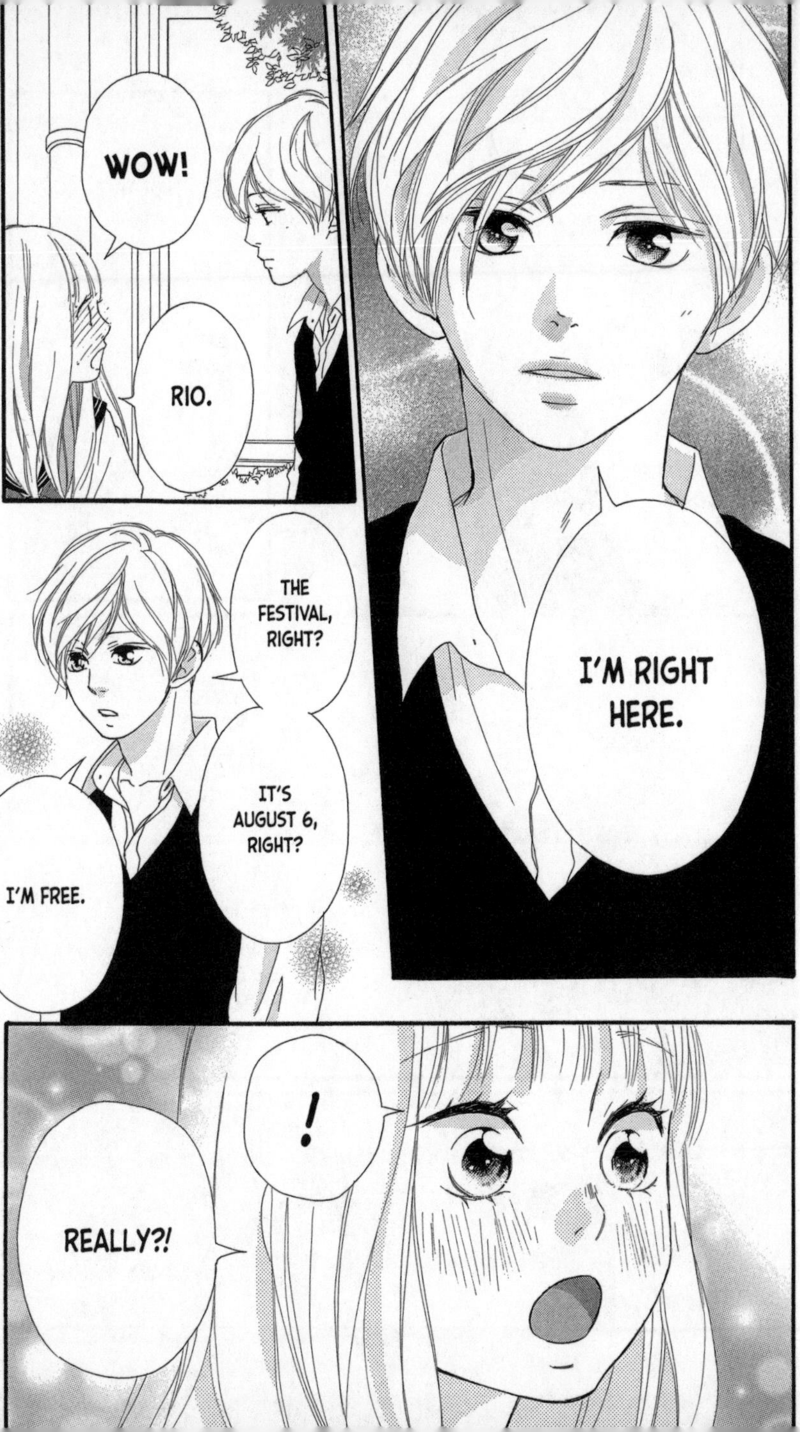
I'M RIGHT HERE.
WOW!
RIO.
THE FESTIVAL, RIGHT?
IT'S AUGUST 6, RIGHT?
I'M FREE.
!
REALLY?!

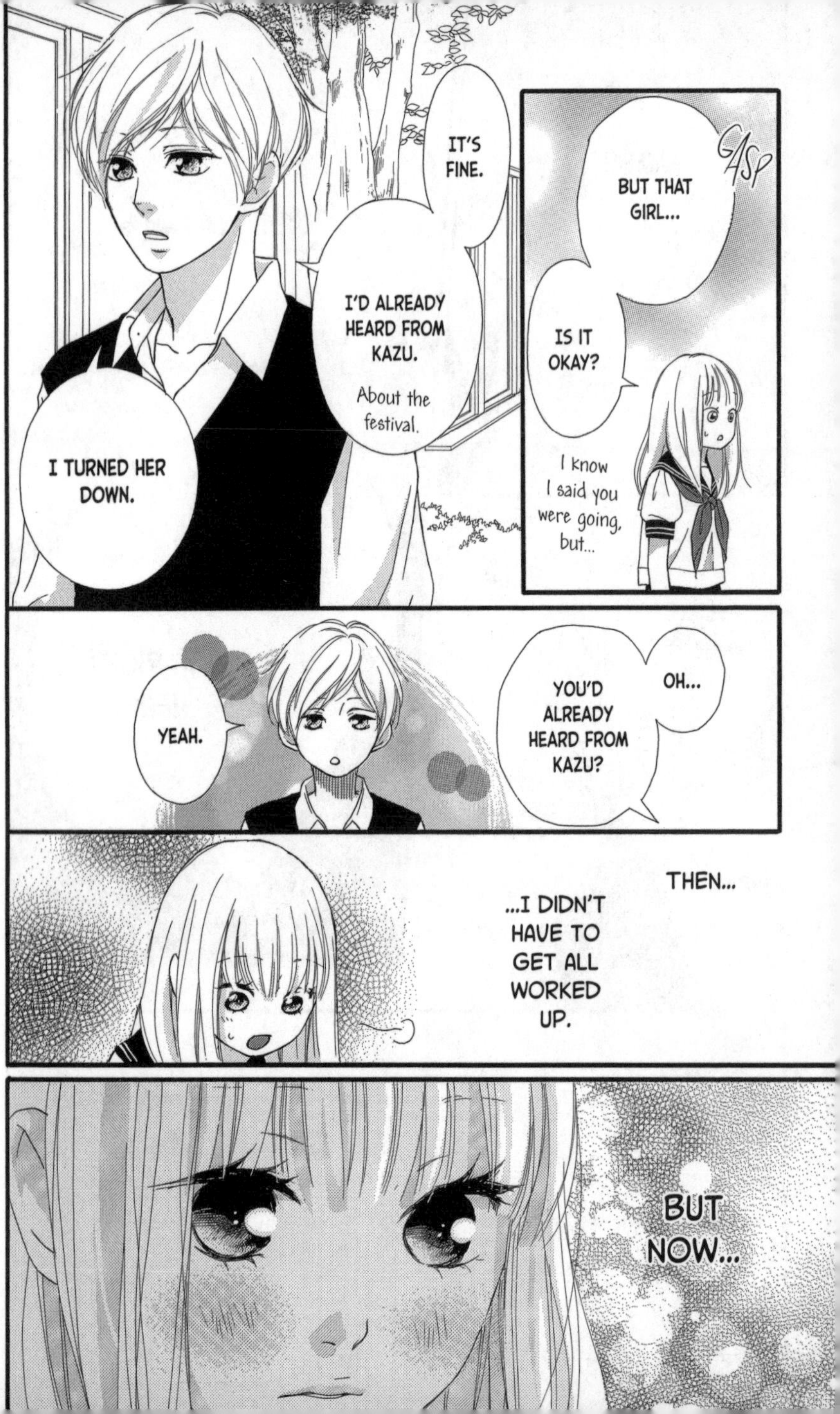
GASP
BUT THAT GIRL...
IS IT OKAY?
I know I said you were going, but...
IT'S FINE.
I'D ALREADY HEARD FROM KAZU.
About the festival.
I TURNED HER DOWN.
OH...
YOU'D ALREADY HEARD FROM KAZU?
YEAH.
THEN...
...I DIDN'T HAVE TO GET ALL WORKED UP.
BUT NOW...

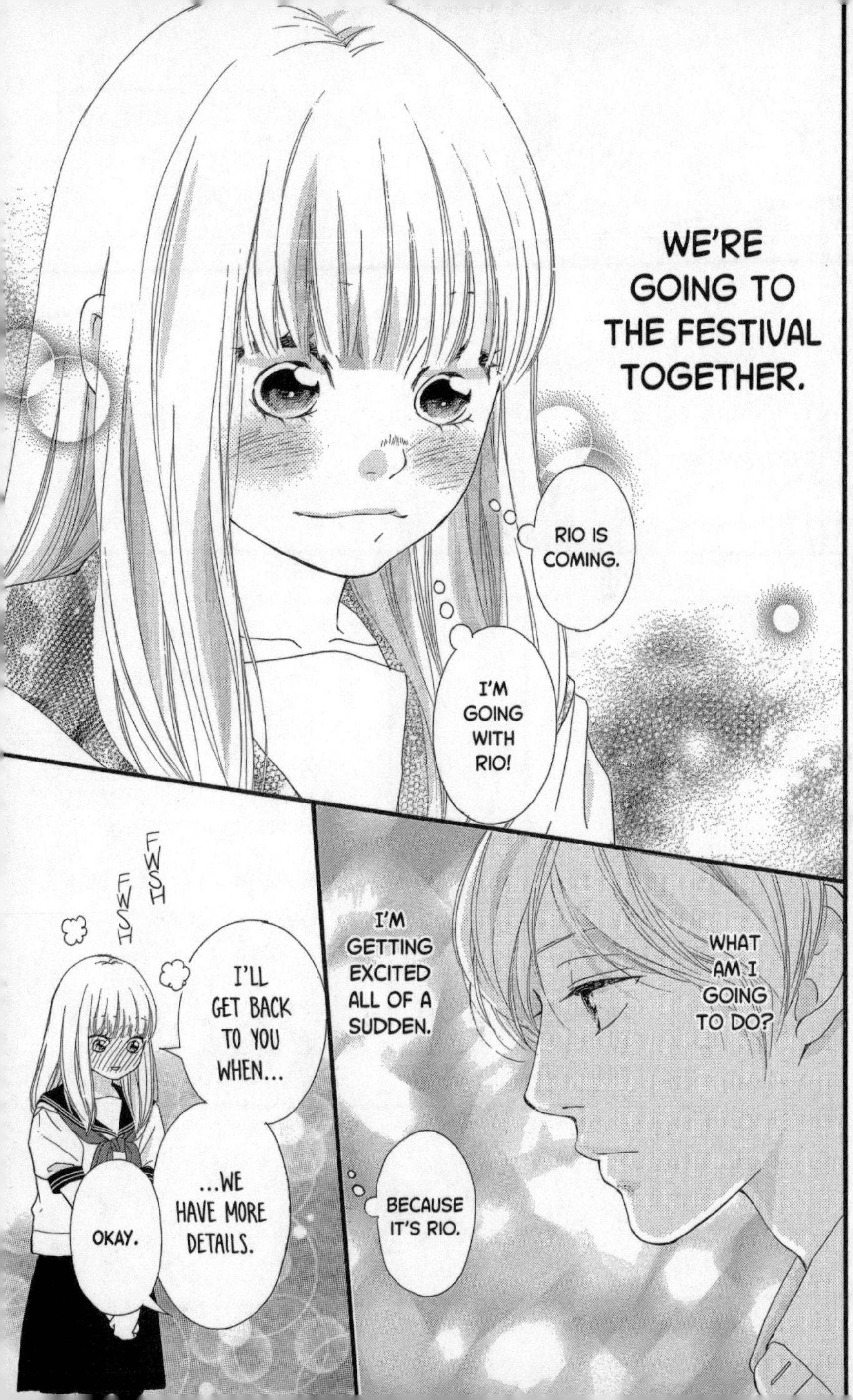
WE'RE GOING TO THE FESTIVAL TOGETHER.
RIO IS COMING.
I'M GOING WITH RIO!
WHAT AM I GOING TO DO?
I'M GETTING EXCITED ALL OF A SUDDEN.
BECAUSE IT'S RIO.
FWSH
FWSH
I'LL GET BACK TO YOU WHEN...
...WE HAVE MORE DETAILS.
OKAY.

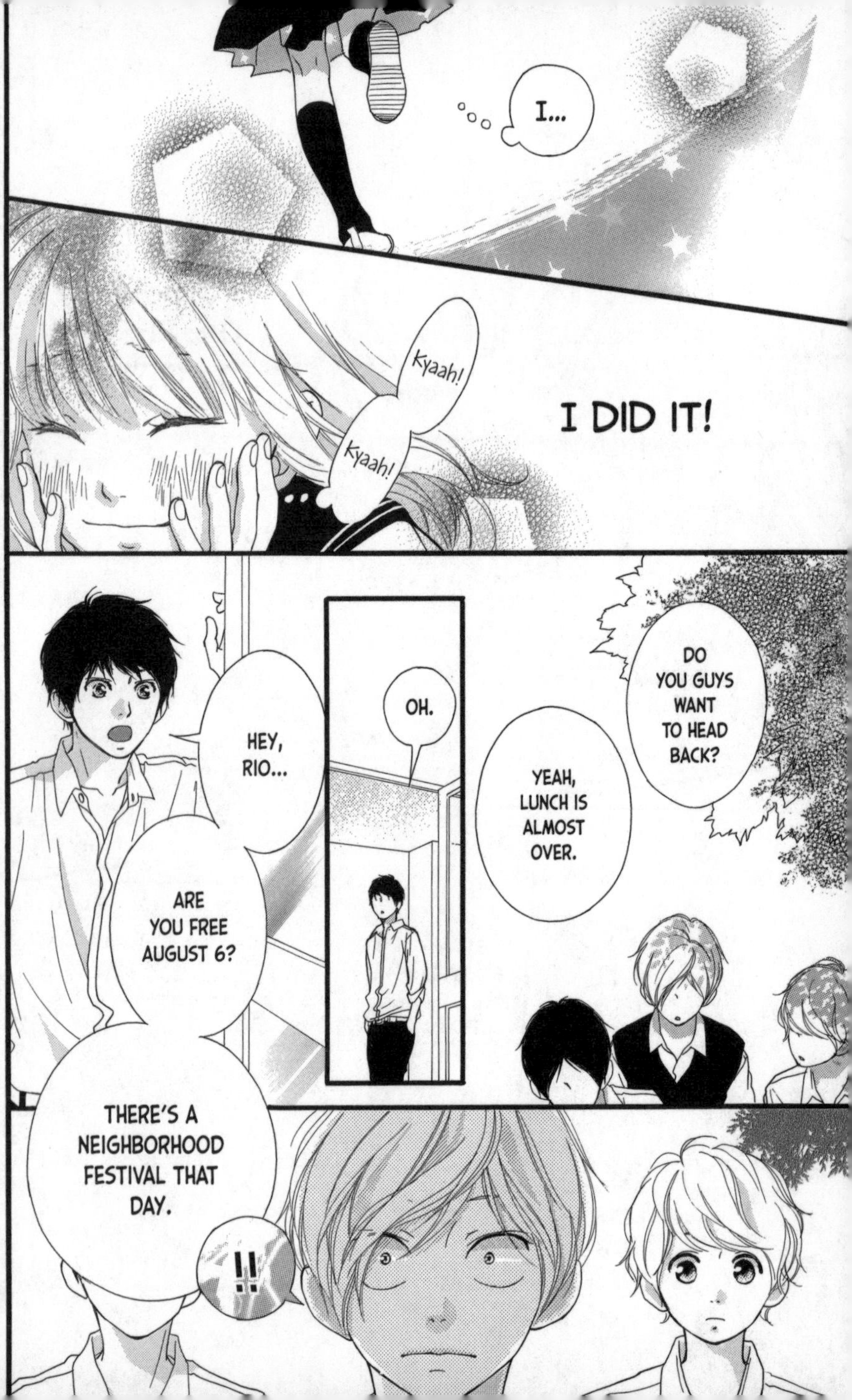
I...
I DID IT!
Kyaah!
Kyaah!
DO YOU GUYS WANT TO HEAD BACK?
YEAH, LUNCH IS ALMOST OVER.
OH.
HEY, RIO...
ARE YOU FREE AUGUST 6?
THERE'S A NEIGHBORHOOD FESTIVAL THAT DAY.
!!

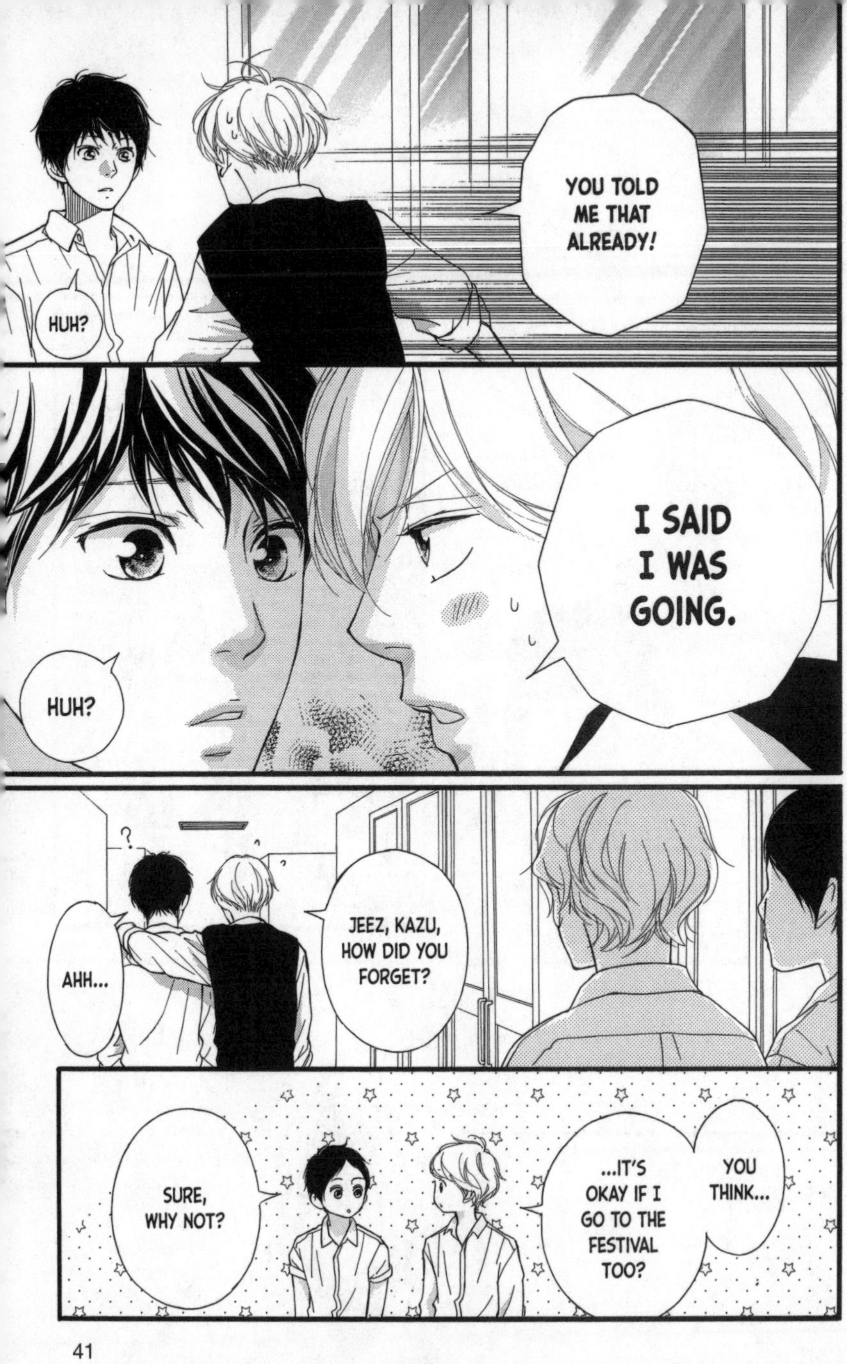
YOU TOLD ME THAT ALREADY!
HUH?
I SAID I WAS GOING.
HUH?
JEEZ, KAZU, HOW DID YOU FORGET?
AHH...
YOU THINK...
...IT'S OKAY IF I GO TO THE FESTIVAL TOO?
SURE, WHY NOT?

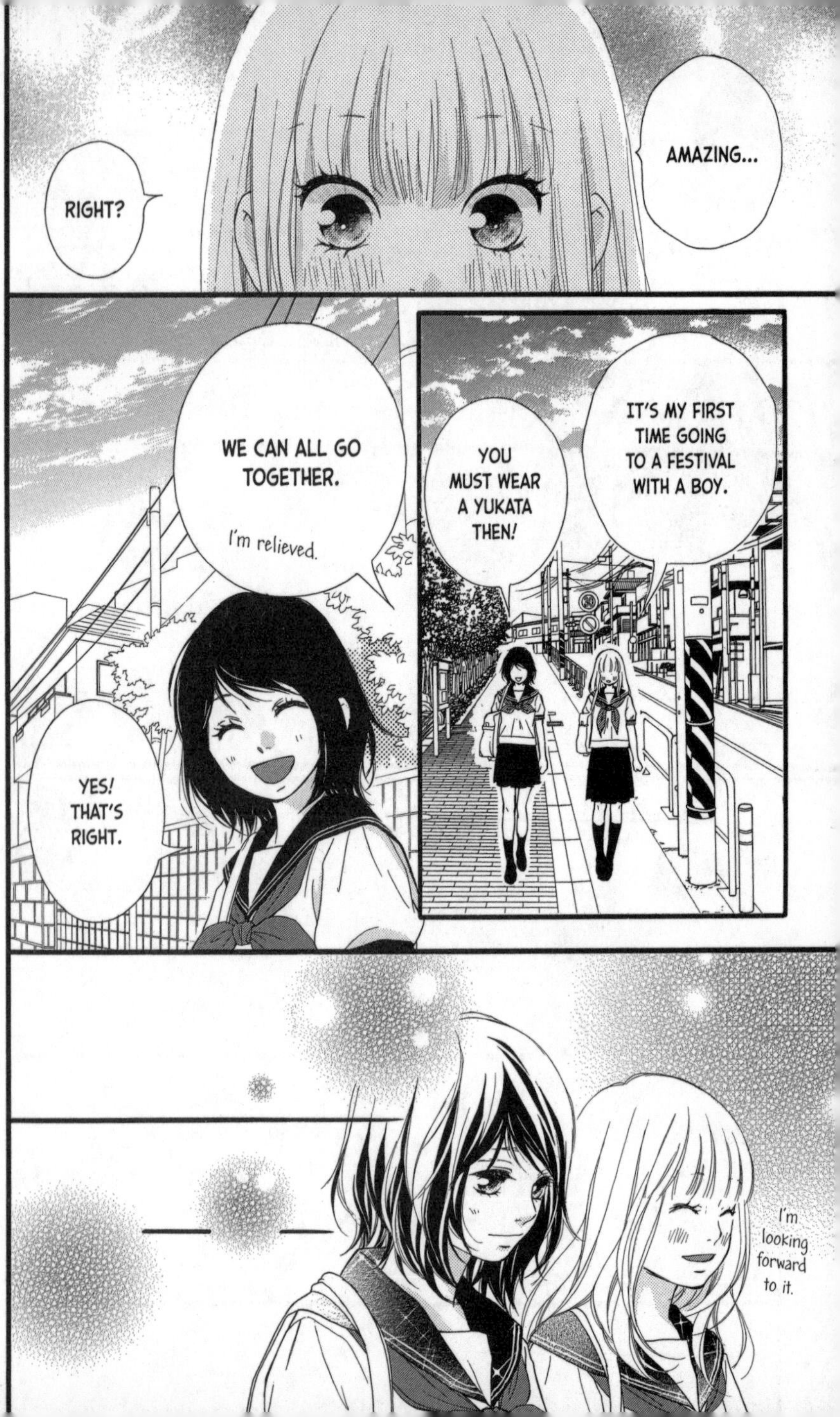
AMAZING...
RIGHT?
IT'S MY FIRST TIME GOING TO A FESTIVAL WITH A BOY.
YOU MUST WEAR A YUKATA THEN!
WE CAN ALL GO TOGETHER.
I'm relieved.
YES! THAT'S RIGHT.
I'm looking forward to it.

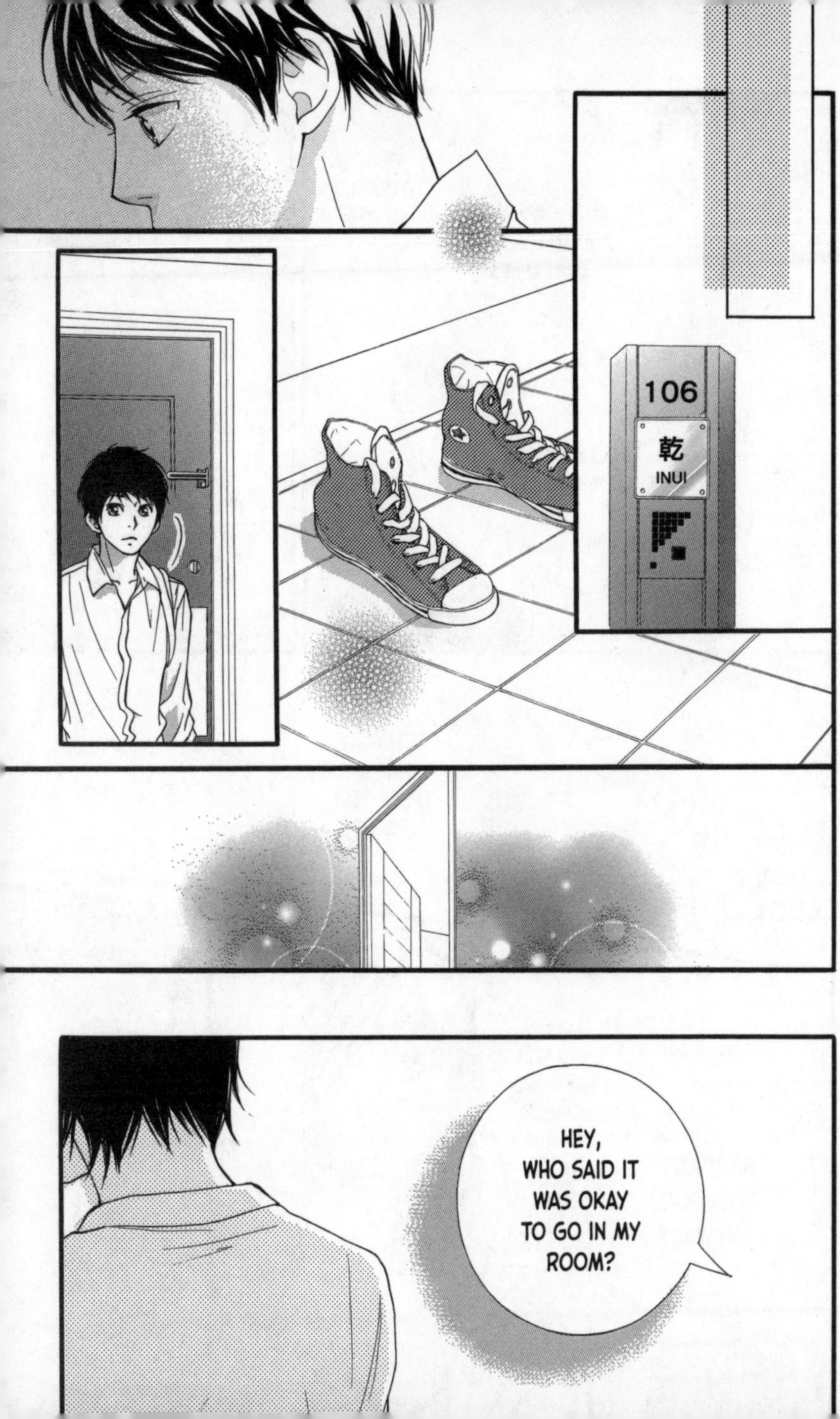
106
乾
INUI
HEY, WHO SAID IT WAS OKAY TO GO IN MY ROOM?

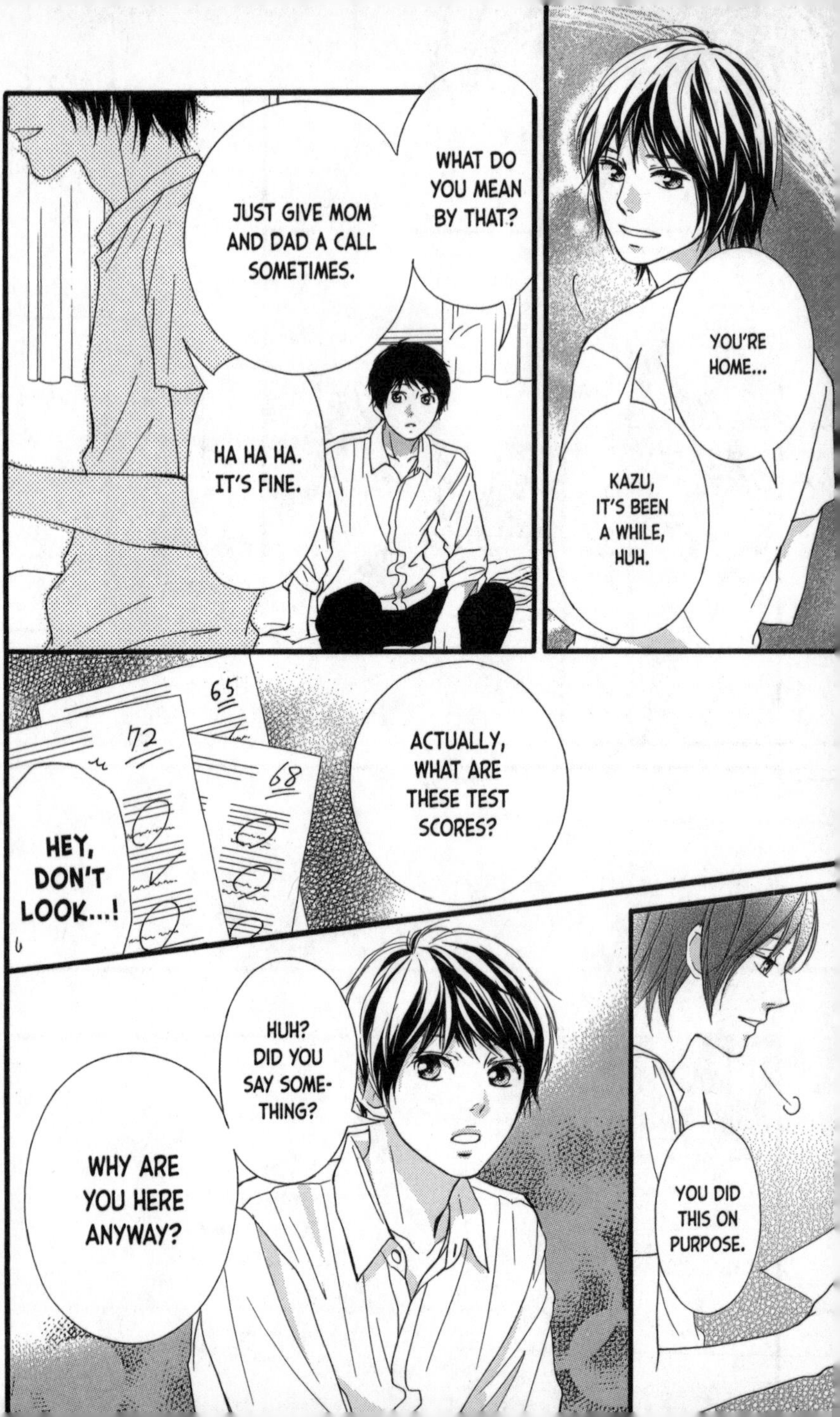

YOU'RE HOME...
KAZU, IT'S BEEN A WHILE, HUH.
WHAT DO YOU MEAN BY THAT?
JUST GIVE MOM AND DAD A CALL SOMETIMES.
HA HA HA. IT'S FINE.
65
72
68
ACTUALLY, WHAT ARE THESE TEST SCORES?
HEY, DON'T LOOK...!
YOU DID THIS ON PURPOSE.
HUH? DID YOU SAY SOME-THING?
WHY ARE YOU HERE ANYWAY?

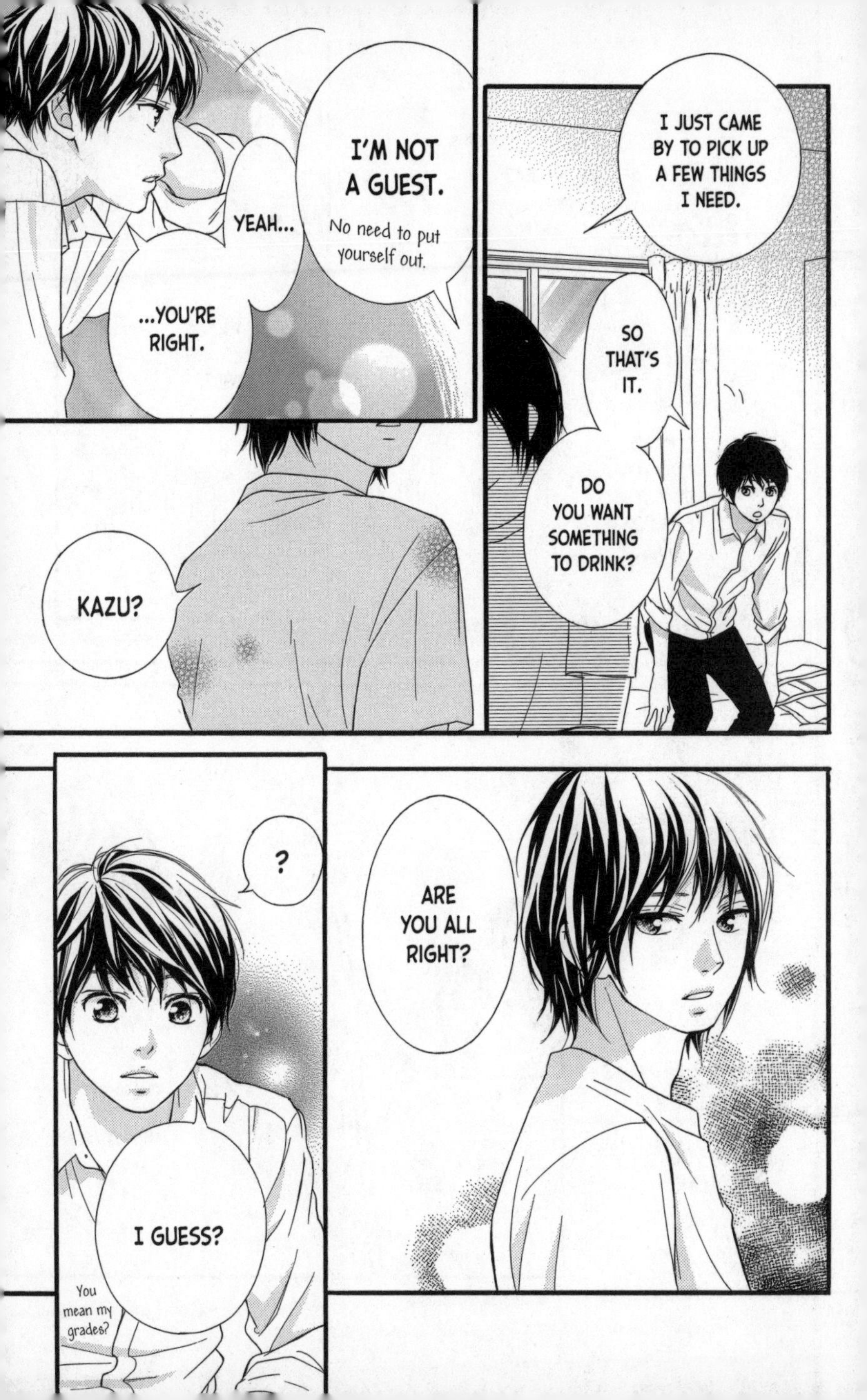
I JUST CAME BY TO PICK UP A FEW THINGS I NEED.
SO THAT'S IT.
DO YOU WANT SOMETHING TO DRINK?
I'M NOT A GUEST.
No need to put yourself out.
YEAH...
...YOU'RE RIGHT.
KAZU?
ARE YOU ALL RIGHT?
?
I GUESS?
You mean my grades?

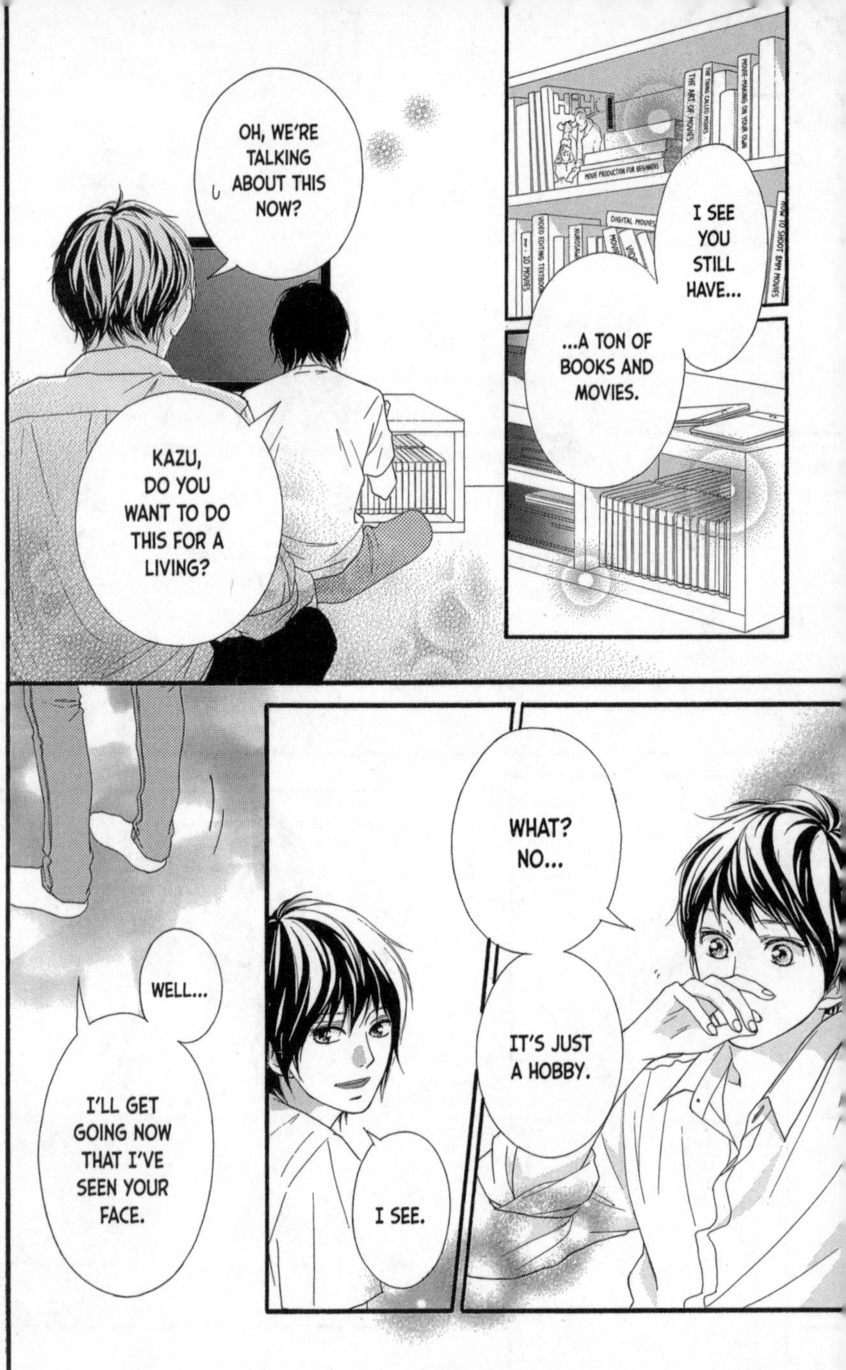
THE THING CALLED MOVIES
THE ART OF MOVIES
MOVIE-MAKING ON YOUR OWN
MOVIE PRODUCTION FOR BEGINNERS
DIGITAL MOVIES
HOW TO SHOOT 8MM MOVIES
I SEE YOU STILL HAVE...
...A TON OF BOOKS AND MOVIES.
OH, WE'RE TALKING ABOUT THIS NOW?
KAZU, DO YOU WANT TO DO THIS FOR A LIVING?
WHAT? NO...
IT'S JUST A HOBBY.
I SEE.
WELL...
I'LL GET GOING NOW THAT I'VE SEEN YOUR FACE.

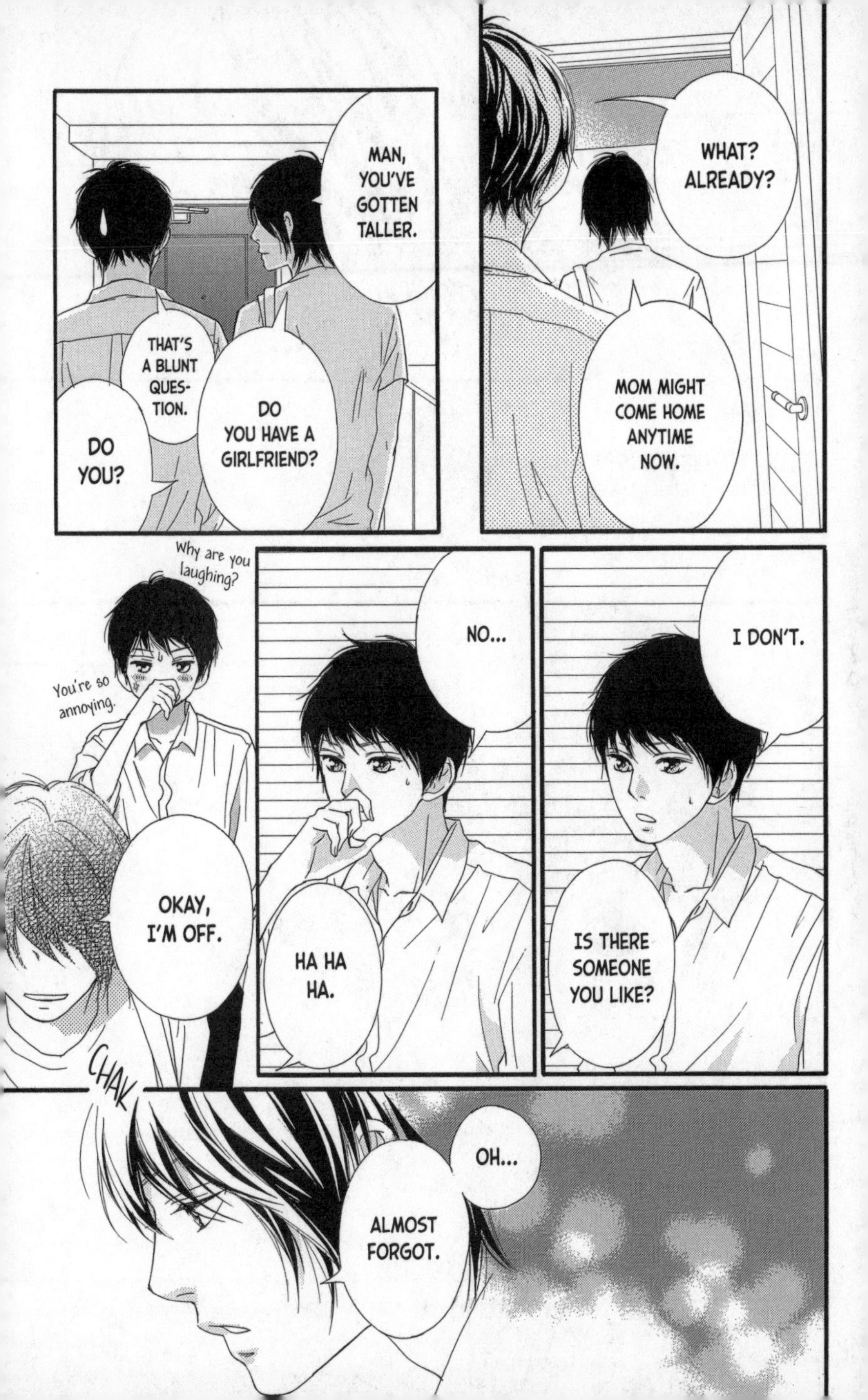
WHAT? ALREADY?
MOM MIGHT COME HOME ANYTIME NOW.
MAN, YOU'VE GOTTEN TALLER.
DO YOU HAVE A GIRLFRIEND?
THAT'S A BLUNT QUES-TION.
DO YOU?
I DON'T.
IS THERE SOMEONE YOU LIKE?
NO...
HA HA HA.
Why are you laughing?
You're so annoying.
OKAY, I'M OFF.
CHAK
OH...
ALMOST FORGOT.

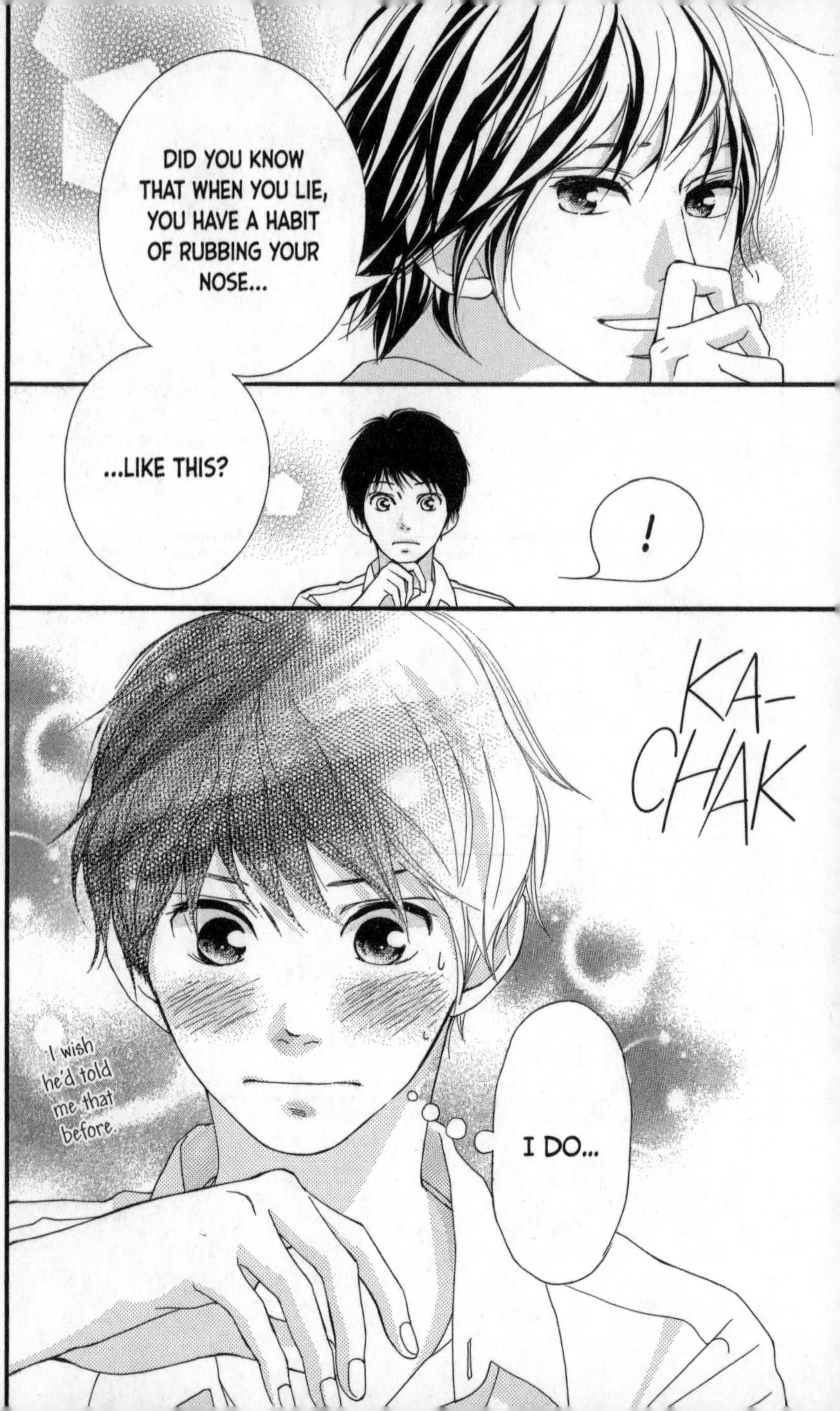
DID YOU KNOW THAT WHEN YOU LIE, YOU HAVE A HABIT OF RUBBING YOUR NOSE...
...LIKE THIS?
!
KA-CHAK
I DO...
I wish he'd told me that before.

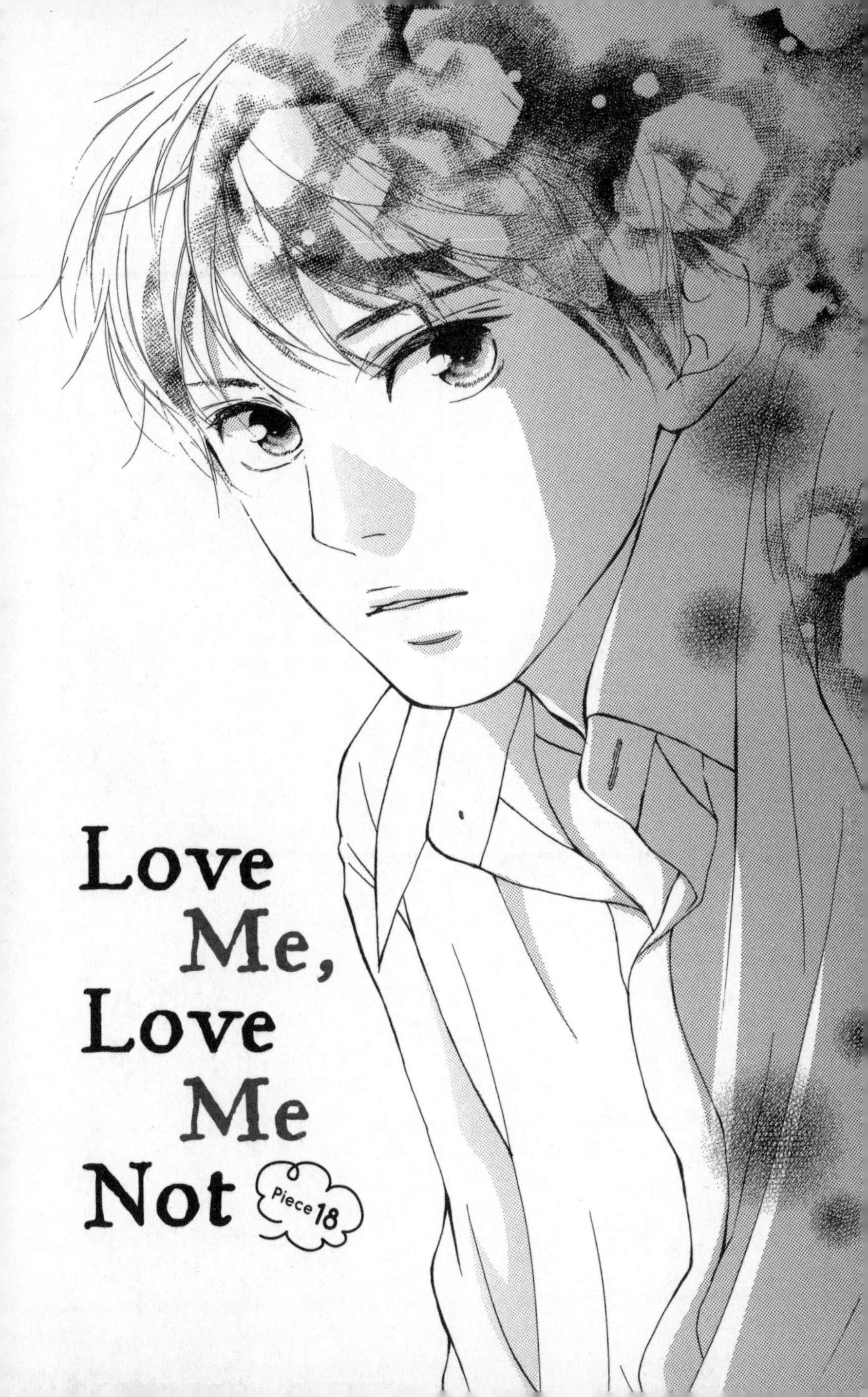
Love Me, Love Me Not
Piece 18

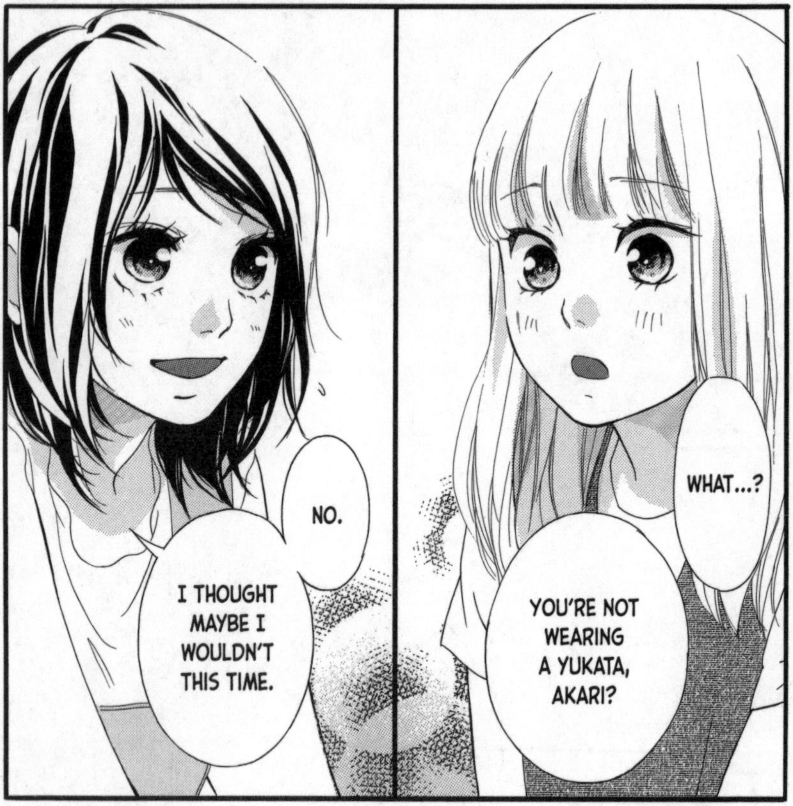
WHAT...?
YOU'RE NOT WEARING A YUKATA, AKARI?
NO.
I THOUGHT MAYBE I WOULDN'T THIS TIME.

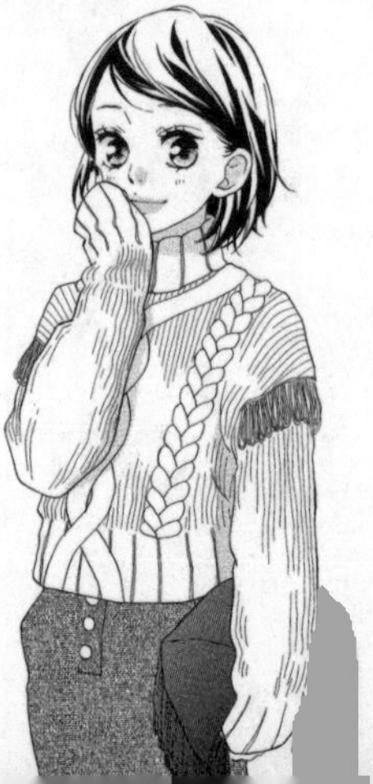

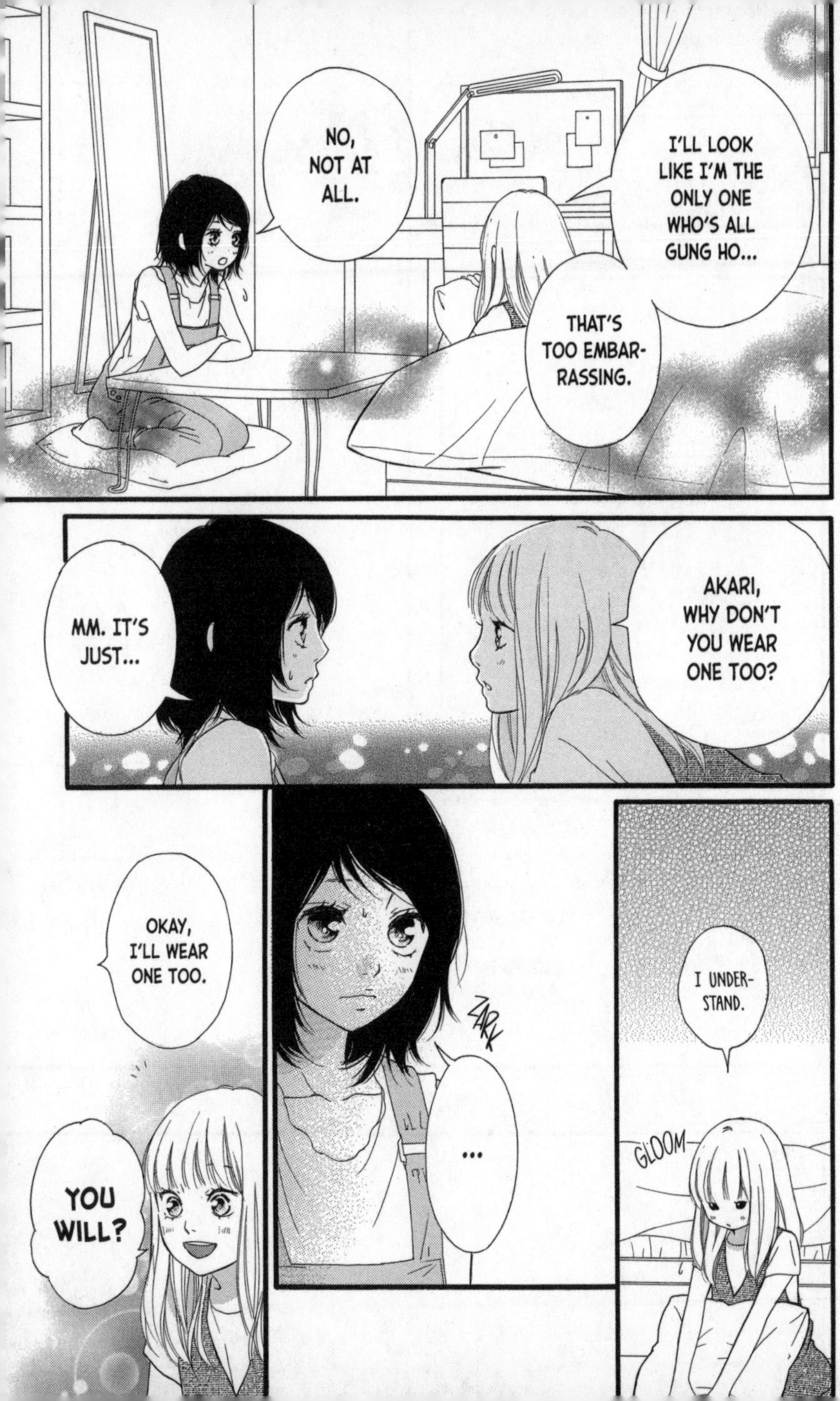
I'LL LOOK LIKE I'M THE ONLY ONE WHO'S ALL GUNG HO...
THAT'S TOO EMBARRASSING.
NO, NOT AT ALL.
AKARI, WHY DON'T YOU WEAR ONE TOO?
MM. IT'S JUST...
I UNDERSTAND.
GLOOM
ZARK
...
OKAY, I'LL WEAR ONE TOO.
YOU WILL?

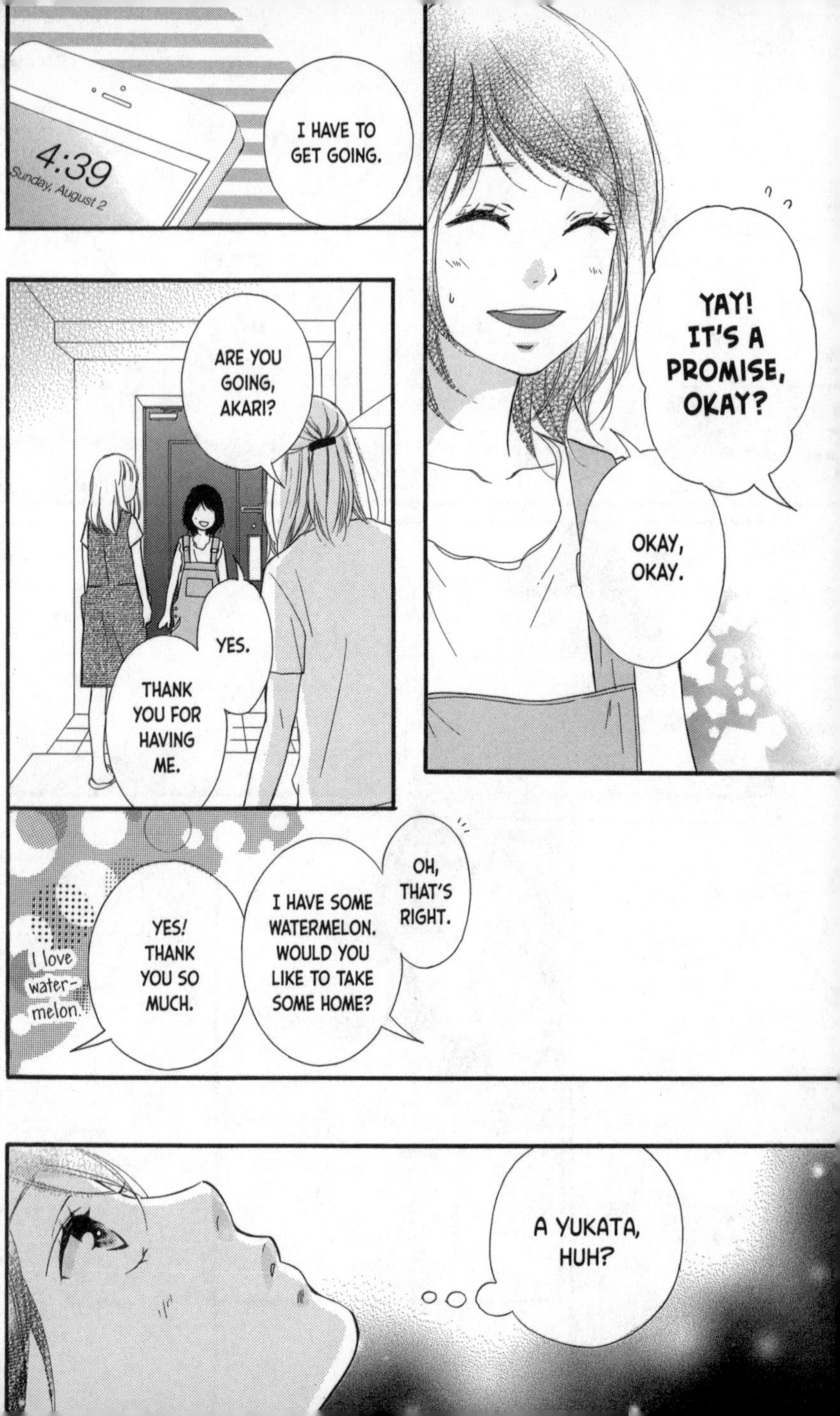
YAY! IT'S A PROMISE, OKAY?
OKAY, OKAY.
4:39
Sunday, August 2
I HAVE TO GET GOING.
ARE YOU GOING, AKARI?
YES.
THANK YOU FOR HAVING ME.
OH, THAT'S RIGHT.
I HAVE SOME WATERMELON. WOULD YOU LIKE TO TAKE SOME HOME?
YES! THANK YOU SO MUCH.
I love water-melon.
A YUKATA, HUH?

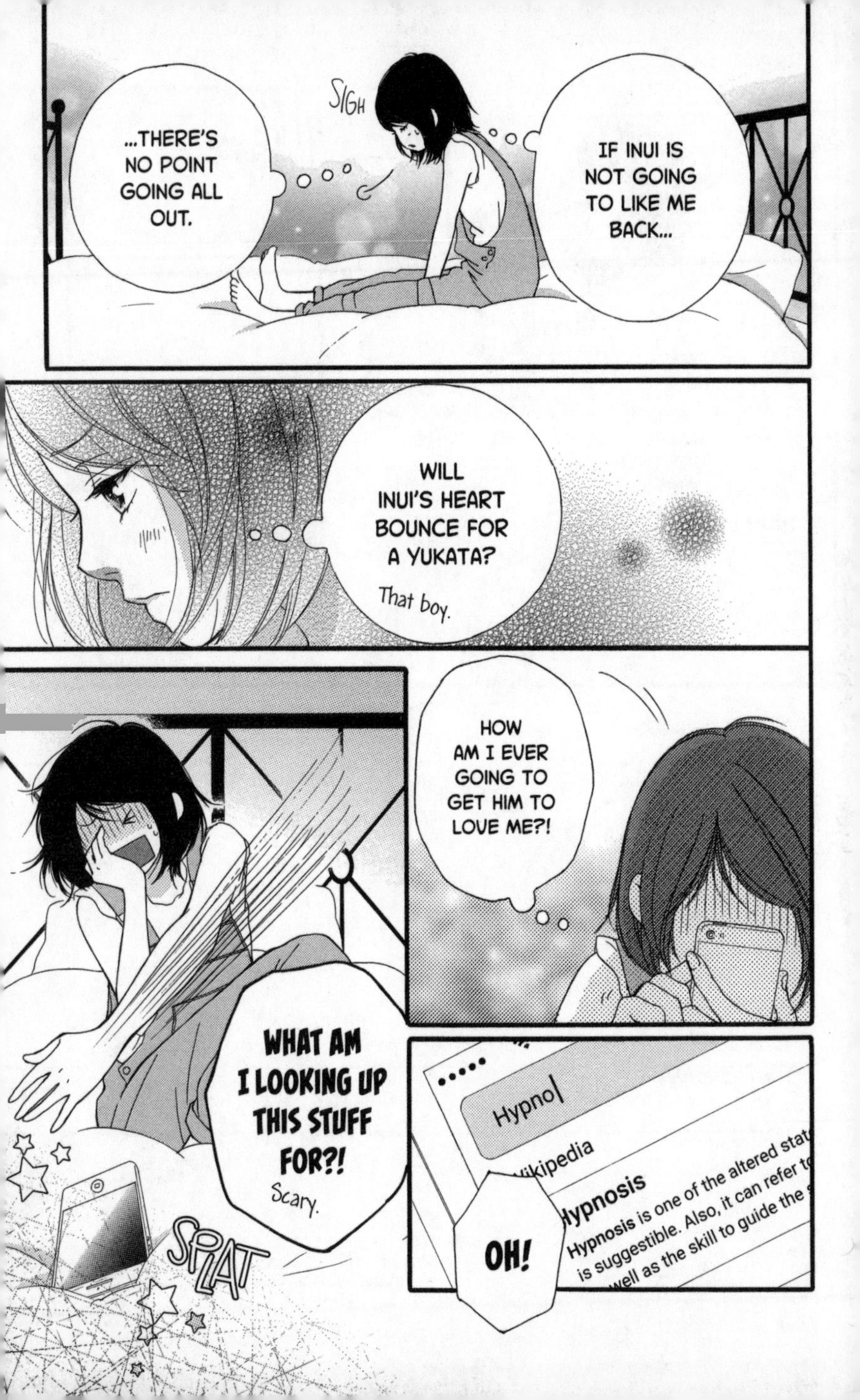
IF INUI IS NOT GOING TO LIKE ME BACK...
SIGH
...THERE'S NO POINT GOING ALL OUT.
WILL INUI'S HEART BOUNCE FOR A YUKATA?
That boy.
HOW AM I EVER GOING TO GET HIM TO LOVE ME?!
Hypno
ikipedia
Hypnosis
Hypnosis is one of the altered stat
is suggestible. Also, it can refer t
well as the skill to guide the
OH!
WHAT AM I LOOKING UP THIS STUFF FOR?!
Scary.
SPLAT

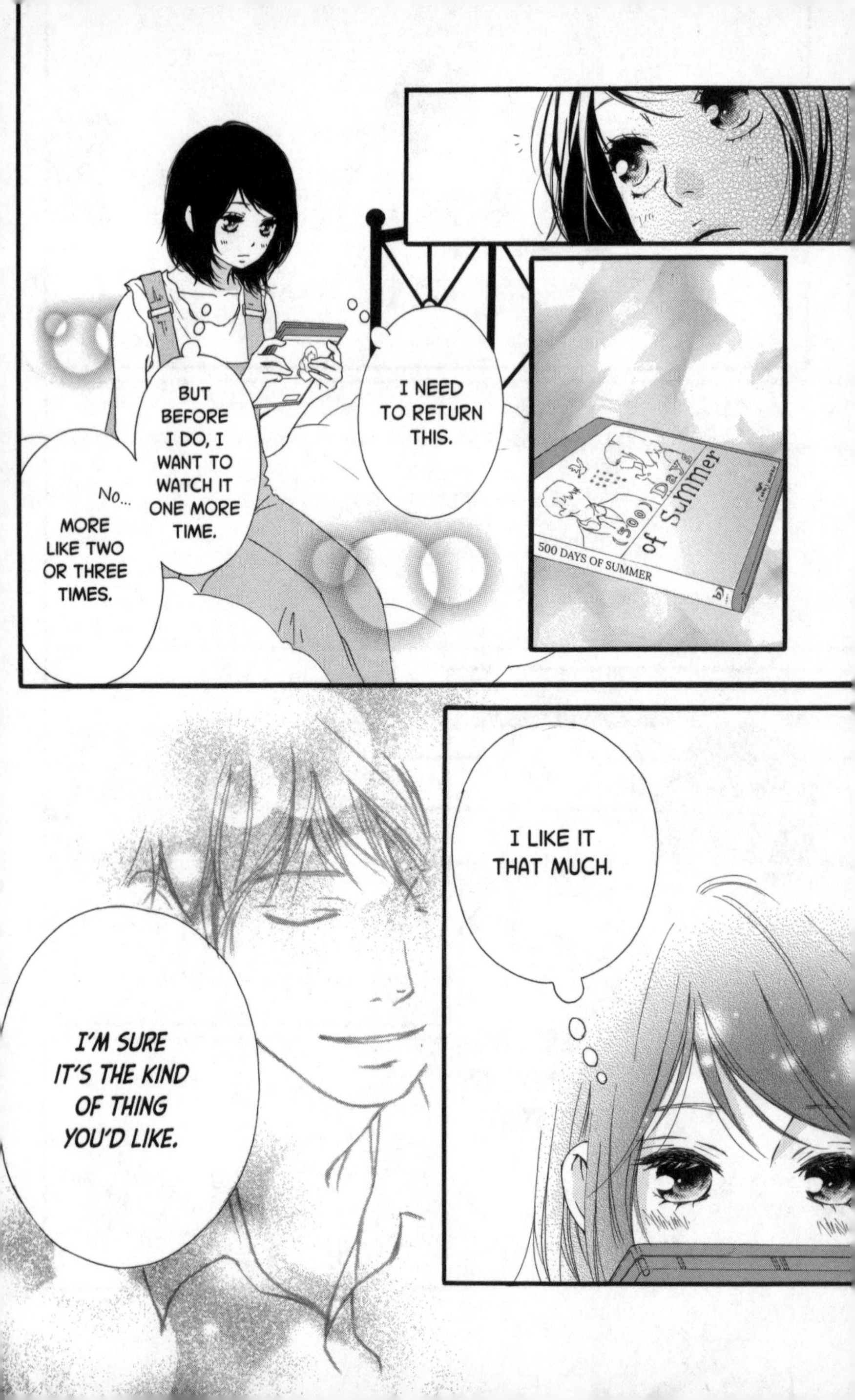
(500) Days of Summer
500 DAYS OF SUMMER
I NEED TO RETURN THIS.
BUT BEFORE I DO, I WANT TO WATCH IT ONE MORE TIME.
No... MORE LIKE TWO OR THREE TIMES.
I LIKE IT THAT MUCH.
I'M SURE IT'S THE KIND OF THING YOU'D LIKE.

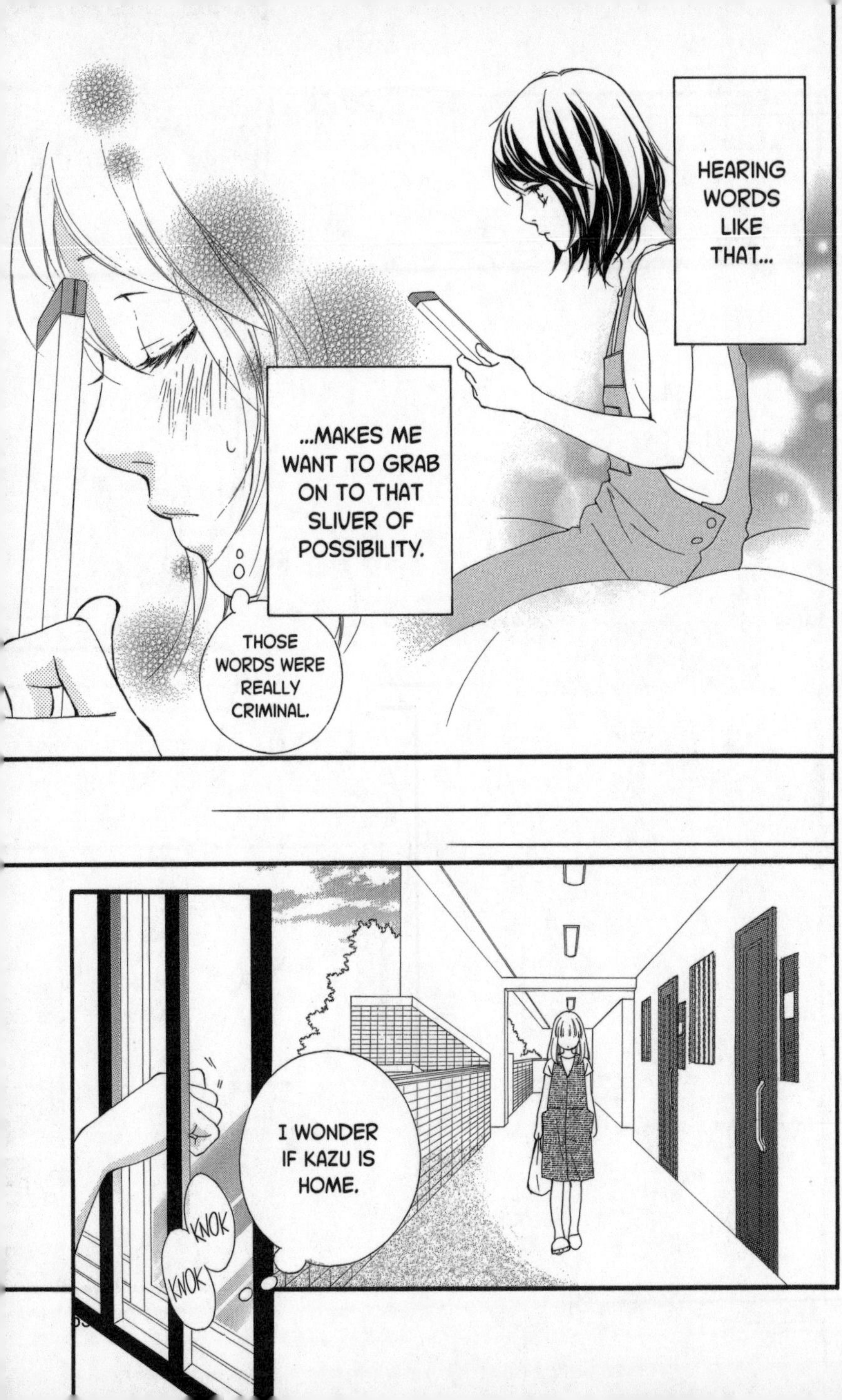
HEARING WORDS LIKE THAT...
...MAKES ME WANT TO GRAB ON TO THAT SLIVER OF POSSIBILITY.
THOSE WORDS WERE REALLY CRIMINAL.
I WONDER IF KAZU IS HOME.
KNOK
KNOK

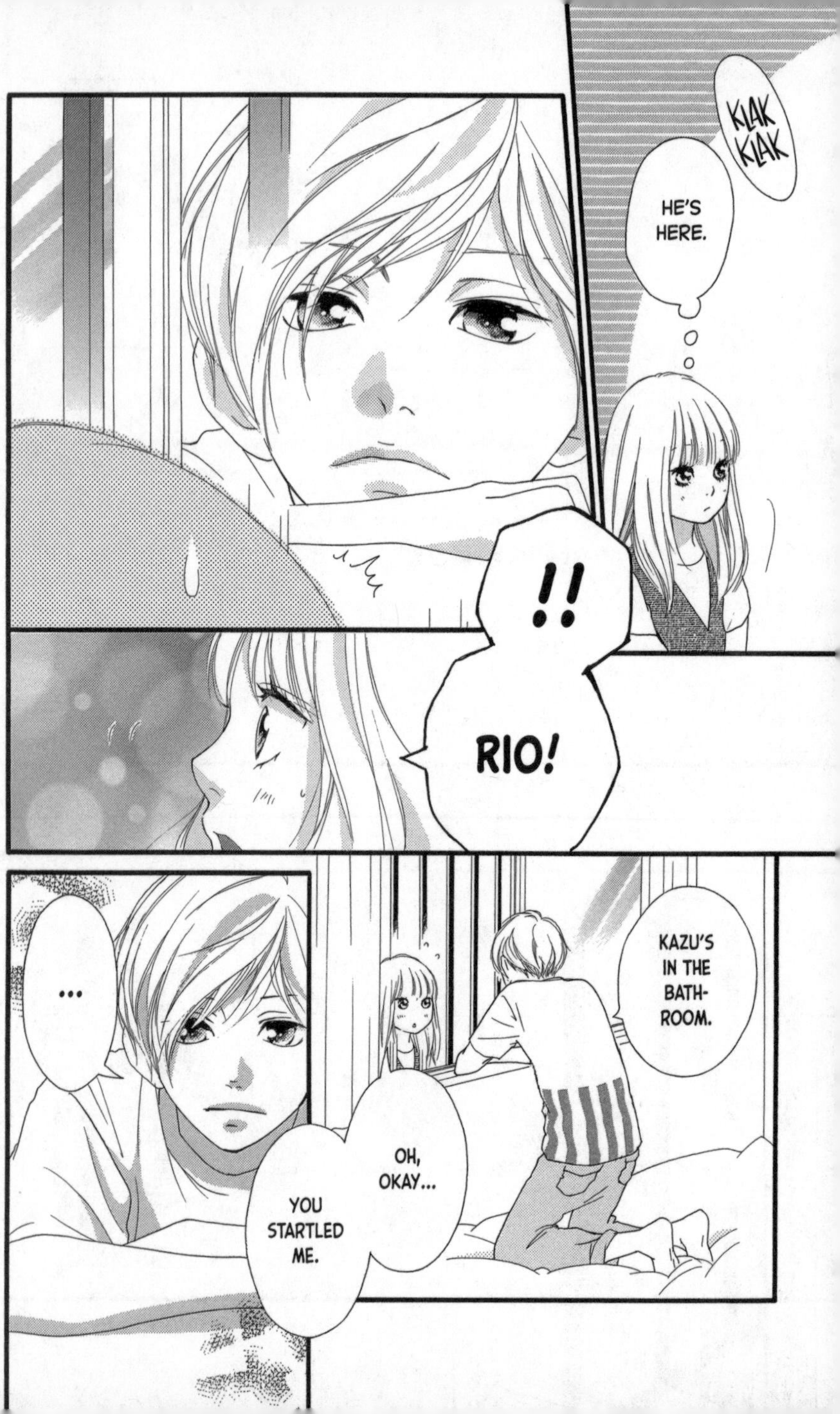
KLAK KLAK
HE'S HERE.
!!
RIO!
KAZU'S IN THE BATH-ROOM.
OH, OKAY...
YOU STARTLED ME.
...

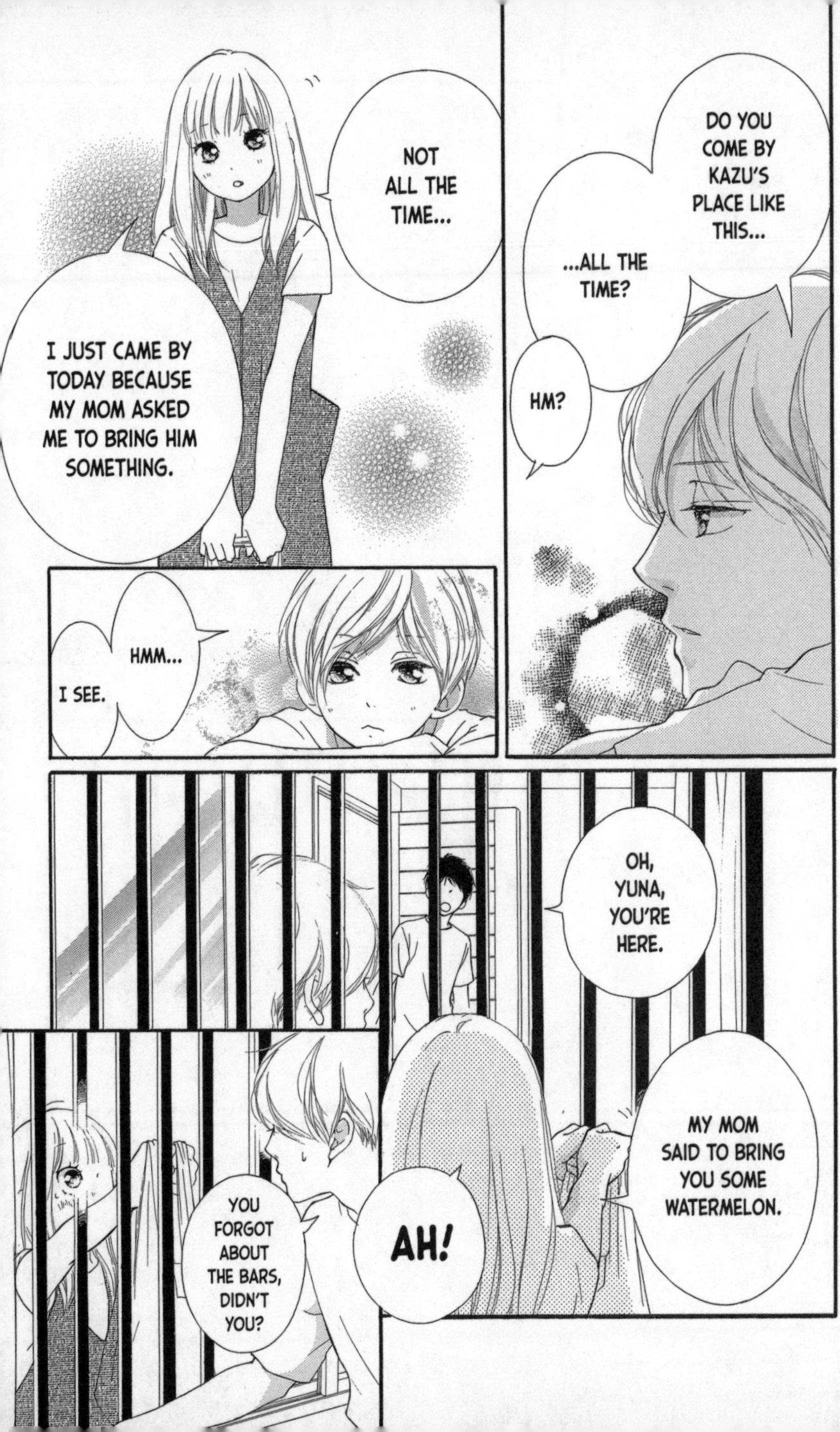
DO YOU COME BY KAZU'S PLACE LIKE THIS...
...ALL THE TIME?
HM?
NOT ALL THE TIME...
I JUST CAME BY TODAY BECAUSE MY MOM ASKED ME TO BRING HIM SOMETHING.
HMM...
I SEE.
OH, YUNA, YOU'RE HERE.
MY MOM SAID TO BRING YOU SOME WATERMELON.
AH!
YOU FORGOT ABOUT THE BARS, DIDN'T YOU?

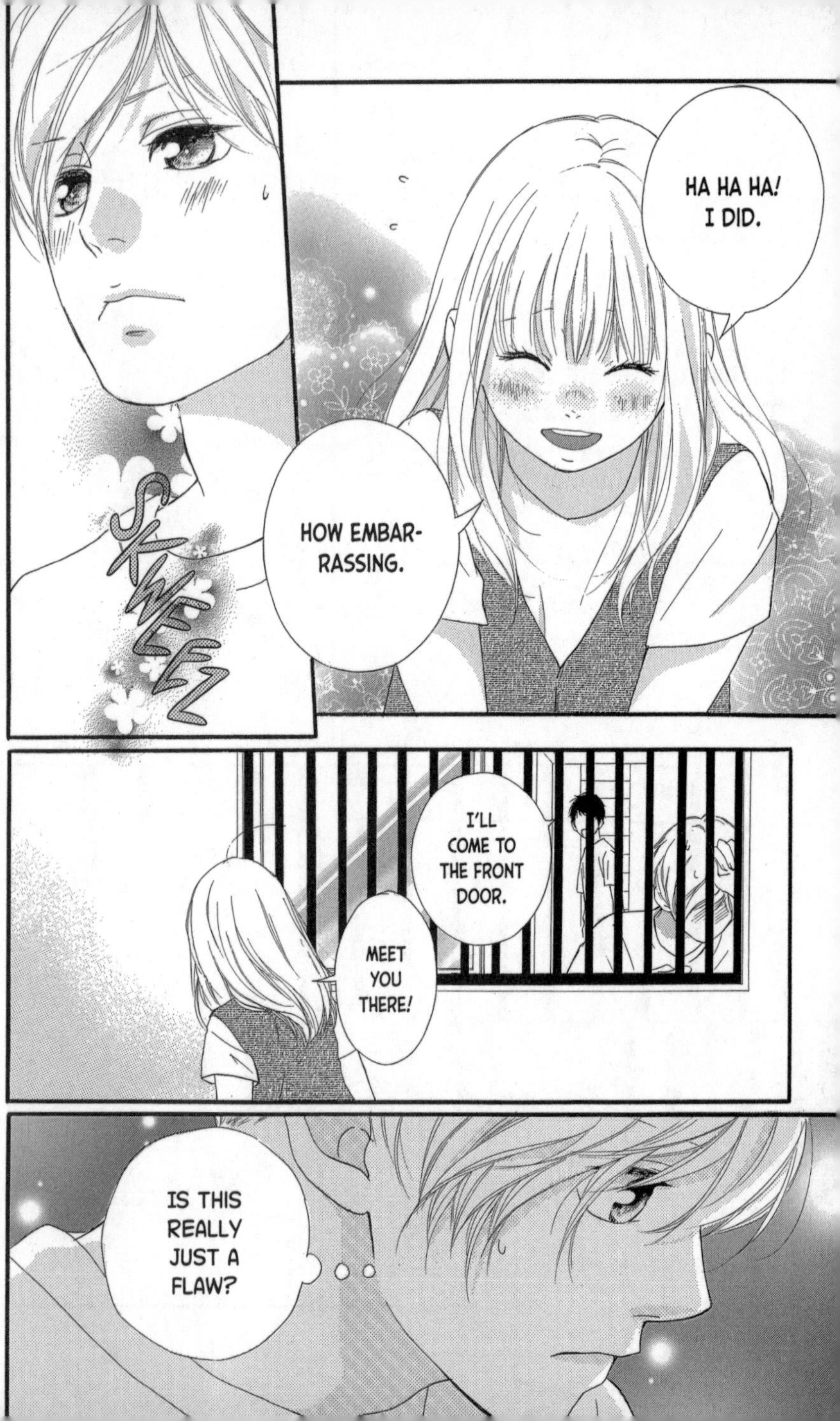
HA HA HA! I DID.
HOW EMBAR-RASSING.
SKWEEZ
I'LL COME TO THE FRONT DOOR.
MEET YOU THERE!
IS THIS REALLY JUST A FLAW?

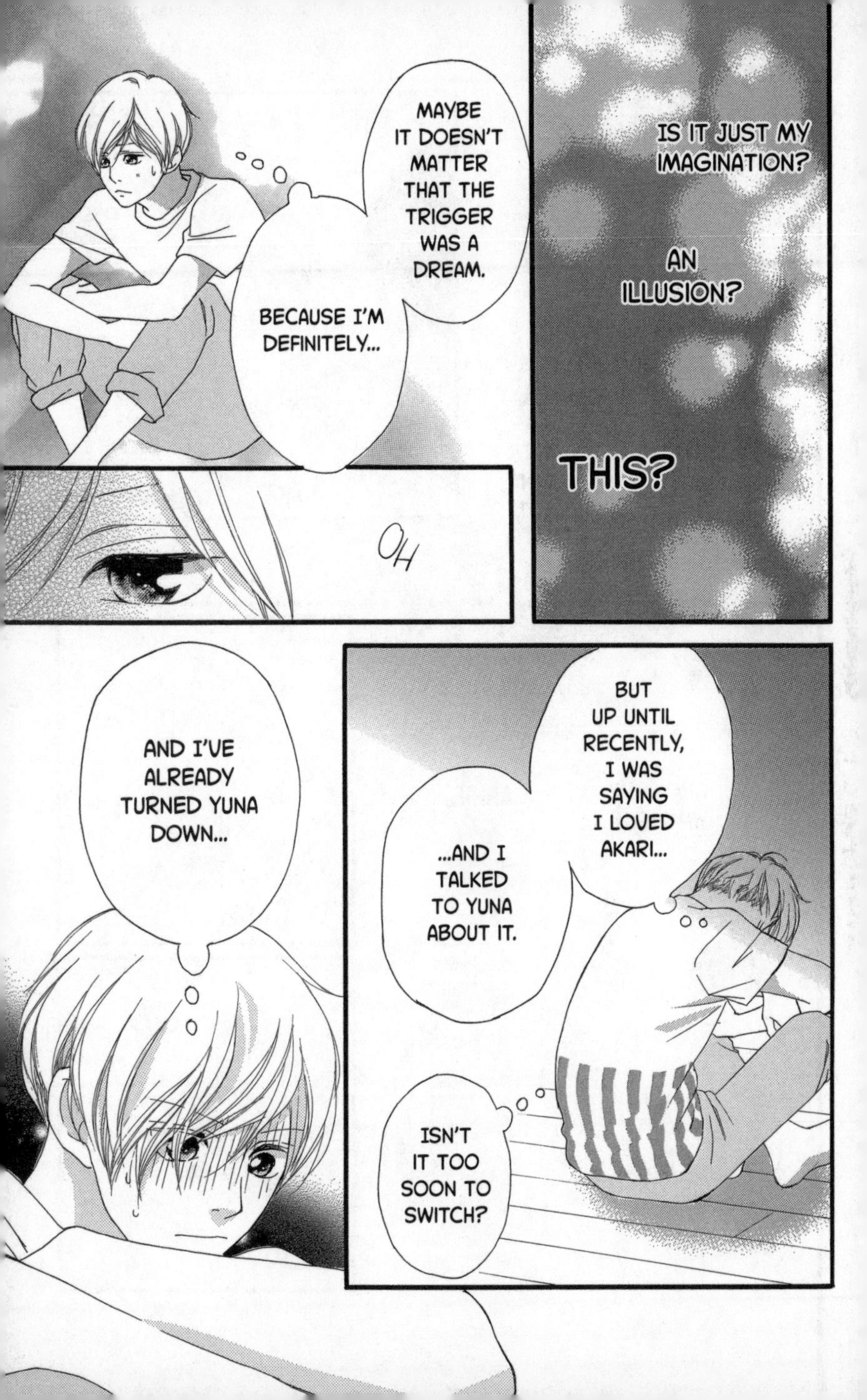
IS IT JUST MY IMAGINATION?
AN ILLUSION?
THIS?
MAYBE IT DOESN'T MATTER THAT THE TRIGGER WAS A DREAM.
BECAUSE I'M DEFINITELY...
OH
BUT UP UNTIL RECENTLY, I WAS SAYING I LOVED AKARI...
...AND I TALKED TO YUNA ABOUT IT.
ISN'T IT TOO SOON TO SWITCH?
AND I'VE ALREADY TURNED YUNA DOWN...

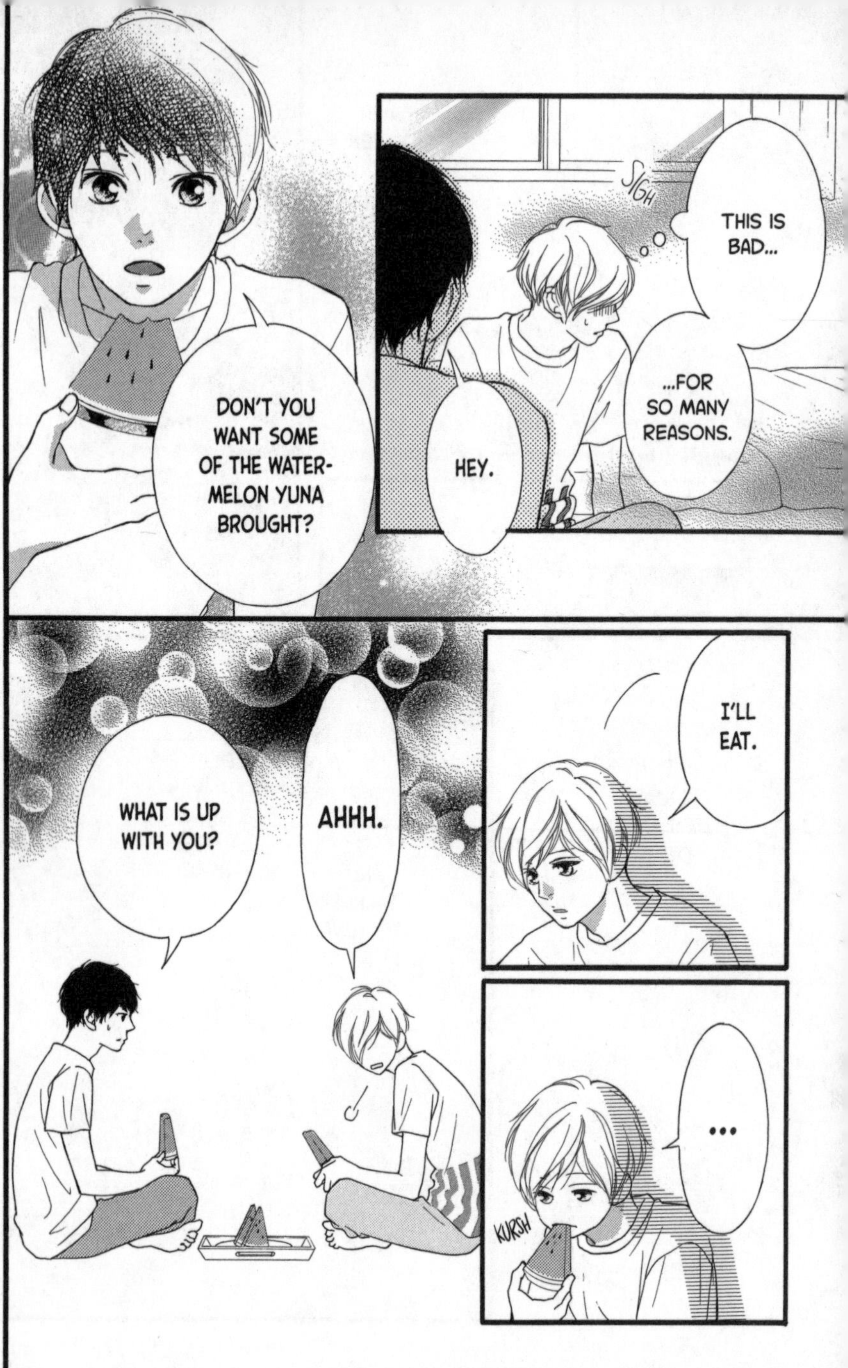
SIGH
THIS IS BAD...
...FOR SO MANY REASONS.
HEY.
DON'T YOU WANT SOME OF THE WATER-MELON YUNA BROUGHT?
I'LL EAT.
...
KURSH
AHHH.
WHAT IS UP WITH YOU?

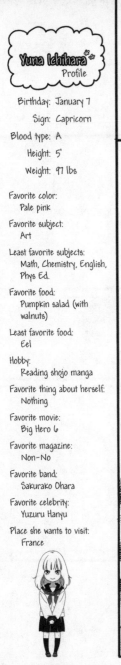

Yuna Ichihara Profile

Birthday: January 7

Sign: Capricorn

Blood type: A

Height: 5'

Weight: 97 lbs

Favorite color:
Pale pink

Favorite subject:
Art

Least favorite subjects:
Math, Chemistry, English, Phys Ed.

Favorite food:
Pumpkin salad (with walnuts)

Least favorite food:
Eel

Hobby:
Reading shojo manga

Favorite thing about herself:
Nothing

Favorite movie:
Big Hero 6

Favorite magazine:
Non-No

Favorite band:
Sakurako Ohara

Favorite celebrity:
Yuzuru Hanyu

Place she wants to visit:
France

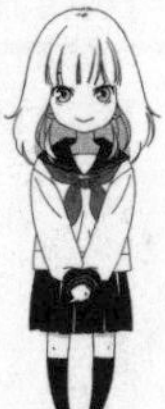

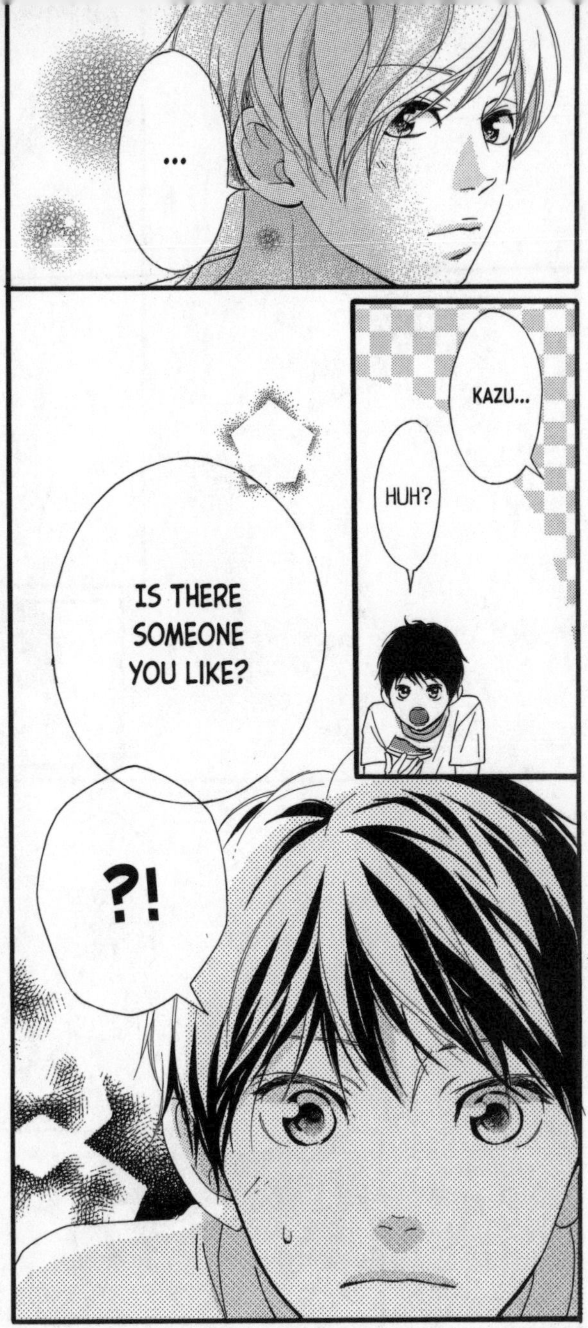
...
KAZU...
HUH?
IS THERE SOMEONE YOU LIKE?
?!

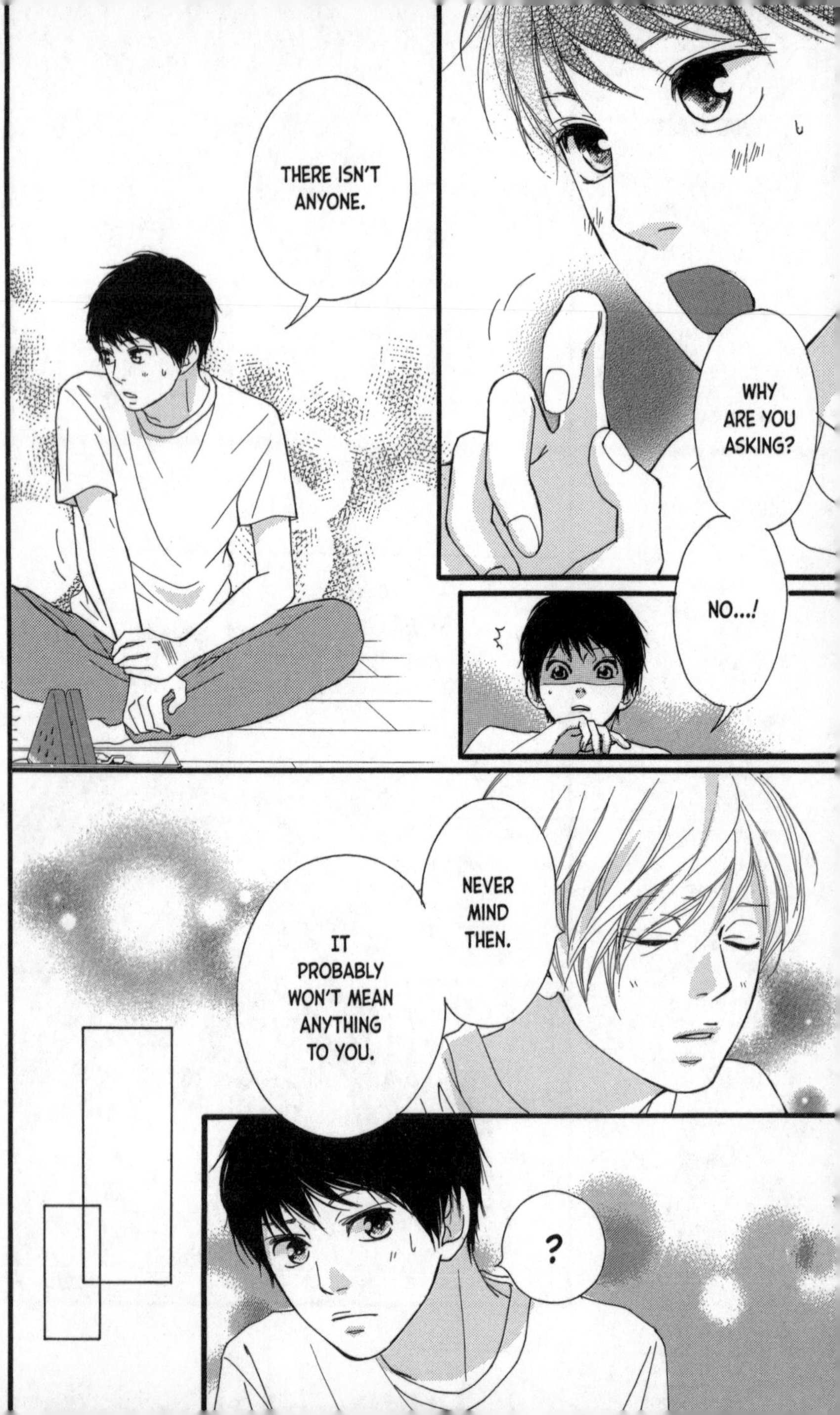
WHY ARE YOU ASKING?
NO...!
THERE ISN'T ANYONE.
NEVER MIND THEN.
IT PROBABLY WON'T MEAN ANYTHING TO YOU.
?

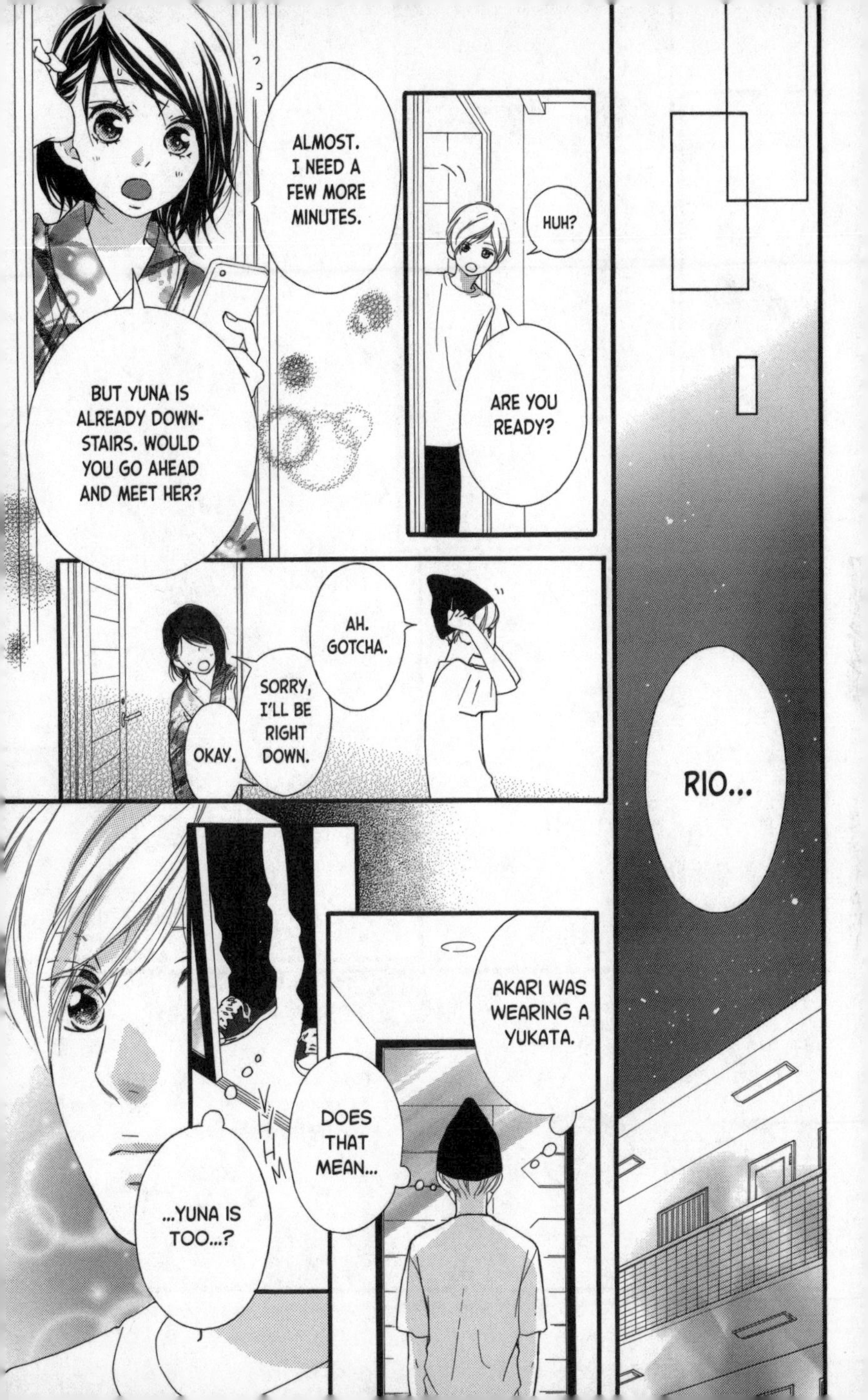
RIO...
HUH?
ARE YOU READY?
ALMOST. I NEED A FEW MORE MINUTES.
BUT YUNA IS ALREADY DOWN-STAIRS. WOULD YOU GO AHEAD AND MEET HER?
AH. GOTCHA.
SORRY, I'LL BE RIGHT DOWN.
OKAY.
AKARI WAS WEARING A YUKATA.
DOES THAT MEAN...
VHHM
...YUNA IS TOO...?

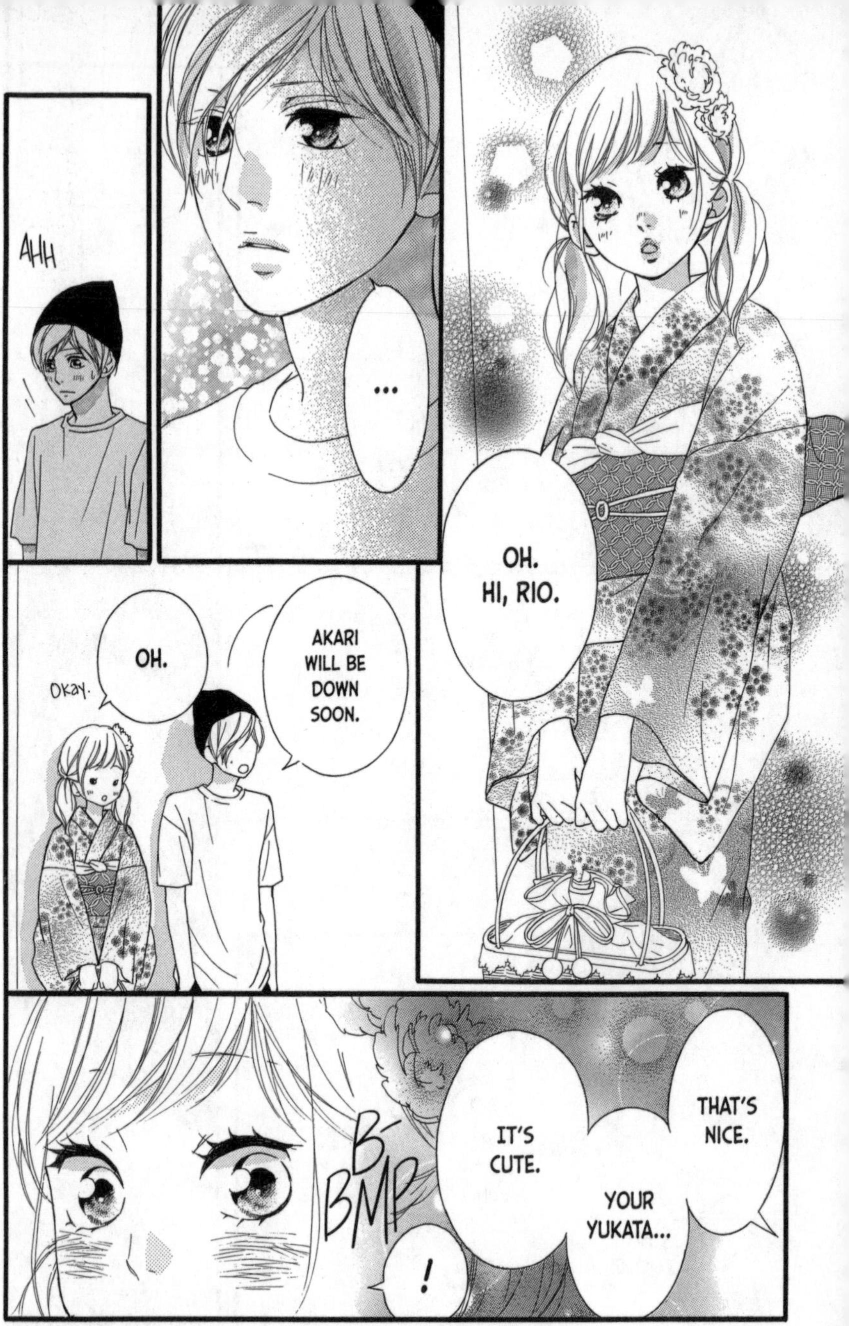
OH.
HI, RIO.
...
AHH
AKARI WILL BE DOWN SOON.
OH.
Okay.
THAT'S NICE.
YOUR YUKATA...
IT'S CUTE.
B-BMP
!

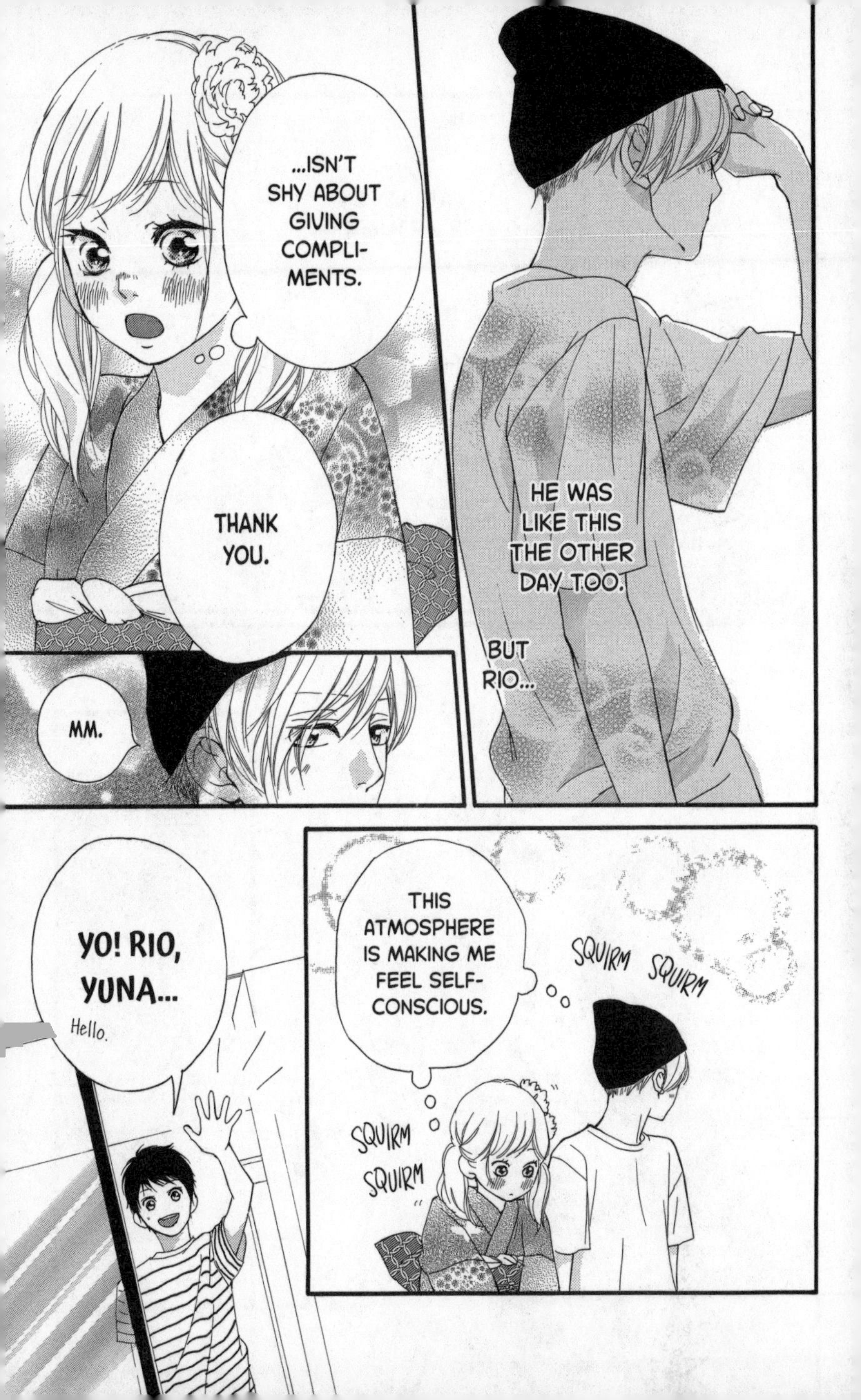
HE WAS LIKE THIS THE OTHER DAY TOO.
BUT RIO...
...ISN'T SHY ABOUT GIVING COMPLIMENTS.
THANK YOU.
MM.
SQUIRM SQUIRM
THIS ATMOSPHERE IS MAKING ME FEEL SELF-CONSCIOUS.
SQUIRM SQUIRM
YO! RIO, YUNA...
Hello.

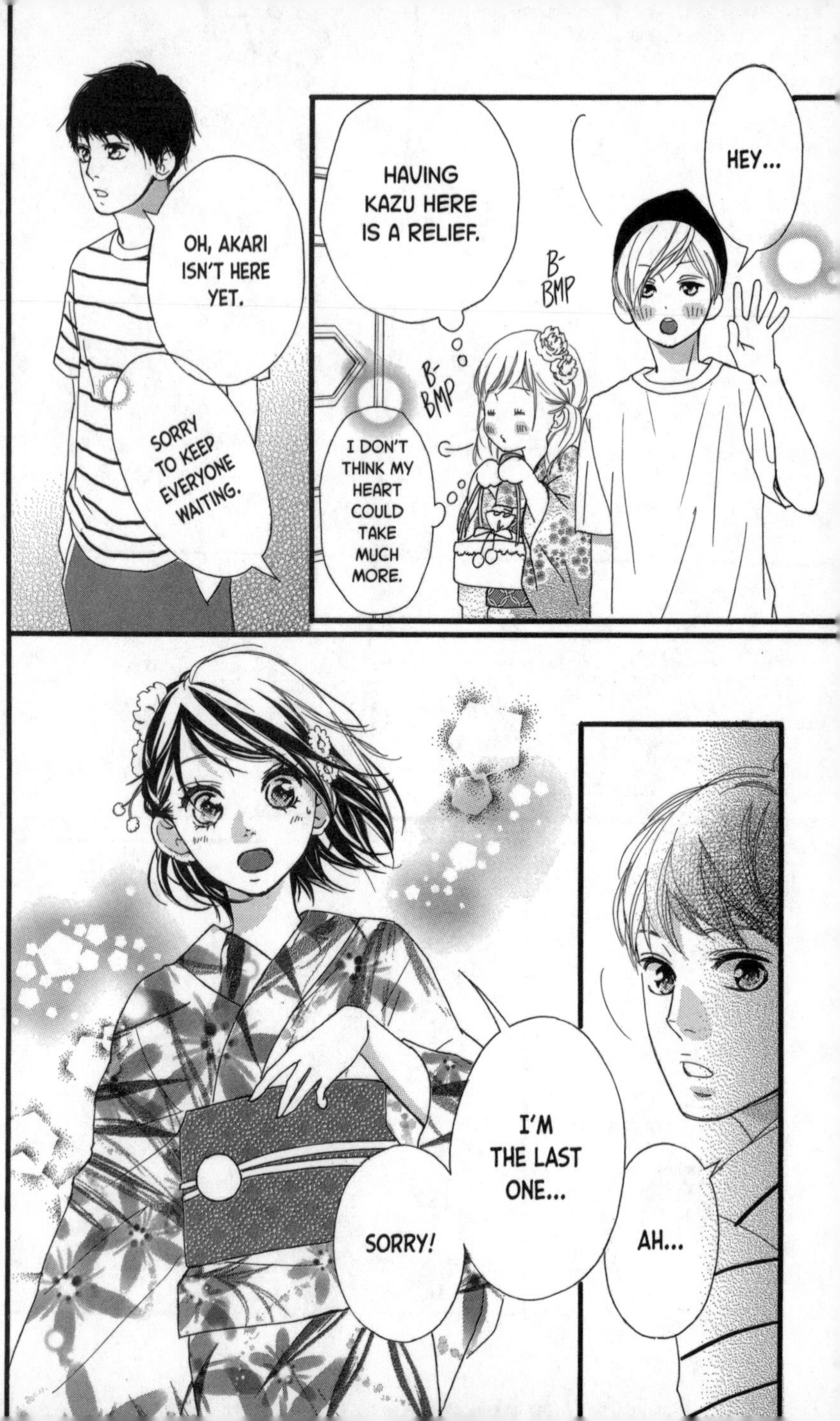
HEY...
HAVING KAZU HERE IS A RELIEF.
B-BMP
B-BMP
I DON'T THINK MY HEART COULD TAKE MUCH MORE.
OH, AKARI ISN'T HERE YET.
SORRY TO KEEP EVERYONE WAITING.
AH...
I'M THE LAST ONE...
SORRY!

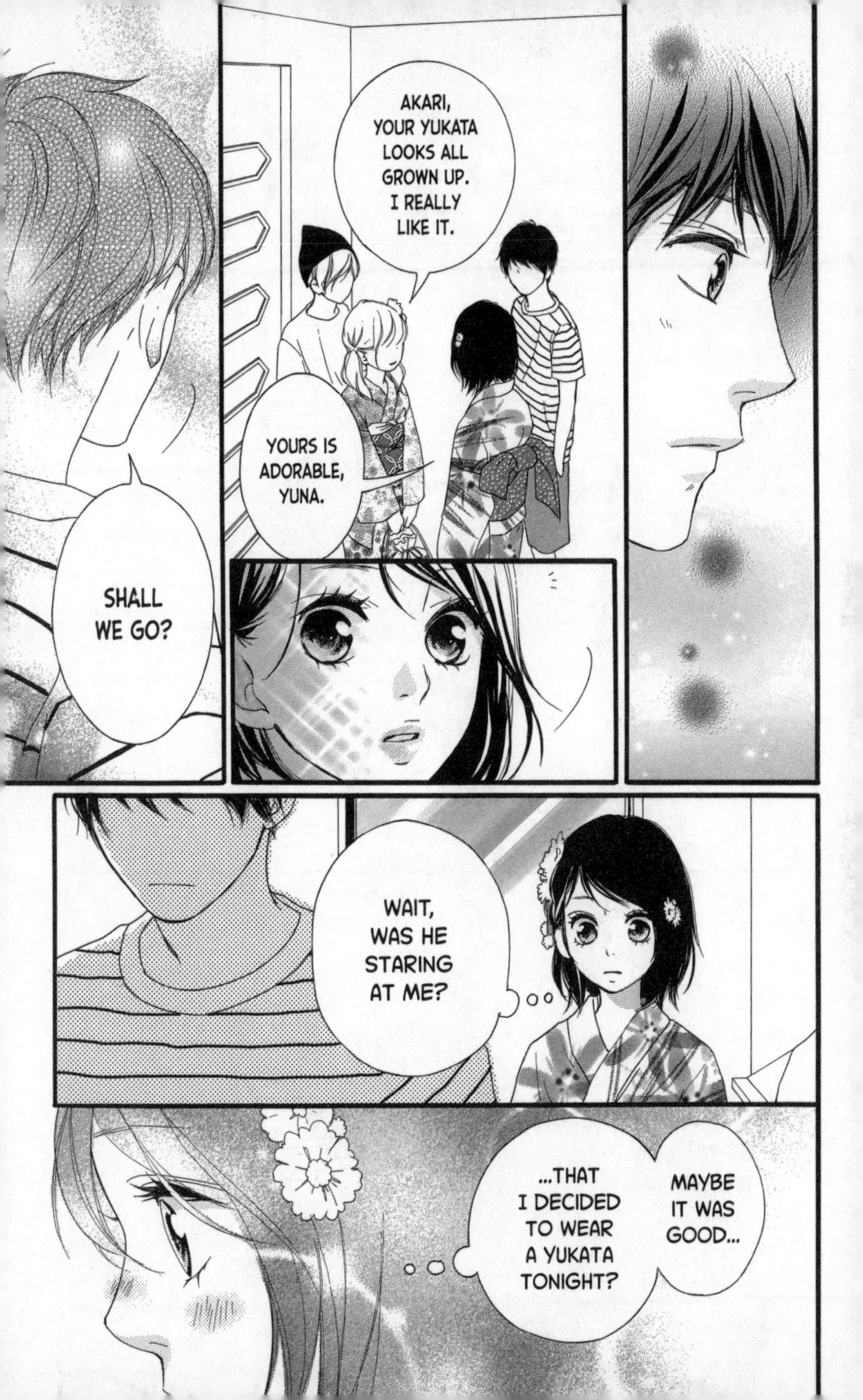
AKARI, YOUR YUKATA LOOKS ALL GROWN UP. I REALLY LIKE IT.
YOURS IS ADORABLE, YUNA.
SHALL WE GO?
WAIT, WAS HE STARING AT ME?
MAYBE IT WAS GOOD...
...THAT I DECIDED TO WEAR A YUKATA TONIGHT?

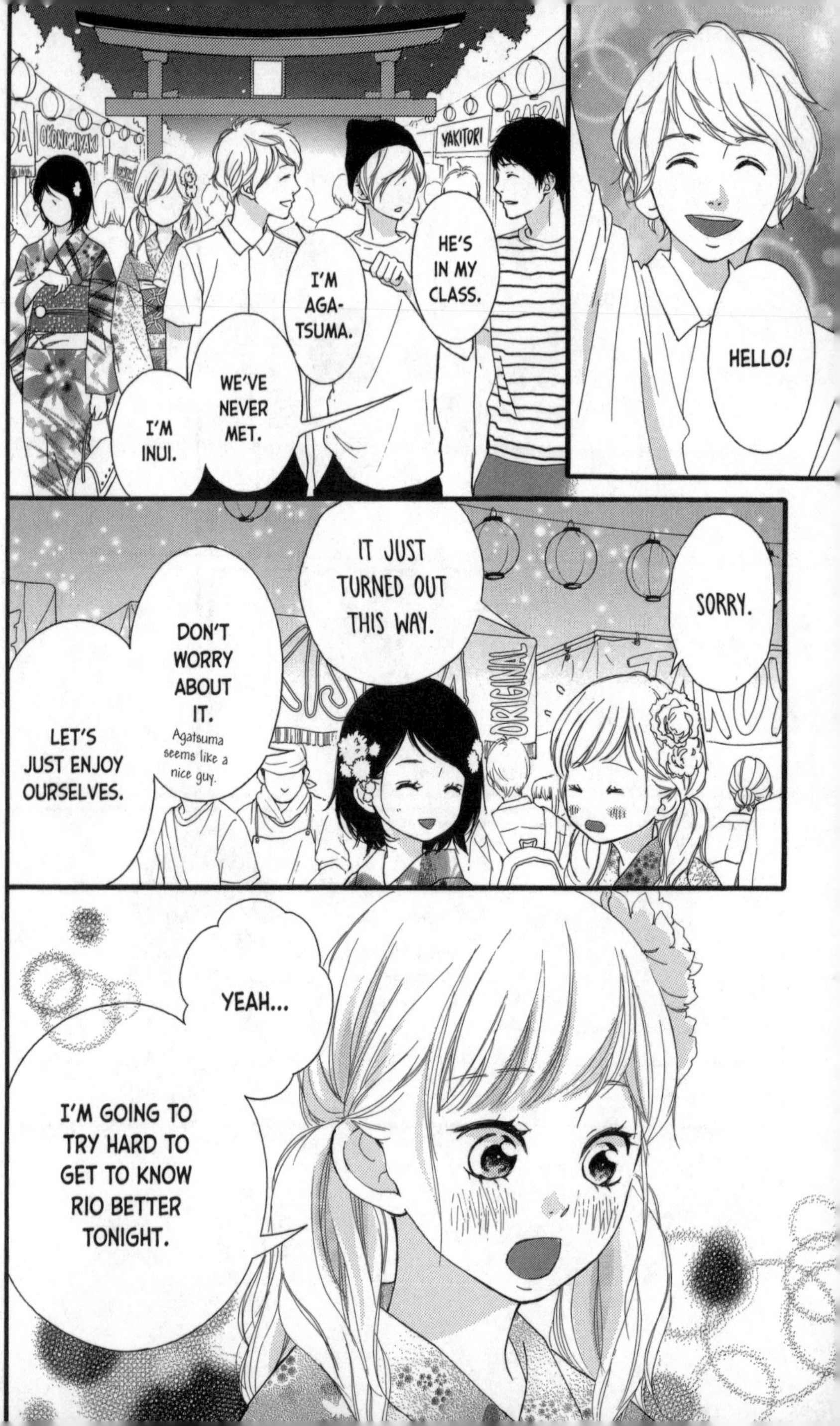
HELLO!
HE'S IN MY CLASS.
I'M AGA-TSUMA.
YAKITORI
OKONOMIYAKI
WE'VE NEVER MET.
I'M INUI.
SORRY.
IT JUST TURNED OUT THIS WAY.
ORIGINAL
DON'T WORRY ABOUT IT.
Agatsuma seems like a nice guy.
LET'S JUST ENJOY OURSELVES.
YEAH...
I'M GOING TO TRY HARD TO GET TO KNOW RIO BETTER TONIGHT.

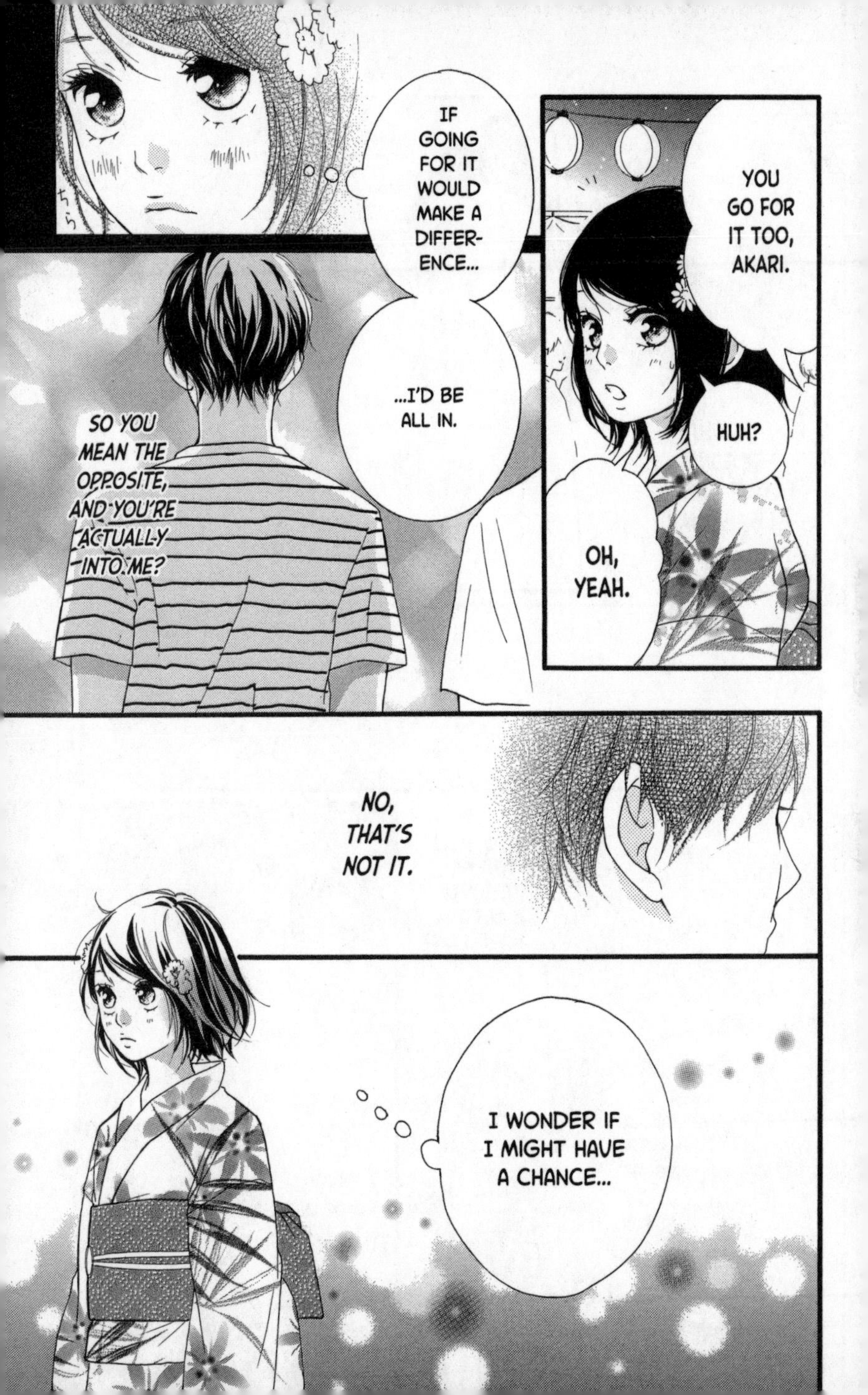
YOU GO FOR IT TOO, AKARI.
HUH?
OH, YEAH.
IF GOING FOR IT WOULD MAKE A DIFFERENCE...
ちら
...I'D BE ALL IN.
SO YOU MEAN THE OPPOSITE, AND YOU'RE ACTUALLY INTO ME?
NO, THAT'S NOT IT.
I WONDER IF I MIGHT HAVE A CHANCE...

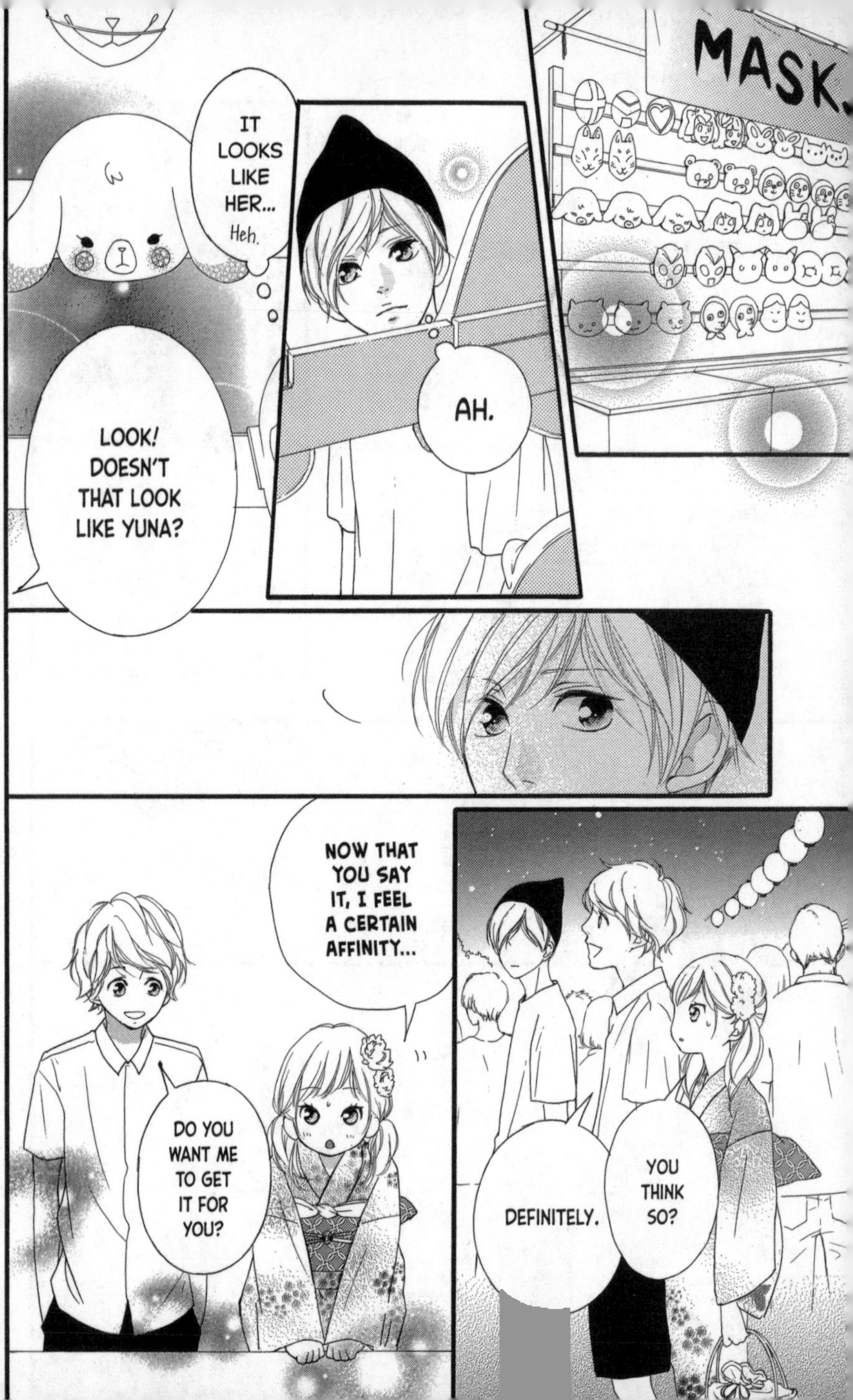
MASK.
LOOK! DOESN'T THAT LOOK LIKE YUNA?
AH.
IT LOOKS LIKE HER... Heh.
YOU THINK SO?
DEFINITELY.
NOW THAT YOU SAY IT, I FEEL A CERTAIN AFFINITY...
DO YOU WANT ME TO GET IT FOR YOU?

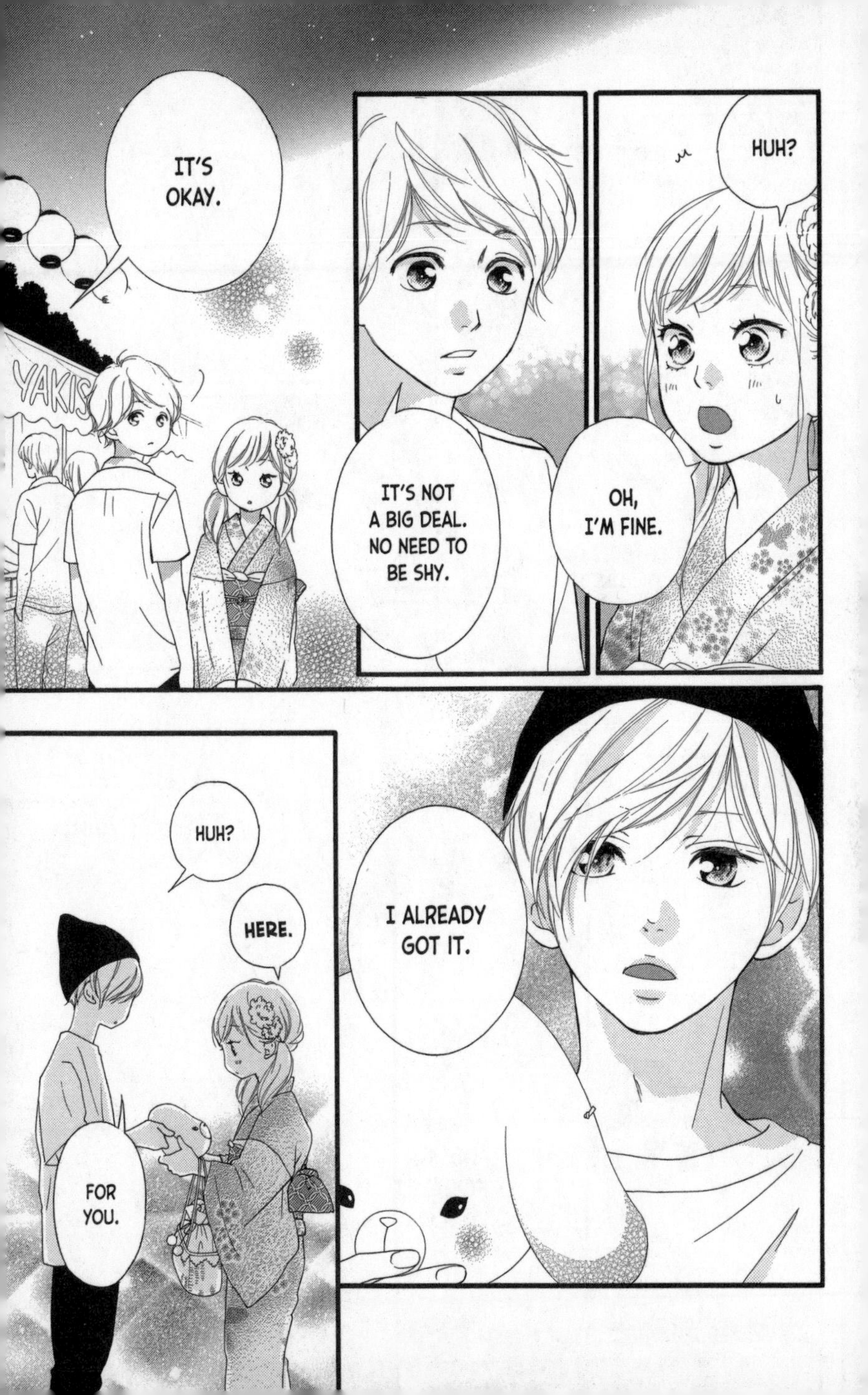
HUH?
OH, I'M FINE.
IT'S NOT A BIG DEAL. NO NEED TO BE SHY.
IT'S OKAY.
YAKIS
I ALREADY GOT IT.
HUH?
HERE.
FOR YOU.

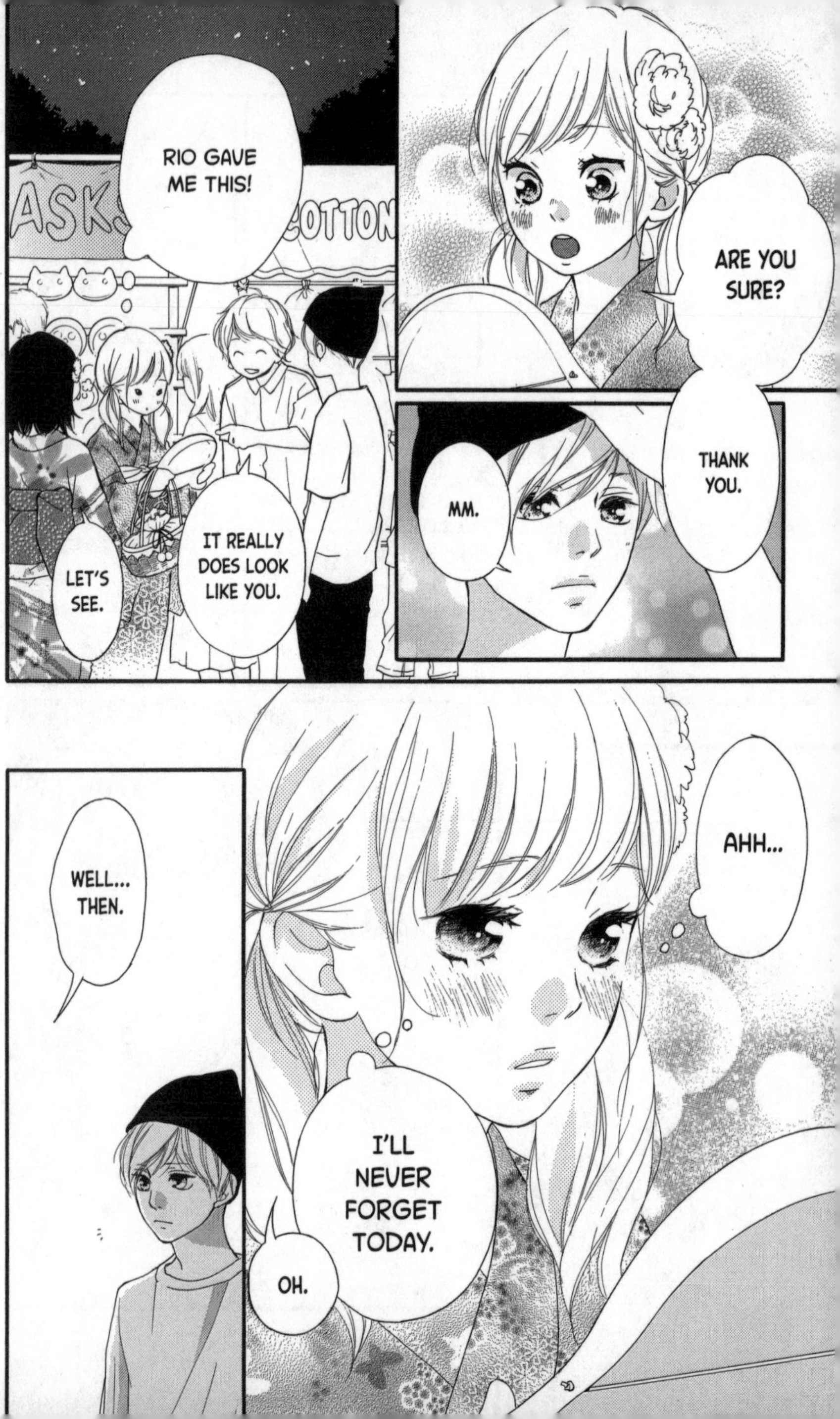
ARE YOU SURE?
THANK YOU.
MM.
RIO GAVE ME THIS!
ASK
COTTON
IT REALLY DOES LOOK LIKE YOU.
LET'S SEE.
AHH...
I'LL NEVER FORGET TODAY.
OH.
WELL... THEN.

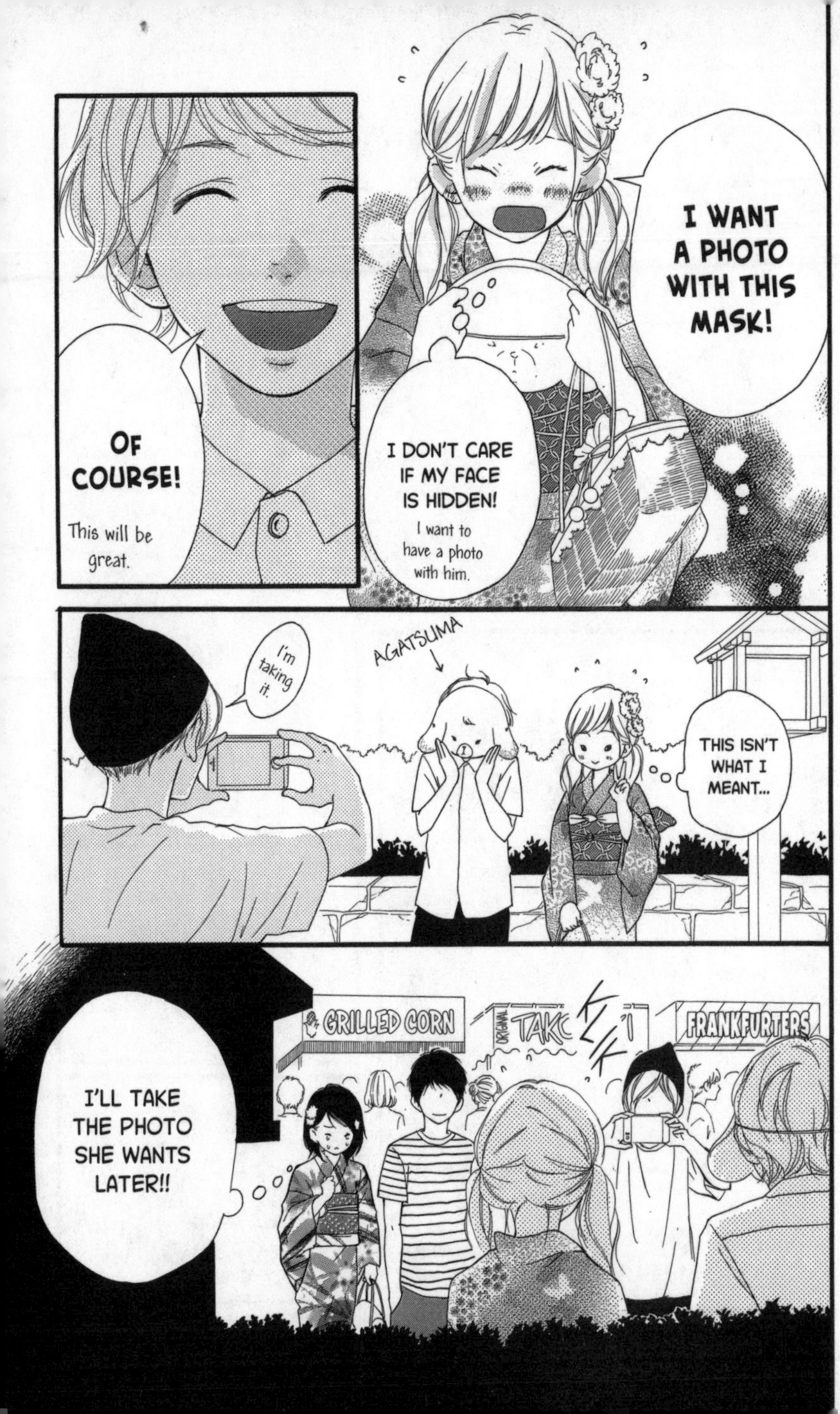
I WANT A PHOTO WITH THIS MASK!
I DON'T CARE IF MY FACE IS HIDDEN!
I want to have a photo with him.
OF COURSE!
This will be great.
THIS ISN'T WHAT I MEANT...
AGATSUMA
I'm taking it.
FRANKFURTERS
KLIK
GRILLED CORN
I'LL TAKE THE PHOTO SHE WANTS LATER!!

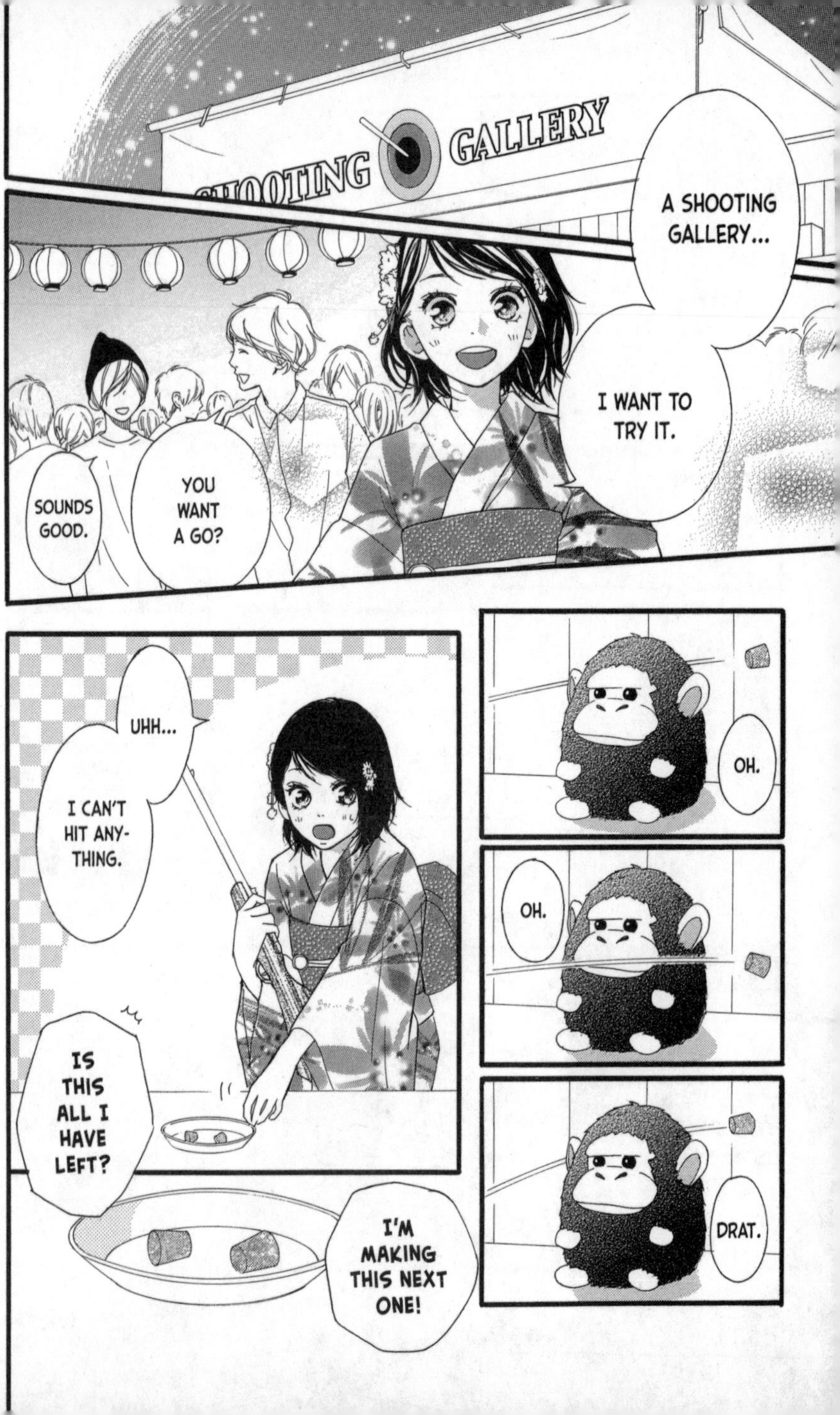
SHOOTING GALLERY
A SHOOTING GALLERY...
I WANT TO TRY IT.
YOU WANT A GO?
SOUNDS GOOD.
OH.
OH.
DRAT.
UHH...
I CAN'T HIT ANY- THING.
IS THIS ALL I HAVE LEFT?
I'M MAKING THIS NEXT ONE!

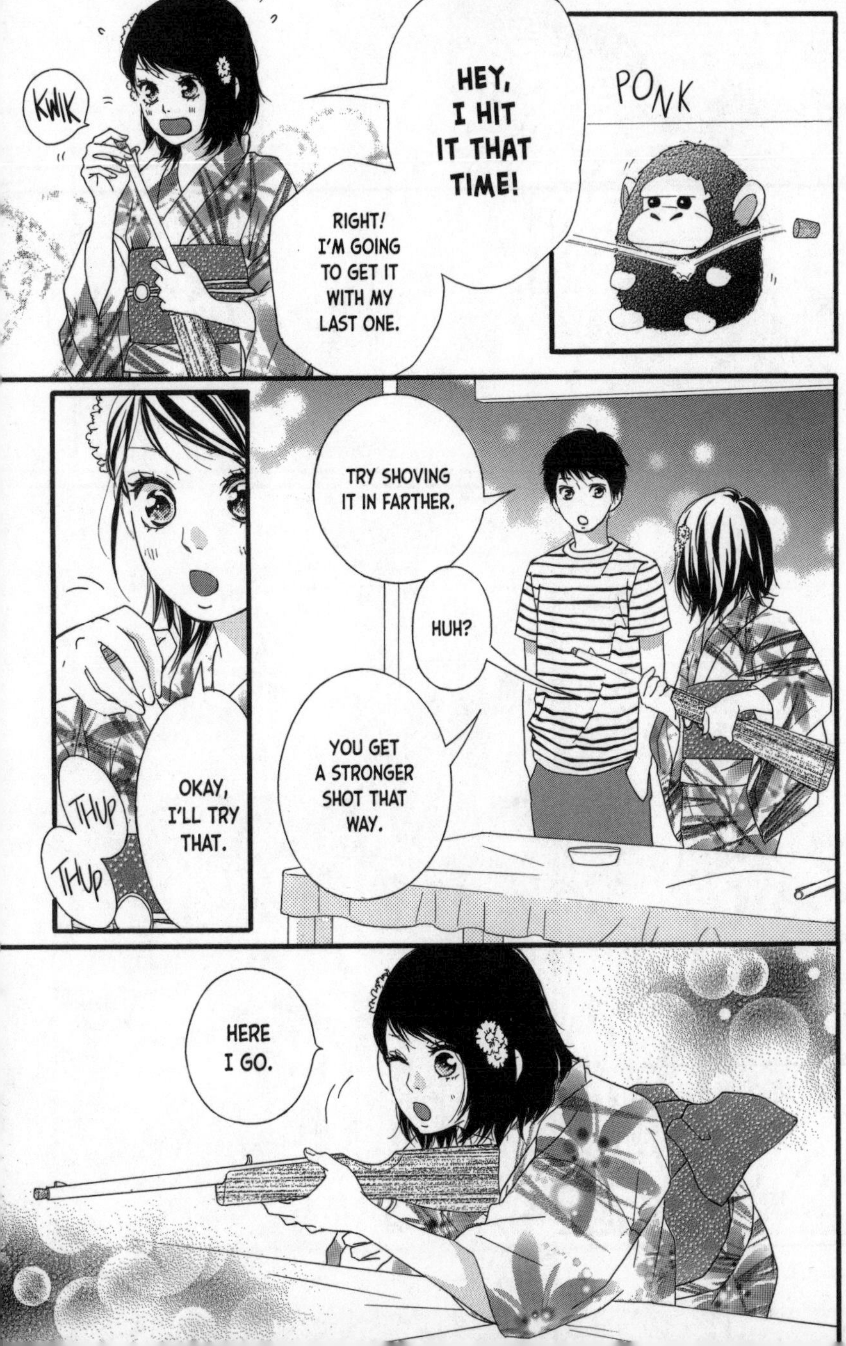
PONK
HEY, I HIT IT THAT TIME!
RIGHT! I'M GOING TO GET IT WITH MY LAST ONE.
KWIK
TRY SHOVING IT IN FARTHER.
HUH?
YOU GET A STRONGER SHOT THAT WAY.
OKAY, I'LL TRY THAT.
THUP
THUP
HERE I GO.

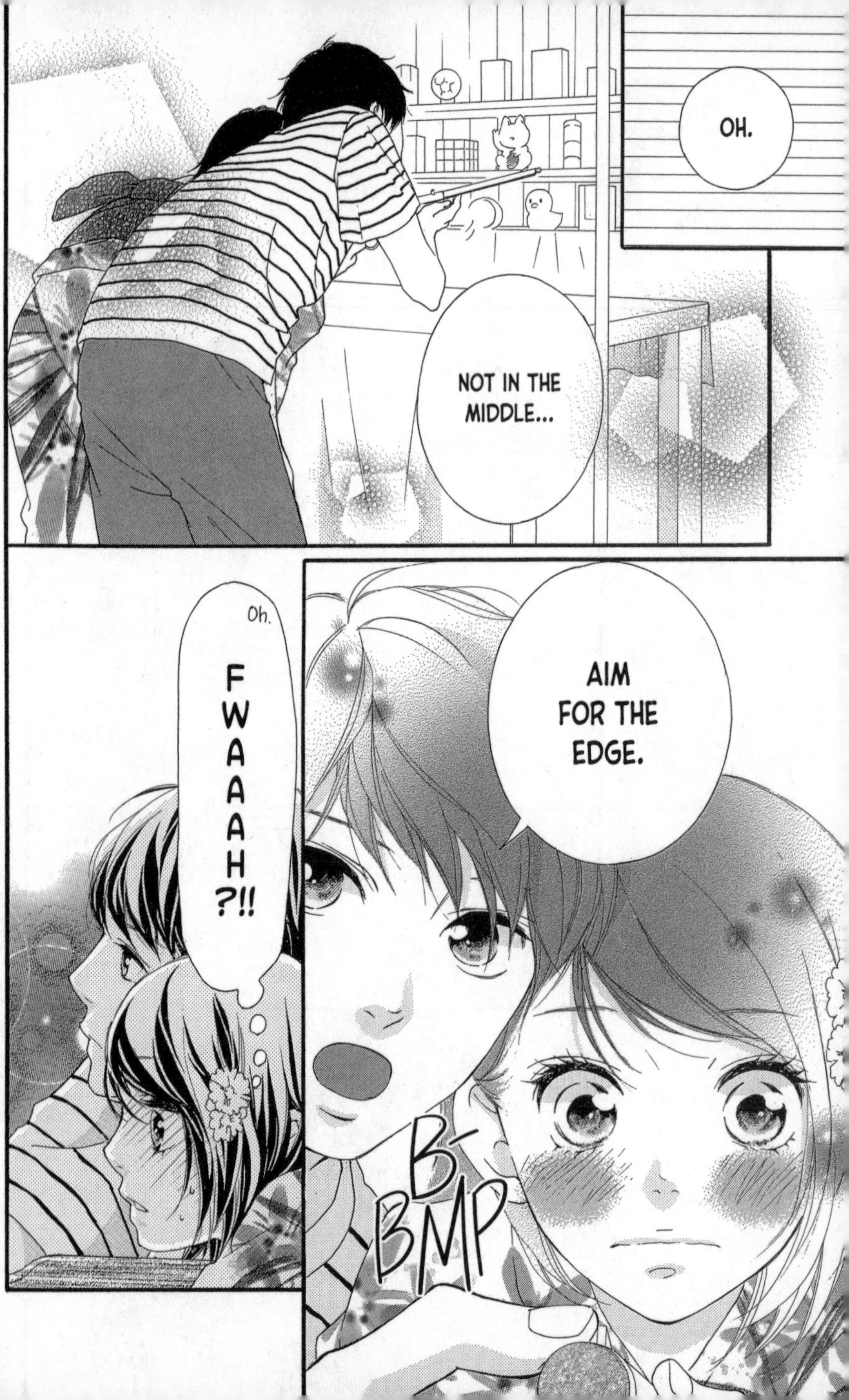
OH.
NOT IN THE MIDDLE...
AIM FOR THE EDGE.
B-BMP
Oh.
FWAAAAH?!!

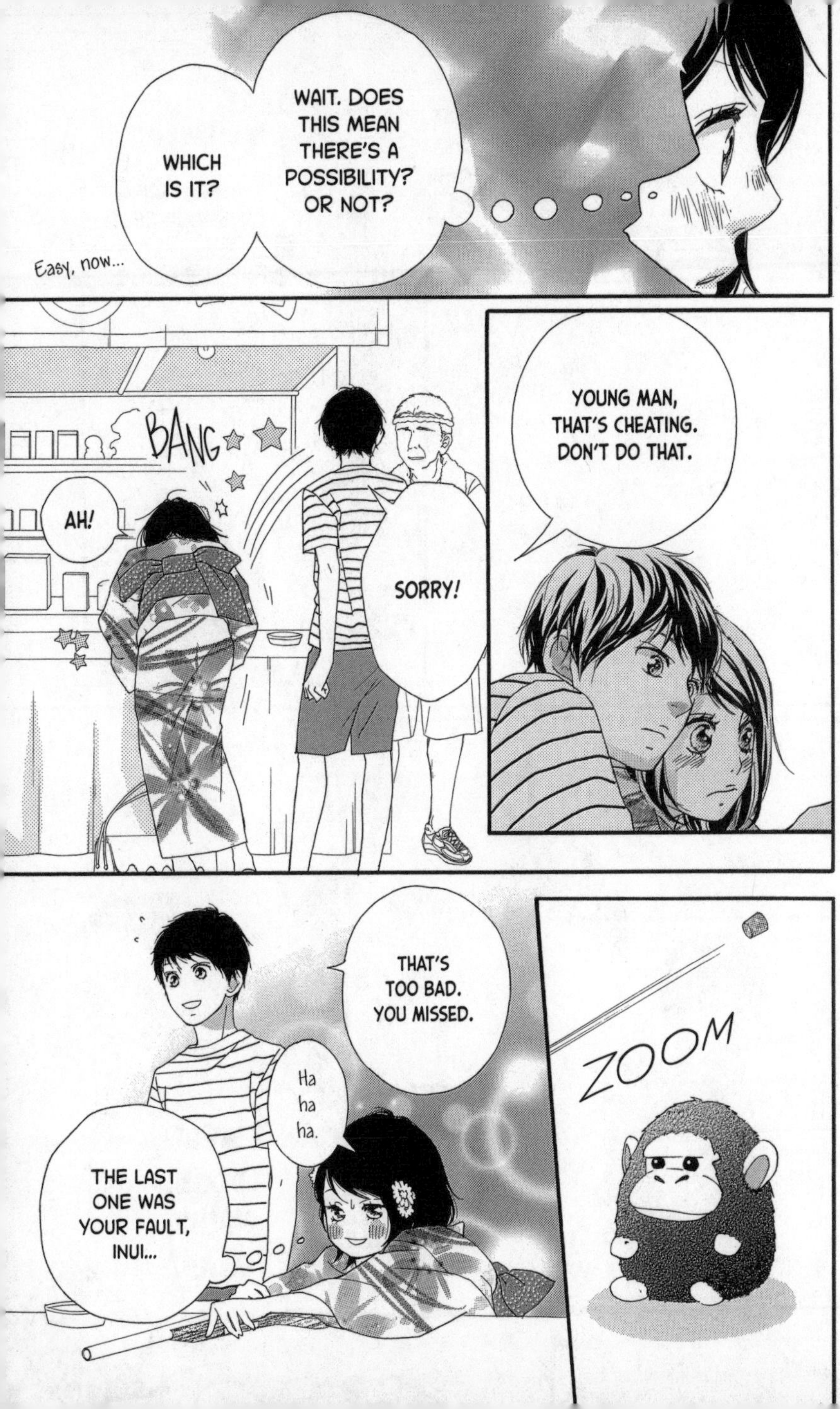
WAIT. DOES THIS MEAN THERE'S A POSSIBILITY? OR NOT?
WHICH IS IT?
Easy, now...
YOUNG MAN, THAT'S CHEATING. DON'T DO THAT.
SORRY!
BANG
AH!
ZOOM
THAT'S TOO BAD. YOU MISSED.
Ha ha ha.
THE LAST ONE WAS YOUR FAULT, INUI...

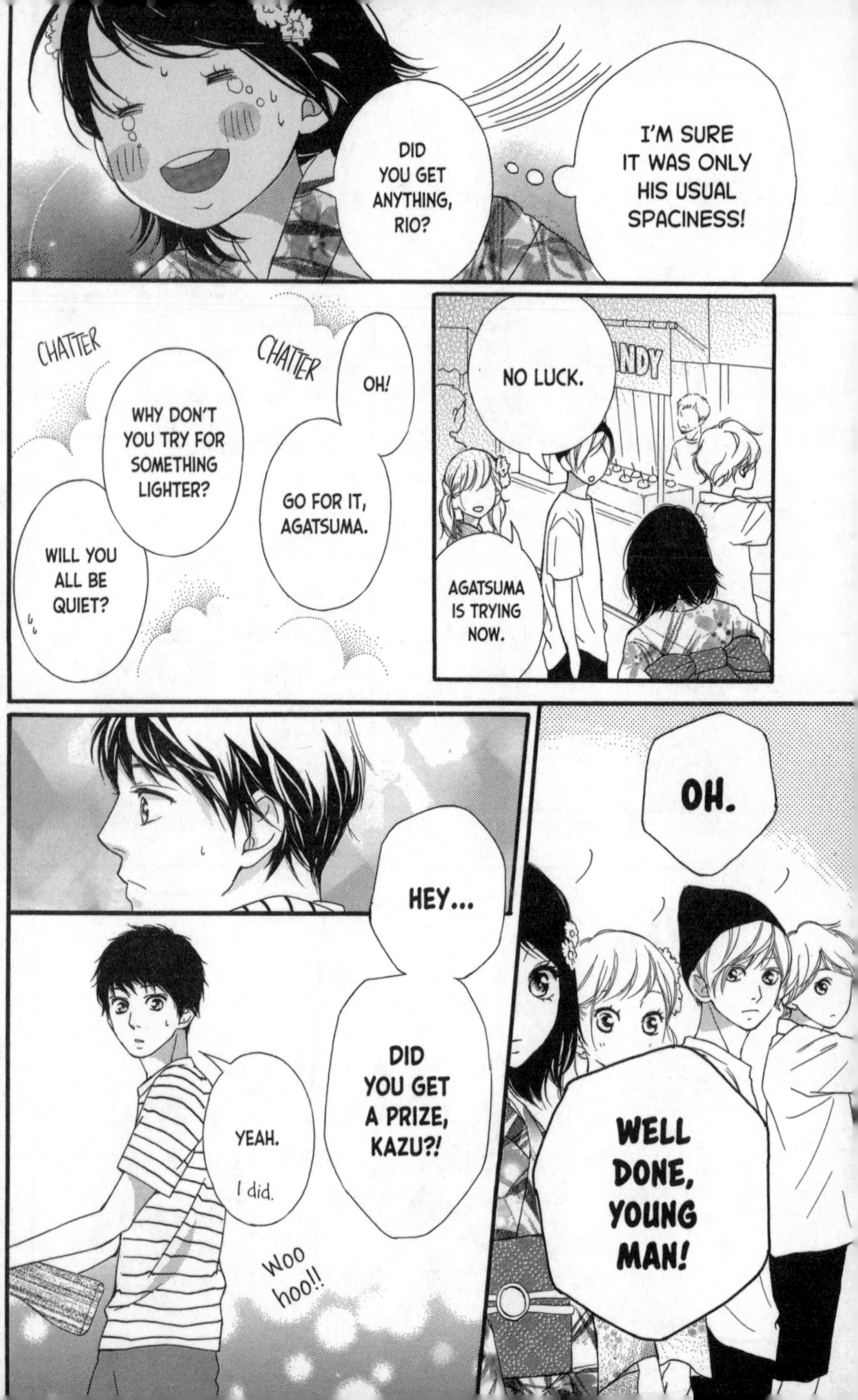
I'M SURE IT WAS ONLY HIS USUAL SPACINESS!
DID YOU GET ANYTHING, RIO?
NO LUCK.
AGATSUMA IS TRYING NOW.
OH!
GO FOR IT, AGATSUMA.
CHATTER
CHATTER
WHY DON'T YOU TRY FOR SOMETHING LIGHTER?
WILL YOU ALL BE QUIET?
OH.
HEY...
DID YOU GET A PRIZE, KAZU?!
WELL DONE, YOUNG MAN!
YEAH.
I did.
Woo hoo!!

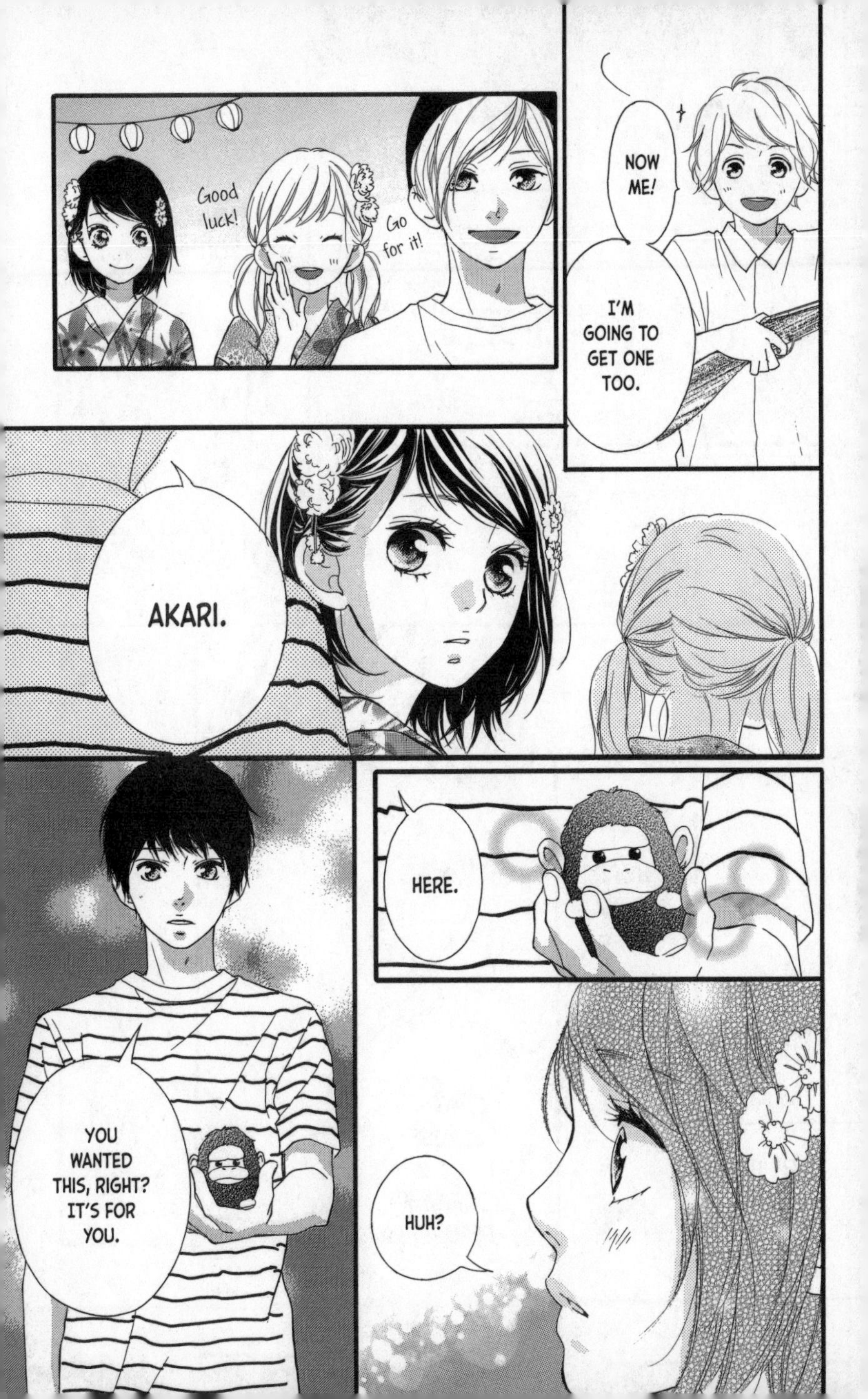
NOW ME!
I'M GOING TO GET ONE TOO.
Go for it!
Good luck!
AKARI.
HERE.
HUH?
YOU WANTED THIS, RIGHT? IT'S FOR YOU.

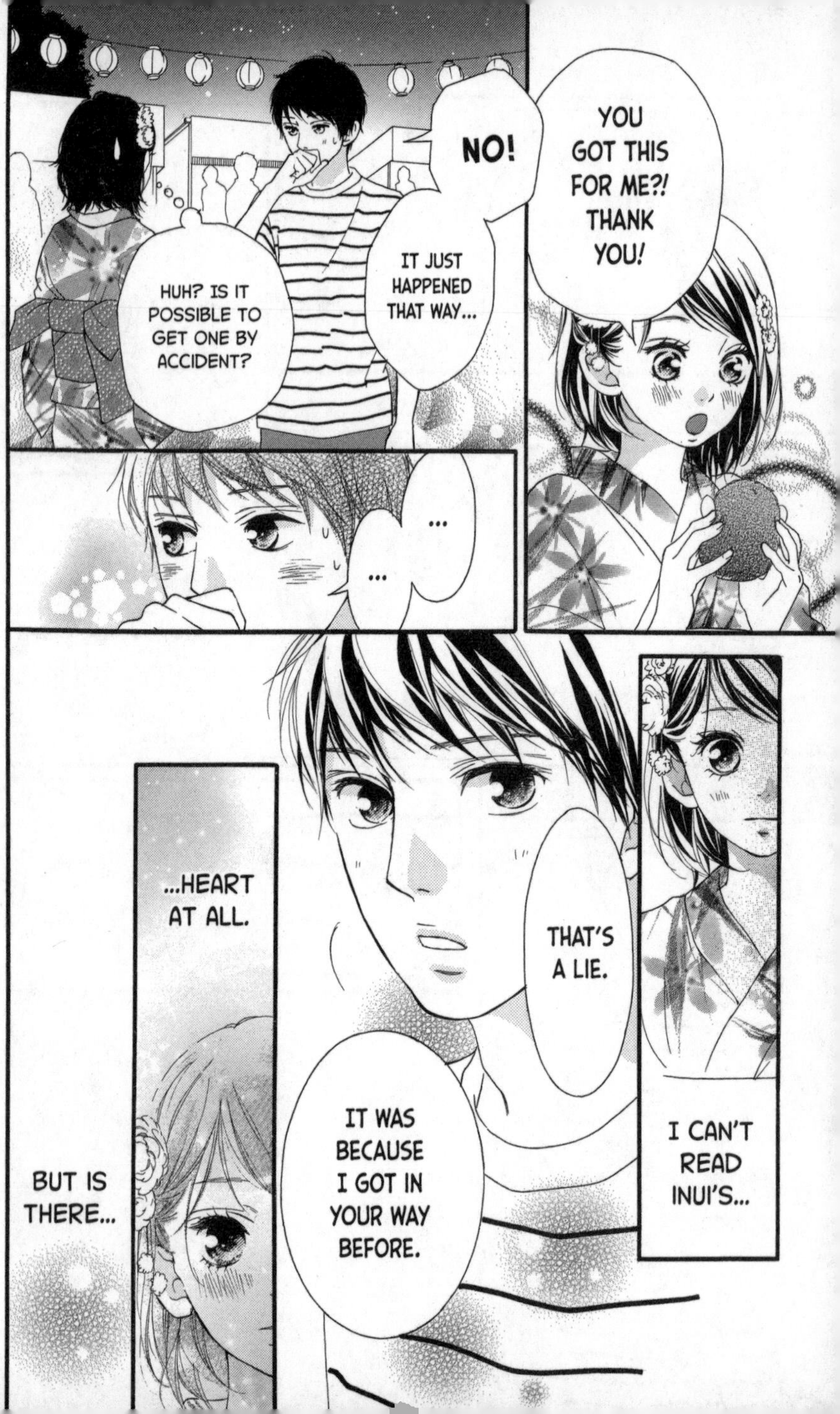
YOU GOT THIS FOR ME?! THANK YOU!
NO!
IT JUST HAPPENED THAT WAY...
HUH? IS IT POSSIBLE TO GET ONE BY ACCIDENT?
...
...
I CAN'T READ INUI'S...
THAT'S A LIE.
IT WAS BECAUSE I GOT IN YOUR WAY BEFORE.
...HEART AT ALL.
BUT IS THERE...

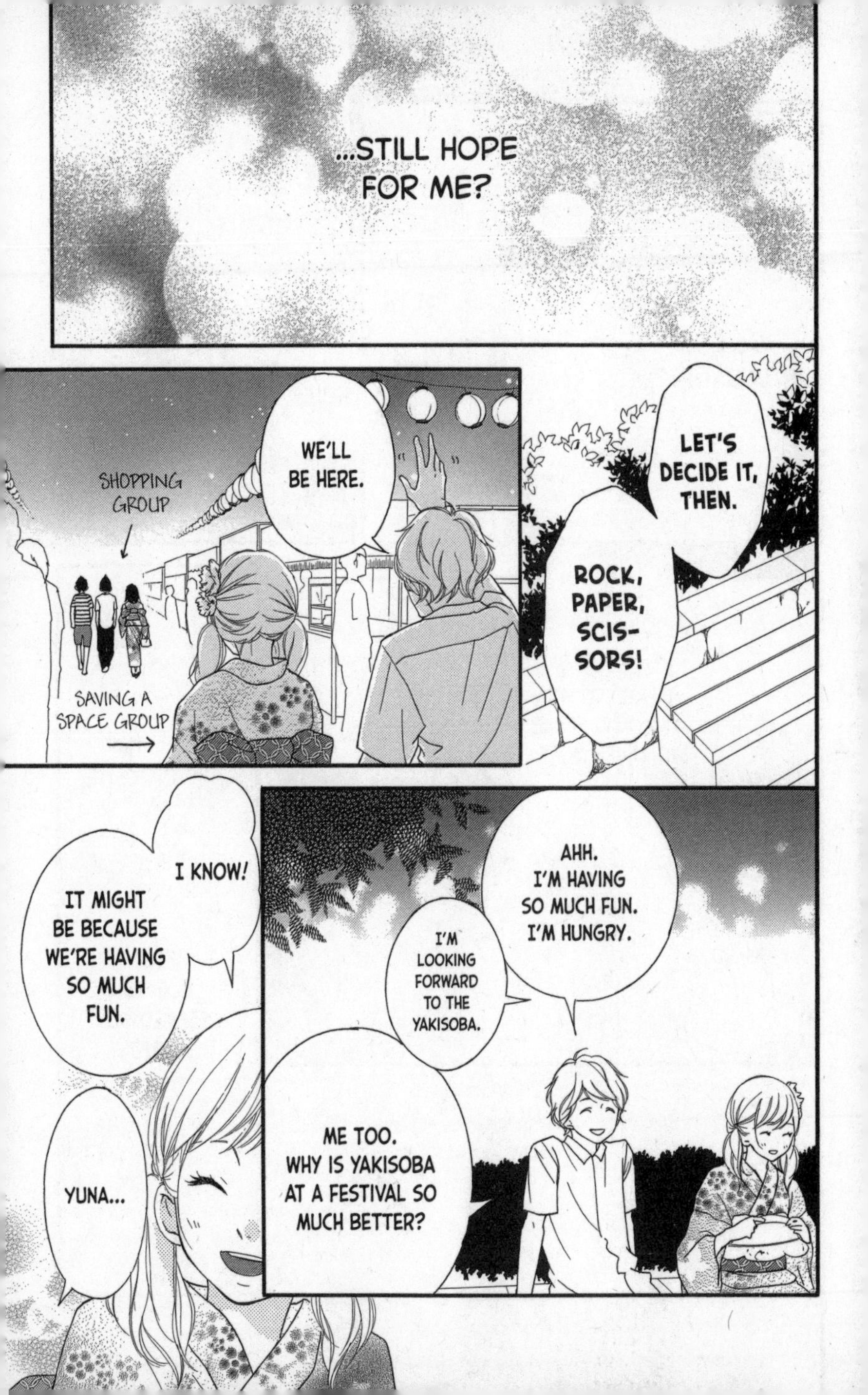
...STILL HOPE FOR ME?
LET'S DECIDE IT, THEN.
ROCK, PAPER, SCIS-SORS!
WE'LL BE HERE.
SHOPPING GROUP
SAVING A SPACE GROUP
AHH. I'M HAVING SO MUCH FUN. I'M HUNGRY.
I'M LOOKING FORWARD TO THE YAKISOBA.
ME TOO. WHY IS YAKISOBA AT A FESTIVAL SO MUCH BETTER?
I KNOW!
IT MIGHT BE BECAUSE WE'RE HAVING SO MUCH FUN.
YUNA...

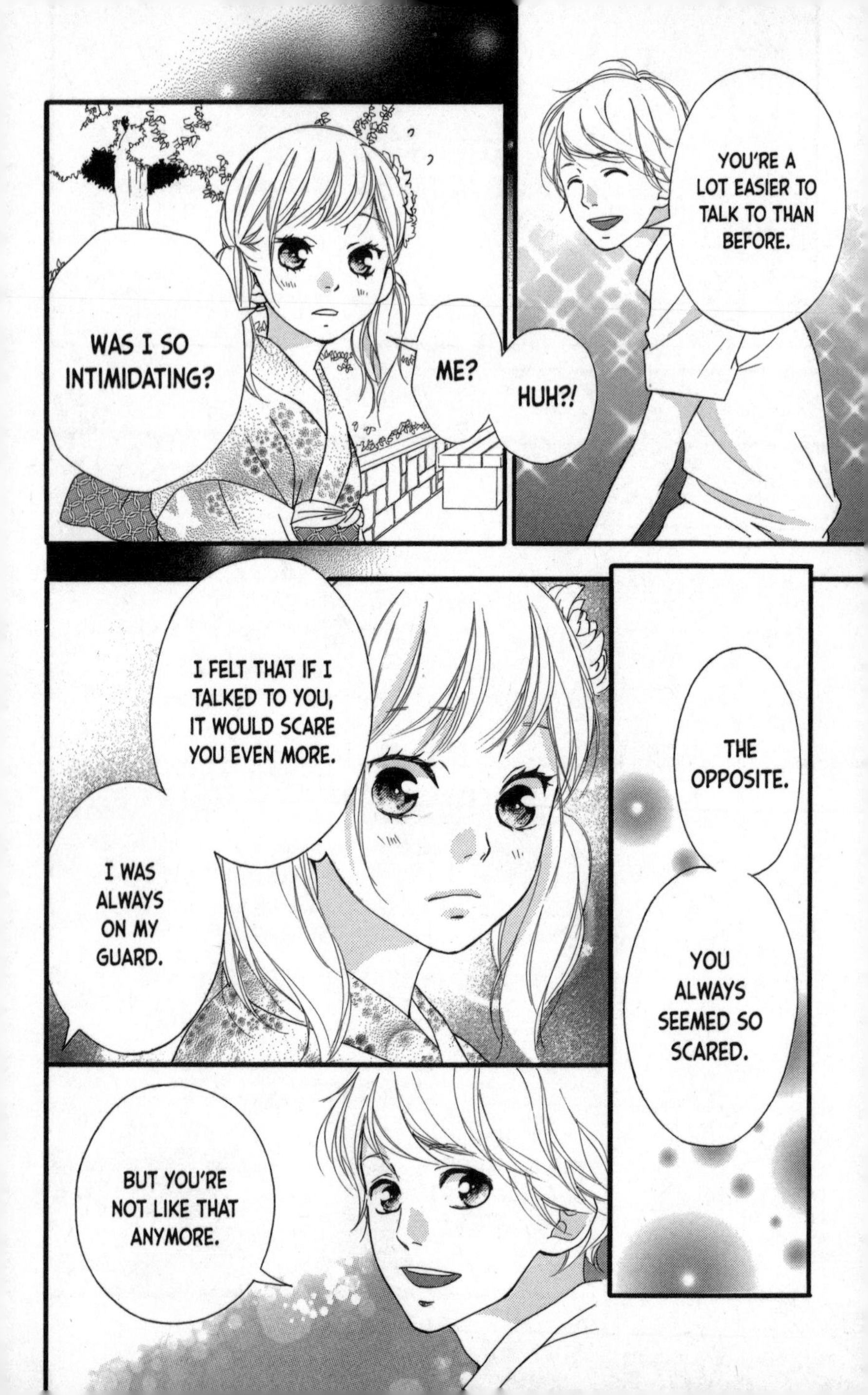
YOU'RE A LOT EASIER TO TALK TO THAN BEFORE.
HUH?!
ME?
WAS I SO INTIMIDATING?
THE OPPOSITE.
YOU ALWAYS SEEMED SO SCARED.
I FELT THAT IF I TALKED TO YOU, IT WOULD SCARE YOU EVEN MORE.
I WAS ALWAYS ON MY GUARD.
BUT YOU'RE NOT LIKE THAT ANYMORE.

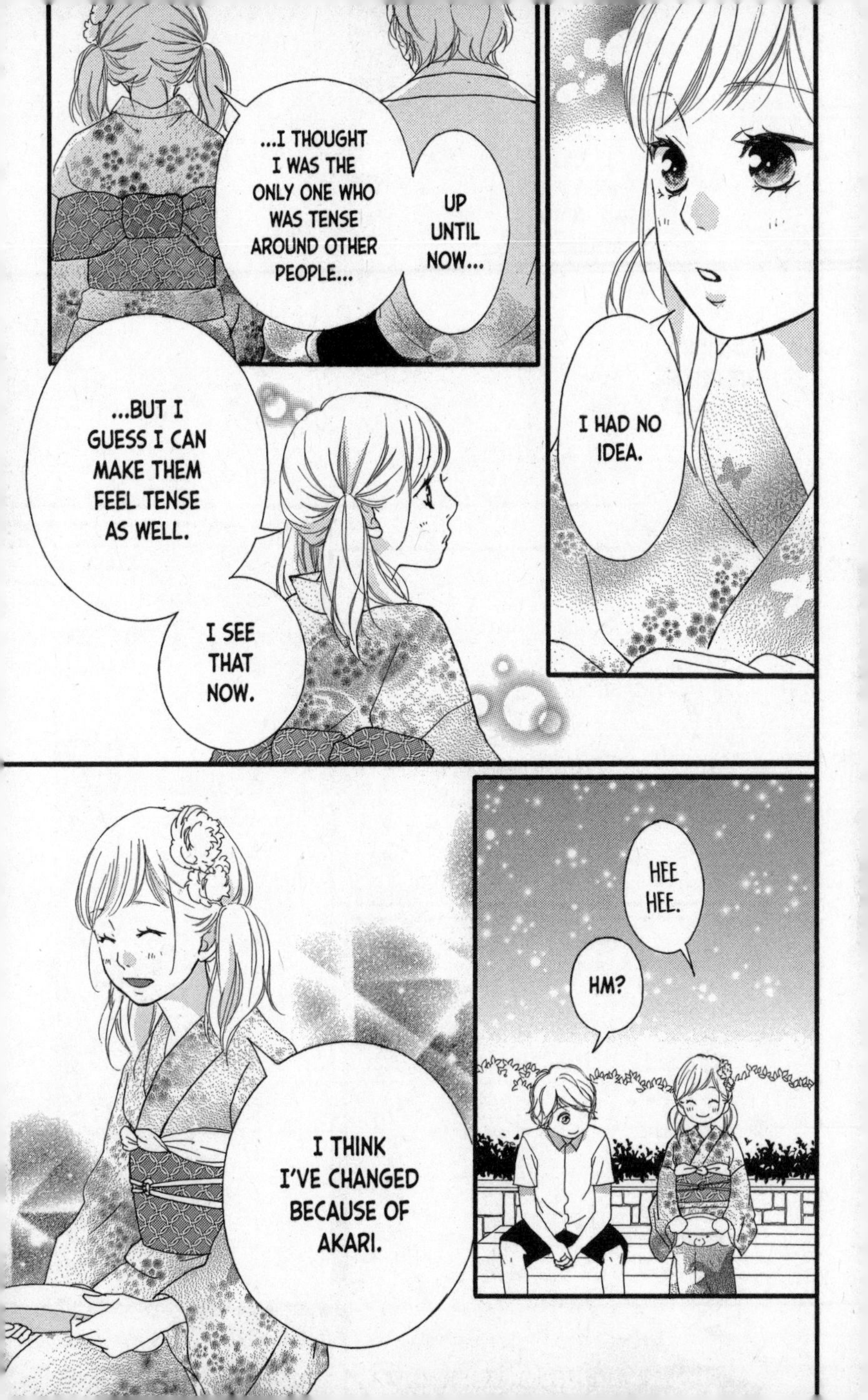
I HAD NO IDEA.
UP UNTIL NOW...
...I THOUGHT I WAS THE ONLY ONE WHO WAS TENSE AROUND OTHER PEOPLE...
...BUT I GUESS I CAN MAKE THEM FEEL TENSE AS WELL.
I SEE THAT NOW.
HEE HEE.
HM?
I THINK I'VE CHANGED BECAUSE OF AKARI.

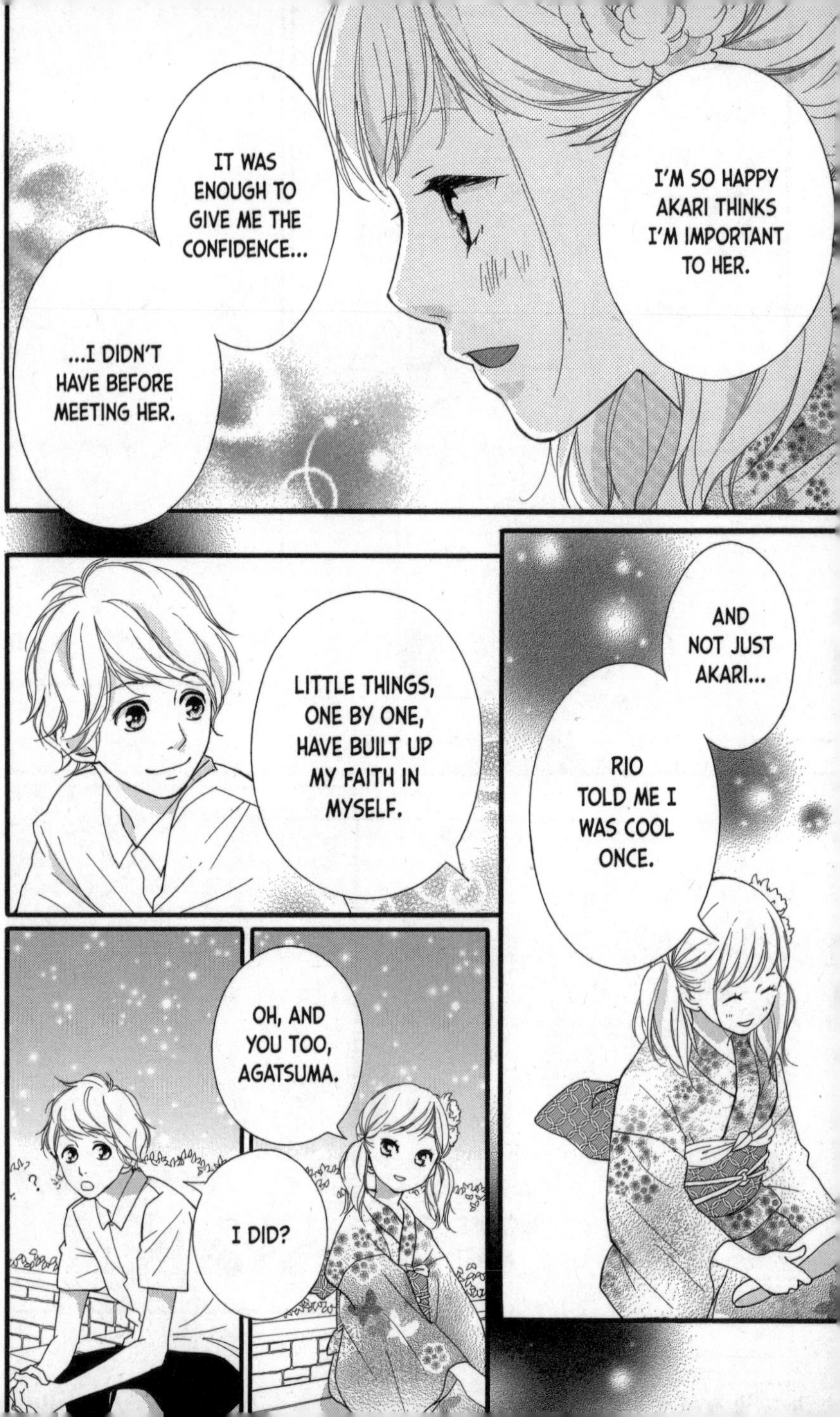
I'M SO HAPPY AKARI THINKS I'M IMPORTANT TO HER.
IT WAS ENOUGH TO GIVE ME THE CONFIDENCE...
...I DIDN'T HAVE BEFORE MEETING HER.
AND NOT JUST AKARI...
RIO TOLD ME I WAS COOL ONCE.
LITTLE THINGS, ONE BY ONE, HAVE BUILT UP MY FAITH IN MYSELF.
OH, AND YOU TOO, AGATSUMA.
I DID?

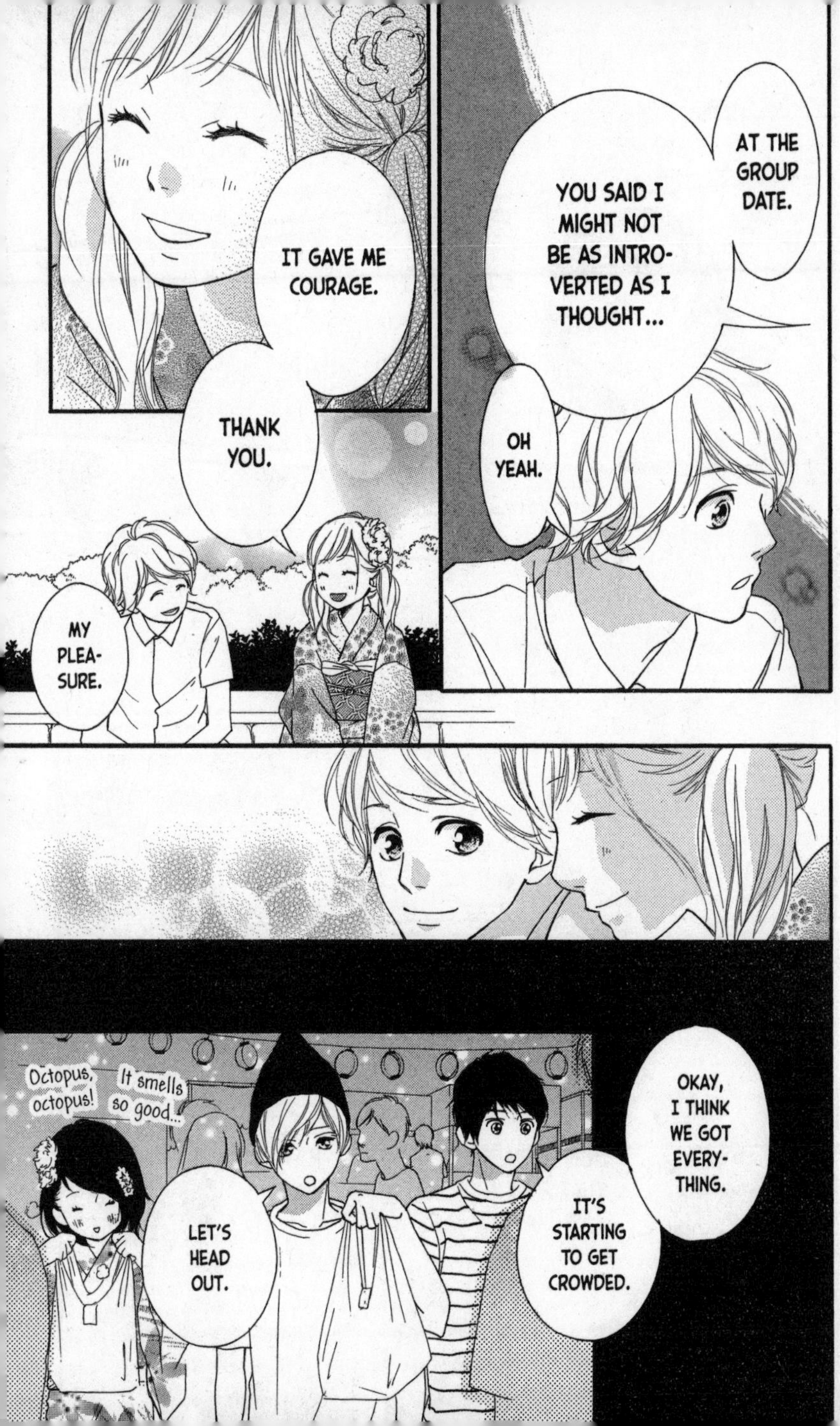
AT THE GROUP DATE.
YOU SAID I MIGHT NOT BE AS INTRO-VERTED AS I THOUGHT...
OH YEAH.
IT GAVE ME COURAGE.
THANK YOU.
MY PLEA-SURE.
OKAY, I THINK WE GOT EVERY-THING.
IT'S STARTING TO GET CROWDED.
LET'S HEAD OUT.
It smells so good...
Octopus, octopus!

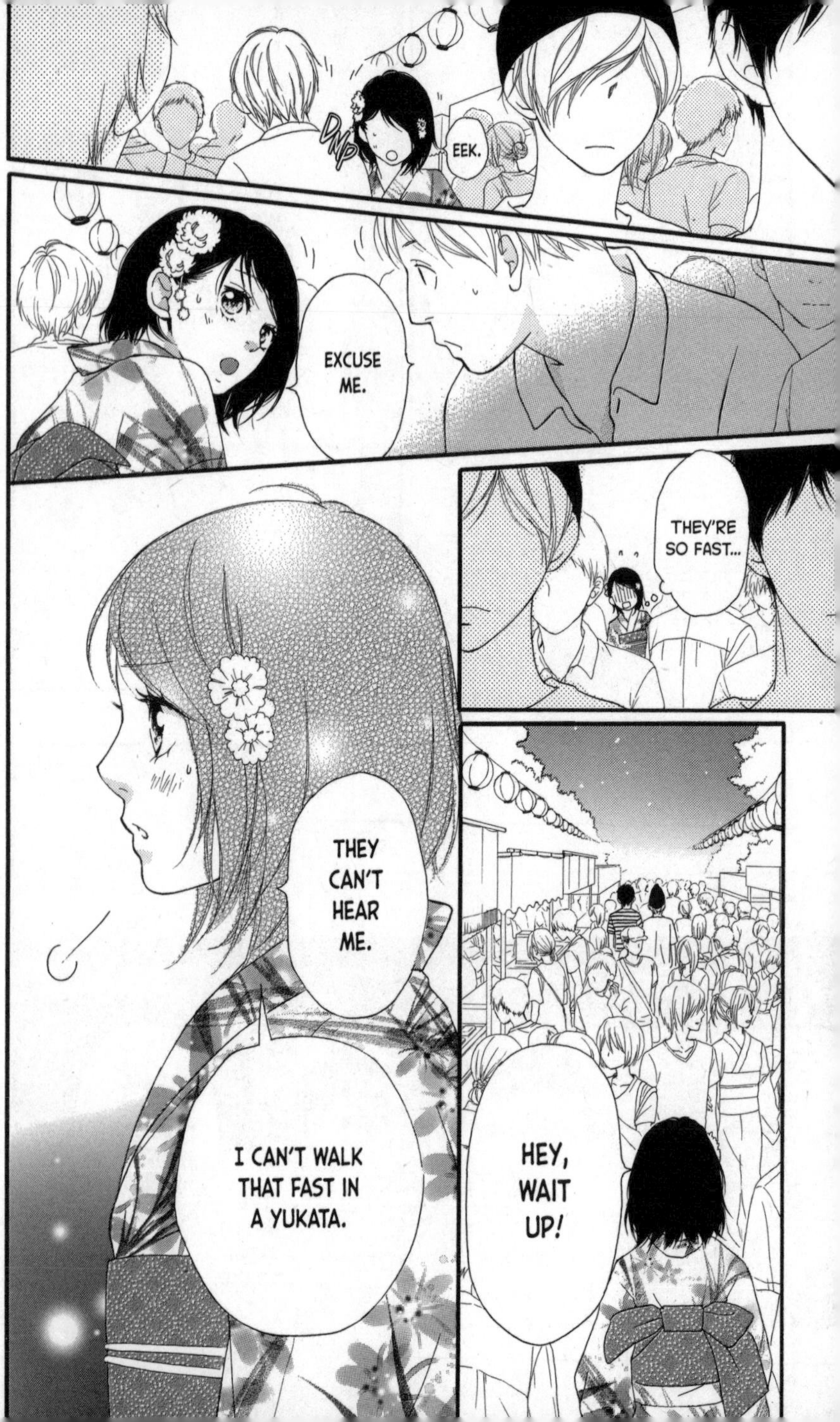
EEK.
DNP
EXCUSE ME.
THEY'RE SO FAST...
HEY, WAIT UP!
THEY CAN'T HEAR ME.
I CAN'T WALK THAT FAST IN A YUKATA.

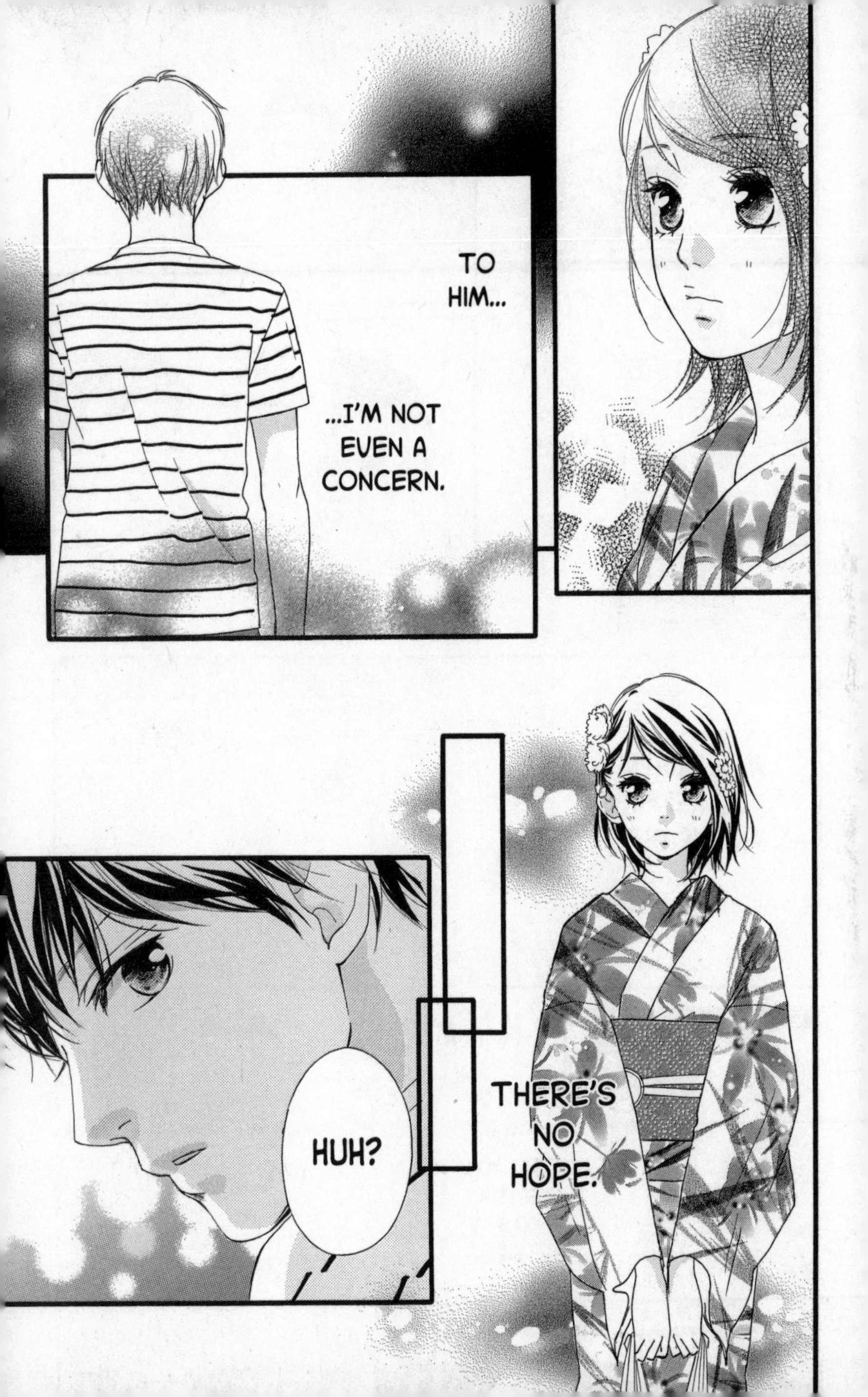
TO HIM...
...I'M NOT EVEN A CONCERN.
THERE'S NO HOPE.
HUH?

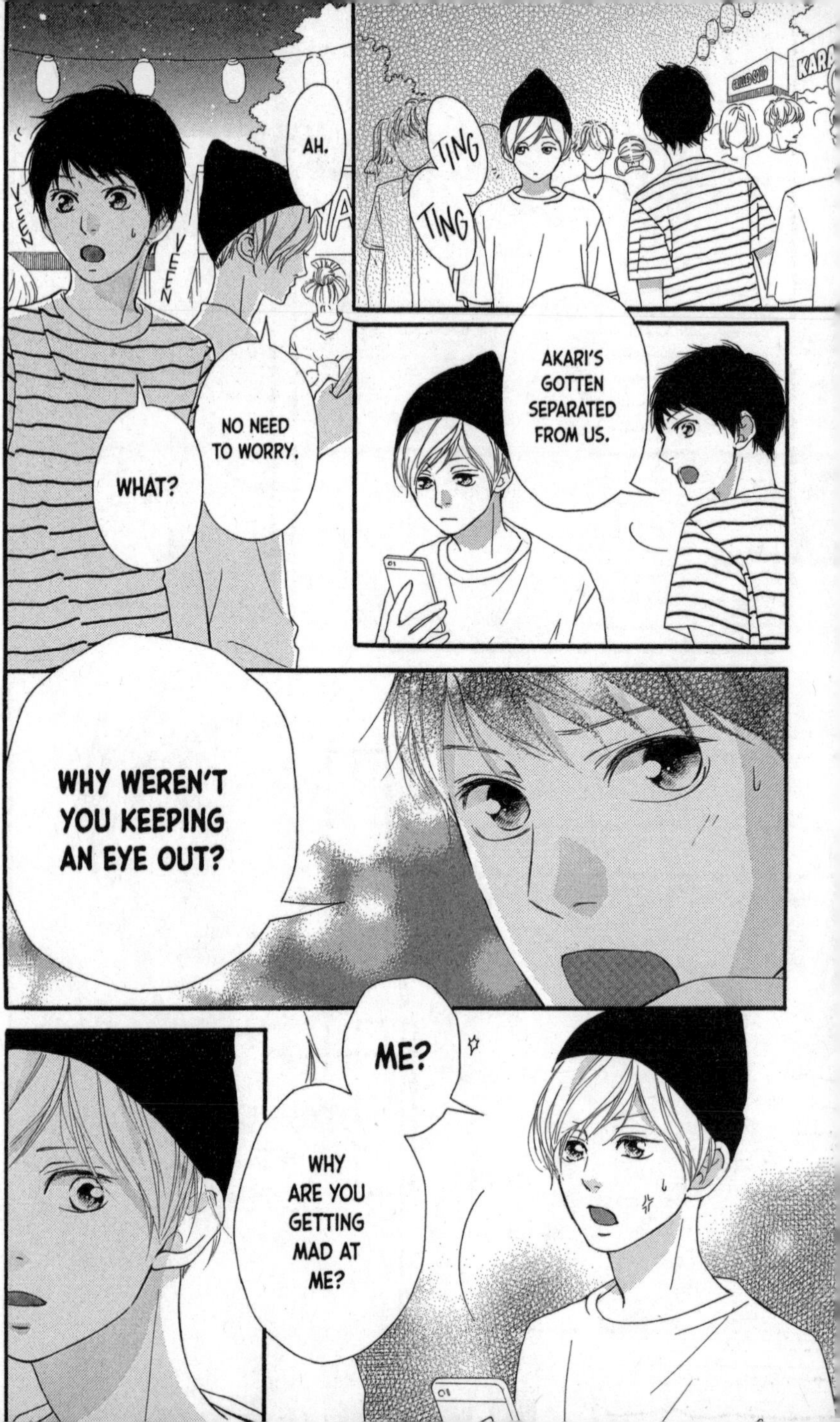
KARA
TING
TING
AKARI'S GOTTEN SEPARATED FROM US.
AH.
VEEN
VEEN
NO NEED TO WORRY.
WHAT?
WHY WEREN'T YOU KEEPING AN EYE OUT?
ME?
WHY ARE YOU GETTING MAD AT ME?

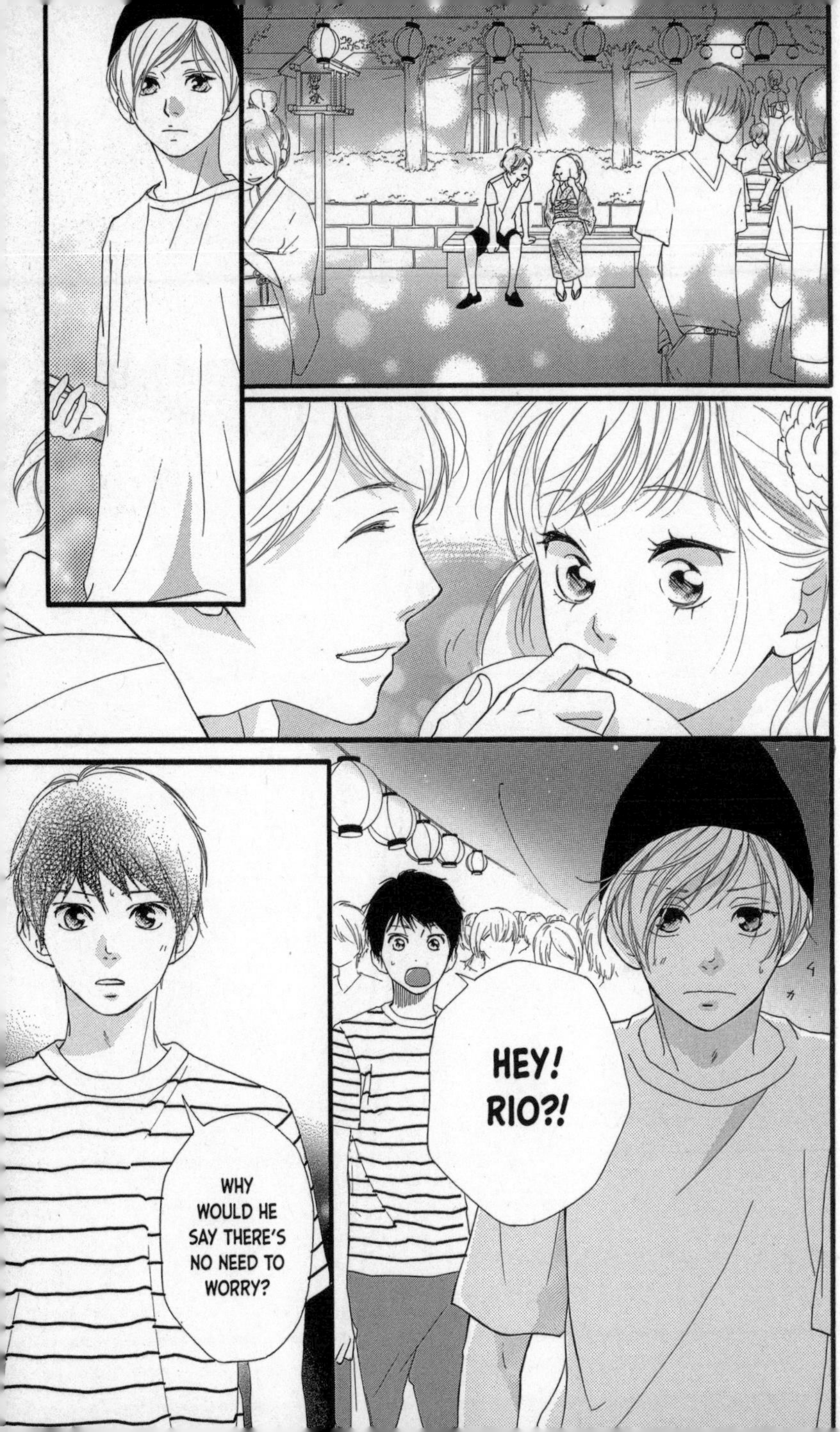
HEY! RIO?!
WHY WOULD HE SAY THERE'S NO NEED TO WORRY?

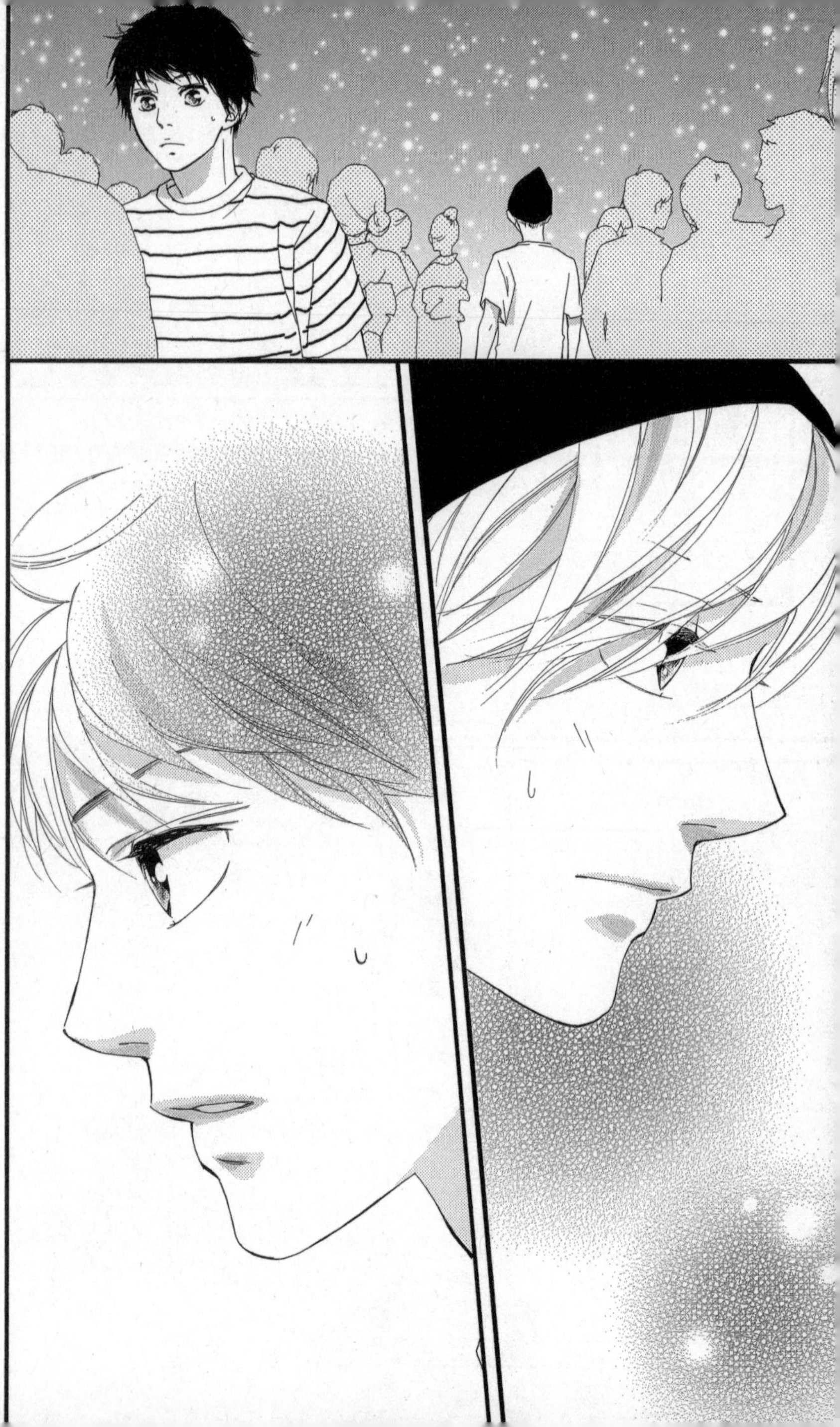

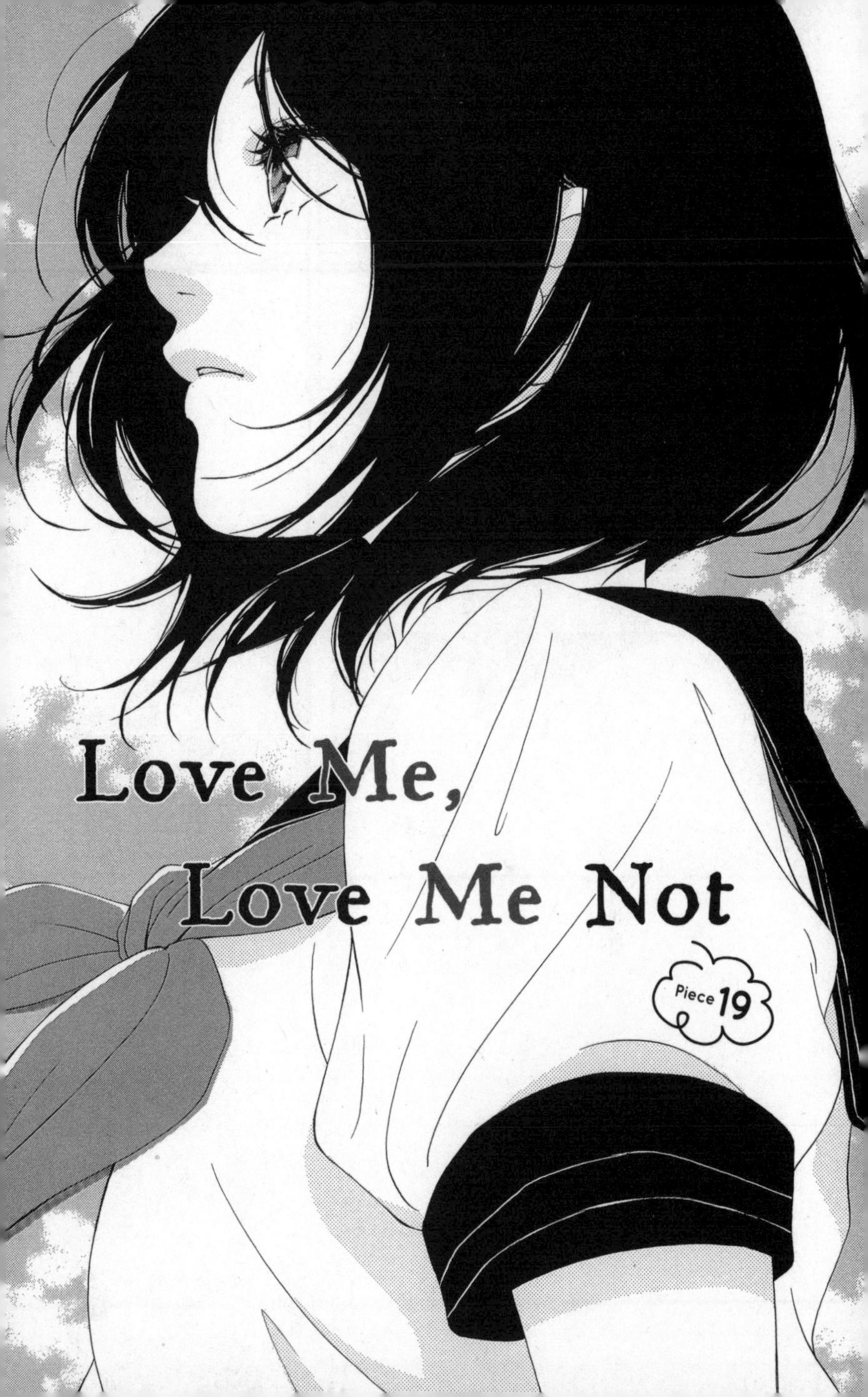
Love Me,
Love Me Not
Piece 19

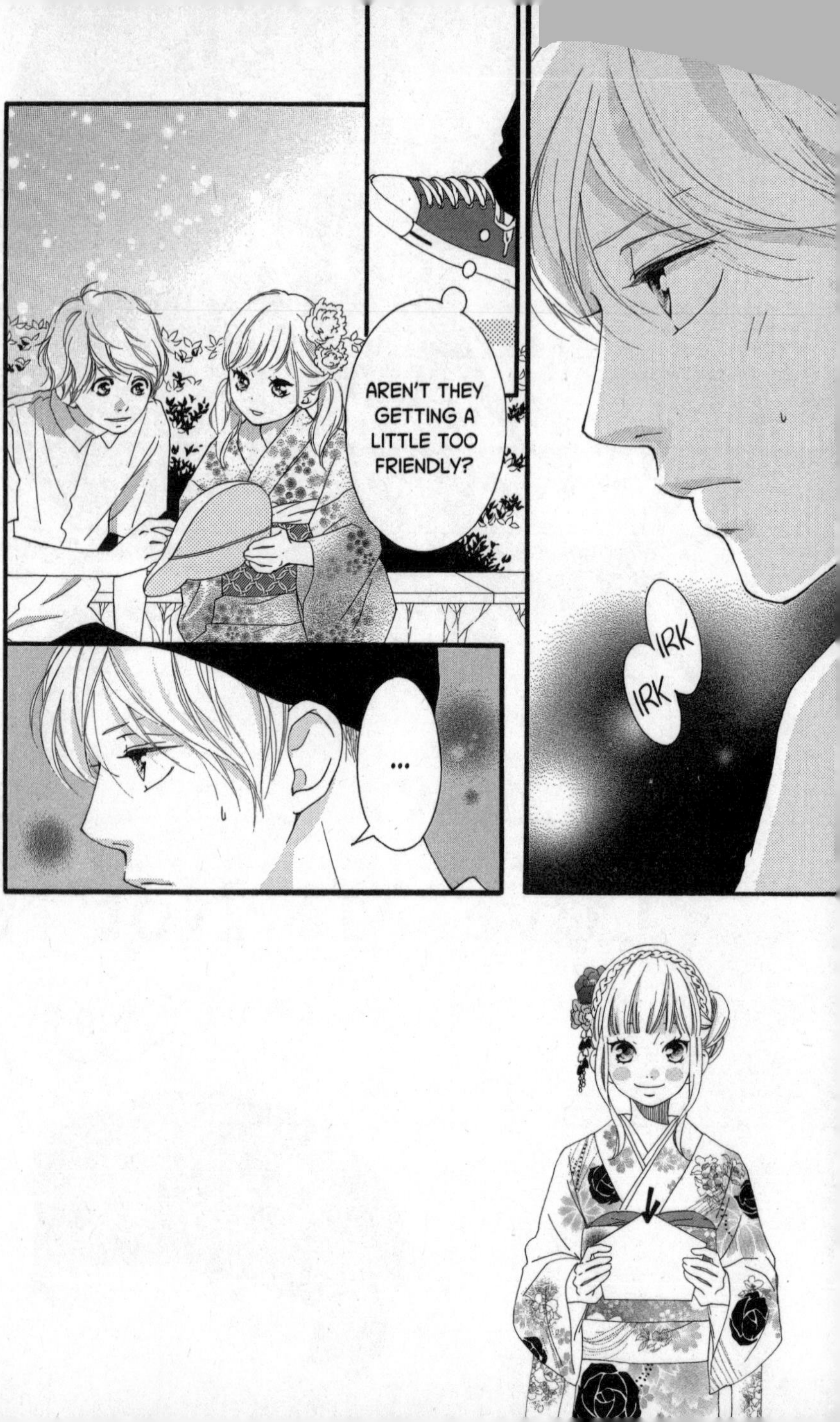
IRK
IRK
AREN'T THEY GETTING A LITTLE TOO FRIENDLY?
...

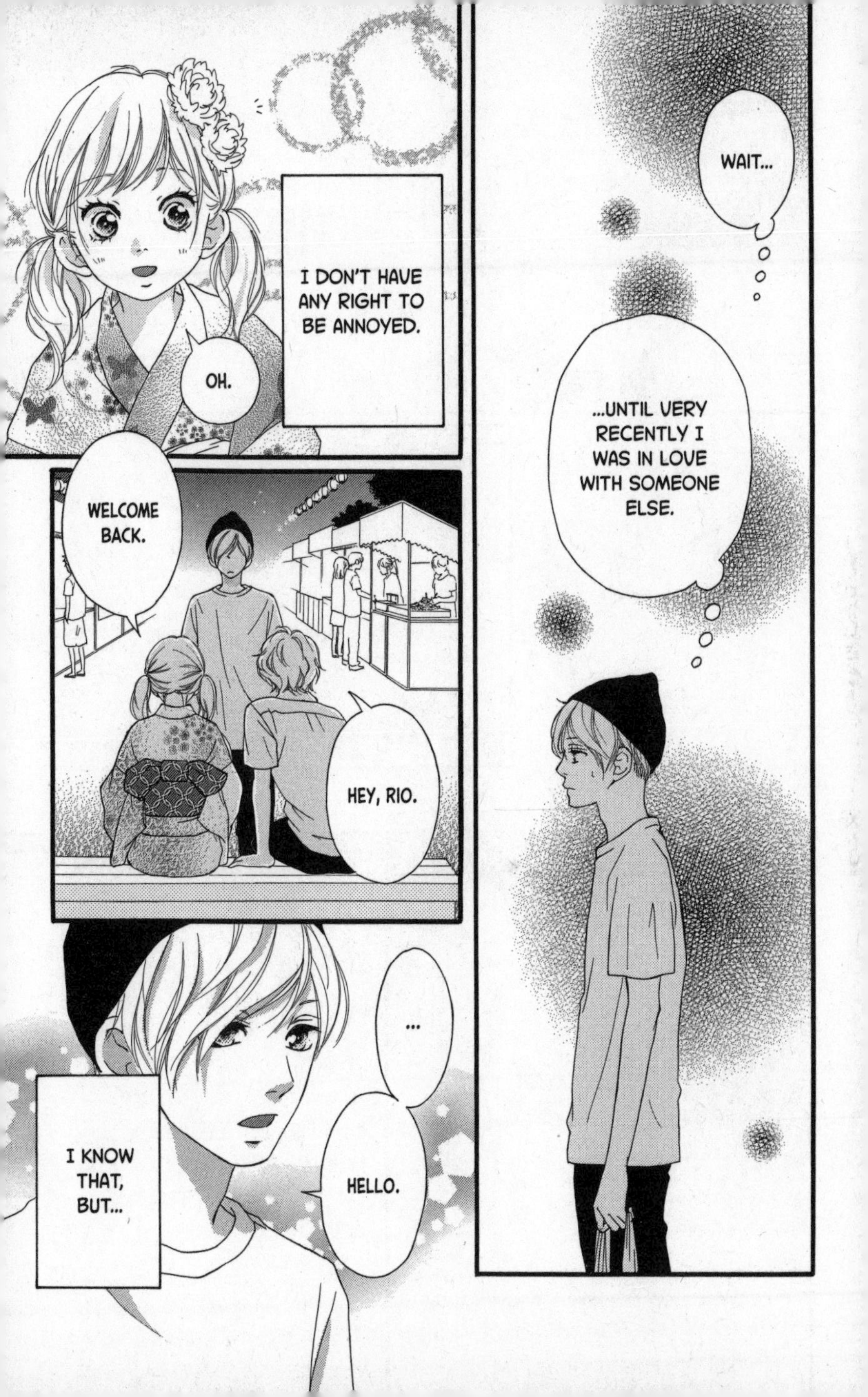
WAIT...
...UNTIL VERY RECENTLY I WAS IN LOVE WITH SOMEONE ELSE.
I DON'T HAVE ANY RIGHT TO BE ANNOYED.
OH.
WELCOME BACK.
HEY, RIO.
...
HELLO.
I KNOW THAT, BUT...

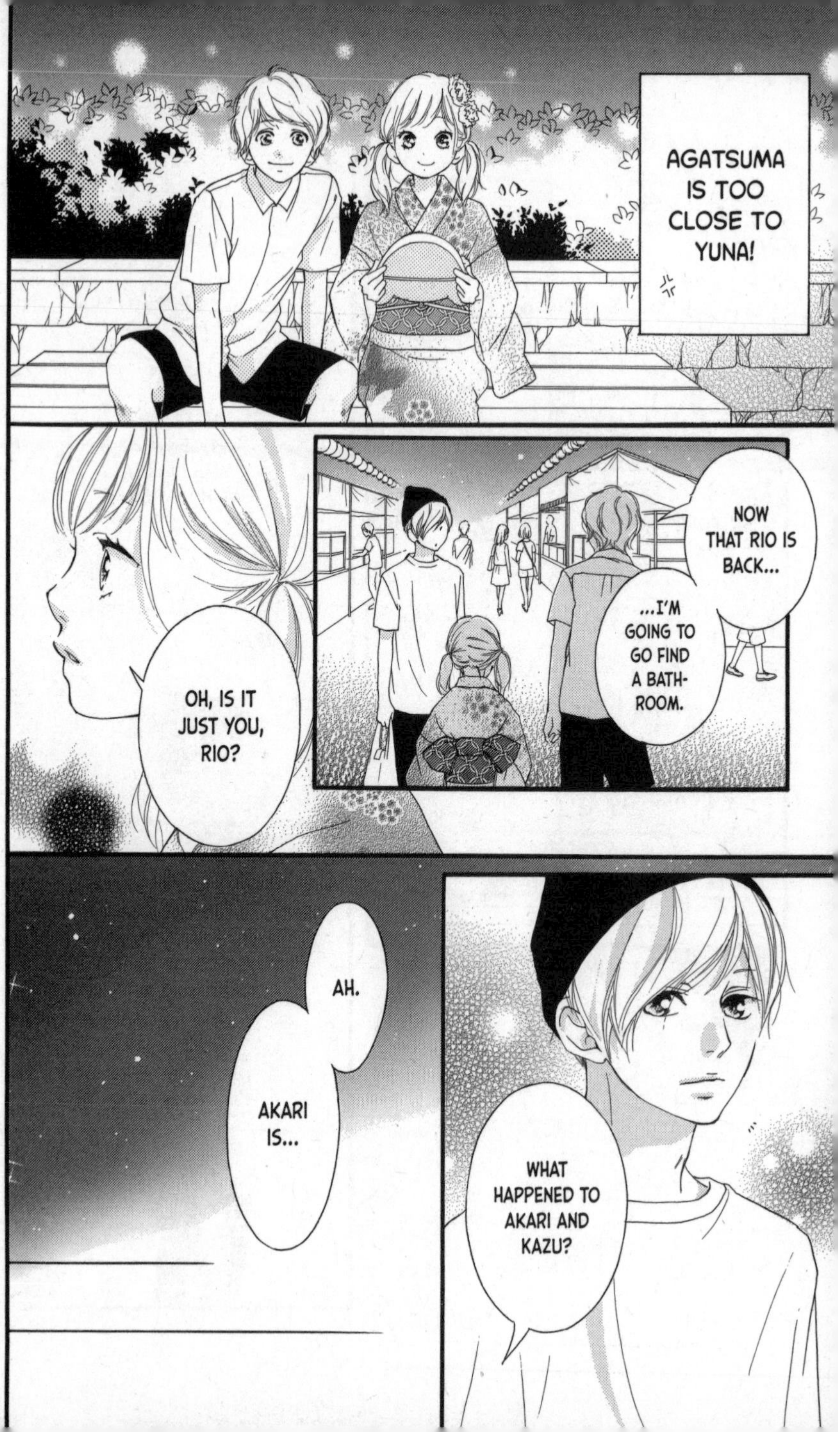
AGATSUMA IS TOO CLOSE TO YUNA!
NOW THAT RIO IS BACK...
...I'M GOING TO GO FIND A BATH-ROOM.
OH, IS IT JUST YOU, RIO?
WHAT HAPPENED TO AKARI AND KAZU?
AH.
AKARI IS...

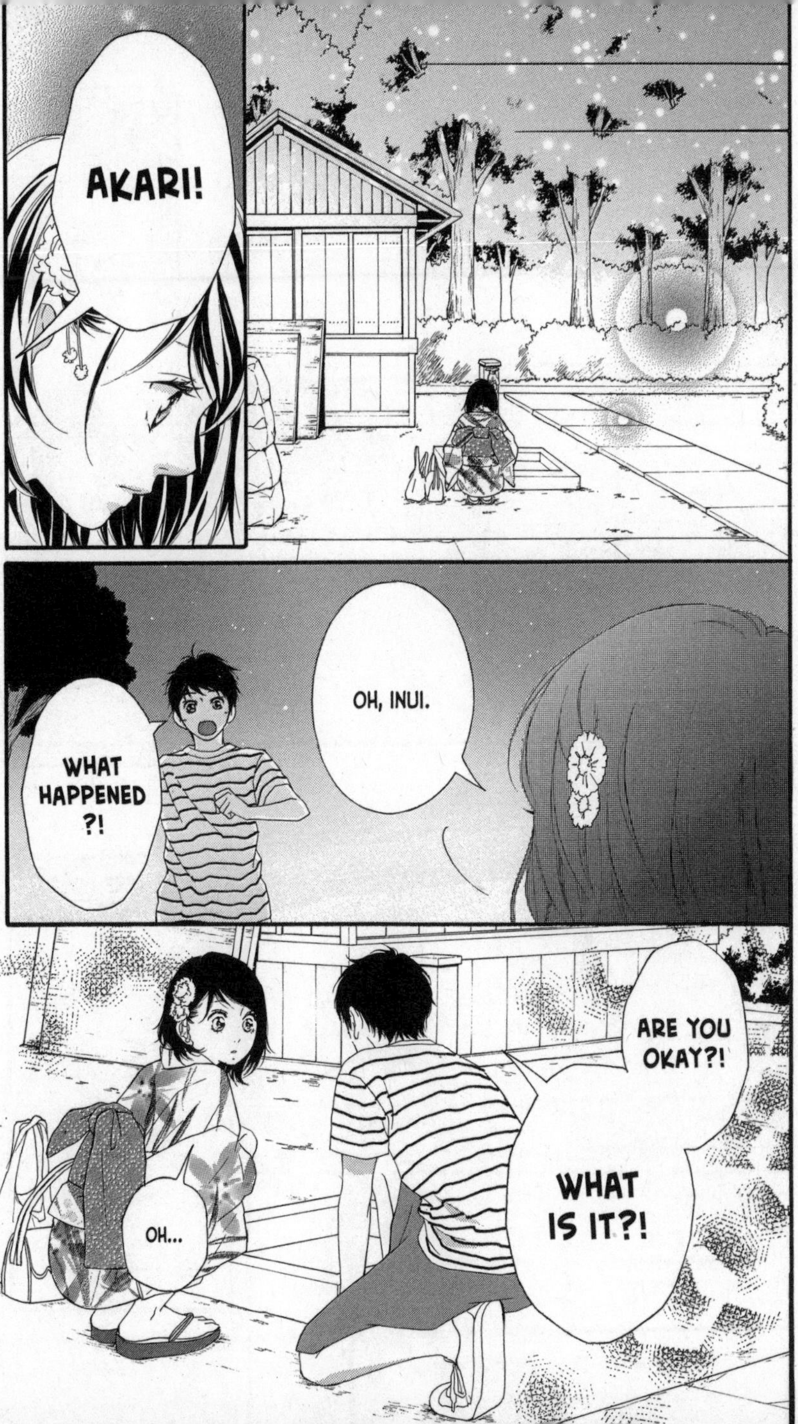
AKARI!
OH, INUI.
WHAT HAPPENED ?!
ARE YOU OKAY?!
WHAT IS IT?!
OH...

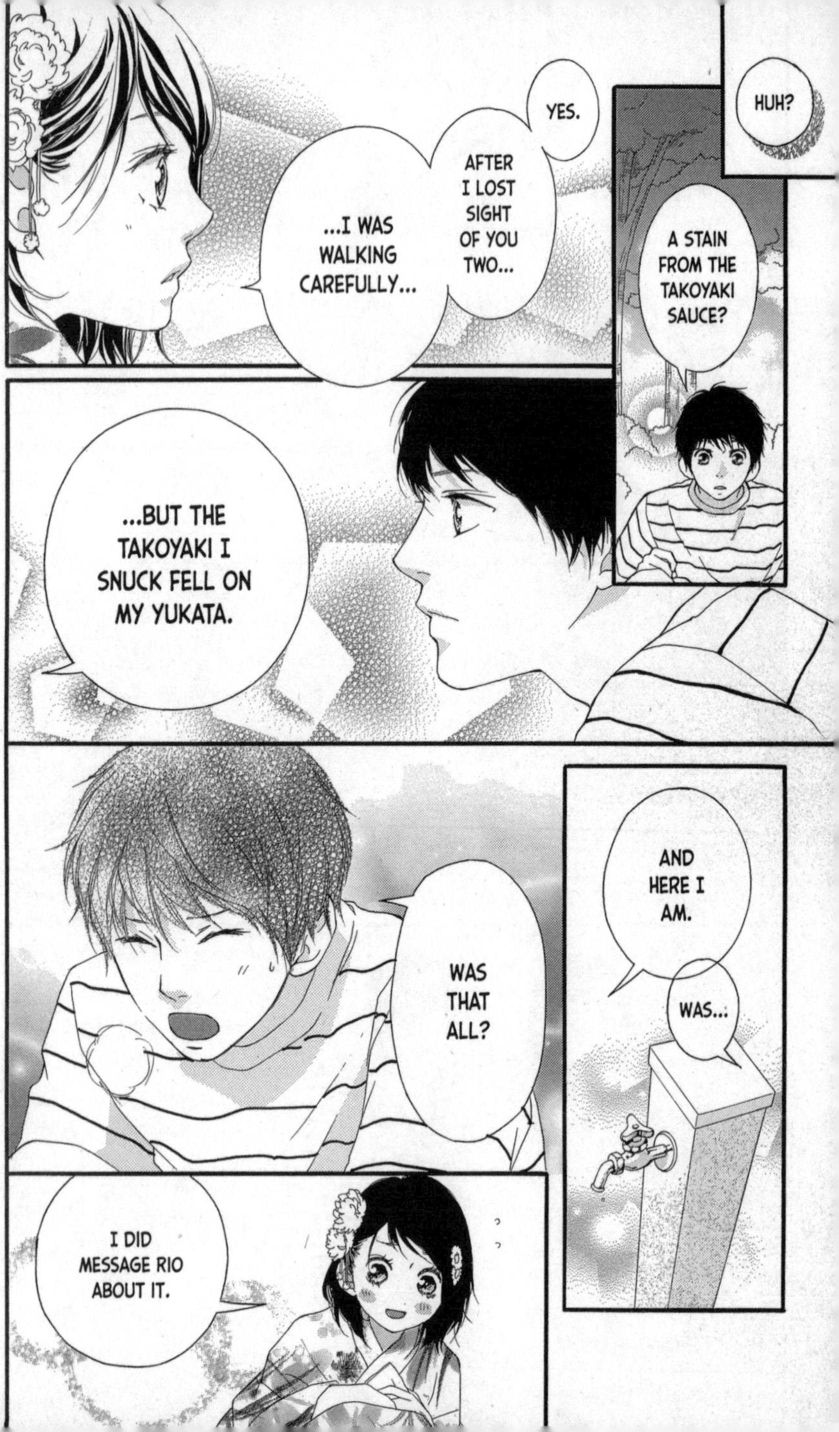
HUH?
A STAIN FROM THE TAKOYAKI SAUCE?
YES.
AFTER I LOST SIGHT OF YOU TWO...
...I WAS WALKING CAREFULLY...
...BUT THE TAKOYAKI I SNUCK FELL ON MY YUKATA.
AND HERE I AM.
WAS...
WAS THAT ALL?
I DID MESSAGE RIO ABOUT IT.

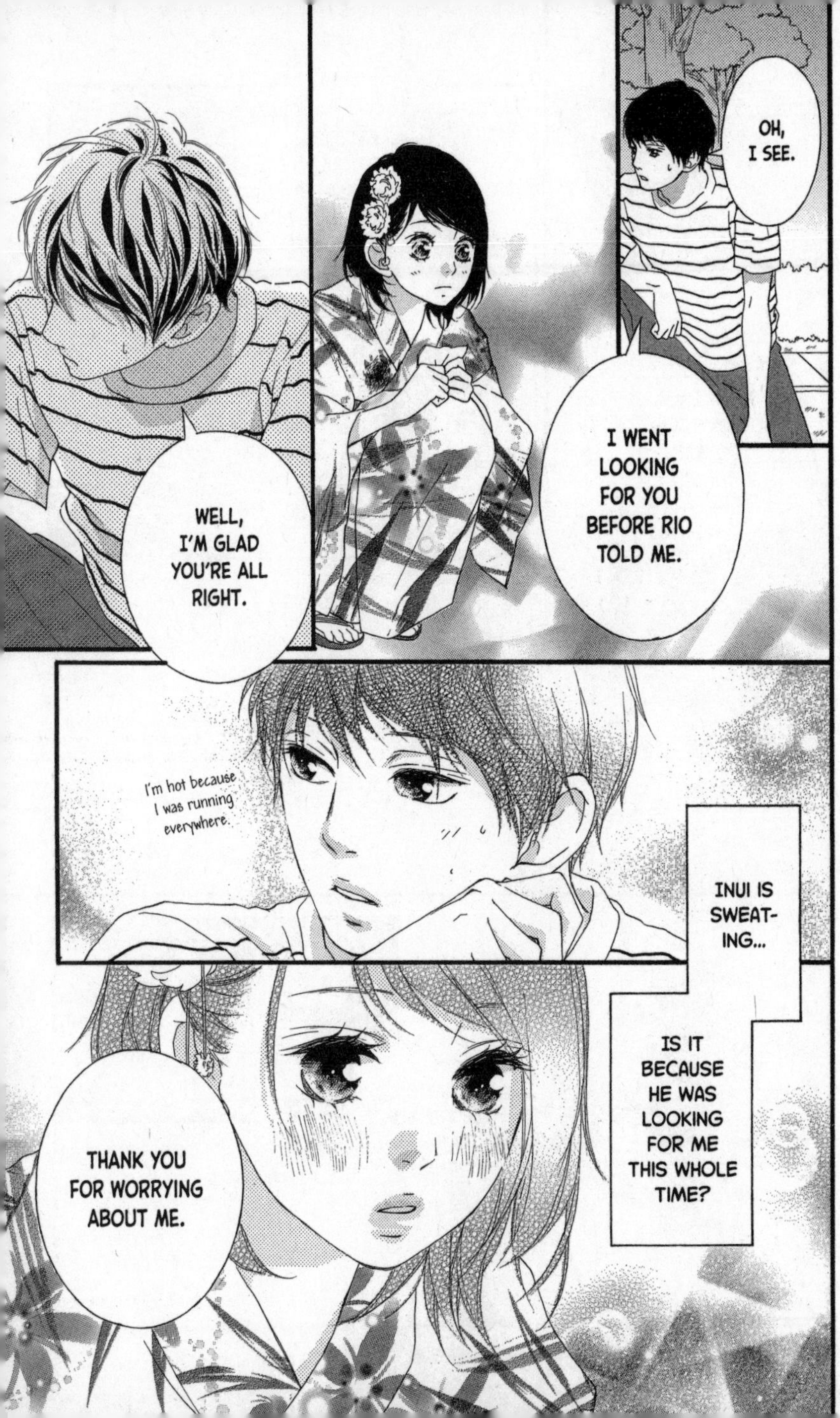
OH, I SEE.
I WENT LOOKING FOR YOU BEFORE RIO TOLD ME.
WELL, I'M GLAD YOU'RE ALL RIGHT.
INUI IS SWEAT-ING...
I'm hot because I was running everywhere.
IS IT BECAUSE HE WAS LOOKING FOR ME THIS WHOLE TIME?
THANK YOU FOR WORRYING ABOUT ME.

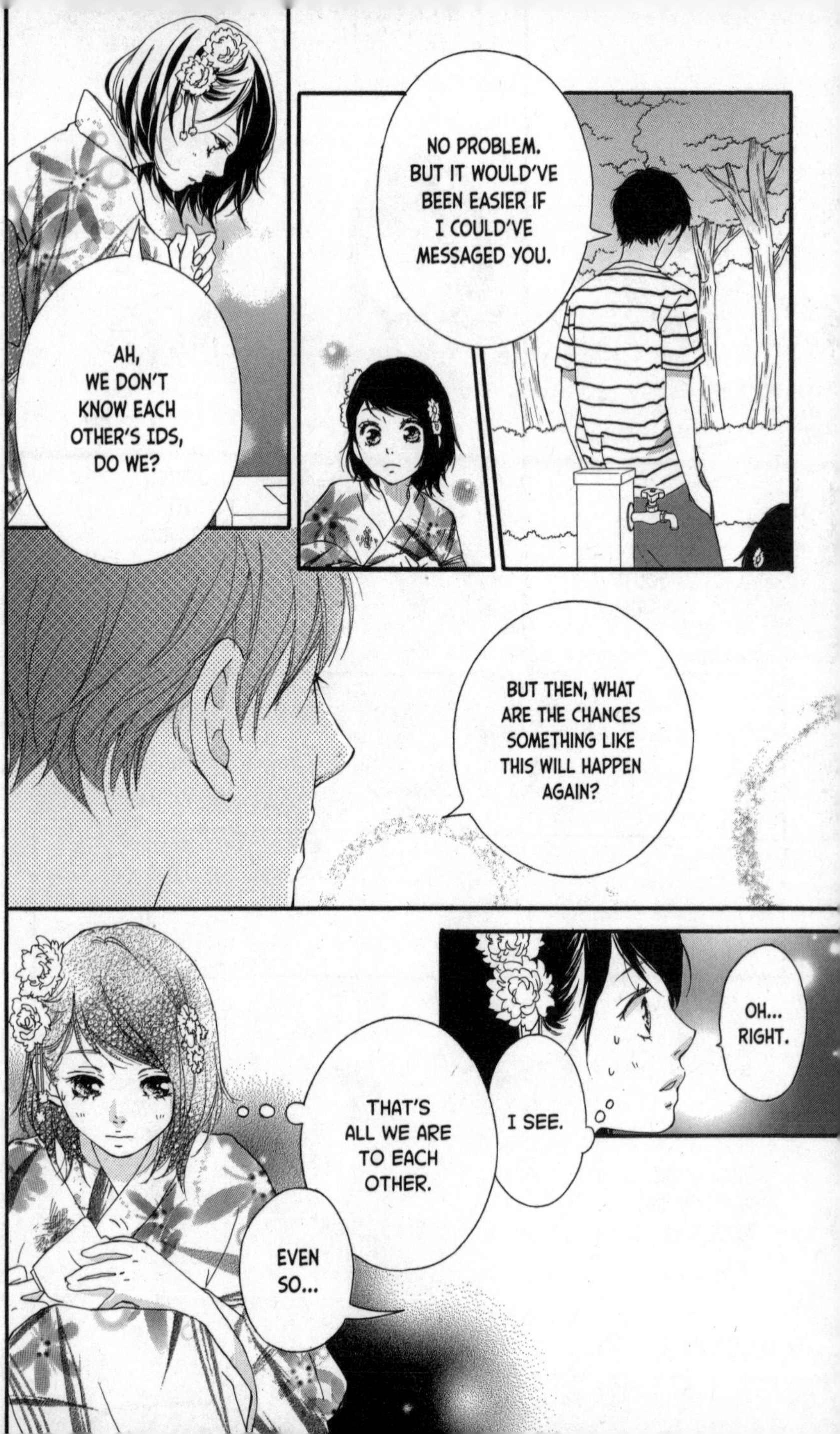
NO PROBLEM. BUT IT WOULD'VE BEEN EASIER IF I COULD'VE MESSAGED YOU.
AH, WE DON'T KNOW EACH OTHER'S IDS, DO WE?
BUT THEN, WHAT ARE THE CHANCES SOMETHING LIKE THIS WILL HAPPEN AGAIN?
OH... RIGHT.
I SEE.
THAT'S ALL WE ARE TO EACH OTHER.
EVEN SO...

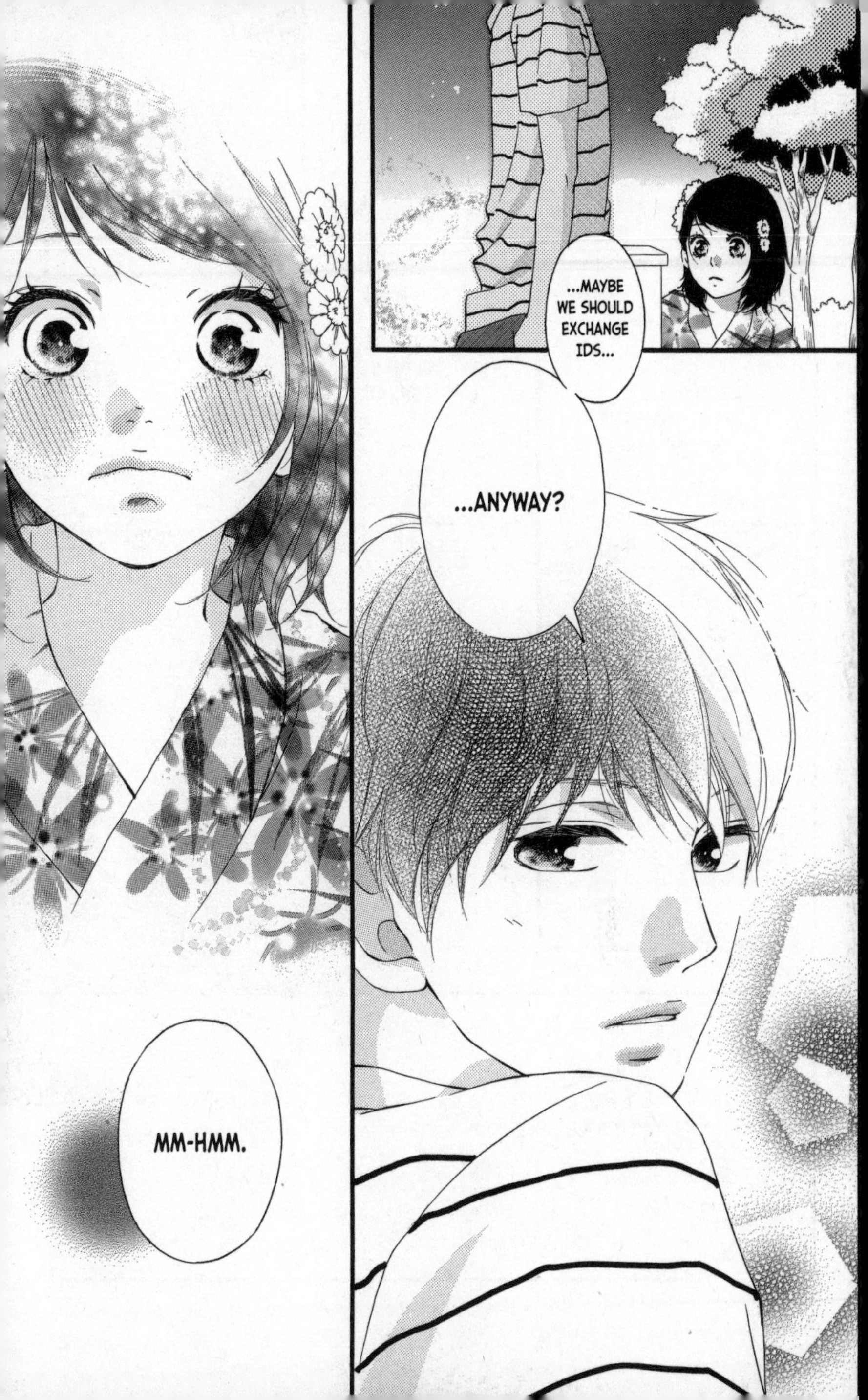
...MAYBE WE SHOULD EXCHANGE IDS...
...ANYWAY?
MM-HMM.

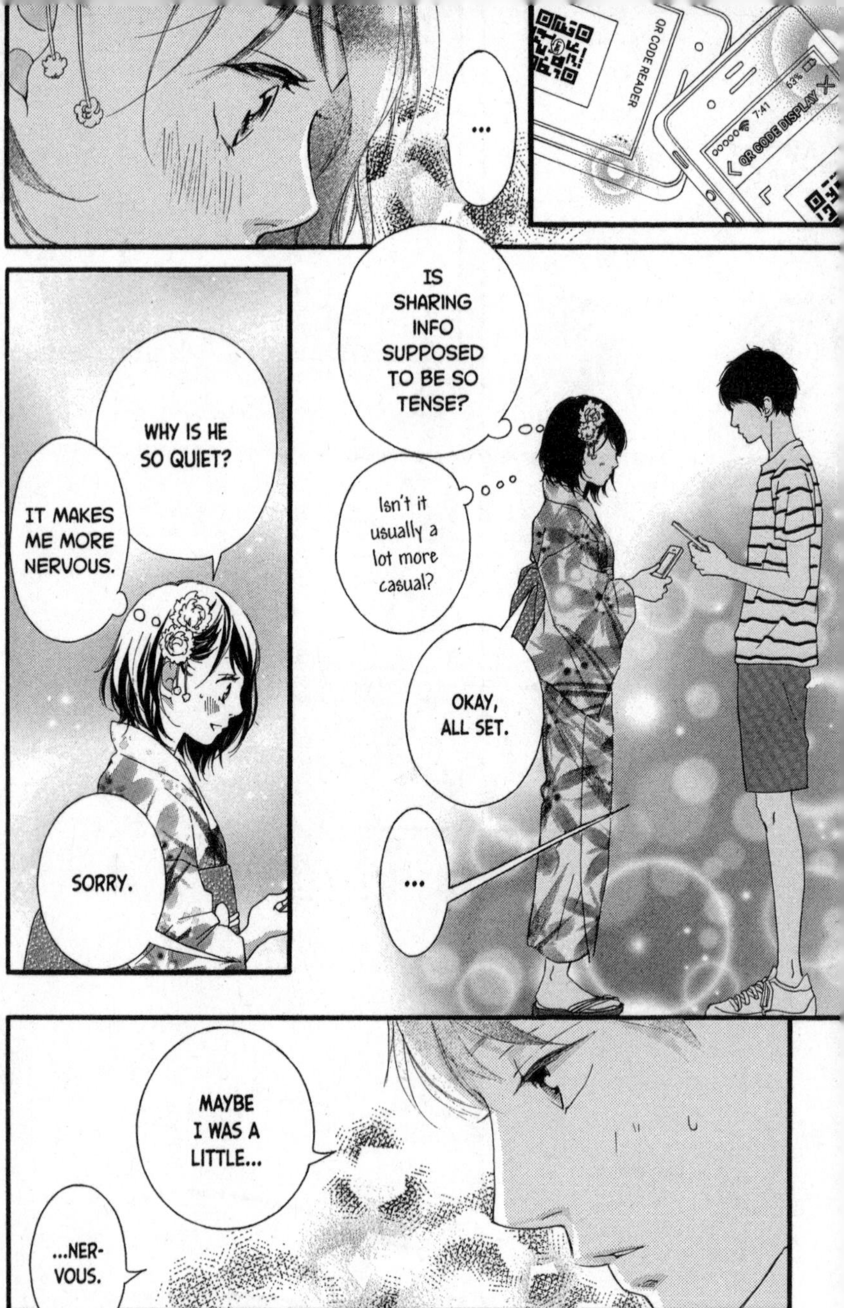
QR CODE READER
QR CODE DISPLAY
...
IS SHARING INFO SUPPOSED TO BE SO TENSE?
Isn't it usually a lot more casual?
OKAY, ALL SET.
...
WHY IS HE SO QUIET?
IT MAKES ME MORE NERVOUS.
SORRY.
MAYBE I WAS A LITTLE...
...NER-VOUS.

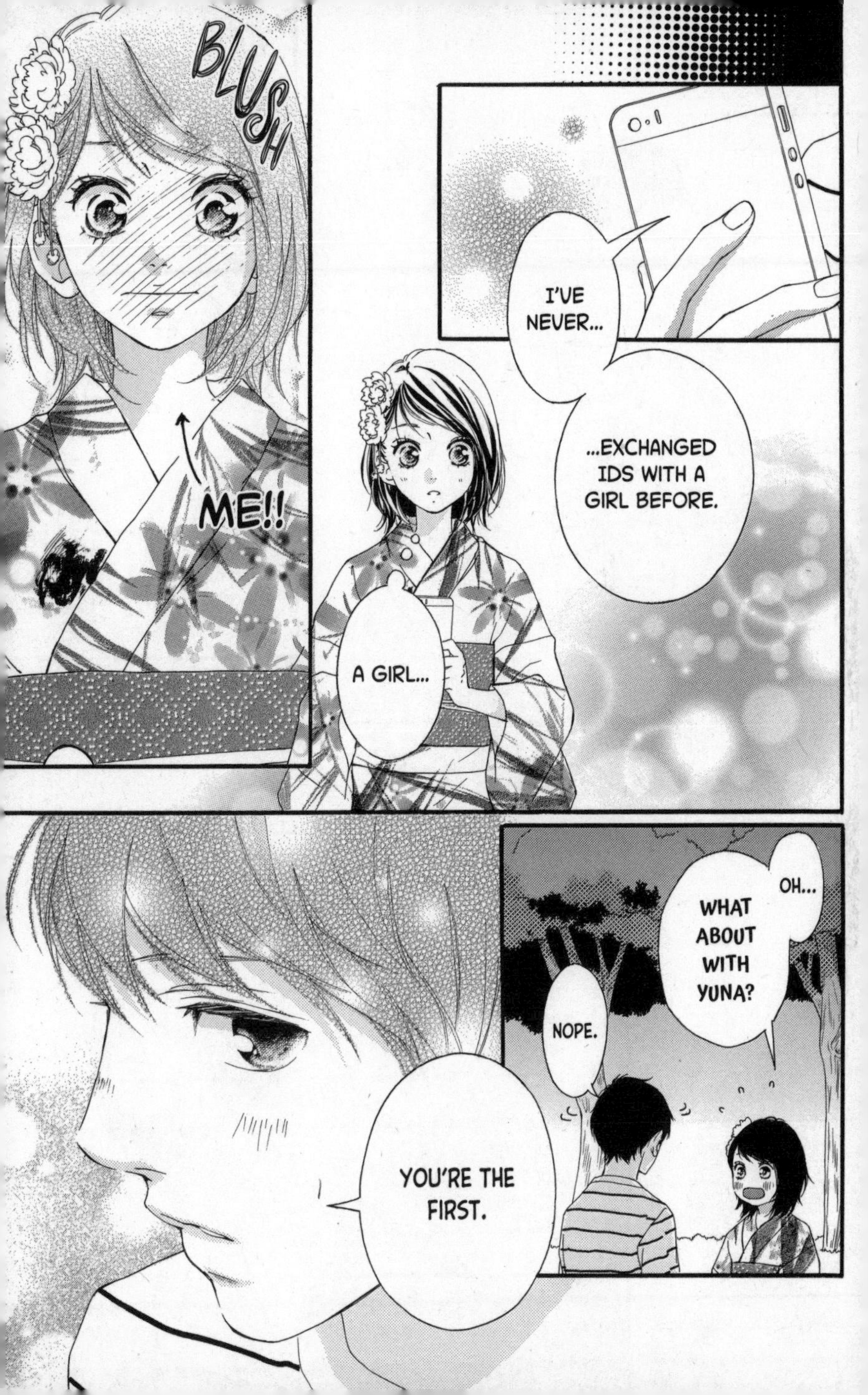
I'VE NEVER...
...EXCHANGED IDS WITH A GIRL BEFORE.
A GIRL...
BLUSH
ME!!
OH...
WHAT ABOUT WITH YUNA?
NOPE.
YOU'RE THE FIRST.

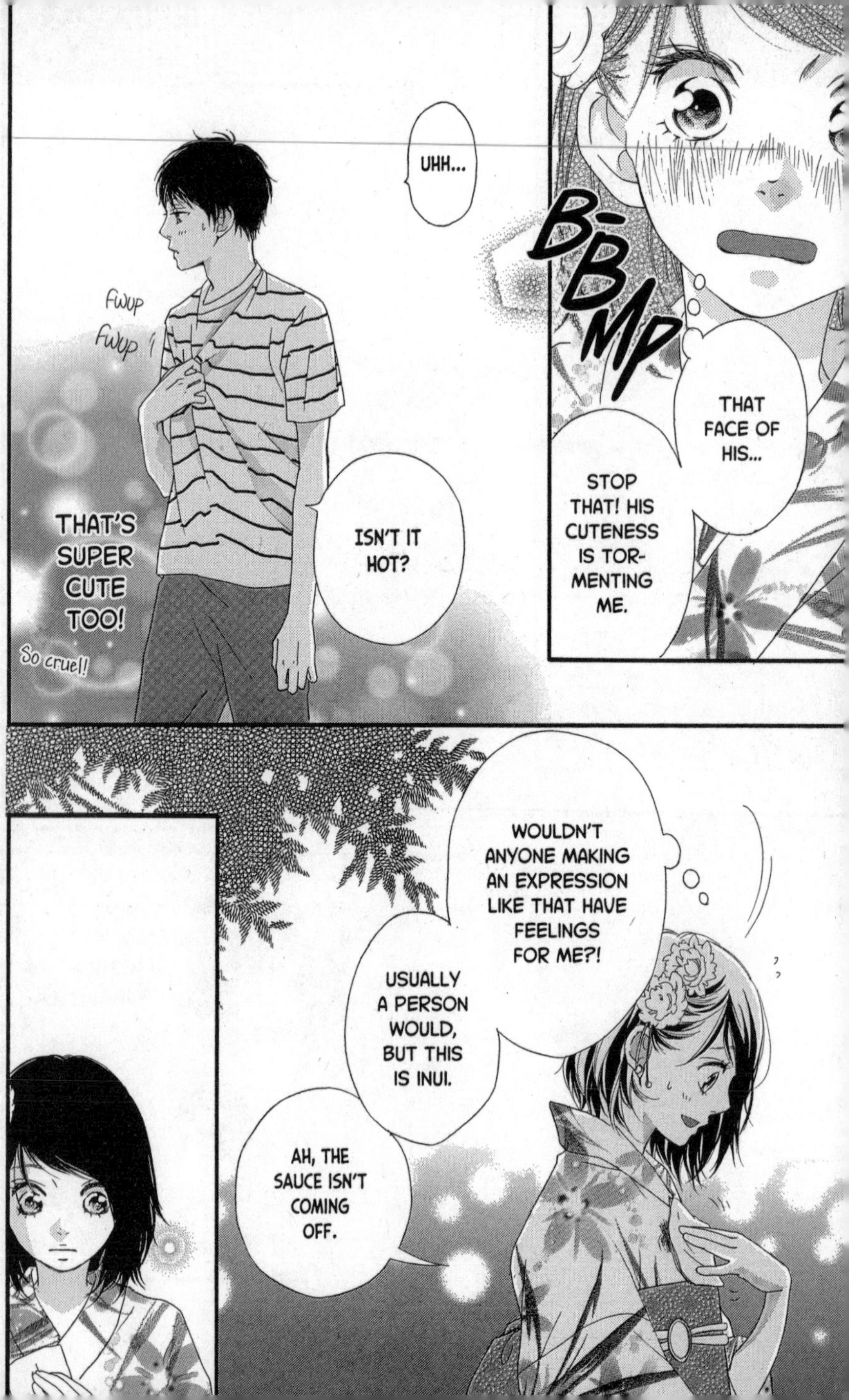
B-BMP
THAT FACE OF HIS...
STOP THAT! HIS CUTENESS IS TOR-MENTING ME.
UHH...
FWUP FWUP
ISN'T IT HOT?
THAT'S SUPER CUTE TOO!
So cruel!
WOULDN'T ANYONE MAKING AN EXPRESSION LIKE THAT HAVE FEELINGS FOR ME?!
USUALLY A PERSON WOULD, BUT THIS IS INUI.
AH, THE SAUCE ISN'T COMING OFF.

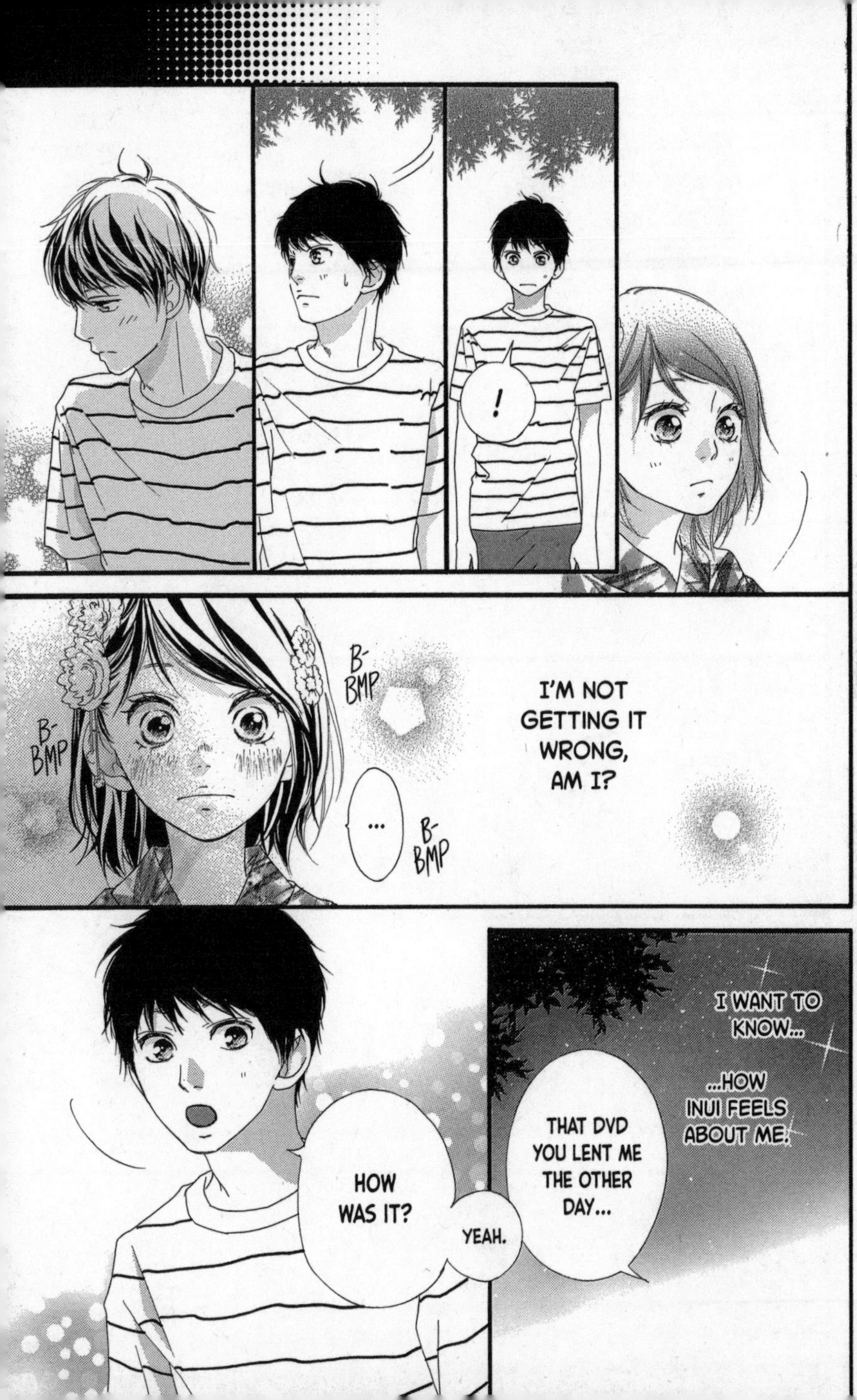
!
I'M NOT GETTING IT WRONG, AM I?
B-BMP
...
B-BMP
B-BMP
I WANT TO KNOW...
...HOW INUI FEELS ABOUT ME.
THAT DVD YOU LENT ME THE OTHER DAY...
YEAH.
HOW WAS IT?

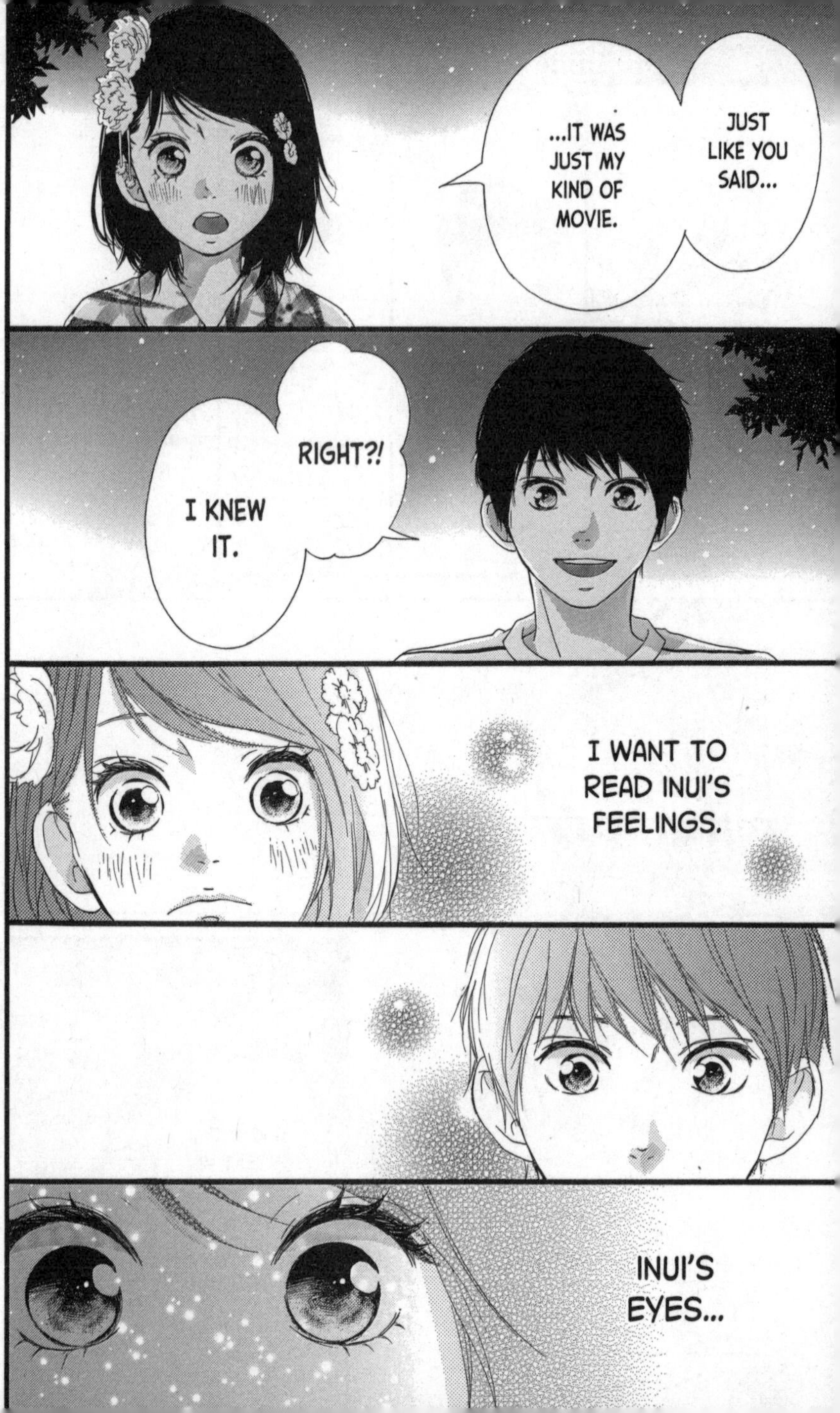
JUST LIKE YOU SAID...
...IT WAS JUST MY KIND OF MOVIE.
RIGHT?!
I KNEW IT.
I WANT TO READ INUI'S FEELINGS.
INUI'S EYES...

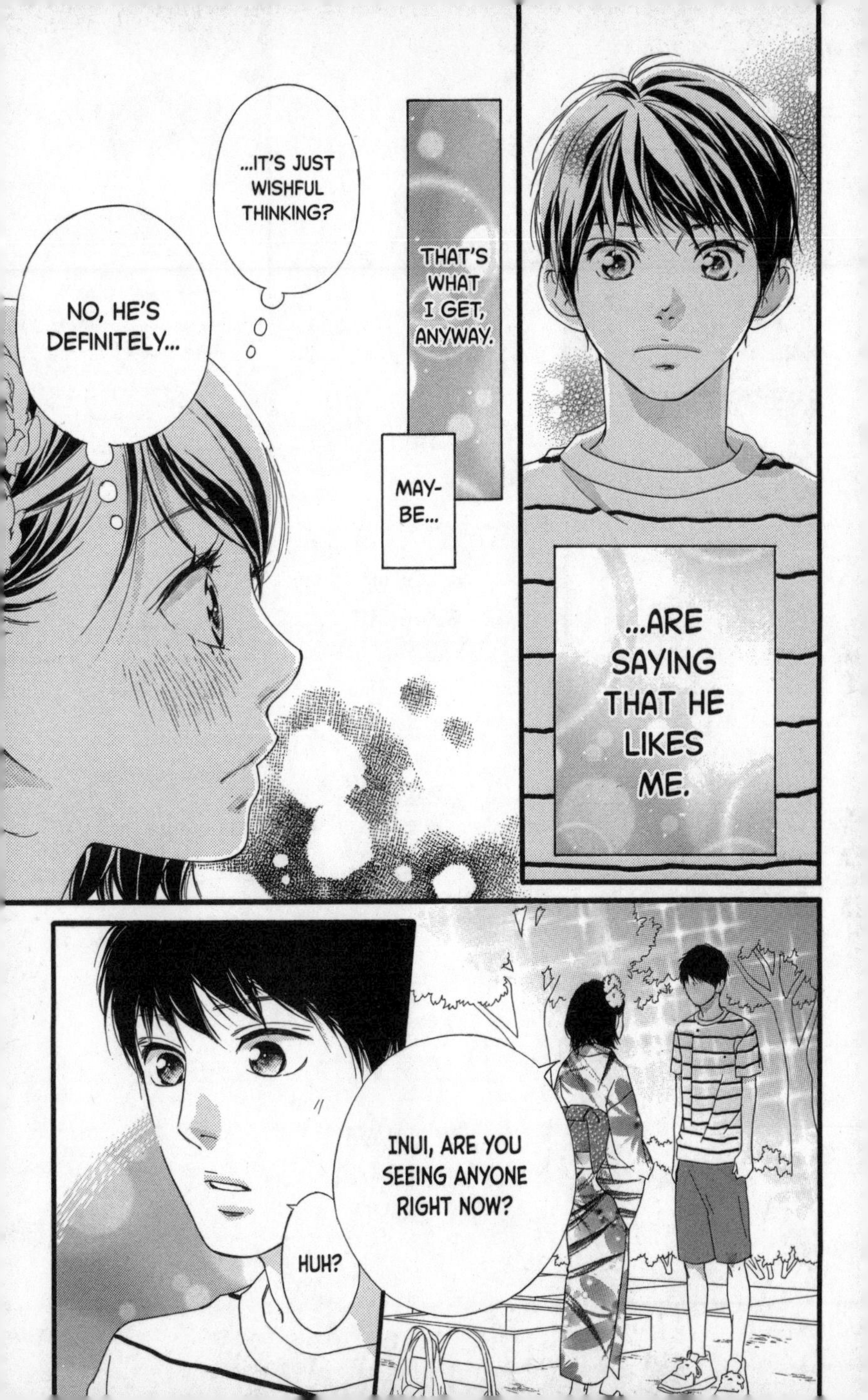

...ARE SAYING THAT HE LIKES ME.
THAT'S WHAT I GET, ANYWAY.
MAY-BE...
...IT'S JUST WISHFUL THINKING?
NO, HE'S DEFINITELY...
INUI, ARE YOU SEEING ANYONE RIGHT NOW?
HUH?

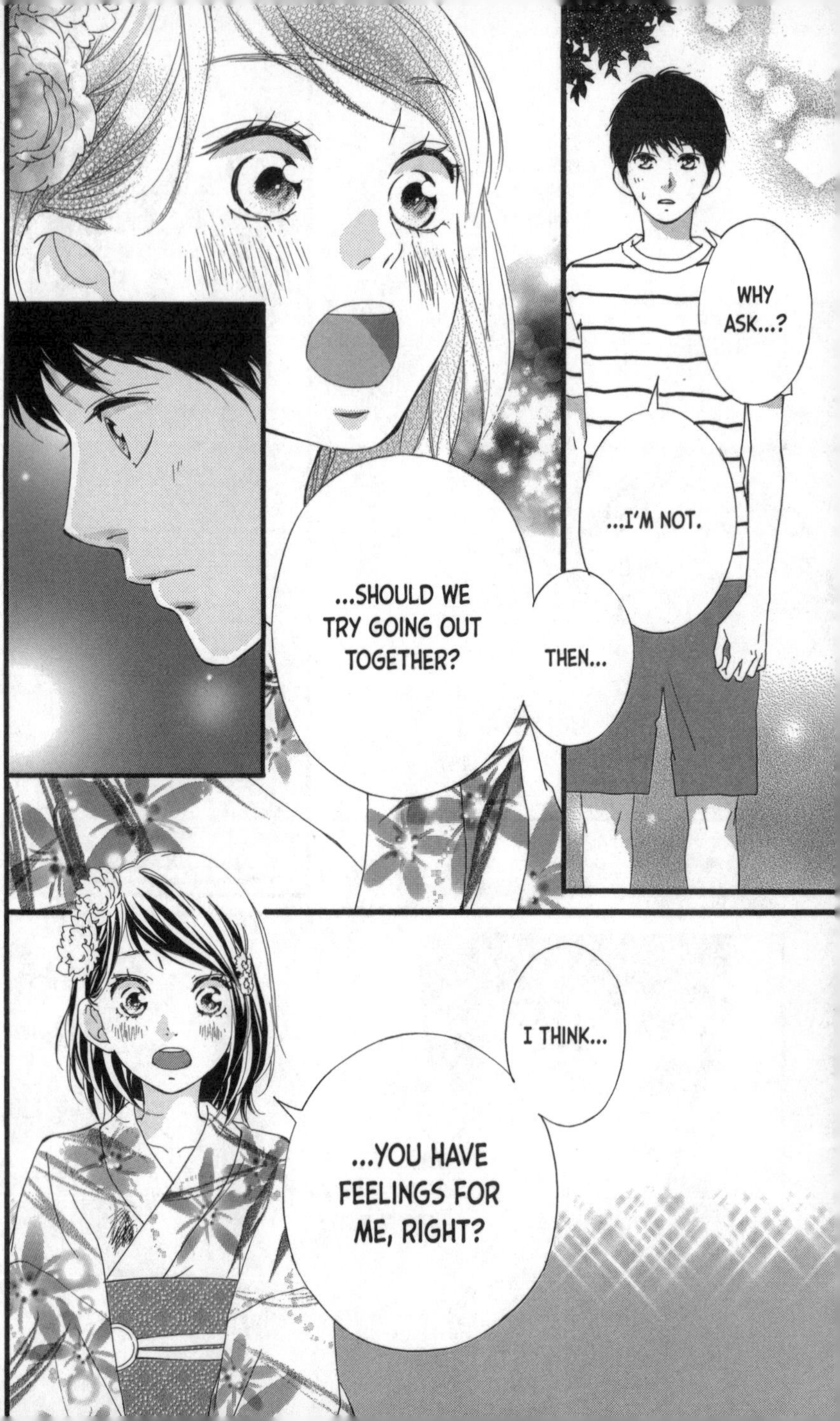
WHY ASK...?
...I'M NOT.
THEN...
...SHOULD WE TRY GOING OUT TOGETHER?
I THINK...
...YOU HAVE FEELINGS FOR ME, RIGHT?

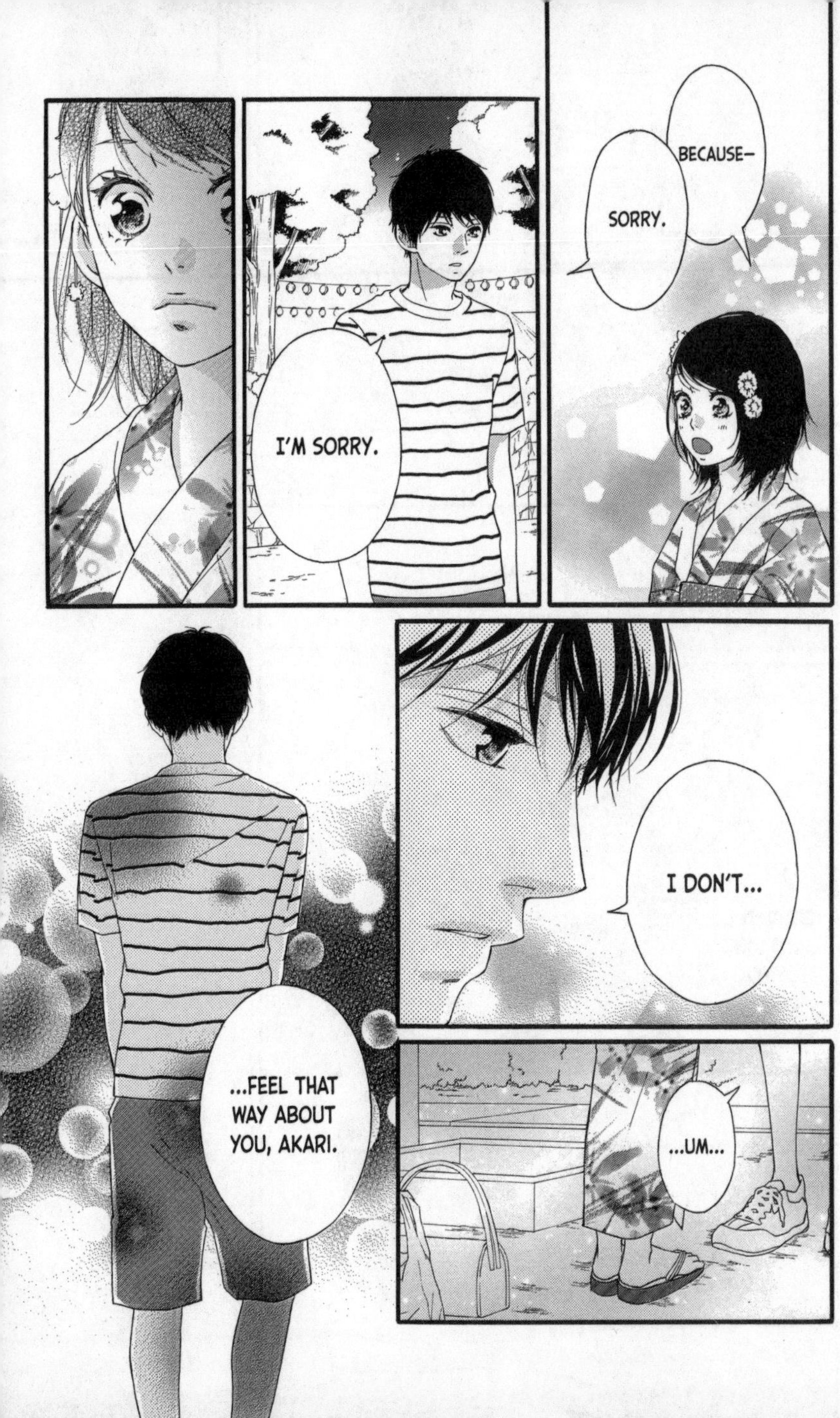
BECAUSE—
SORRY.
I'M SORRY.
I DON'T...
...UM...
...FEEL THAT WAY ABOUT YOU, AKARI.

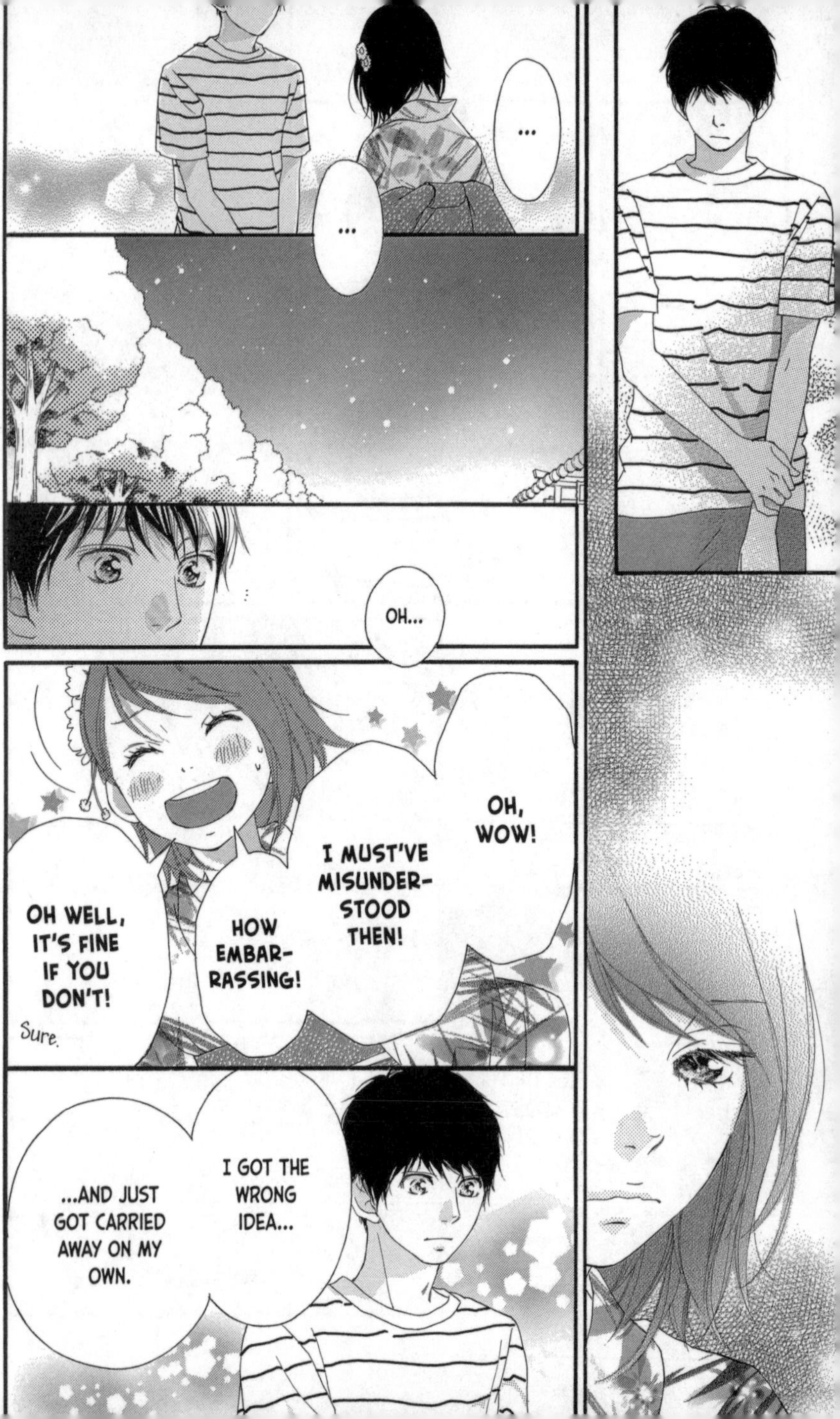
...
...
OH...
OH, WOW!
I MUST'VE MISUNDER-STOOD THEN!
HOW EMBAR-RASSING!
OH WELL, IT'S FINE IF YOU DON'T!
Sure.
I GOT THE WRONG IDEA...
...AND JUST GOT CARRIED AWAY ON MY OWN.

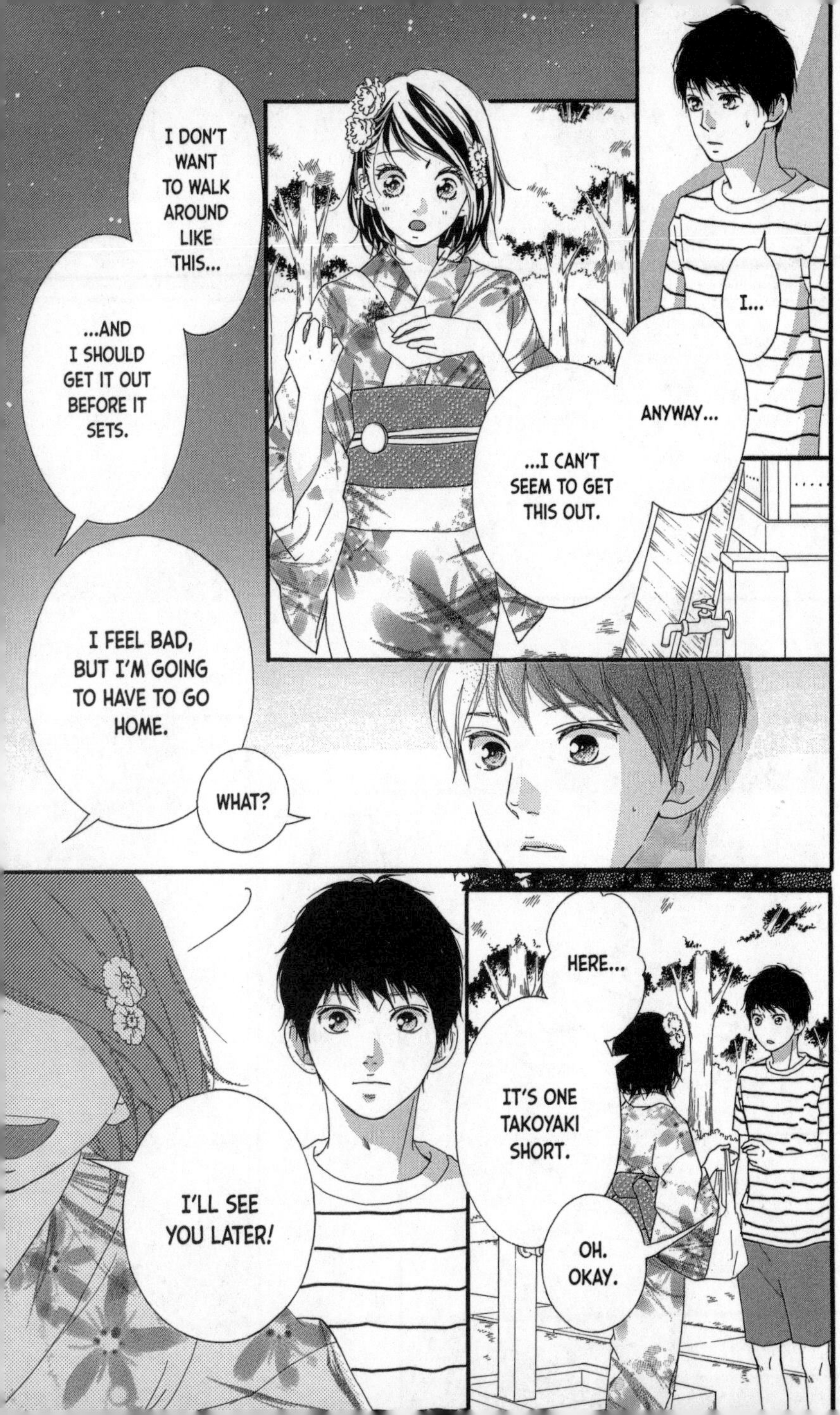
I...
ANYWAY...
...I CAN'T SEEM TO GET THIS OUT.
I DON'T WANT TO WALK AROUND LIKE THIS...
...AND I SHOULD GET IT OUT BEFORE IT SETS.
I FEEL BAD, BUT I'M GOING TO HAVE TO GO HOME.
WHAT?
HERE...
IT'S ONE TAKOYAKI SHORT.
OH. OKAY.
I'LL SEE YOU LATER!

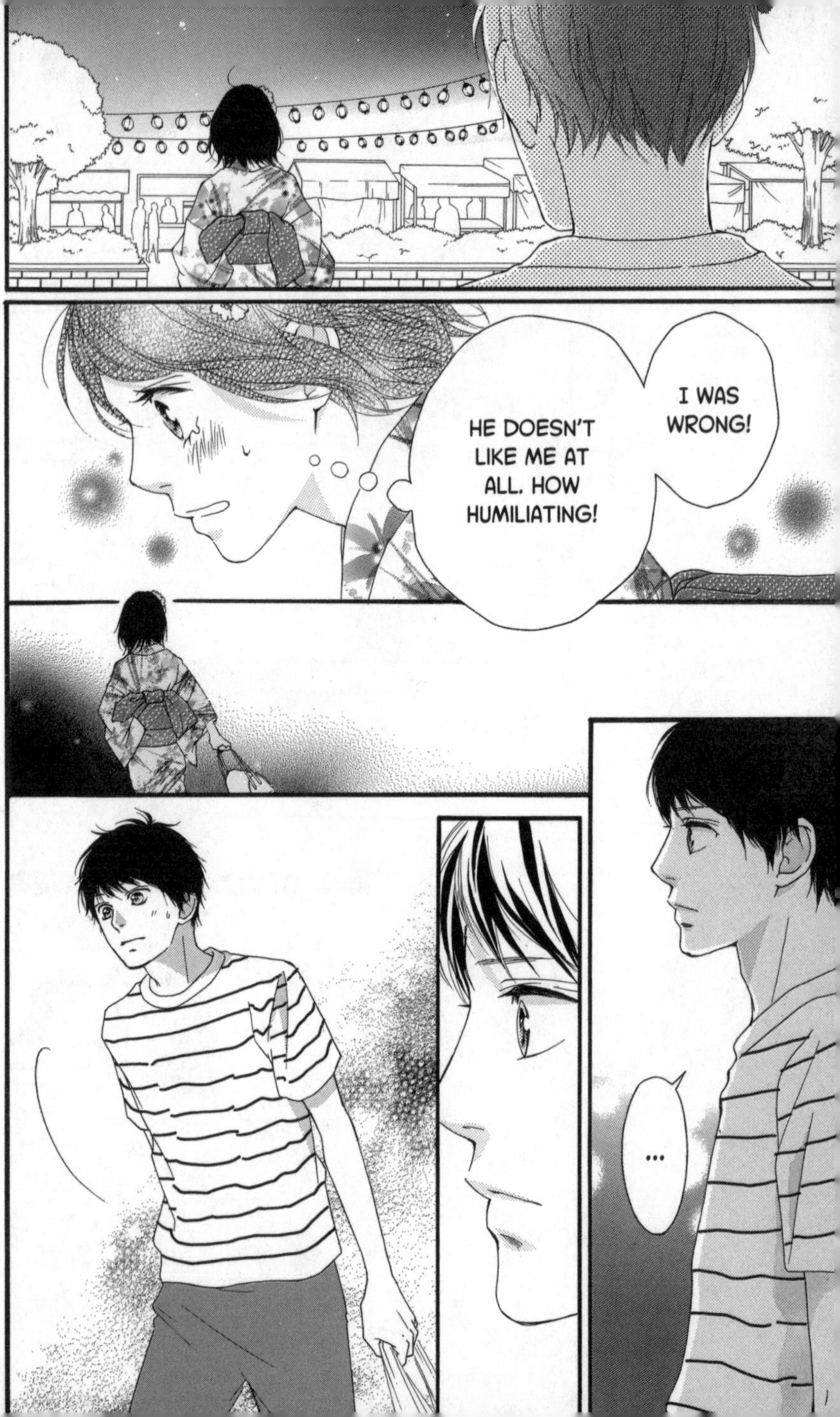
I WAS WRONG!
HE DOESN'T LIKE ME AT ALL. HOW HUMILIATING!
...

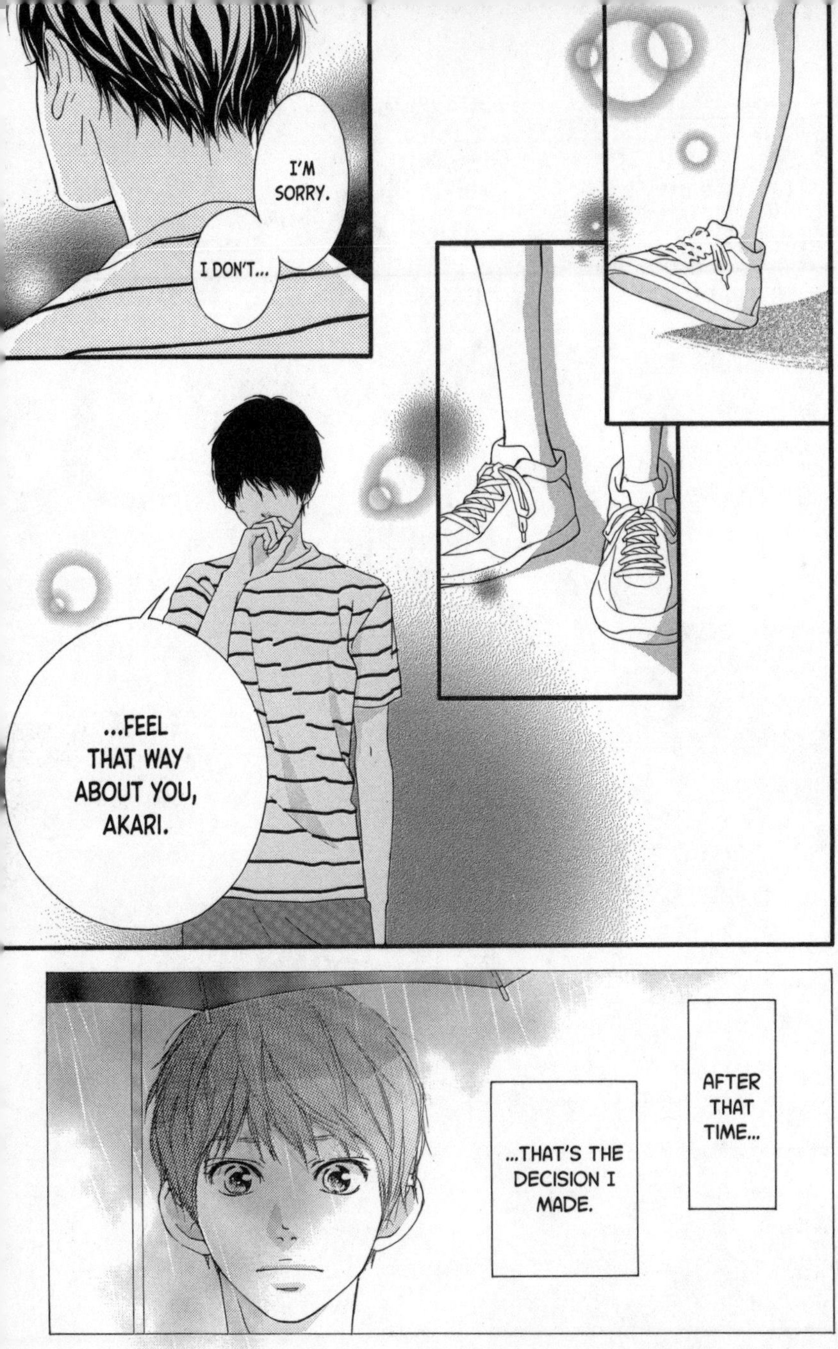
I'M SORRY.
I DON'T...
...FEEL THAT WAY ABOUT YOU, AKARI.
AFTER THAT TIME...
...THAT'S THE DECISION I MADE.

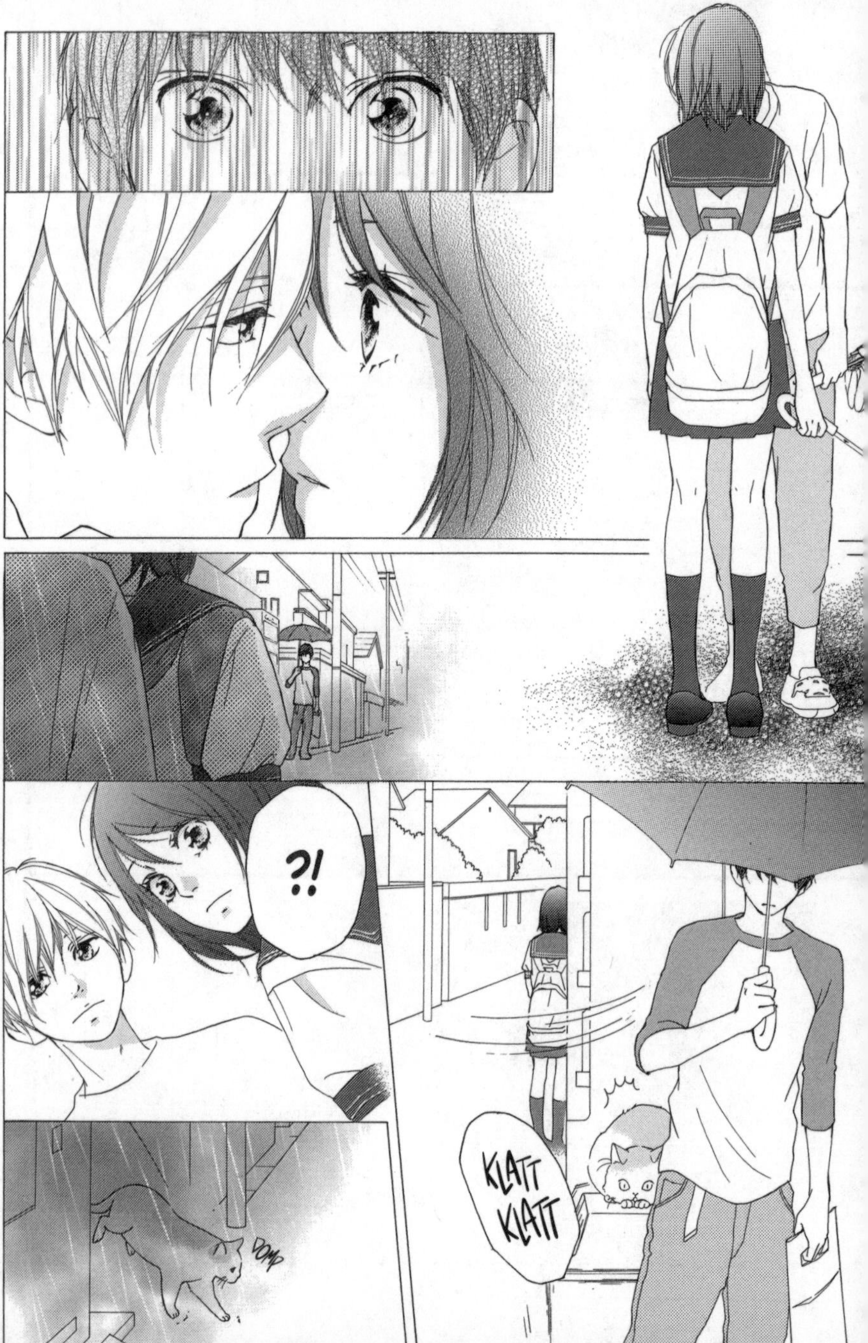
?!
KLATT KLATT
DOMP

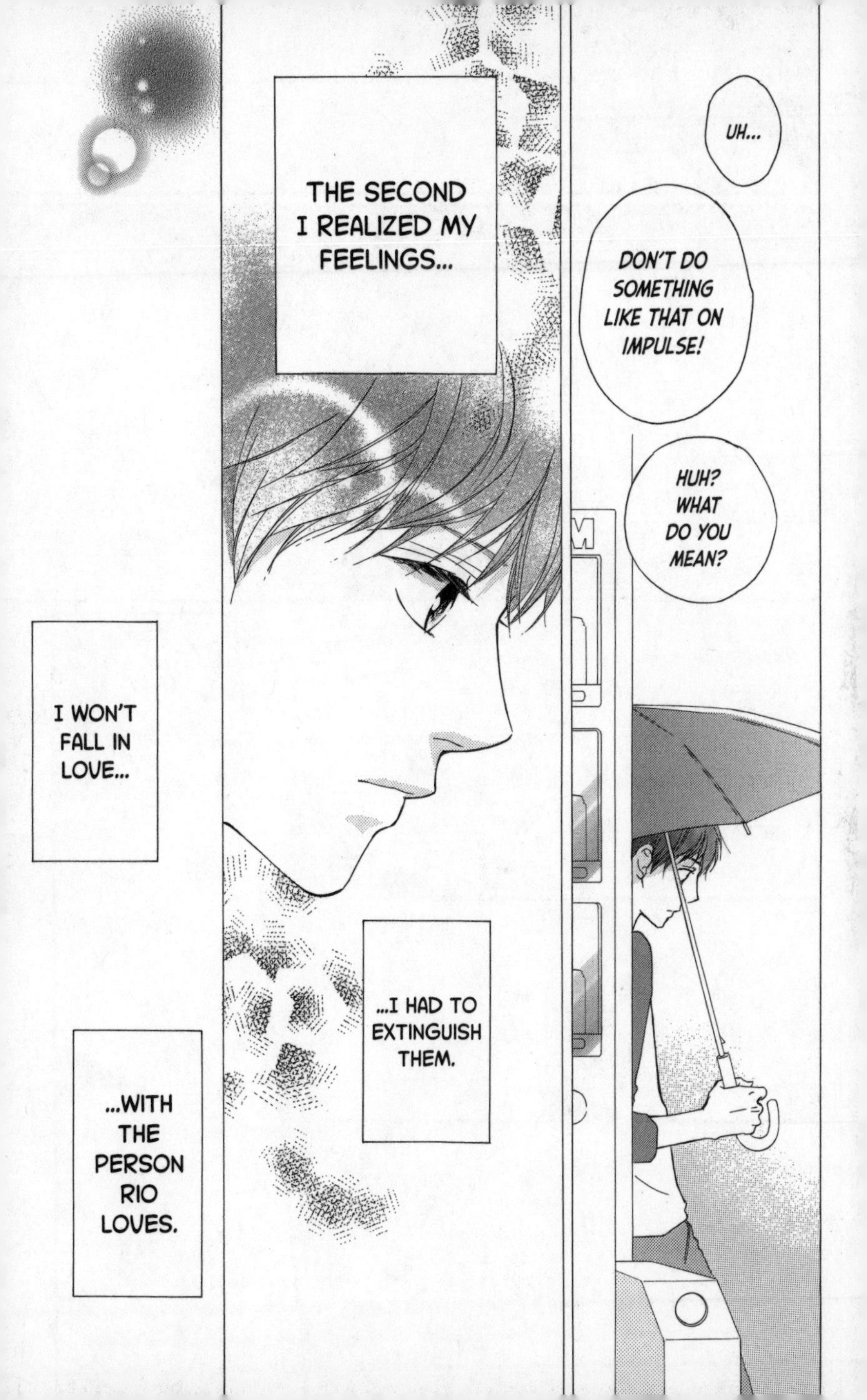
UH...
DON'T DO SOMETHING LIKE THAT ON IMPULSE!
HUH? WHAT DO YOU MEAN?
THE SECOND I REALIZED MY FEELINGS...
...I HAD TO EXTINGUISH THEM.
I WON'T FALL IN LOVE...
...WITH THE PERSON RIO LOVES.

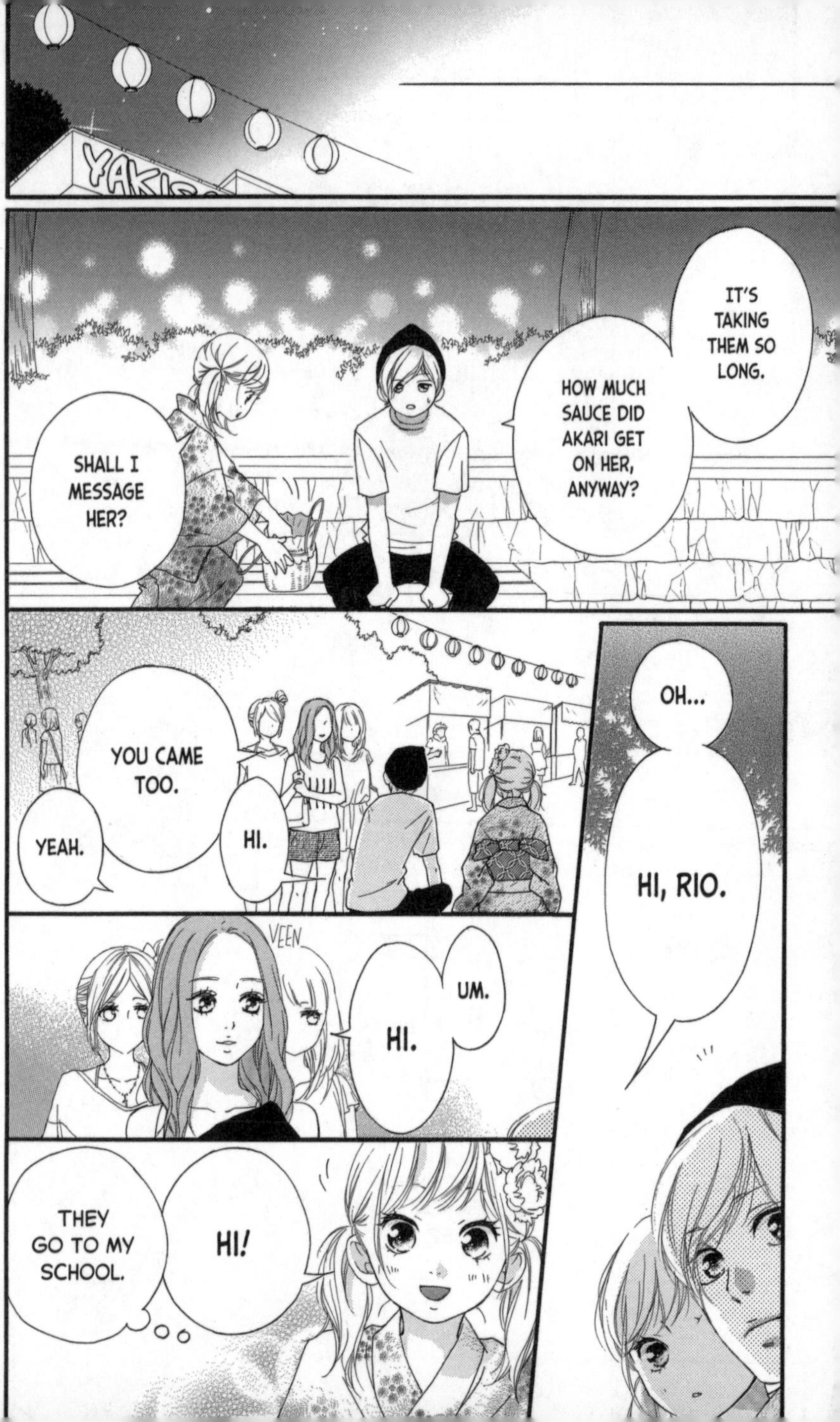
IT'S TAKING THEM SO LONG.
HOW MUCH SAUCE DID AKARI GET ON HER, ANYWAY?
SHALL I MESSAGE HER?
OH...
HI, RIO.
YOU CAME TOO.
HI.
YEAH.
VEEN
UM.
HI.
HI!
THEY GO TO MY SCHOOL.

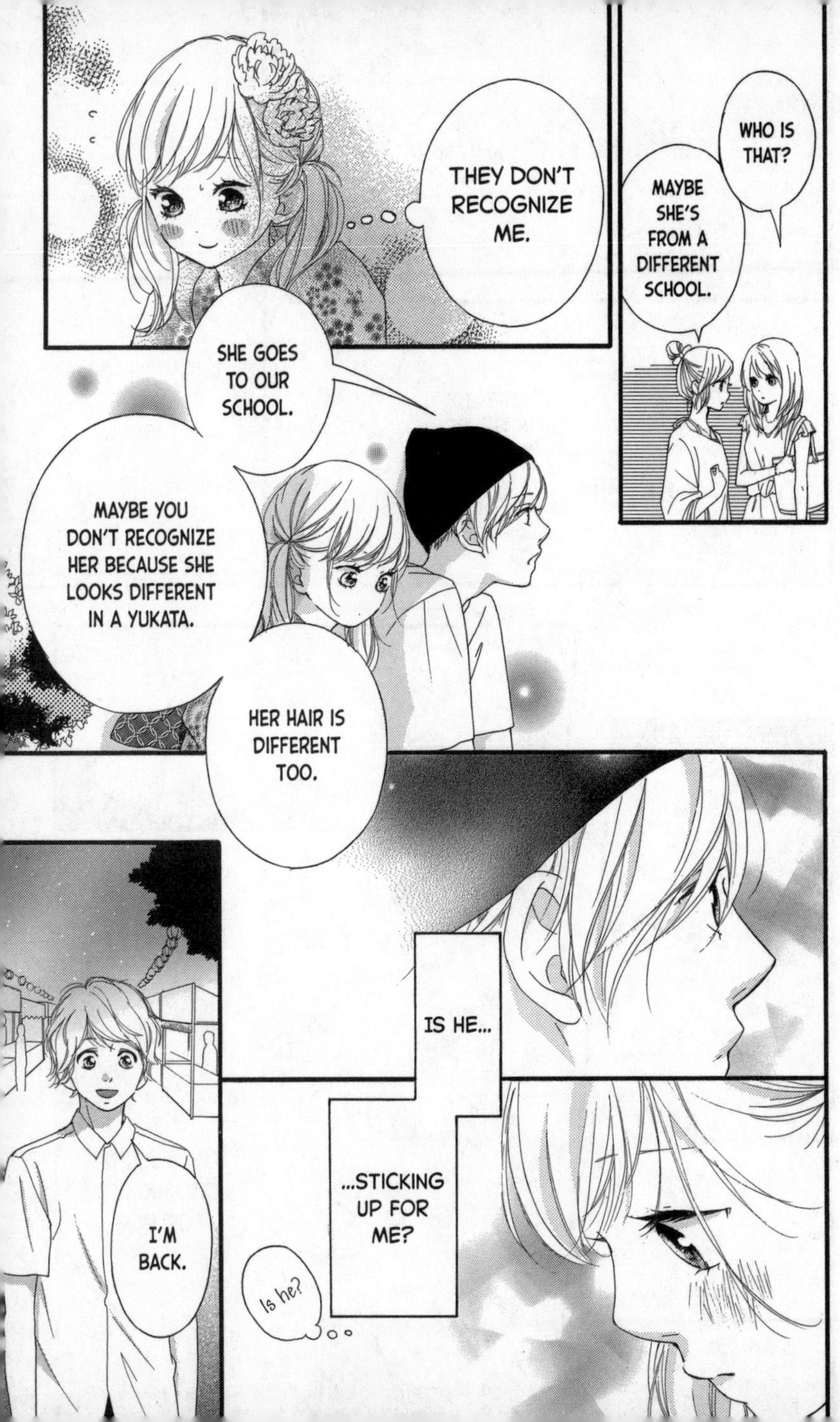
WHO IS THAT?
MAYBE SHE'S FROM A DIFFERENT SCHOOL.
THEY DON'T RECOGNIZE ME.
SHE GOES TO OUR SCHOOL.
MAYBE YOU DON'T RECOGNIZE HER BECAUSE SHE LOOKS DIFFERENT IN A YUKATA.
HER HAIR IS DIFFERENT TOO.
IS HE...
...STICKING UP FOR ME?
Is he?
I'M BACK.

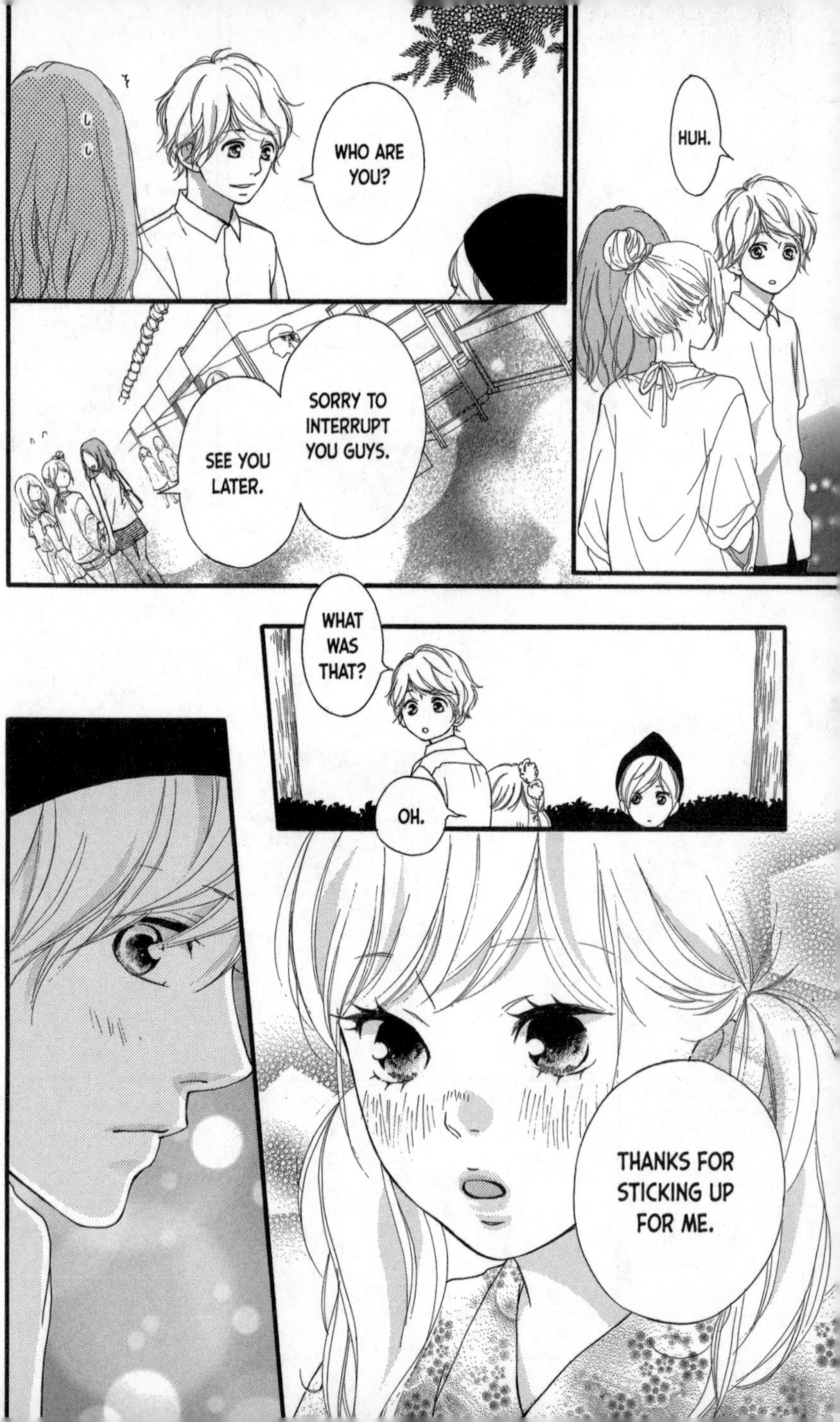
HUH.
WHO ARE YOU?
SORRY TO INTERRUPT YOU GUYS.
SEE YOU LATER.
WHAT WAS THAT?
OH.
THANKS FOR STICKING UP FOR ME.

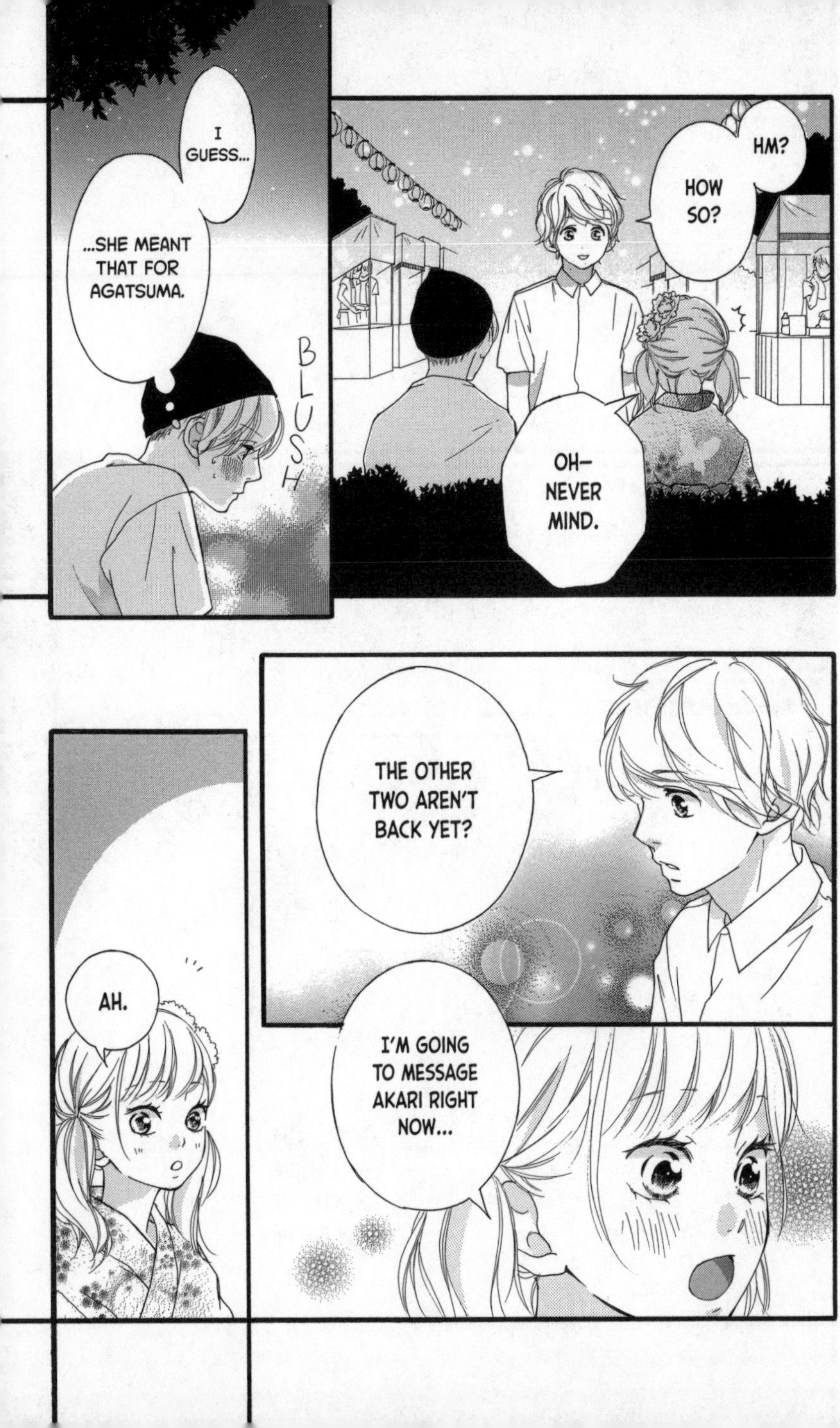
HM?
HOW SO?
OH— NEVER MIND.
I GUESS...
...SHE MEANT THAT FOR AGATSUMA.
BLUSH
THE OTHER TWO AREN'T BACK YET?
I'M GOING TO MESSAGE AKARI RIGHT NOW...
AH.

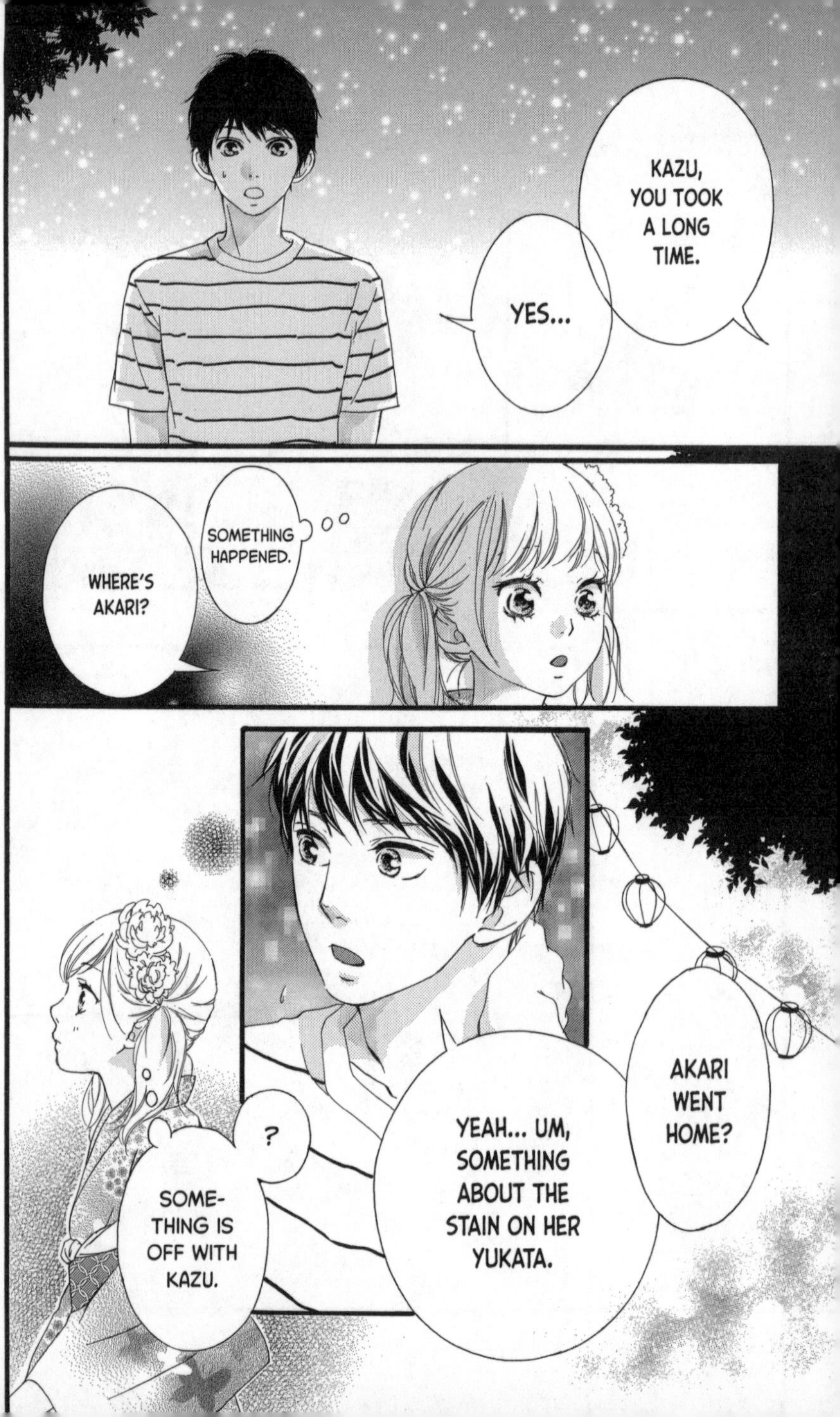
KAZU, YOU TOOK A LONG TIME.
YES...
SOMETHING HAPPENED.
WHERE'S AKARI?
AKARI WENT HOME?
YEAH... UM, SOMETHING ABOUT THE STAIN ON HER YUKATA.
?
SOME-THING IS OFF WITH KAZU.

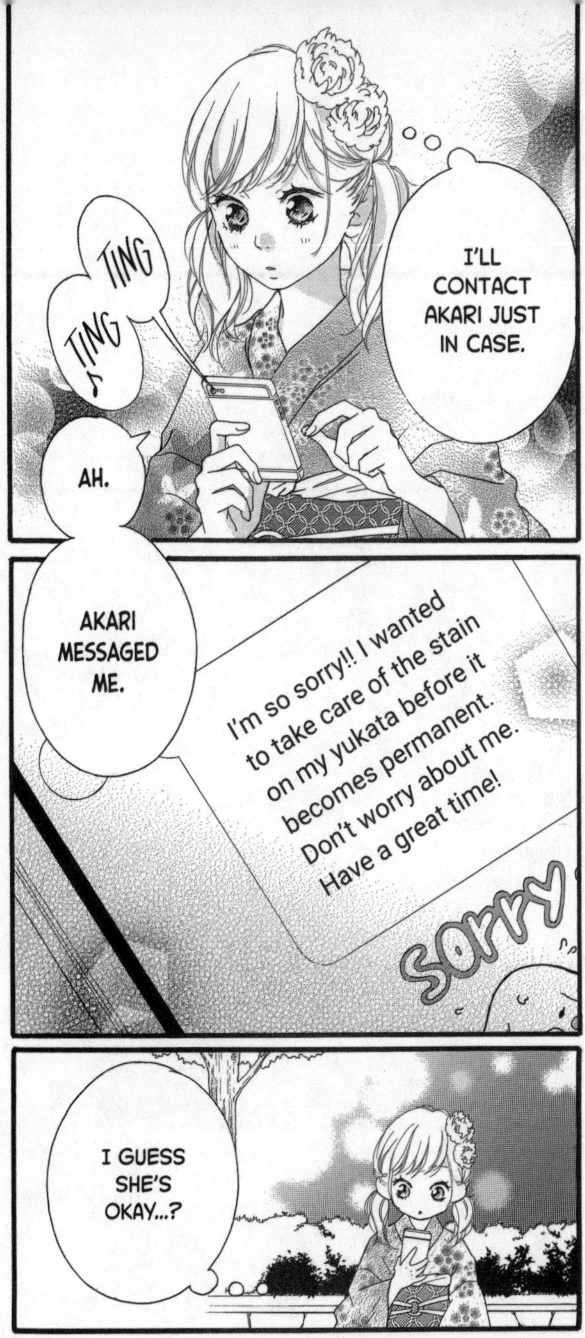
I'LL CONTACT AKARI JUST IN CASE.
TING TING ♪
AH.
AKARI MESSAGED ME.
I'm so sorry!! I wanted to take care of the stain on my yukata before it becomes permanent. Don't worry about me. Have a great time!
sorry
I GUESS SHE'S OKAY...?

Kazuomi Inui ☆ Profile

Birthday: October 6
Sign: Libra
Blood type: B
Height: 5' 8" still growing (definite)
Weight: 134 lbs

Favorite colors:
Blue, khaki

Favorite subject:
Japanese

Least favorite subject:
English

Favorite food:
Curry

Least favorite food:
Nothing in particular

Hobby:
Watching movies

Favorite thing about himself:
Even teeth

Favorite movie:
Enter the Dragon

Favorite magazine:
Eiga Hiho

Favorite band:
Takashi Fujii

Favorite celebrity:
Matsuko Deluxe

Place he wants to visit:
Nowhere in particular

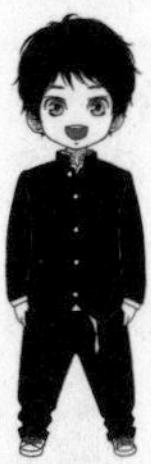

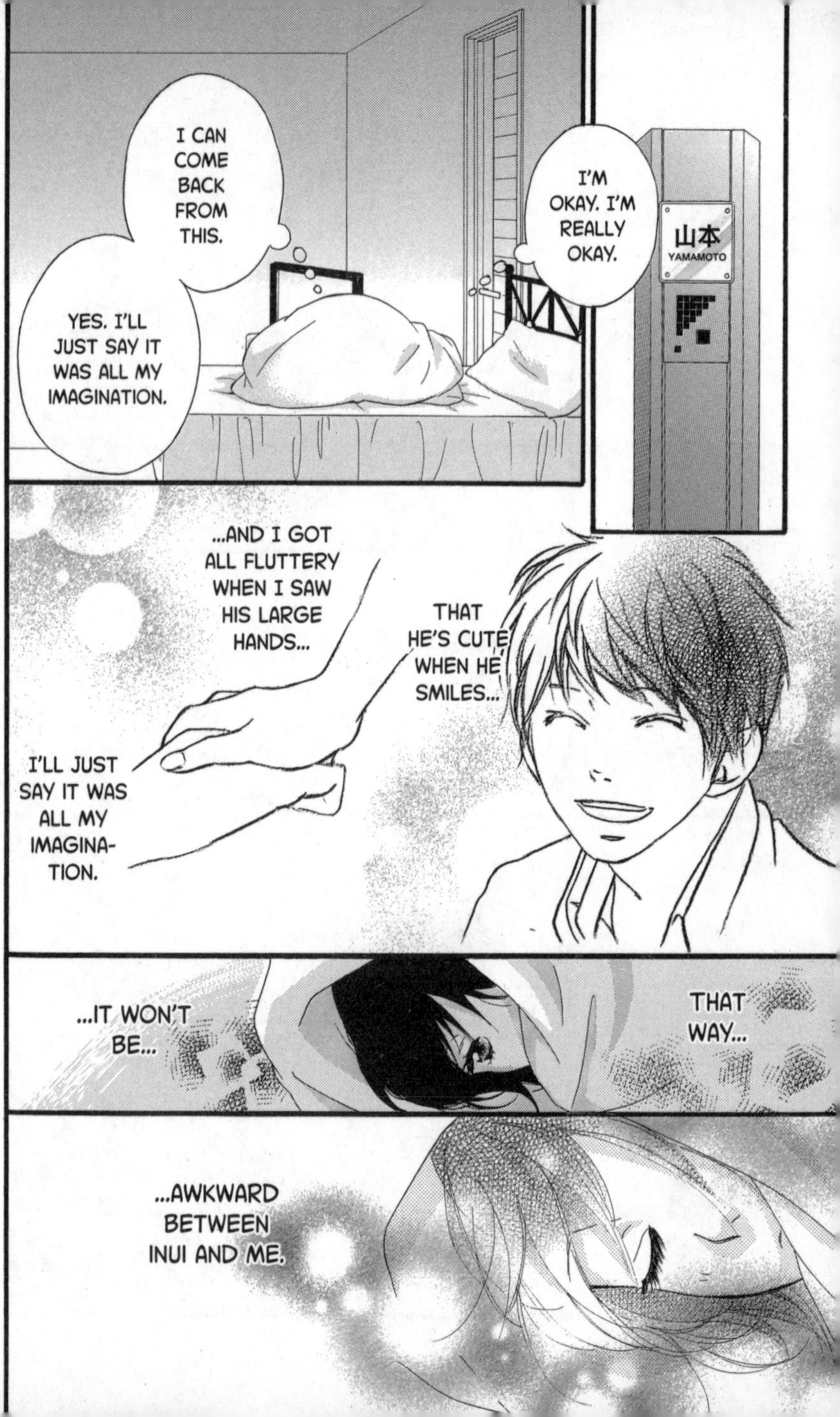
山本
YAMAMOTO
I'M OKAY. I'M REALLY OKAY.
I CAN COME BACK FROM THIS.
YES. I'LL JUST SAY IT WAS ALL MY IMAGINATION.
THAT HE'S CUTE WHEN HE SMILES...
...AND I GOT ALL FLUTTERY WHEN I SAW HIS LARGE HANDS...
I'LL JUST SAY IT WAS ALL MY IMAGINA-TION.
THAT WAY...
...IT WON'T BE...
...AWKWARD BETWEEN INUI AND ME.

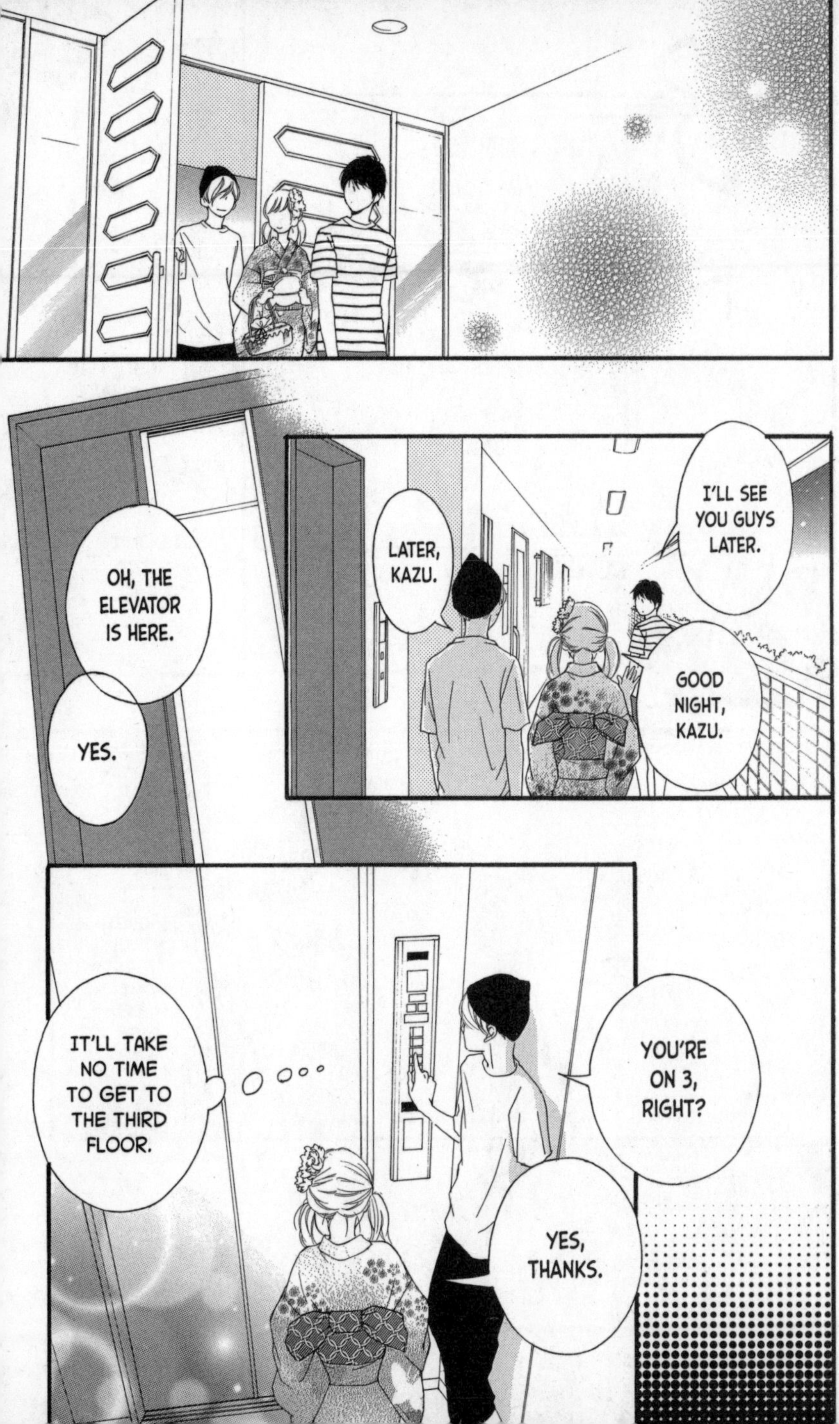
I'LL SEE YOU GUYS LATER.
LATER, KAZU.
GOOD NIGHT, KAZU.
OH, THE ELEVATOR IS HERE.
YES.
YOU'RE ON 3, RIGHT?
YES, THANKS.
IT'LL TAKE NO TIME TO GET TO THE THIRD FLOOR.

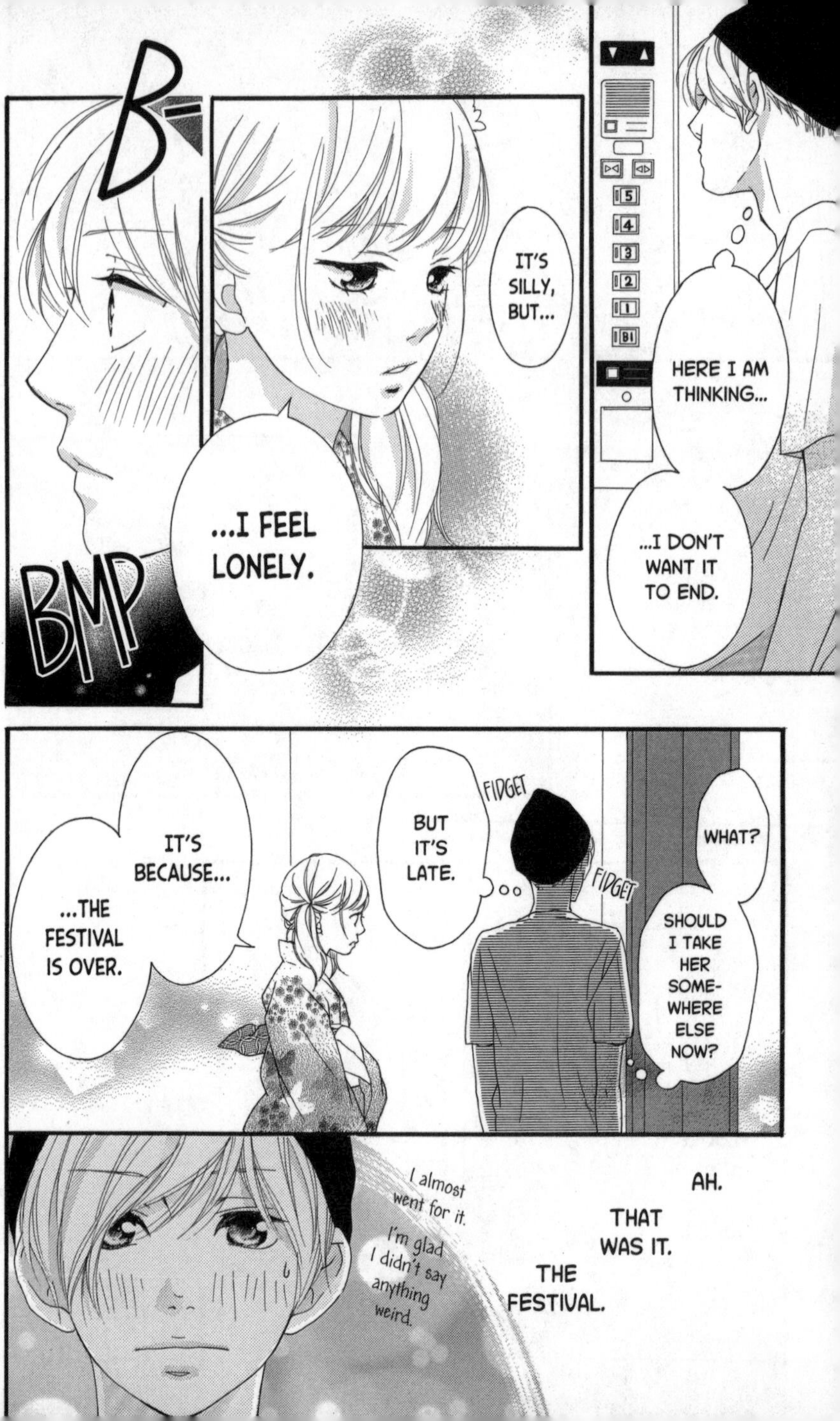
HERE I AM THINKING...
...I DON'T WANT IT TO END.
IT'S SILLY, BUT...
B-
BMP
...I FEEL LONELY.
WHAT?
SHOULD I TAKE HER SOME-WHERE ELSE NOW?
FIDGET
FIDGET
BUT IT'S LATE.
IT'S BECAUSE...
...THE FESTIVAL IS OVER.
AH.
THAT WAS IT.
THE FESTIVAL.
I almost went for it.
I'm glad I didn't say anything weird.

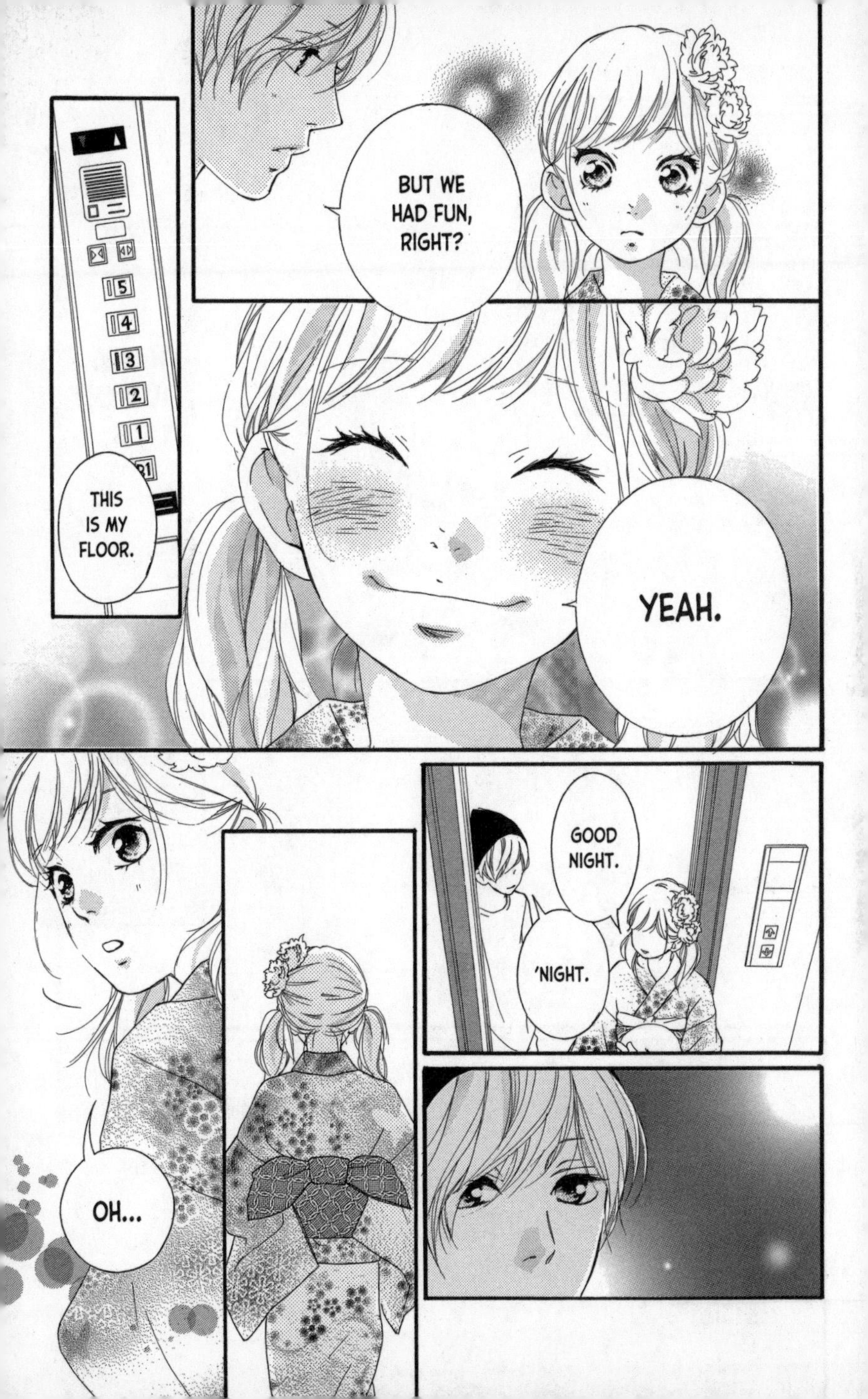
BUT WE HAD FUN, RIGHT?
YEAH.
THIS IS MY FLOOR.
GOOD NIGHT.
'NIGHT.
OH...

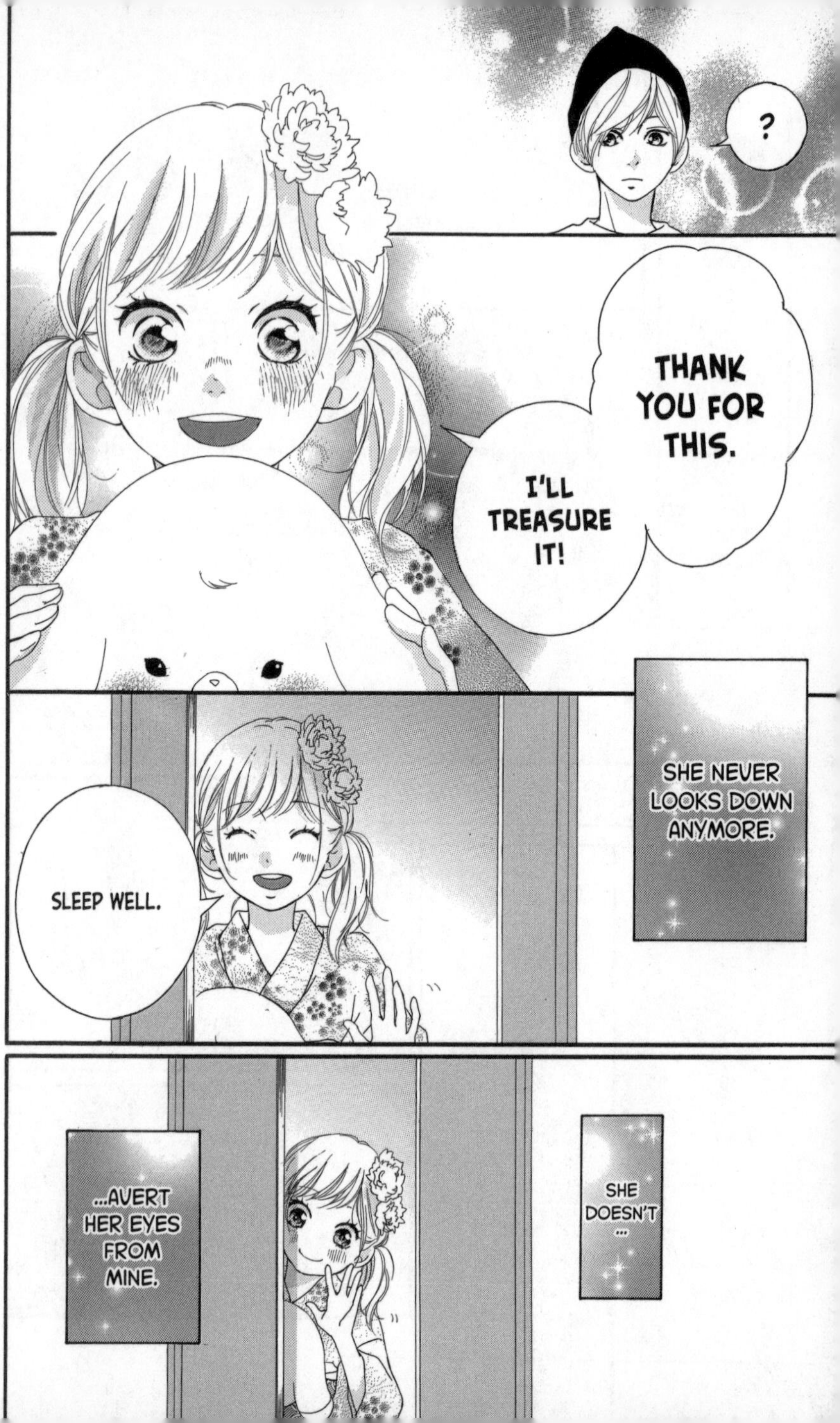
?
THANK YOU FOR THIS.
I'LL TREASURE IT!
SHE NEVER LOOKS DOWN ANYMORE.
SLEEP WELL.
SHE DOESN'T...
...AVERT HER EYES FROM MINE.

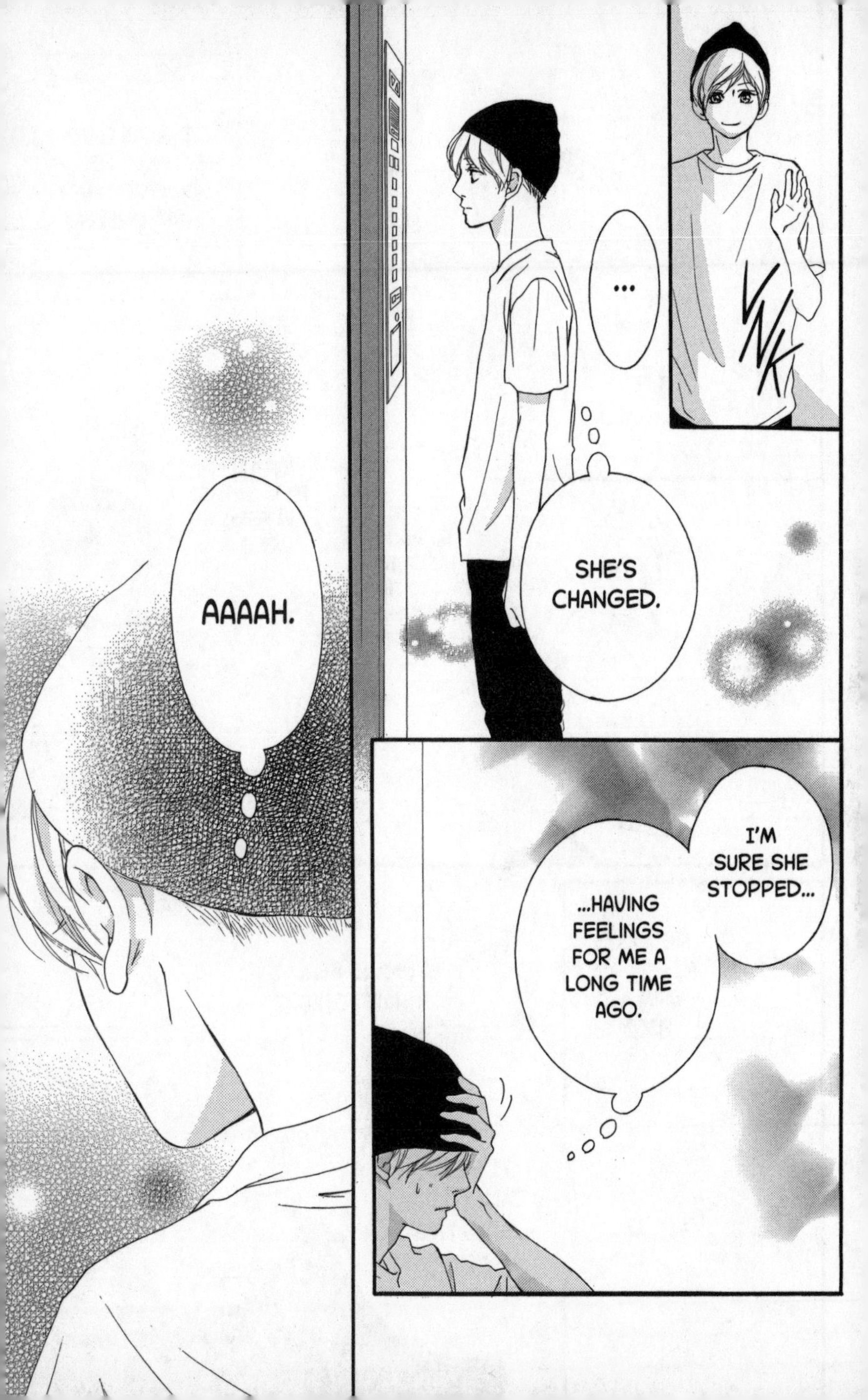
VNK
...
SHE'S CHANGED.
I'M SURE SHE STOPPED...
...HAVING FEELINGS FOR ME A LONG TIME AGO.
AAAAH.

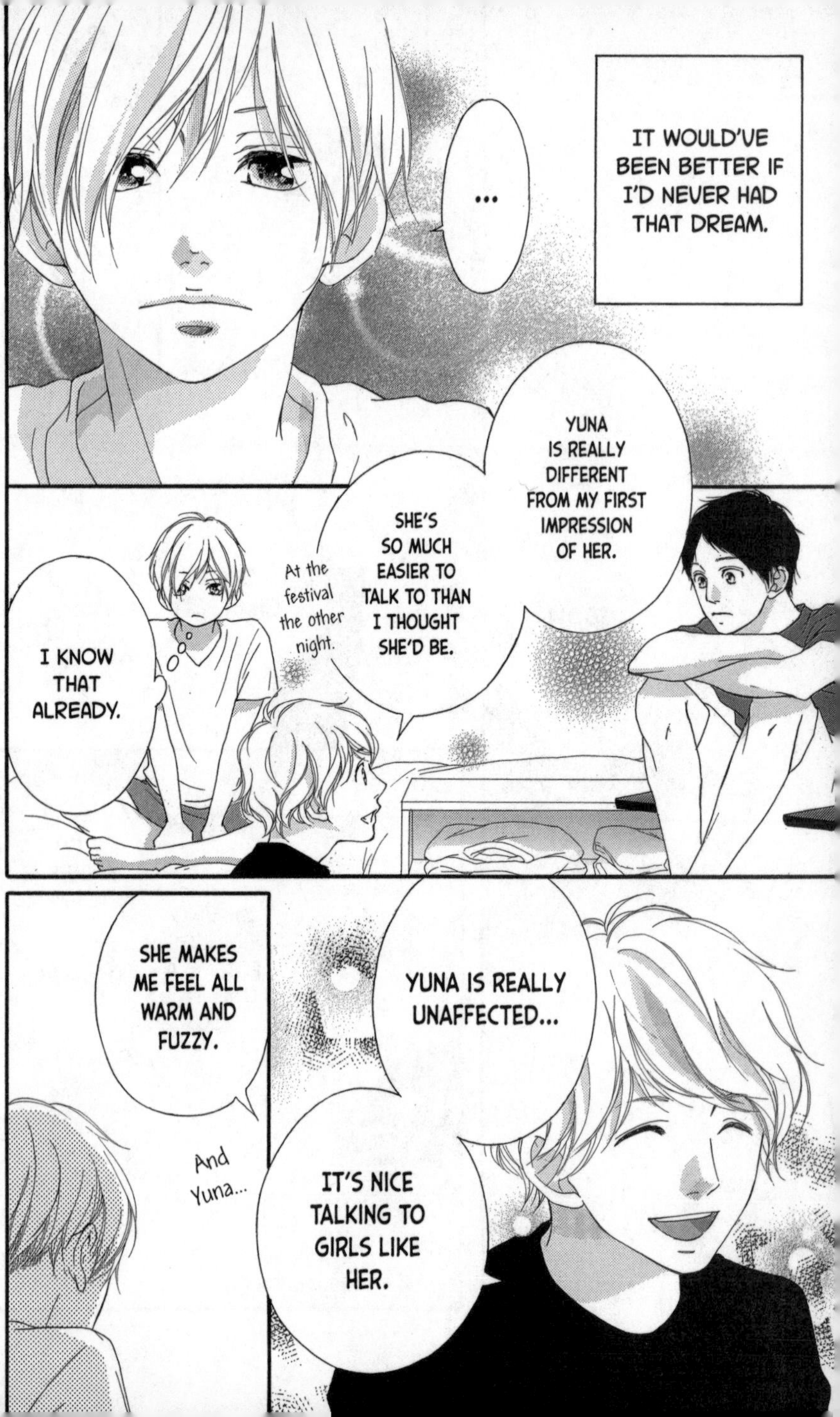
IT WOULD'VE BEEN BETTER IF I'D NEVER HAD THAT DREAM.
...
YUNA IS REALLY DIFFERENT FROM MY FIRST IMPRESSION OF HER.
SHE'S SO MUCH EASIER TO TALK TO THAN I THOUGHT SHE'D BE.
At the festival the other night.
I KNOW THAT ALREADY.
YUNA IS REALLY UNAFFECTED...
IT'S NICE TALKING TO GIRLS LIKE HER.
SHE MAKES ME FEEL ALL WARM AND FUZZY.
And Yuna...

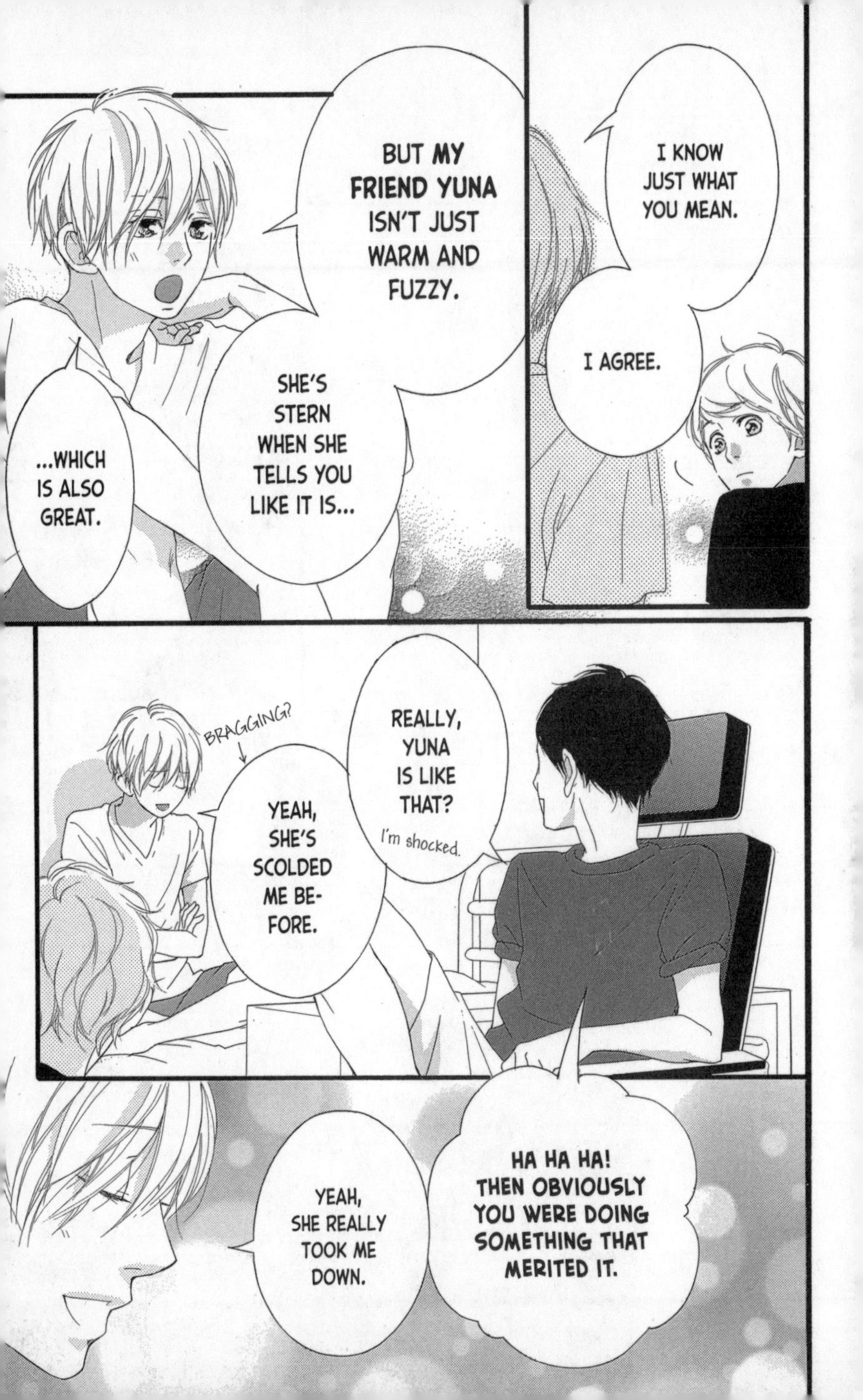
I KNOW JUST WHAT YOU MEAN.
I AGREE.
BUT MY FRIEND YUNA ISN'T JUST WARM AND FUZZY.
SHE'S STERN WHEN SHE TELLS YOU LIKE IT IS...
...WHICH IS ALSO GREAT.
REALLY, YUNA IS LIKE THAT?
I'm shocked.
BRAGGING?
YEAH, SHE'S SCOLDED ME BE-FORE.
HA HA HA! THEN OBVIOUSLY YOU WERE DOING SOMETHING THAT MERITED IT.
YEAH, SHE REALLY TOOK ME DOWN.

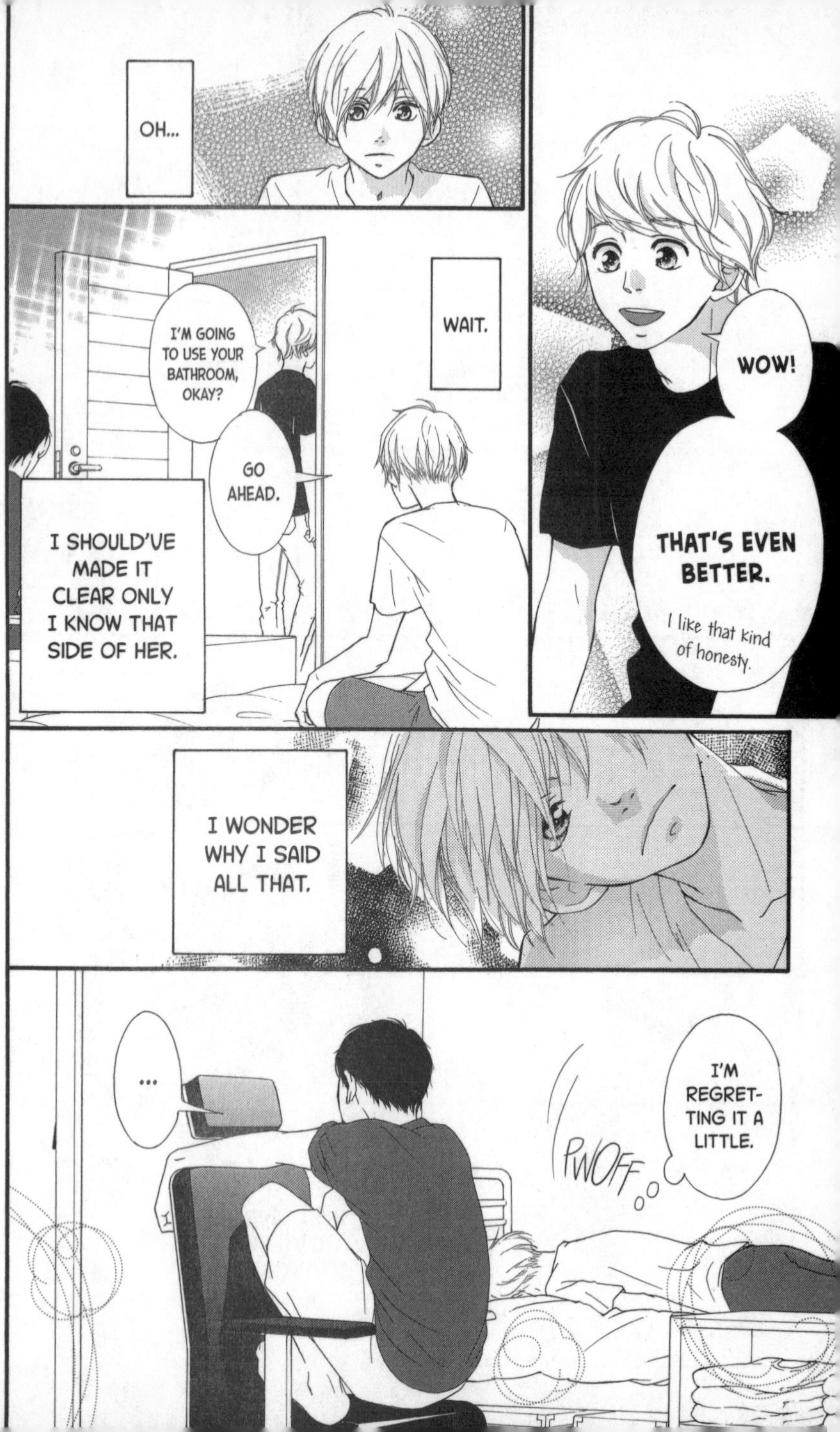
WOW!
THAT'S EVEN BETTER.
I like that kind of honesty.
OH...
WAIT.
I'M GOING TO USE YOUR BATHROOM, OKAY?
GO AHEAD.
I SHOULD'VE MADE IT CLEAR ONLY I KNOW THAT SIDE OF HER.
I WONDER WHY I SAID ALL THAT.
I'M REGRET-TING IT A LITTLE.
PWOFF
...

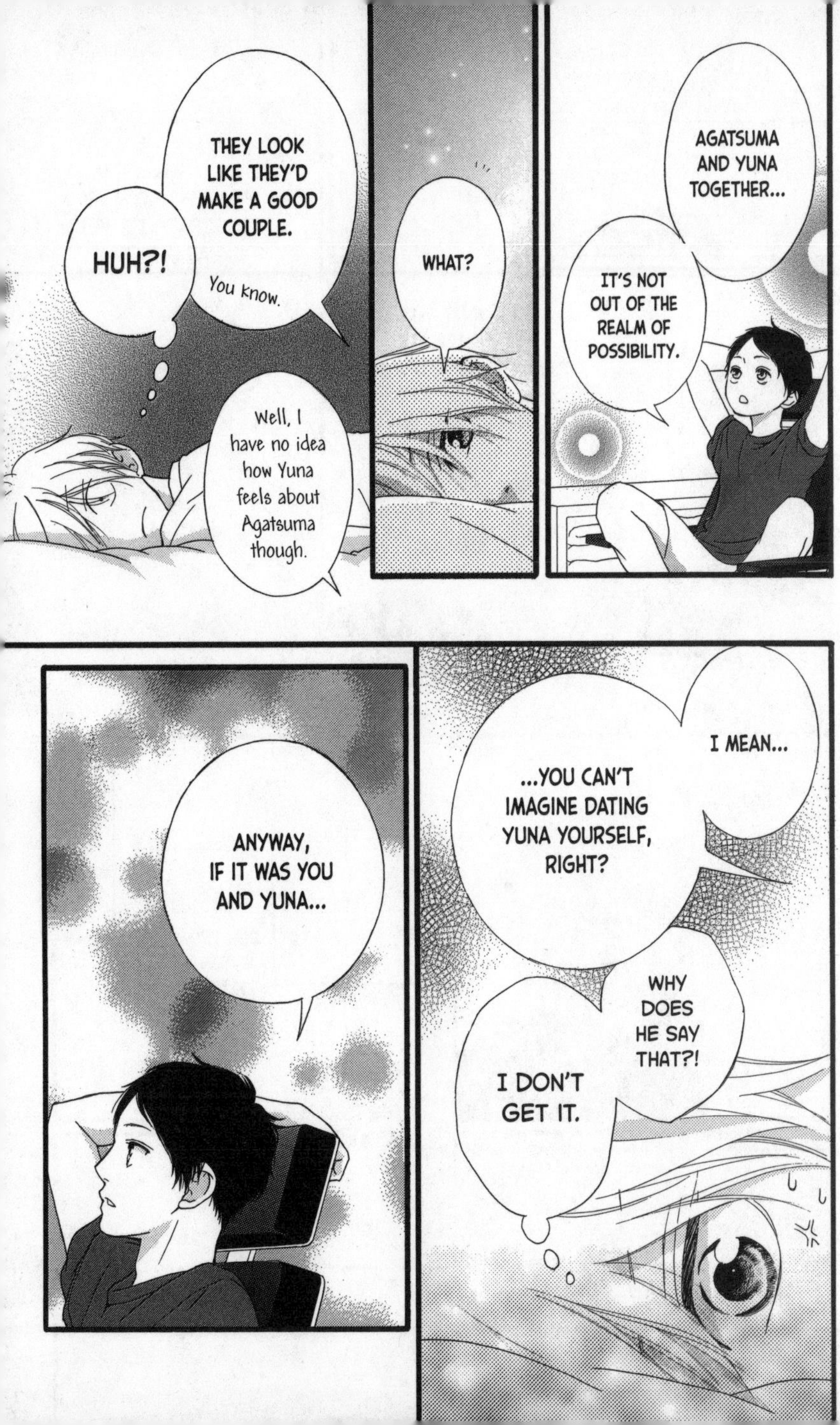
AGATSUMA AND YUNA TOGETHER...
IT'S NOT OUT OF THE REALM OF POSSIBILITY.
WHAT?
THEY LOOK LIKE THEY'D MAKE A GOOD COUPLE.
You know.
HUH?!
Well, I have no idea how Yuna feels about Agatsuma though.
I MEAN...
...YOU CAN'T IMAGINE DATING YUNA YOURSELF, RIGHT?
WHY DOES HE SAY THAT?!
I DON'T GET IT.
ANYWAY, IF IT WAS YOU AND YUNA...

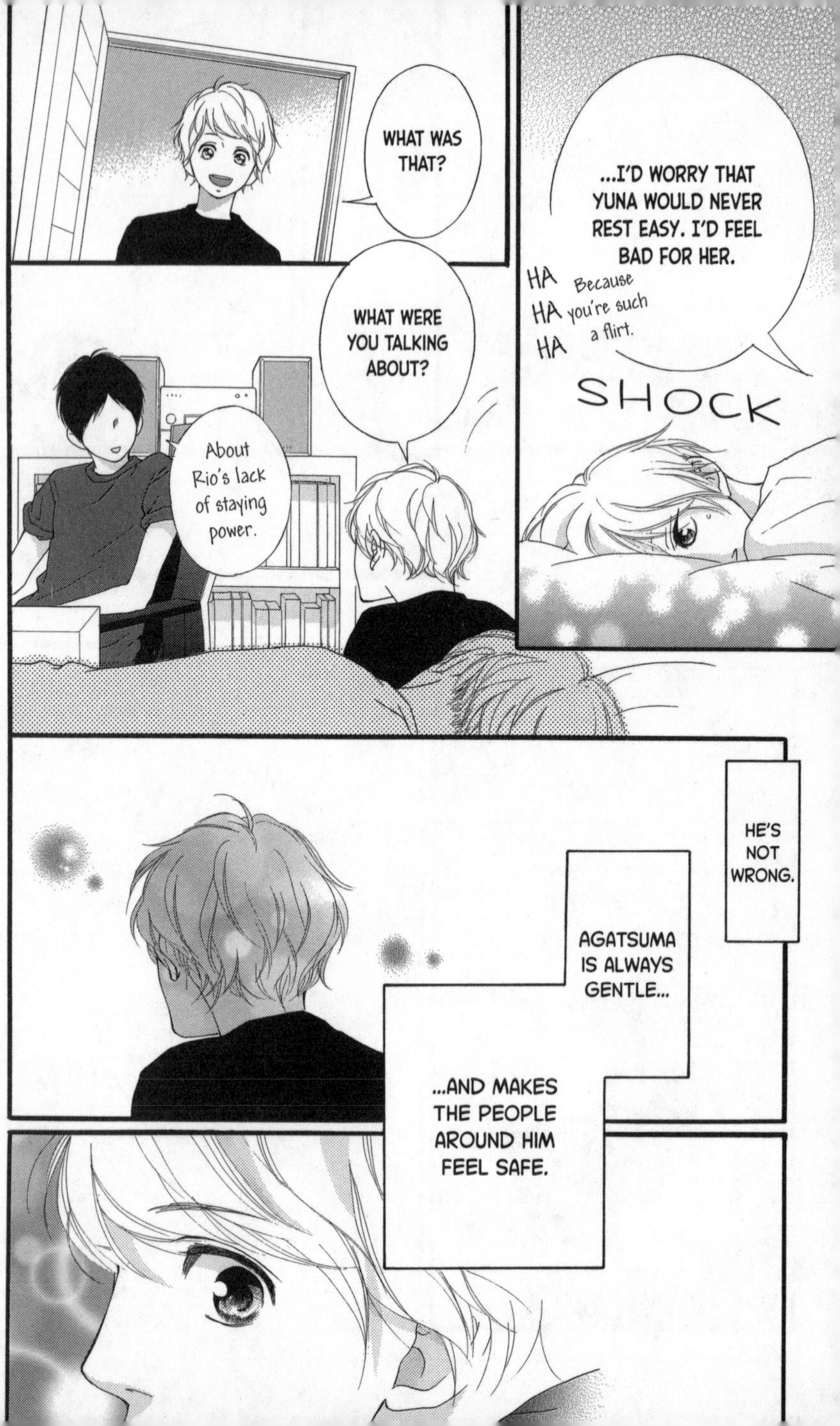
...I'D WORRY THAT YUNA WOULD NEVER REST EASY. I'D FEEL BAD FOR HER.
HA HA HA
Because you're such a flirt.
SHOCK
WHAT WAS THAT?
WHAT WERE YOU TALKING ABOUT?
About Rio's lack of staying power.
HE'S NOT WRONG.
AGATSUMA IS ALWAYS GENTLE...
...AND MAKES THE PEOPLE AROUND HIM FEEL SAFE.

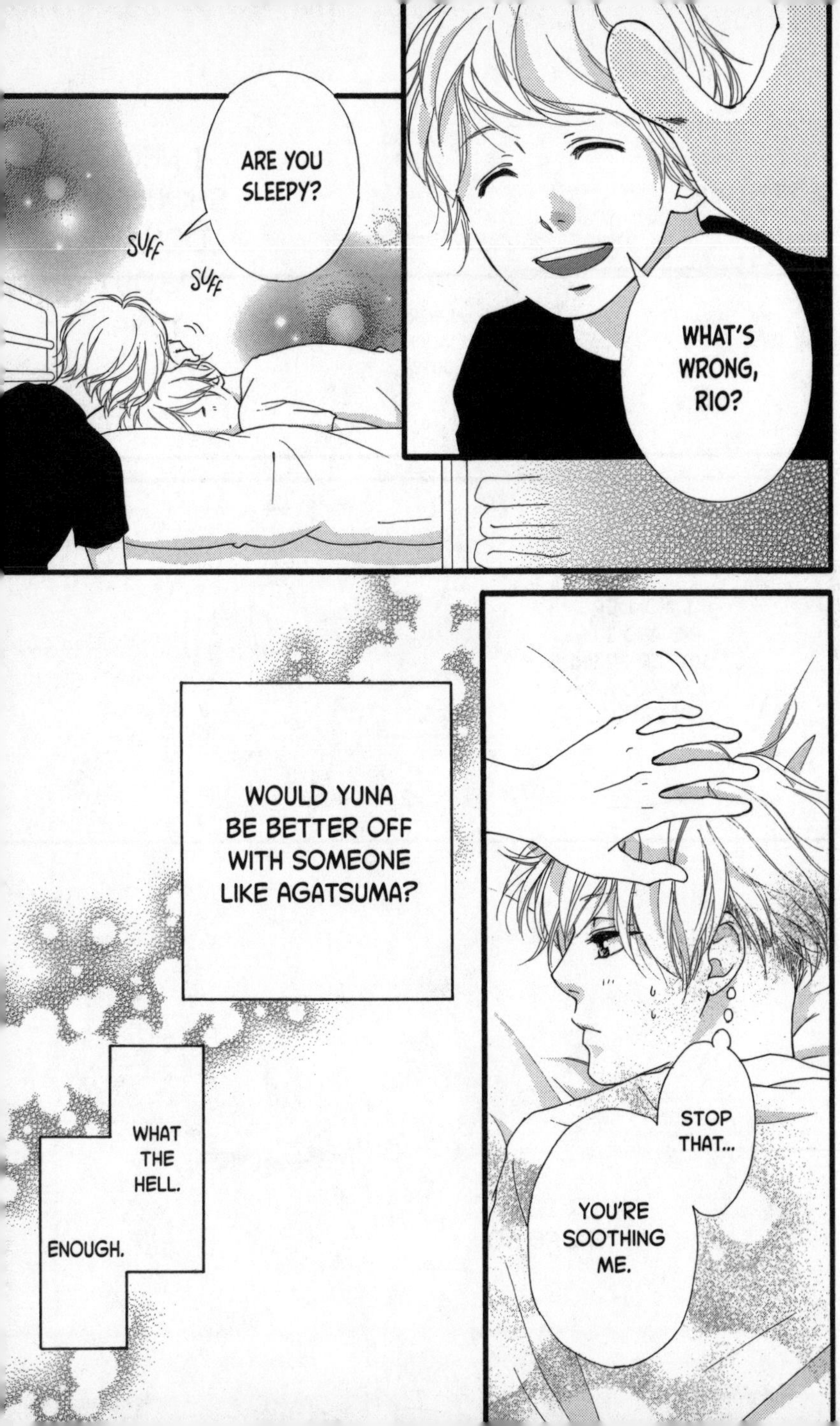
WHAT'S WRONG, RIO?
ARE YOU SLEEPY?
SUFF
SUFF
STOP THAT...
YOU'RE SOOTHING ME.
WOULD YUNA BE BETTER OFF WITH SOMEONE LIKE AGATSUMA?
WHAT THE HELL.
ENOUGH.

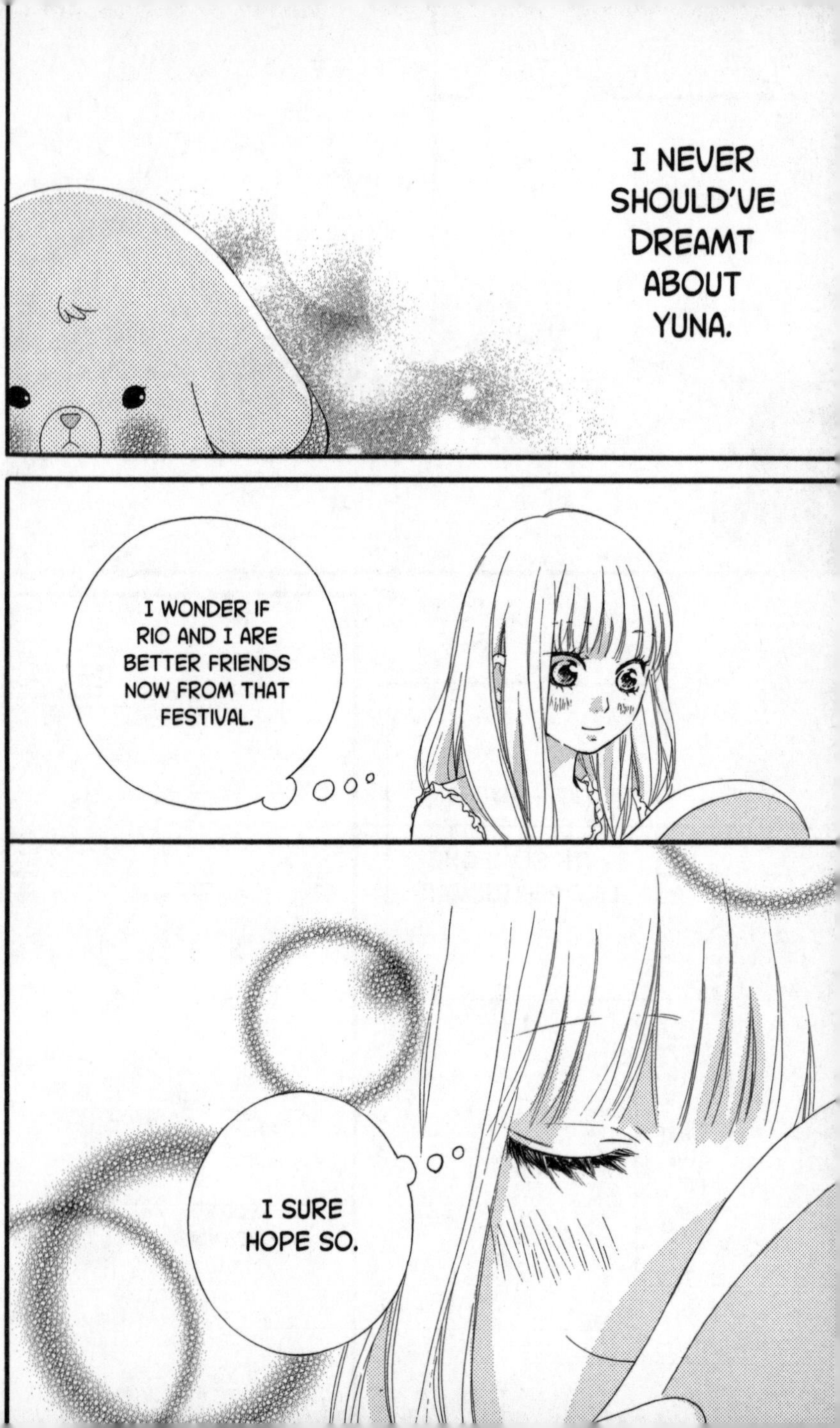
I NEVER SHOULD'VE DREAMT ABOUT YUNA.
I WONDER IF RIO AND I ARE BETTER FRIENDS NOW FROM THAT FESTIVAL.
I SURE HOPE SO.

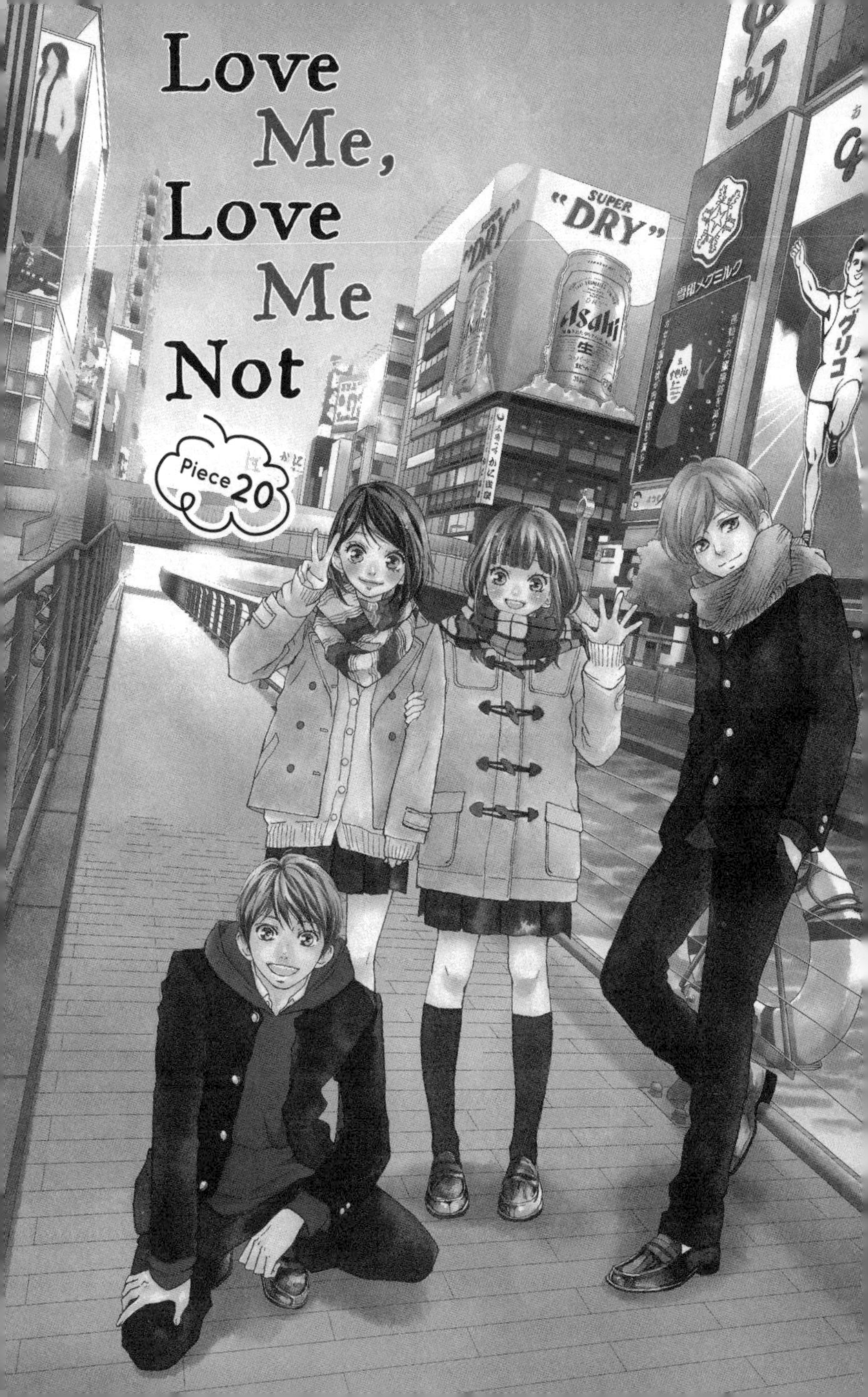
Love Me, Love Me Not
Piece 20
"SUPER DRY"
Asahi

A Thrilling ♡ Kobe Diary

I went to Kobe for a gig. (With F.) As it was my first time travelling for a gig, we decided to go up the day before just in case anything should go wrong. I got train tickets and booked the hotel early. We were all set. It was supposed to be a calm stay in Kobe, but... I lost my cell phone on the first day. I realized right after we got back to the hotel from dinner. My mind went blank! Oh nooo! The e-tickets for the gig were on my phone. We couldn't get in without it! I emptied my bag and looked in every pocket, but it wasn't there. I'd never lost my phone before. Why did this have to be the first? I was in such a panic, I couldn't remember when I had it last, but F. reminded me, "You were on it in the taxi." I calmed down a little and thought, "Maybe it's in that taxi." F. called the taxi company, and they said they'd check and get back to her. She hung up, and we waited. If it wasn't there, then we'd have come all the way to Kobe and back without seeing the gig. Thoughts like that made me panic so much that I ended up grinning instead—a self-defense mechanism to calm myself. Very quickly, we got a call back. So nerve-wracking! F. picked up the call, and I could hear only her voice and not the taxi company. So nerve-wracking! Depending on what F. told me next, I could be headed for hell. I was listening as if in prayer when I hear F. saying, "Oh really? Thank you so much." They had it! Thank you, God! I am so sorry to the driver for being a pain. The gig was great! I won't lose my phone again.

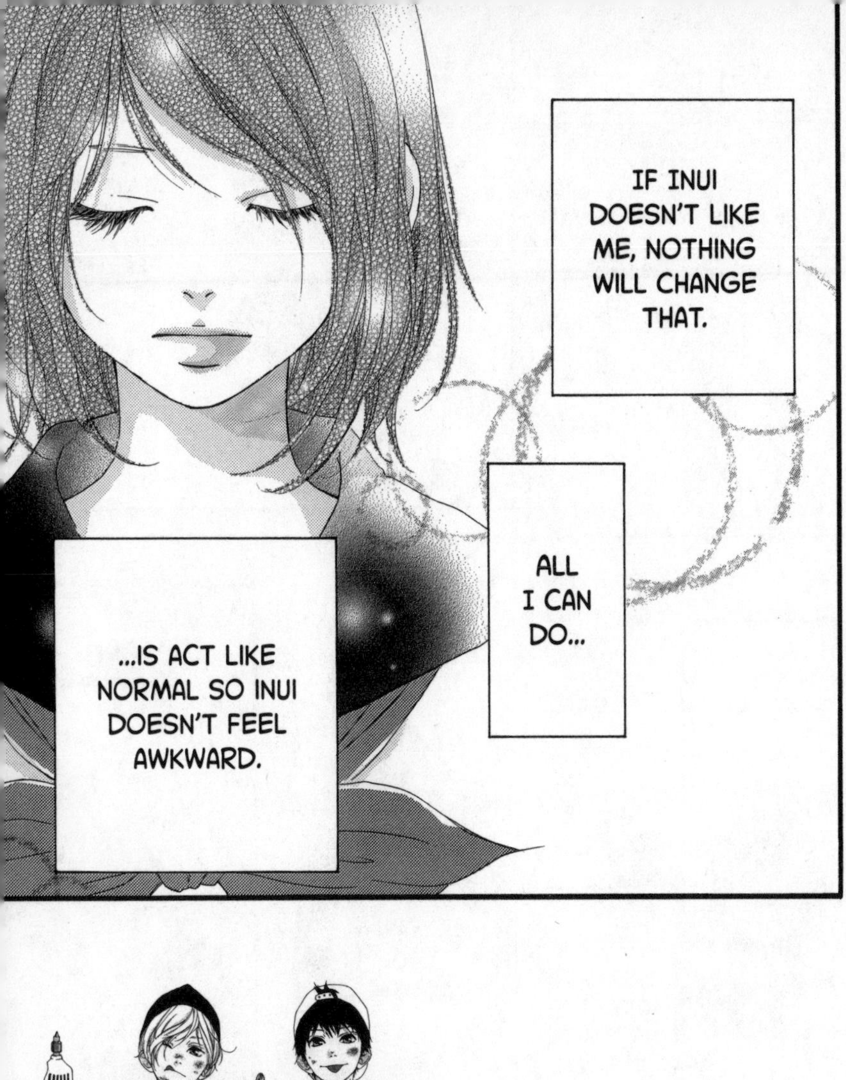
IF INUI DOESN'T LIKE ME, NOTHING WILL CHANGE THAT.
ALL I CAN DO...
...IS ACT LIKE NORMAL SO INUI DOESN'T FEEL AWKWARD.

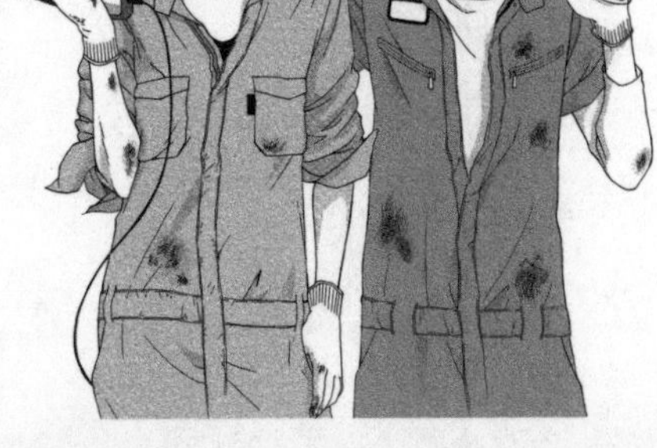

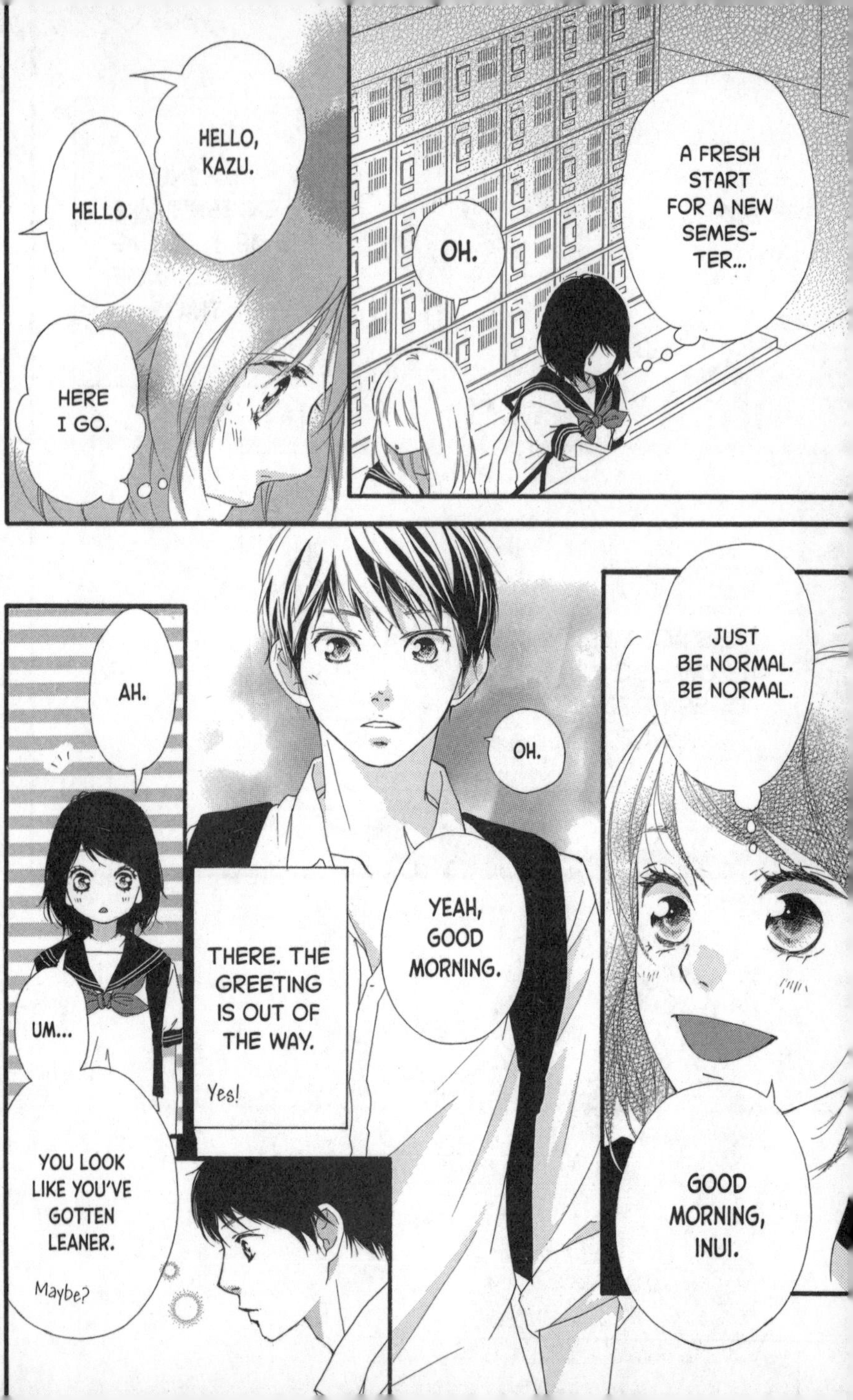
A FRESH START FOR A NEW SEMESTER...
OH.
HELLO, KAZU.
HELLO.
HERE I GO.
JUST BE NORMAL. BE NORMAL.
GOOD MORNING, INUI.
OH.
YEAH, GOOD MORNING.
THERE. THE GREETING IS OUT OF THE WAY.
Yes!
AH.
UM...
YOU LOOK LIKE YOU'VE GOTTEN LEANER.
Maybe?

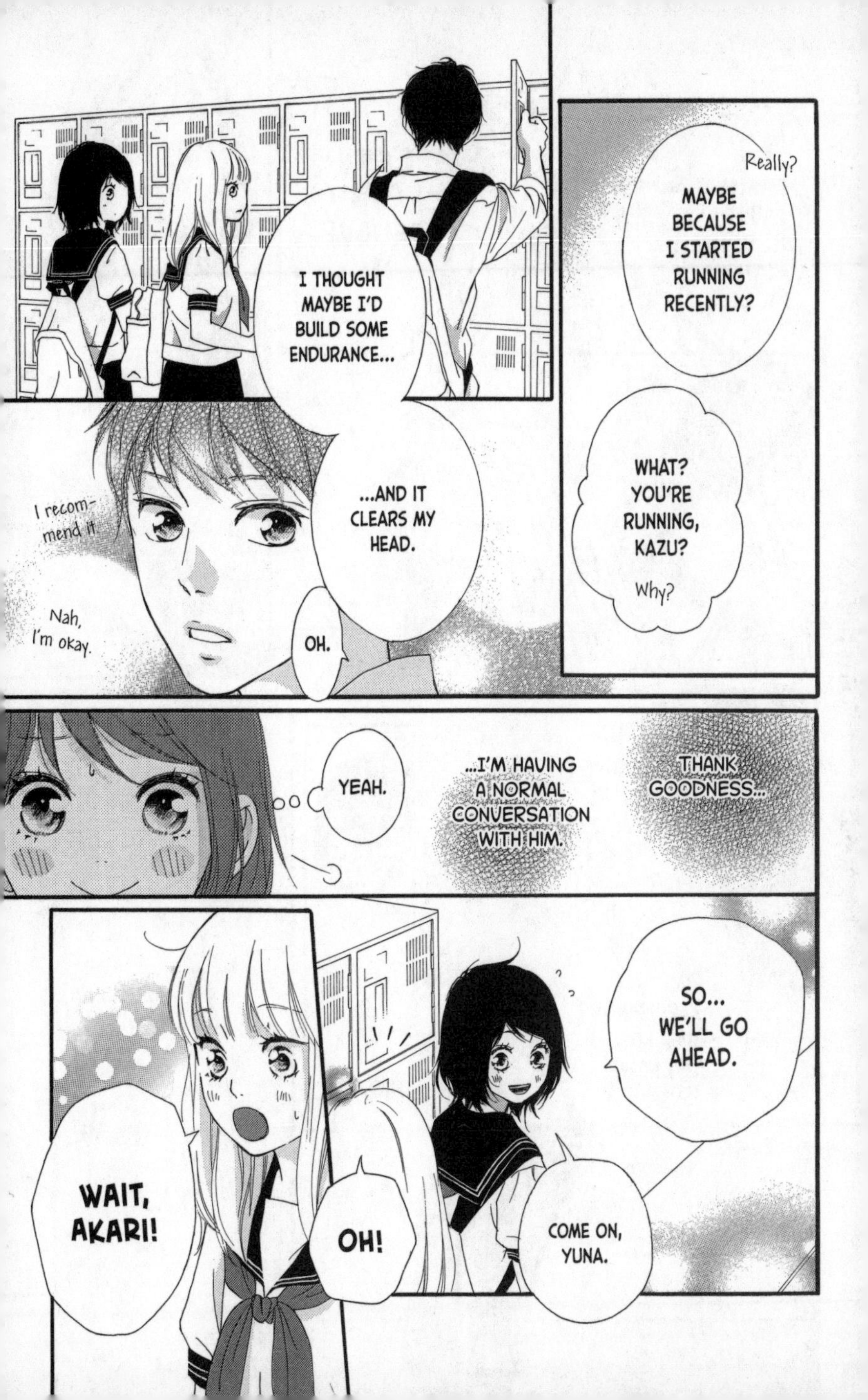
Really?
MAYBE BECAUSE I STARTED RUNNING RECENTLY?
WHAT? YOU'RE RUNNING, KAZU?
Why?
I THOUGHT MAYBE I'D BUILD SOME ENDURANCE...
...AND IT CLEARS MY HEAD.
I recom-mend it
OH.
Nah, I'm okay.
THANK GOODNESS...
...I'M HAVING A NORMAL CONVERSATION WITH HIM.
YEAH.
SO... WE'LL GO AHEAD.
COME ON, YUNA.
OH!
WAIT, AKARI!

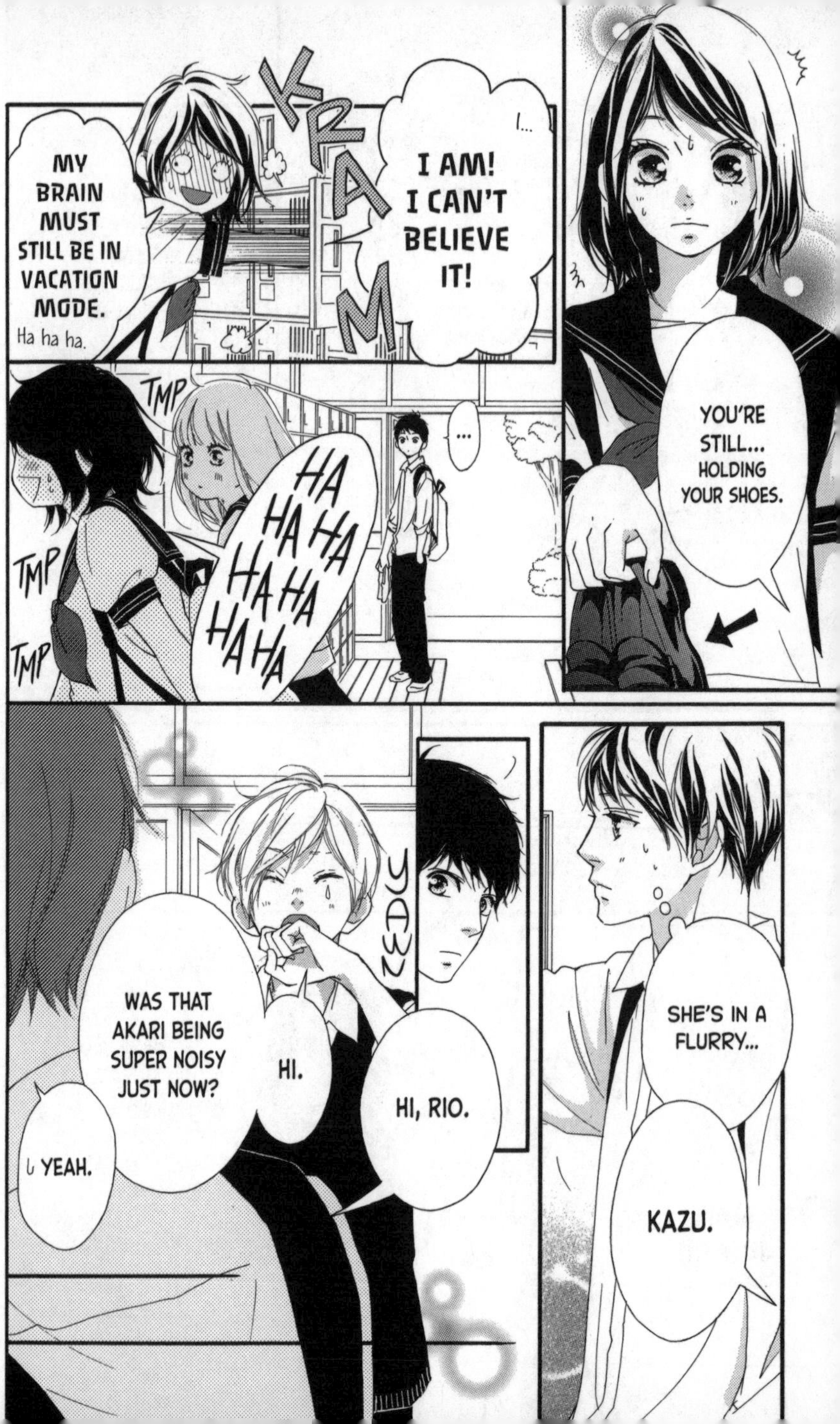
YOU'RE STILL... HOLDING YOUR SHOES.
I...
I AM! I CAN'T BELIEVE IT!
KRAM
MY BRAIN MUST STILL BE IN VACATION MODE.
Ha ha ha.
...
HA HA HA HA HA HA HA HA HA
TMP
TMP
TMP
SHE'S IN A FLURRY...
KAZU.
HI, RIO.
YAWN
HI.
WAS THAT AKARI BEING SUPER NOISY JUST NOW?
YEAH.

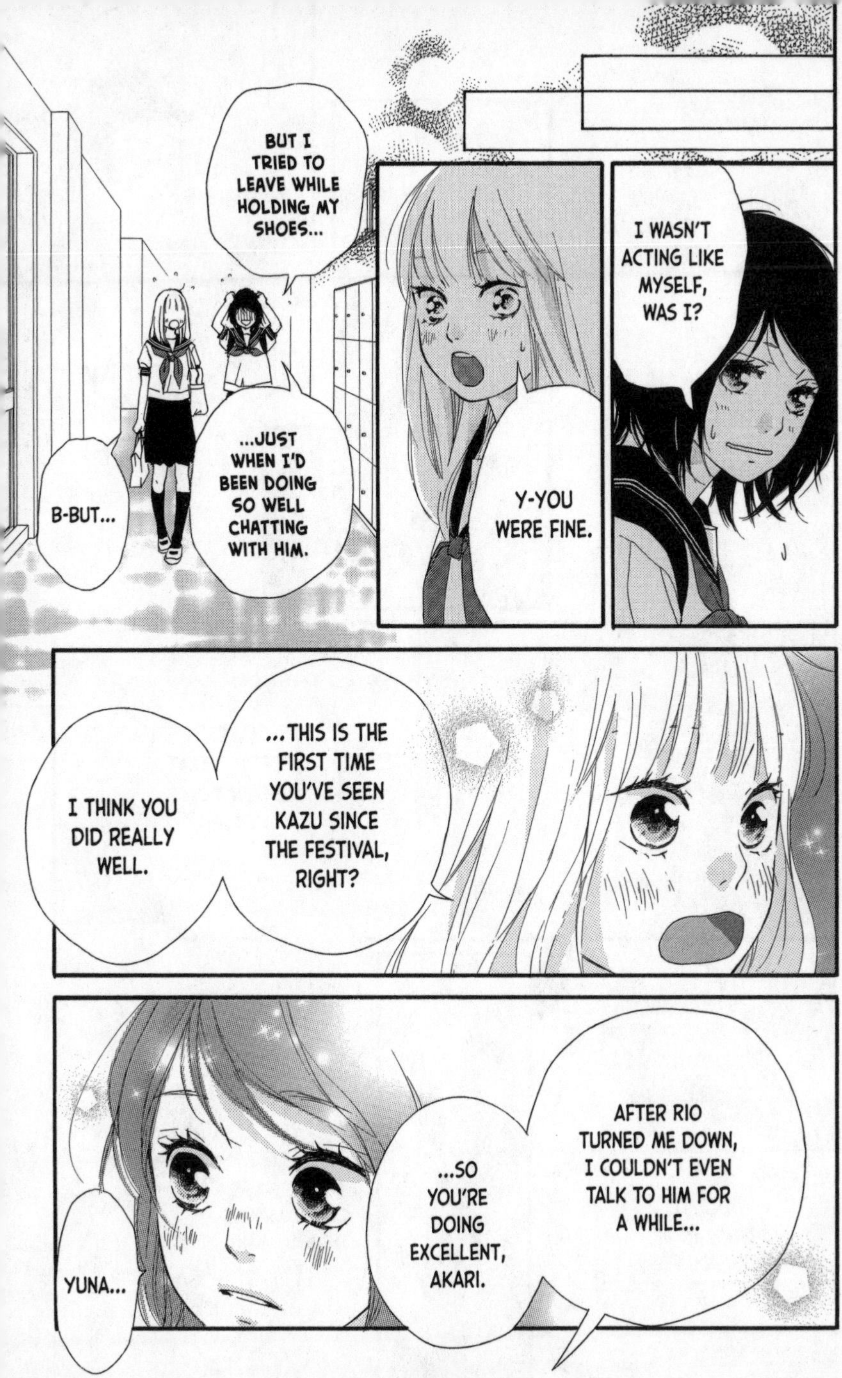
I WASN'T ACTING LIKE MYSELF, WAS I?
Y-YOU WERE FINE.
BUT I TRIED TO LEAVE WHILE HOLDING MY SHOES...
...JUST WHEN I'D BEEN DOING SO WELL CHATTING WITH HIM.
B-BUT...
...THIS IS THE FIRST TIME YOU'VE SEEN KAZU SINCE THE FESTIVAL, RIGHT?
I THINK YOU DID REALLY WELL.
AFTER RIO TURNED ME DOWN, I COULDN'T EVEN TALK TO HIM FOR A WHILE...
...SO YOU'RE DOING EXCELLENT, AKARI.
YUNA...

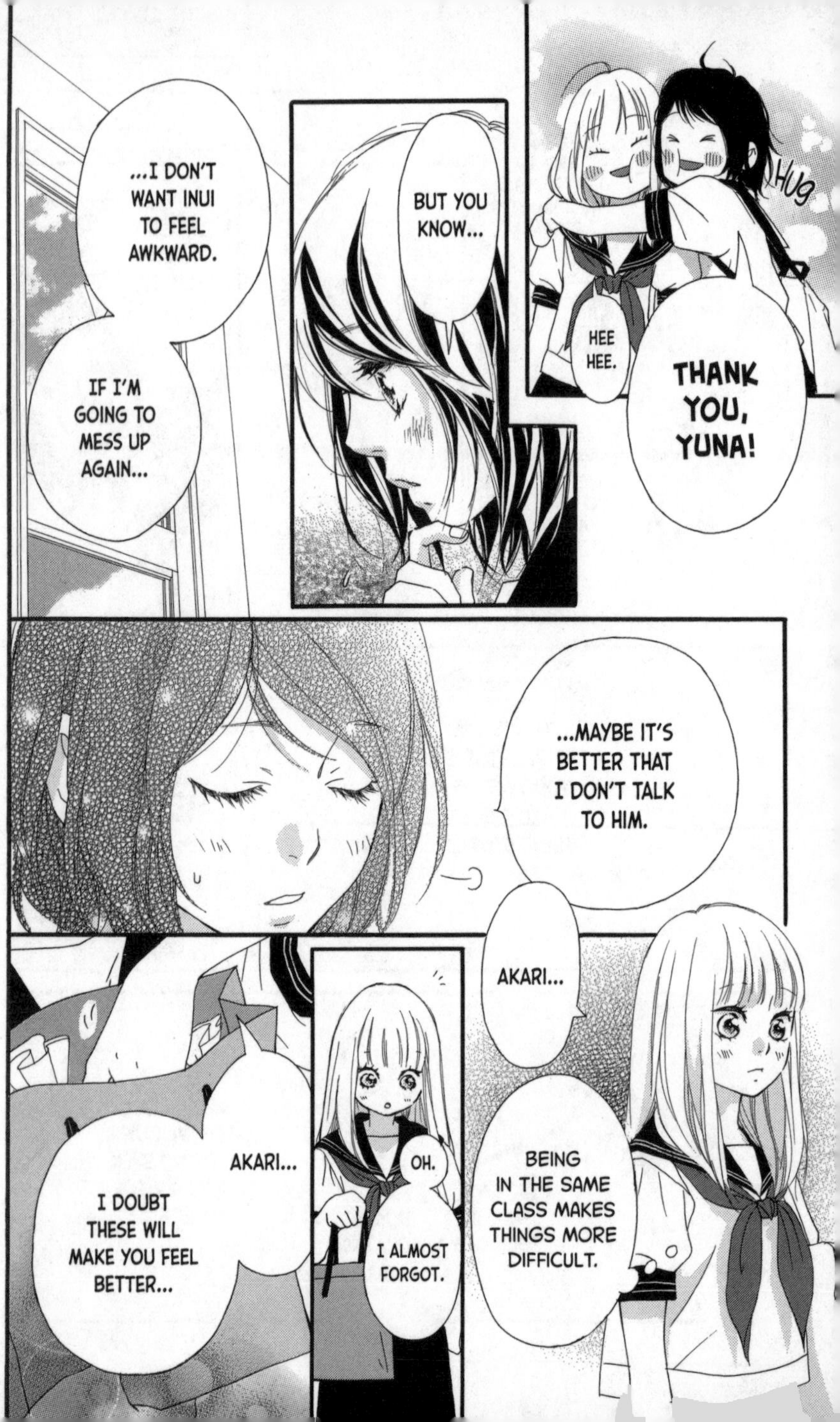
HUG
THANK YOU, YUNA!
HEE HEE.
BUT YOU KNOW...
...I DON'T WANT INUI TO FEEL AWKWARD.
IF I'M GOING TO MESS UP AGAIN...
...MAYBE IT'S BETTER THAT I DON'T TALK TO HIM.
AKARI...
BEING IN THE SAME CLASS MAKES THINGS MORE DIFFICULT.
OH.
I ALMOST FORGOT.
AKARI...
I DOUBT THESE WILL MAKE YOU FEEL BETTER...

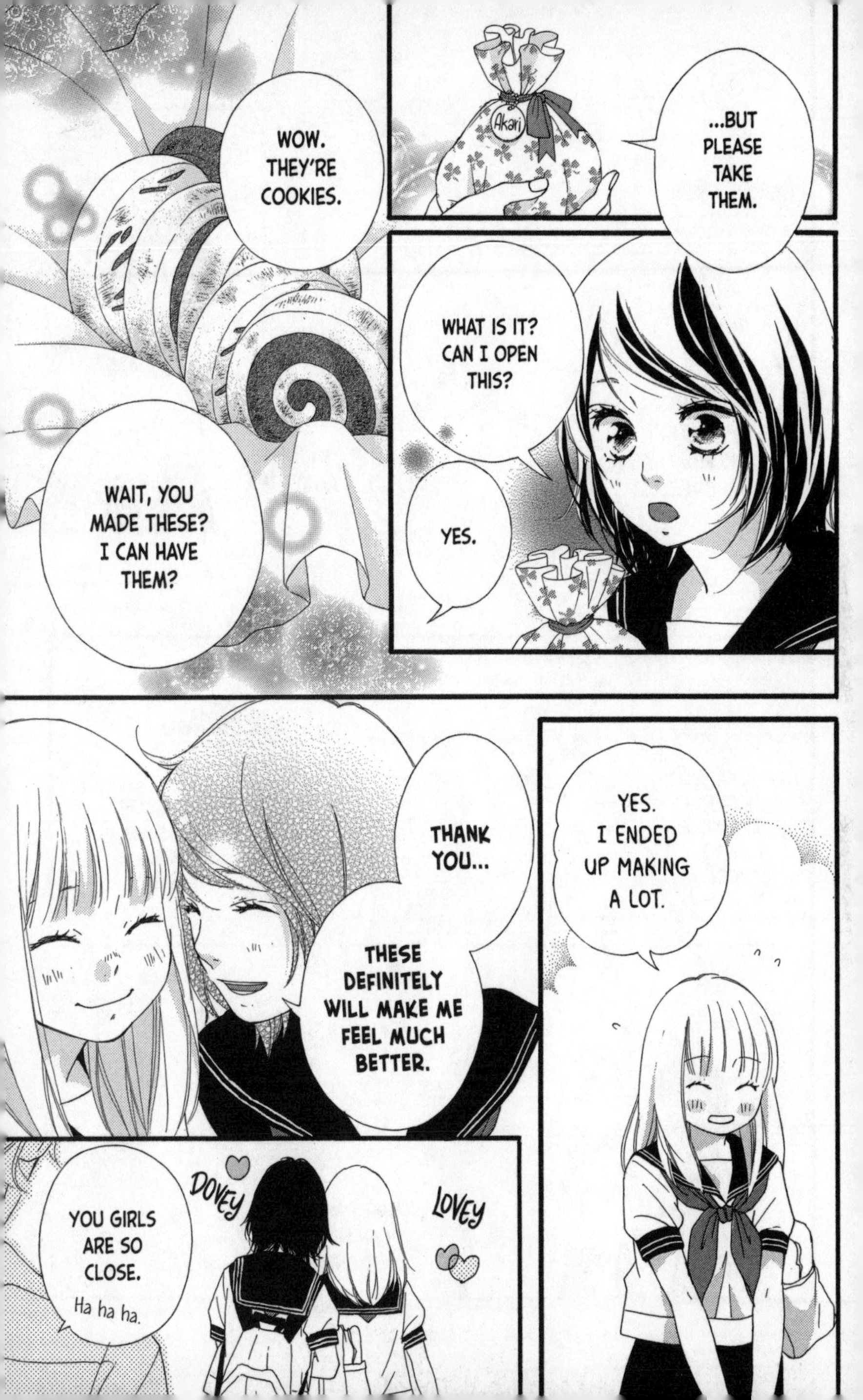
Akari
...BUT PLEASE TAKE THEM.
WHAT IS IT? CAN I OPEN THIS?
YES.
WOW. THEY'RE COOKIES.
WAIT, YOU MADE THESE? I CAN HAVE THEM?
YES. I ENDED UP MAKING A LOT.
THANK YOU...
THESE DEFINITELY WILL MAKE ME FEEL MUCH BETTER.
LOVEY
DOVEY
YOU GIRLS ARE SO CLOSE.
Ha ha ha.

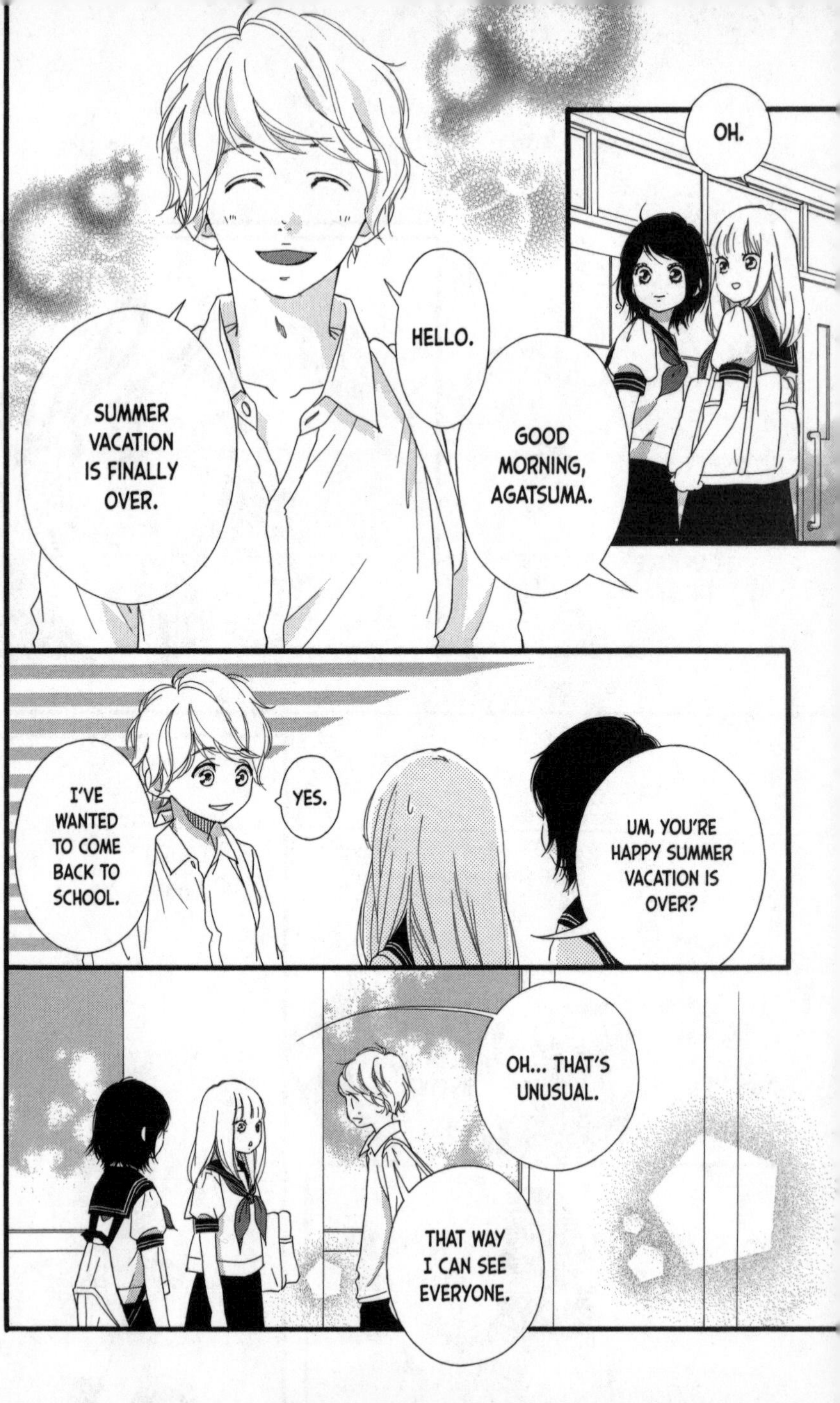
OH.
GOOD MORNING, AGATSUMA.
HELLO.
SUMMER VACATION IS FINALLY OVER.
UM, YOU'RE HAPPY SUMMER VACATION IS OVER?
YES.
I'VE WANTED TO COME BACK TO SCHOOL.
OH... THAT'S UNUSUAL.
THAT WAY I CAN SEE EVERYONE.

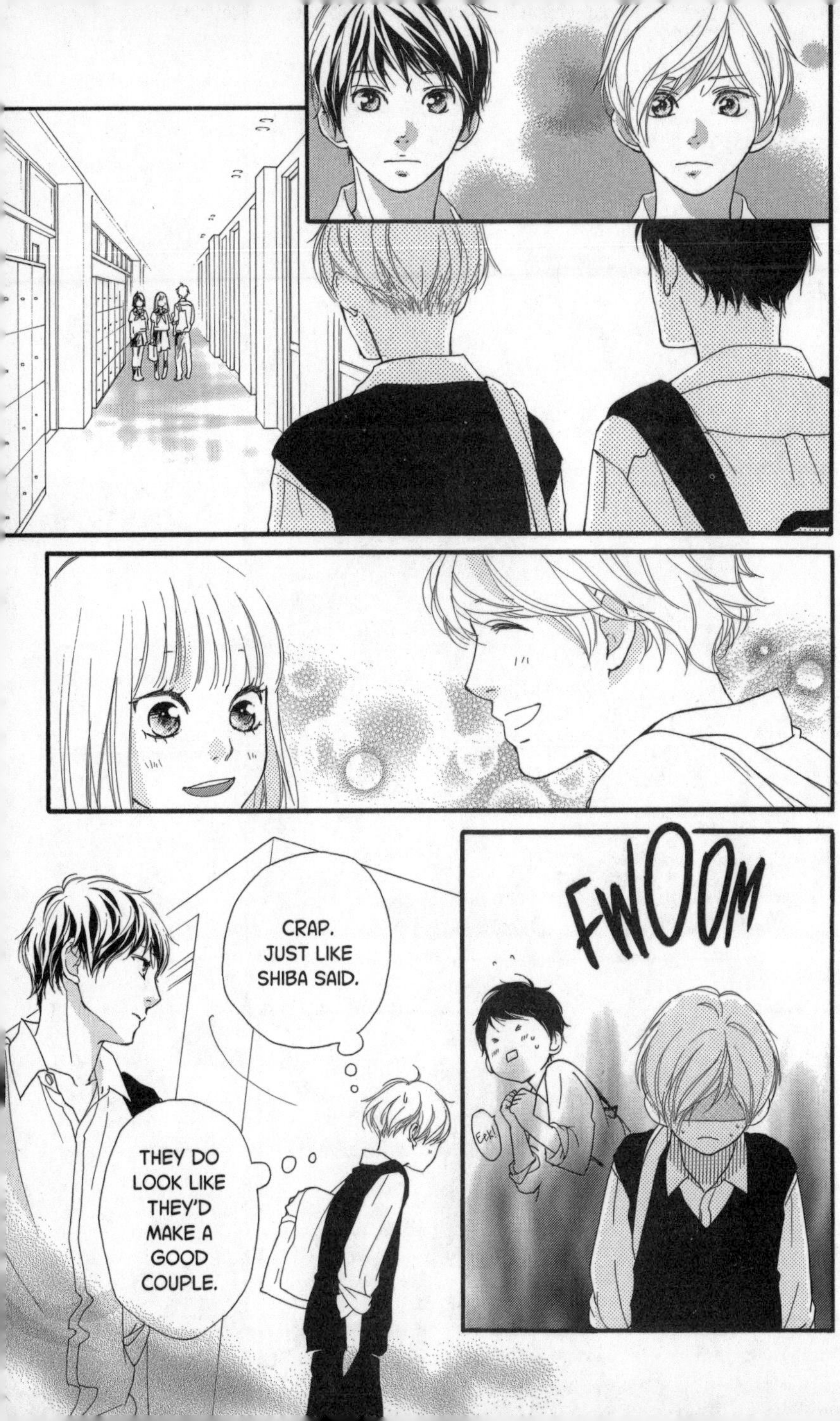
FWOOM
Eek!
CRAP. JUST LIKE SHIBA SAID.
THEY DO LOOK LIKE THEY'D MAKE A GOOD COUPLE.

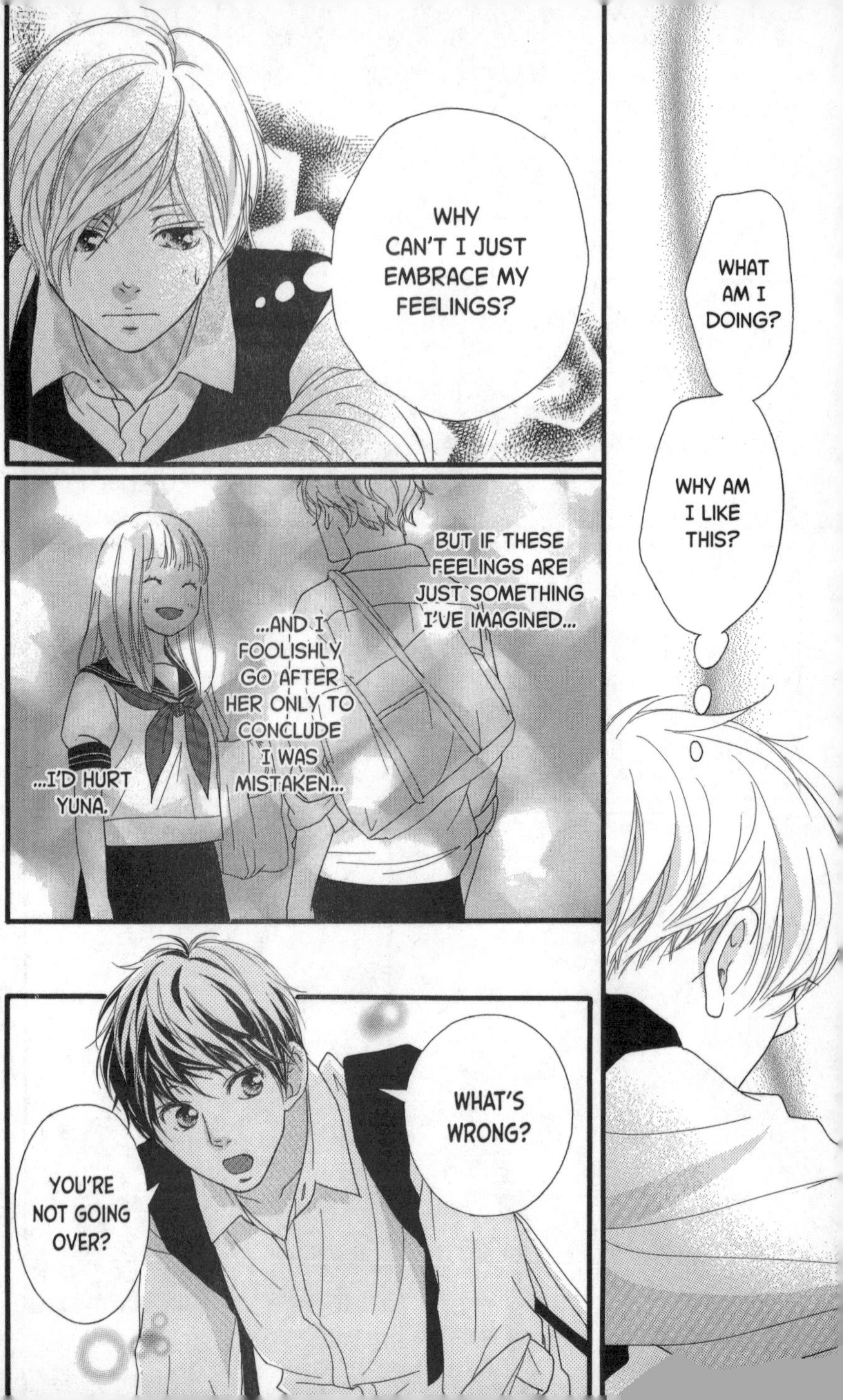
WHAT AM I DOING?
WHY AM I LIKE THIS?
WHY CAN'T I JUST EMBRACE MY FEELINGS?
BUT IF THESE FEELINGS ARE JUST SOMETHING I'VE IMAGINED...
...AND I FOOLISHLY GO AFTER HER ONLY TO CONCLUDE I WAS MISTAKEN...
...I'D HURT YUNA.
WHAT'S WRONG?
YOU'RE NOT GOING OVER?

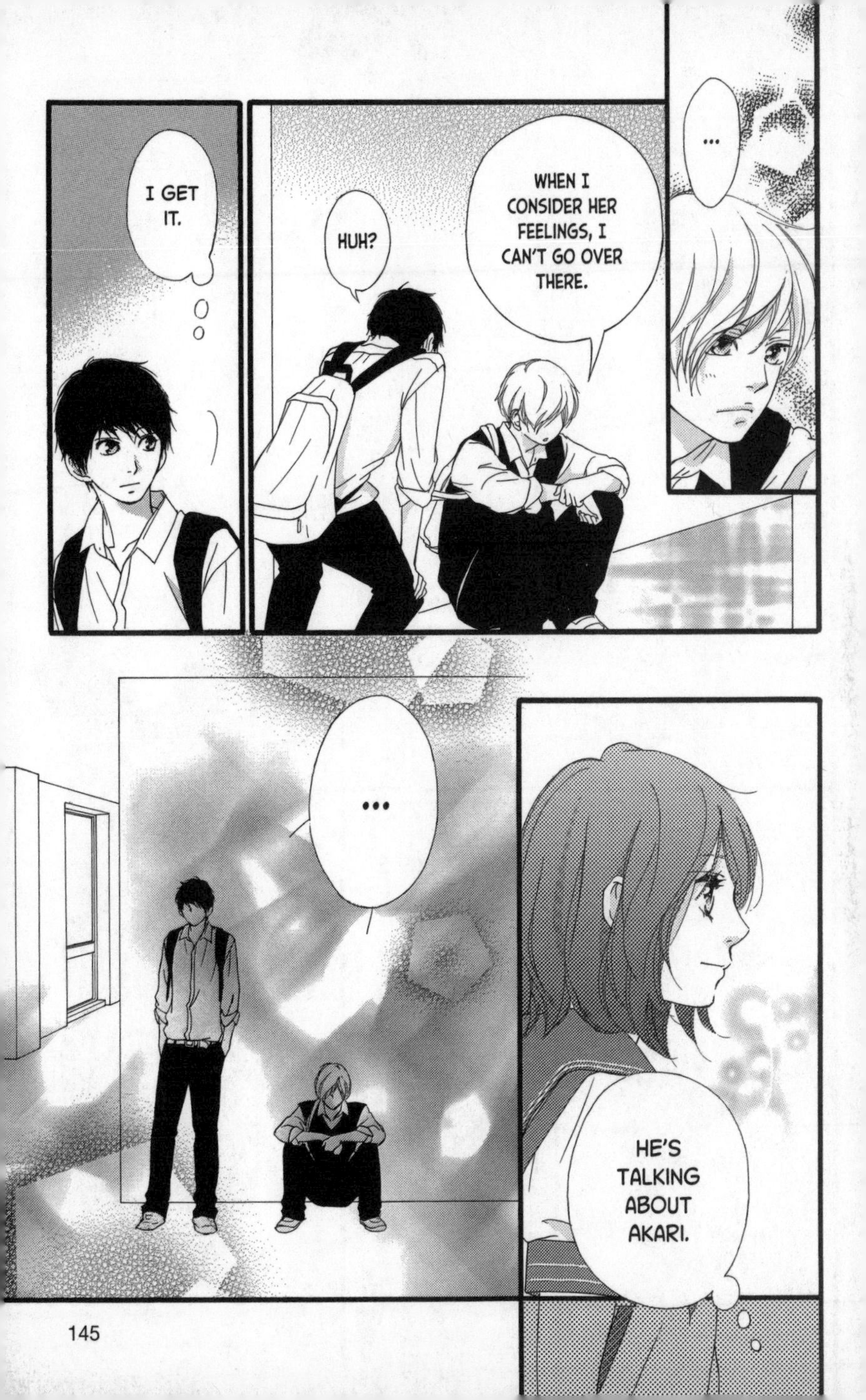
...
WHEN I CONSIDER HER FEELINGS, I CAN'T GO OVER THERE.
HUH?
I GET IT.
HE'S TALKING ABOUT AKARI.
...

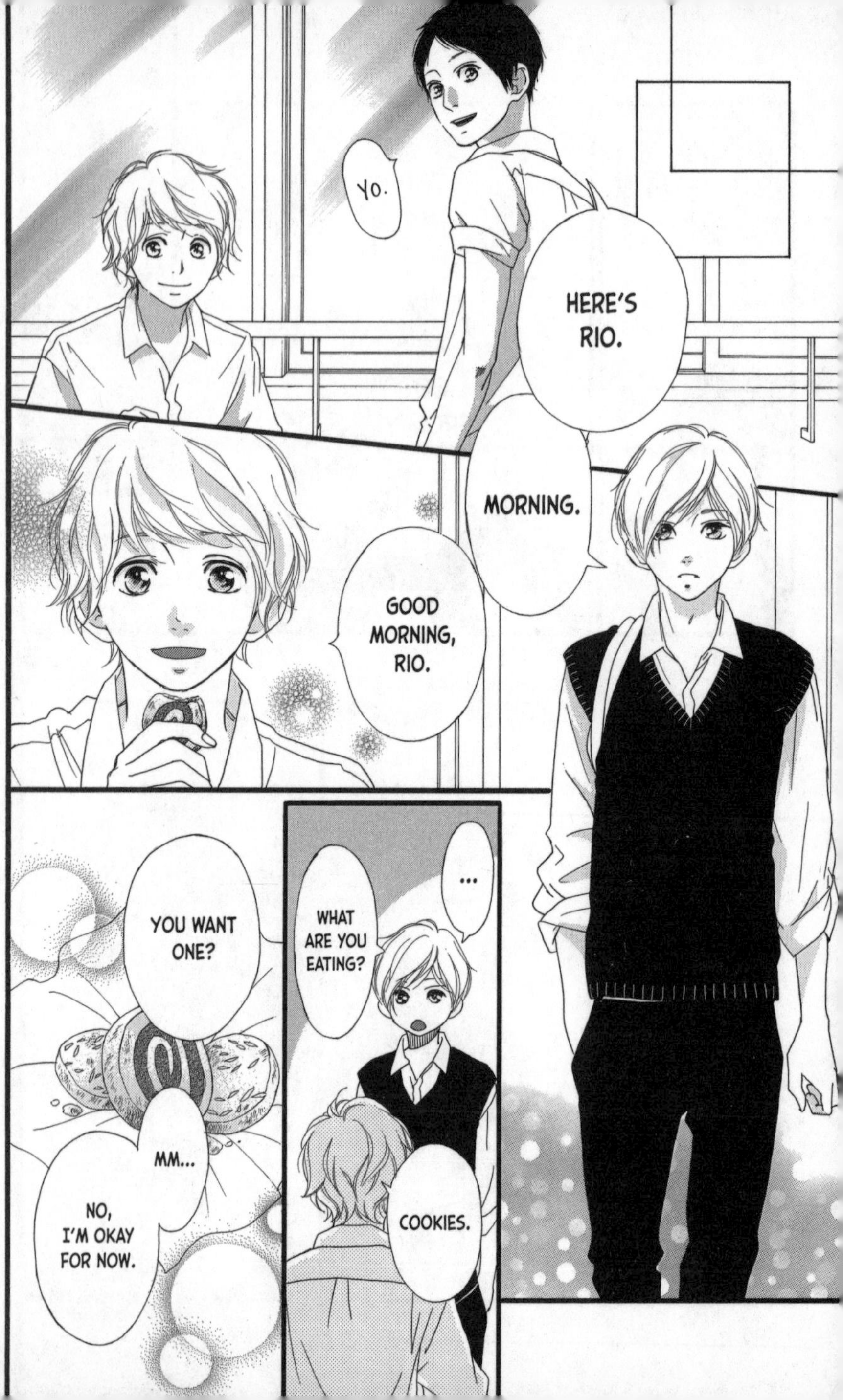
HERE'S RIO.
YO.
MORNING.
GOOD MORNING, RIO.
...
WHAT ARE YOU EATING?
COOKIES.
YOU WANT ONE?
MM...
NO, I'M OKAY FOR NOW.

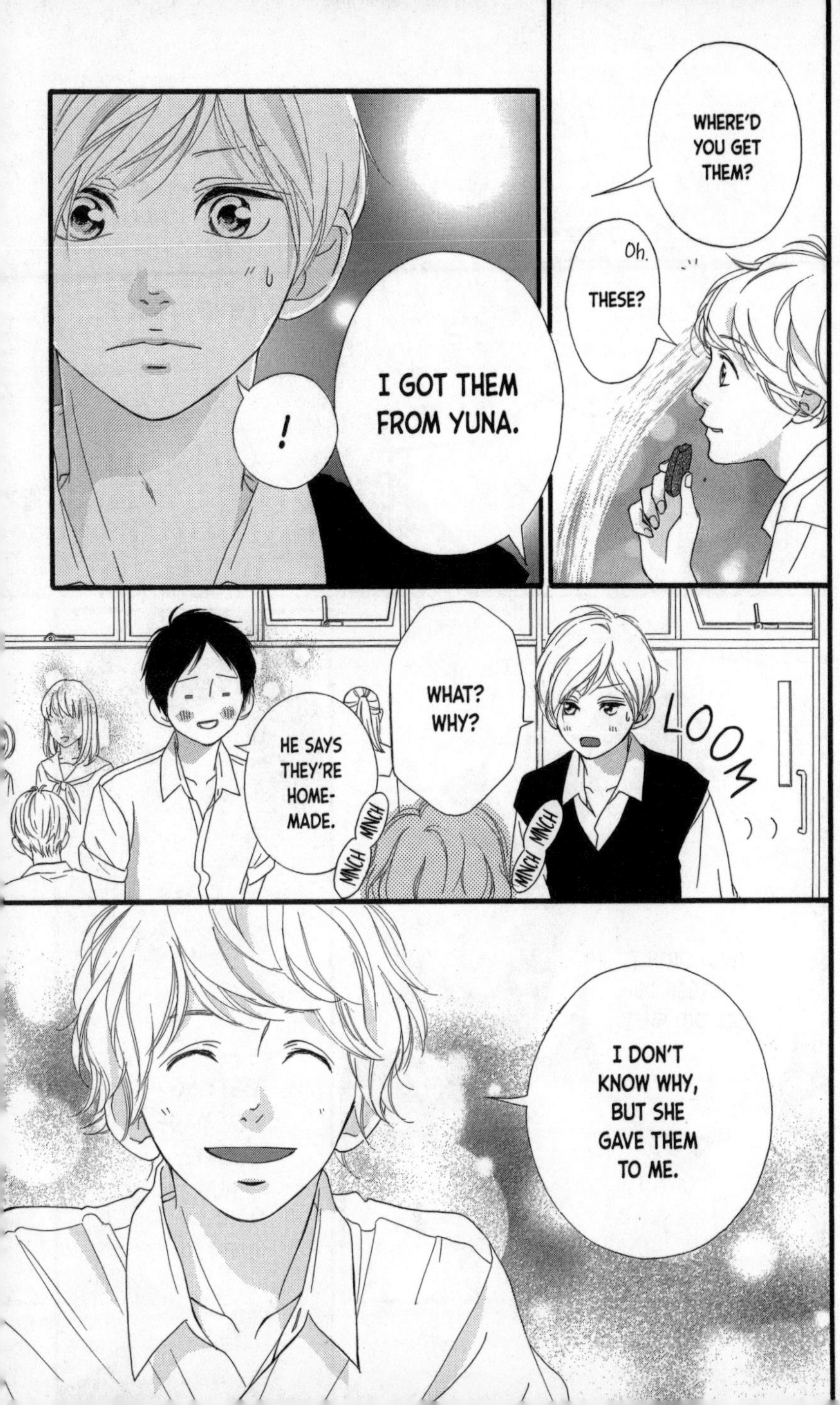
WHERE'D YOU GET THEM?
Oh.
THESE?
I GOT THEM FROM YUNA.
!
LOOM
WHAT? WHY?
MINCH MINCH
HE SAYS THEY'RE HOME-MADE.
MINCH MINCH
I DON'T KNOW WHY, BUT SHE GAVE THEM TO ME.

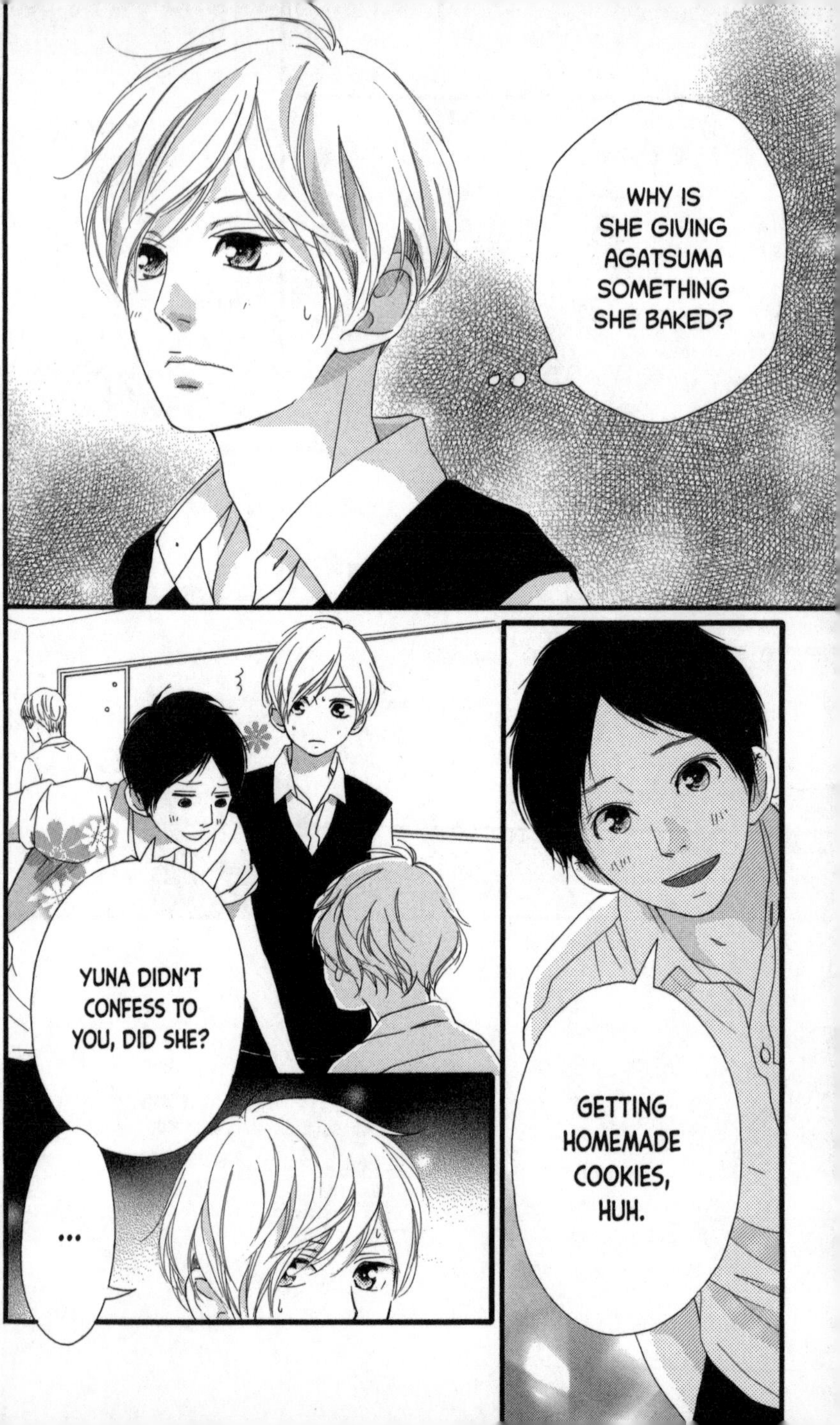
WHY IS SHE GIVING AGATSUMA SOMETHING SHE BAKED?
GETTING HOMEMADE COOKIES, HUH.
YUNA DIDN'T CONFESS TO YOU, DID SHE?
...

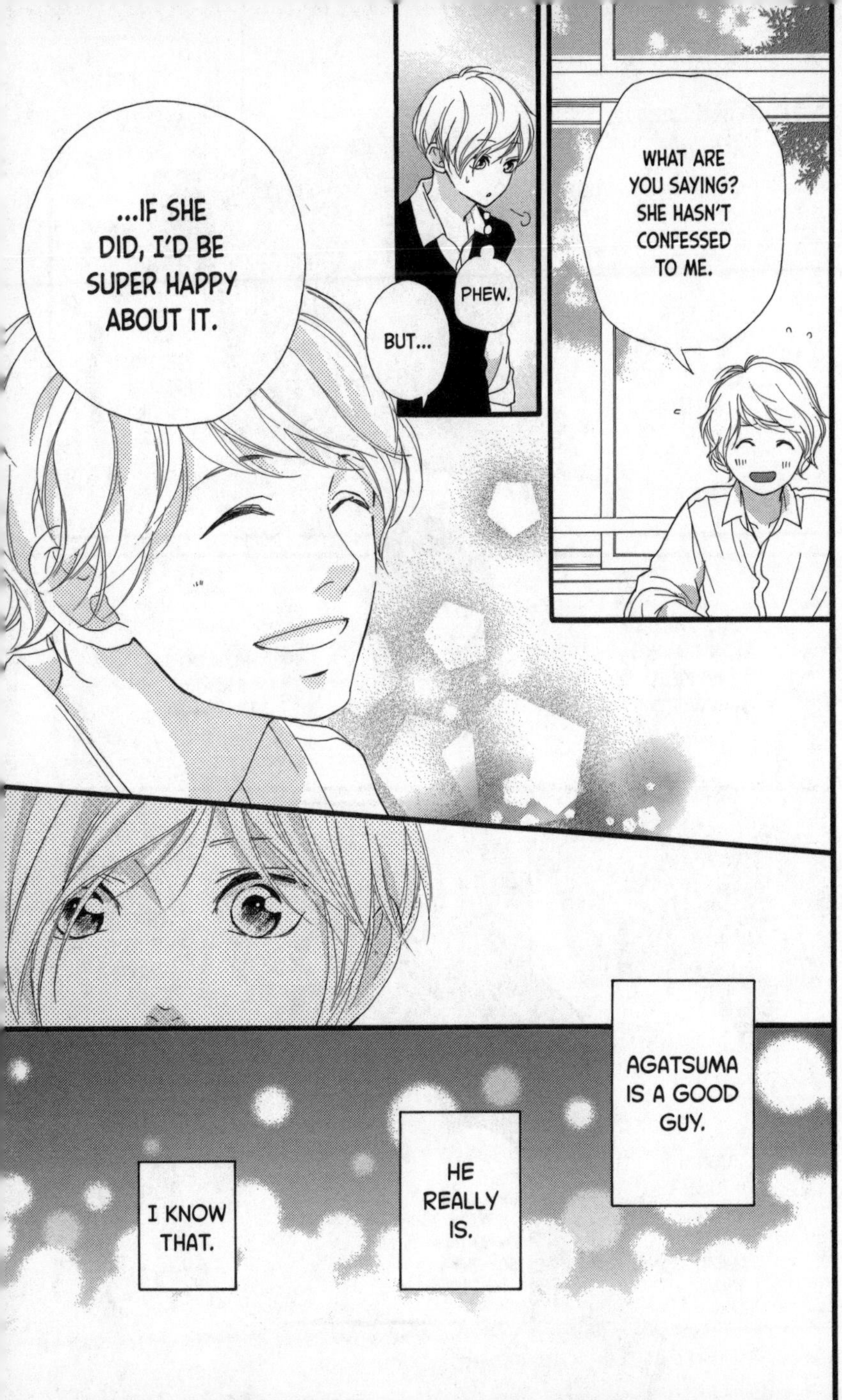
WHAT ARE YOU SAYING? SHE HASN'T CONFESSED TO ME.
PHEW.
BUT...
...IF SHE DID, I'D BE SUPER HAPPY ABOUT IT.
AGATSUMA IS A GOOD GUY.
HE REALLY IS.
I KNOW THAT.

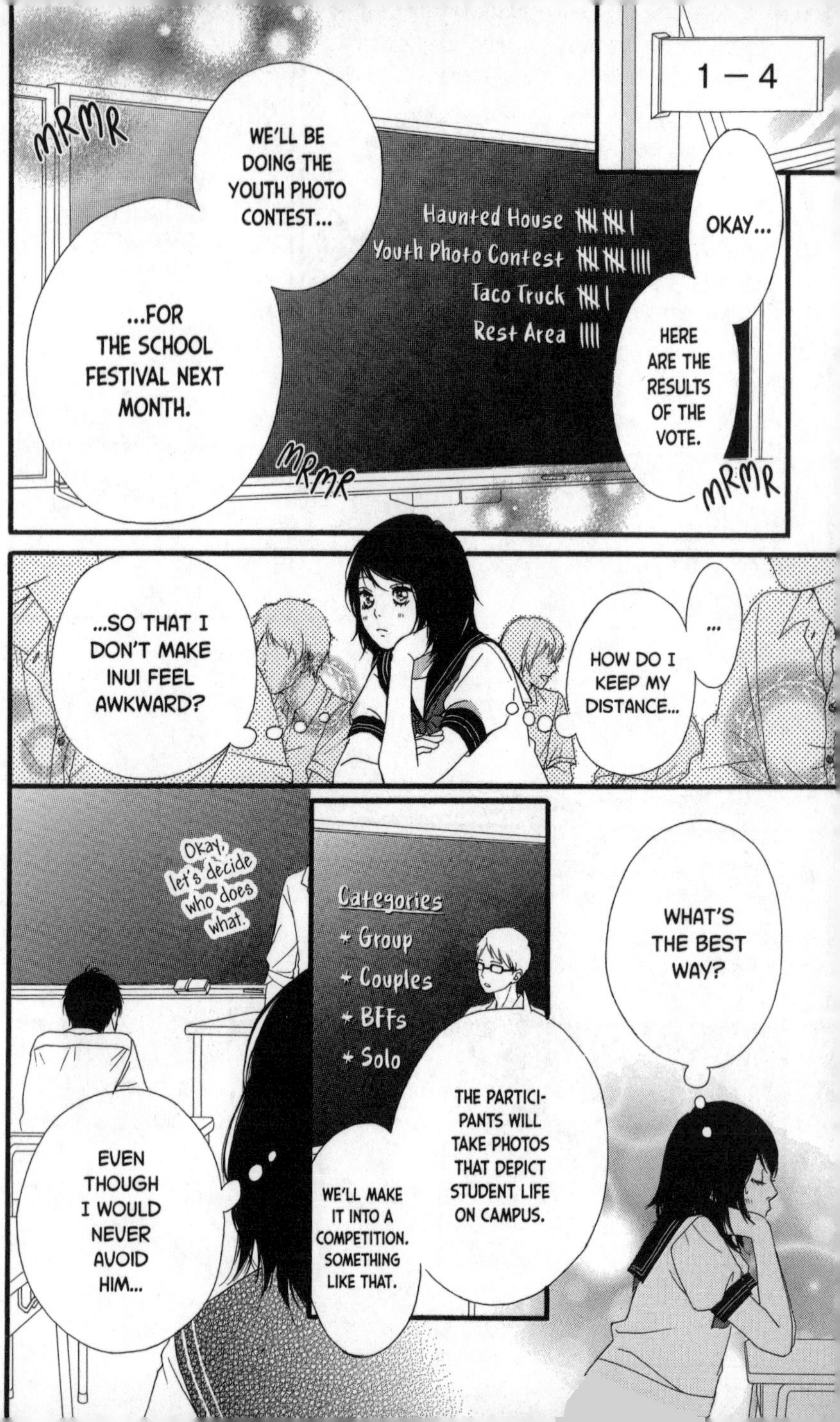
1 — 4
OKAY...
HERE ARE THE RESULTS OF THE VOTE.
MRMR
Haunted House
Youth Photo Contest
Taco Truck
Rest Area
WE'LL BE DOING THE YOUTH PHOTO CONTEST...
...FOR THE SCHOOL FESTIVAL NEXT MONTH.
MRMR
MRMR
...
HOW DO I KEEP MY DISTANCE...
...SO THAT I DON'T MAKE INUI FEEL AWKWARD?
WHAT'S THE BEST WAY?
Categories
★ Group
★ Couples
★ BFFs
★ Solo
THE PARTICI-PANTS WILL TAKE PHOTOS THAT DEPICT STUDENT LIFE ON CAMPUS.
WE'LL MAKE IT INTO A COMPETITION. SOMETHING LIKE THAT.
Okay, let's decide who does what.
EVEN THOUGH I WOULD NEVER AVOID HIM...

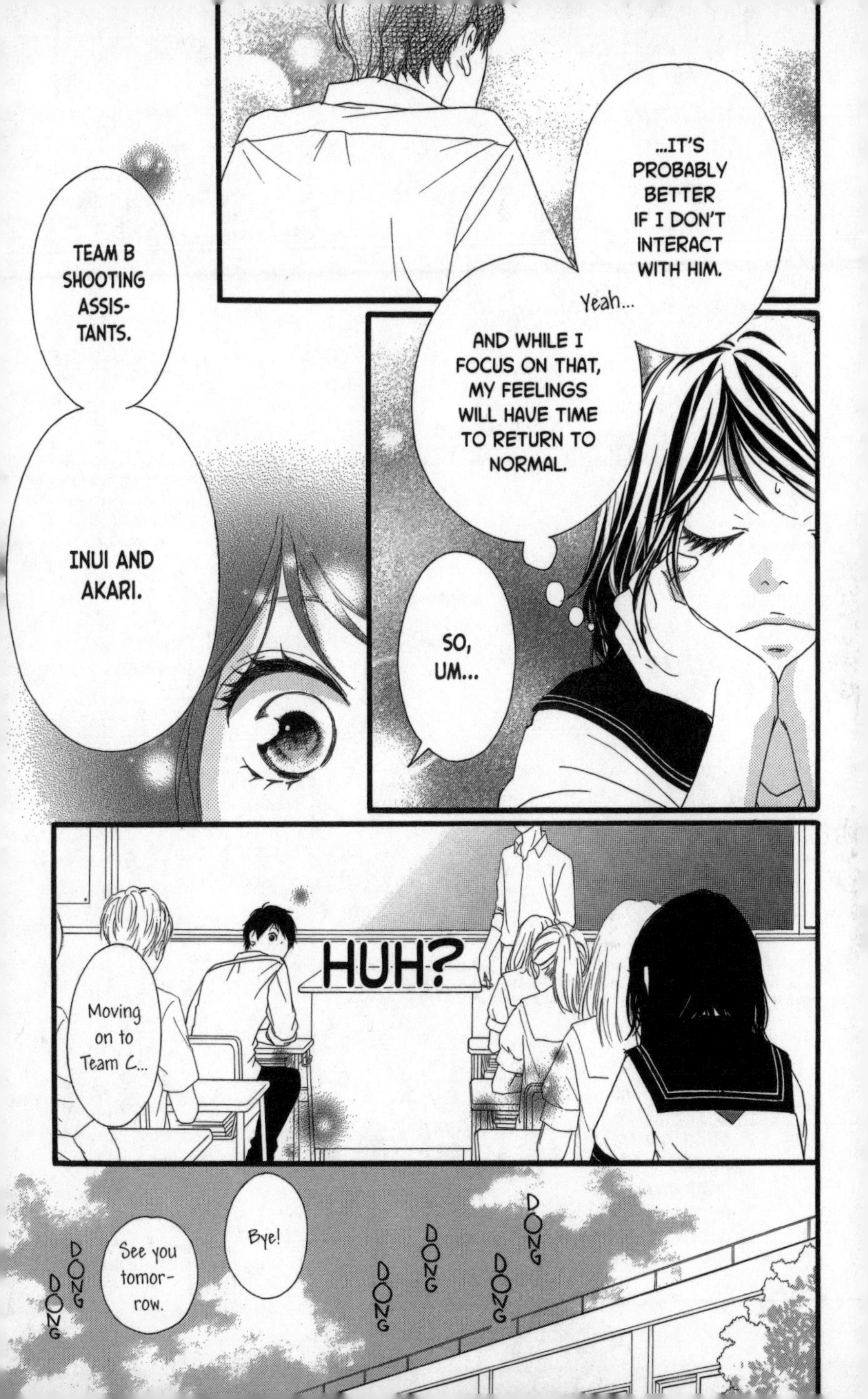
...IT'S PROBABLY BETTER IF I DON'T INTERACT WITH HIM.
Yeah...
AND WHILE I FOCUS ON THAT, MY FEELINGS WILL HAVE TIME TO RETURN TO NORMAL.
SO, UM...
TEAM B SHOOTING ASSIS- TANTS.
INUI AND AKARI.
HUH?
Moving on to Team C...
DONG DONG
DONG DONG
DONG DONG
Bye!
See you tomor- row.
DONG DONG

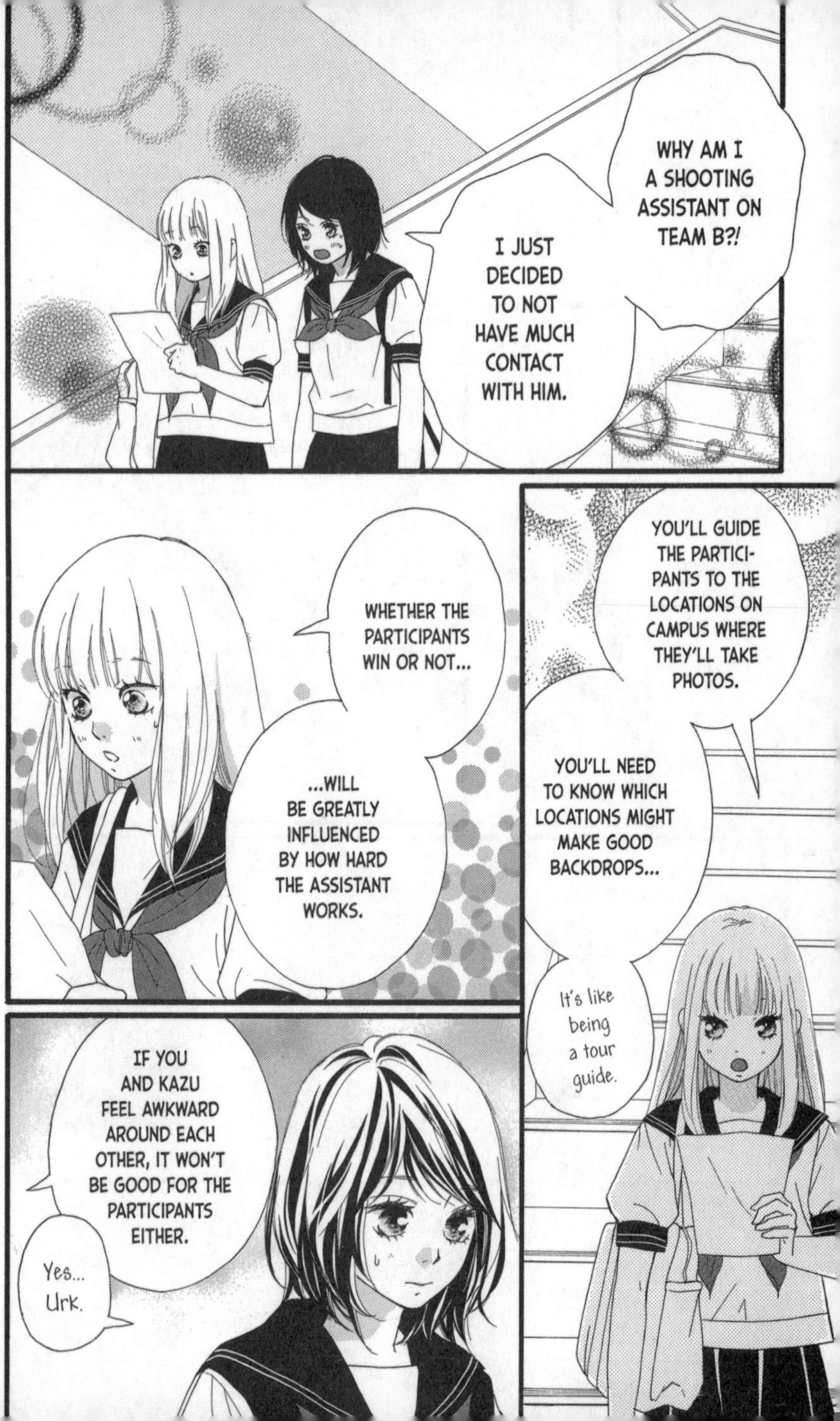
WHY AM I A SHOOTING ASSISTANT ON TEAM B?!
I JUST DECIDED TO NOT HAVE MUCH CONTACT WITH HIM.
YOU'LL GUIDE THE PARTICI-PANTS TO THE LOCATIONS ON CAMPUS WHERE THEY'LL TAKE PHOTOS.
YOU'LL NEED TO KNOW WHICH LOCATIONS MIGHT MAKE GOOD BACKDROPS...
It's like being a tour guide.
WHETHER THE PARTICIPANTS WIN OR NOT...
...WILL BE GREATLY INFLUENCED BY HOW HARD THE ASSISTANT WORKS.
IF YOU AND KAZU FEEL AWKWARD AROUND EACH OTHER, IT WON'T BE GOOD FOR THE PARTICIPANTS EITHER.
Yes... Urk.

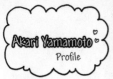

Akari Yamamoto Profile

Birthday: August 17

Sign: Leo

Blood type: O

Height: 5' 2"

Weight: 93 lbs

Favorite colors:
Red, black

Favorite subject:
English

Least favorite subject:
History

Favorite food:
Nashi pear

Least favorite food:
Buri daikon

Hobby:
Collecting nail polish

Favorite thing about herself:
Shape of my nails

Favorite movie:
500 Days of Summer

Favorite magazine:
PERK

Favorite band:
Sakanaction

Favorite celebrity:
Rola

Place she wants to visit:
Florence, Italy

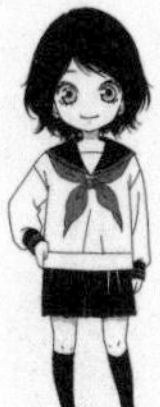

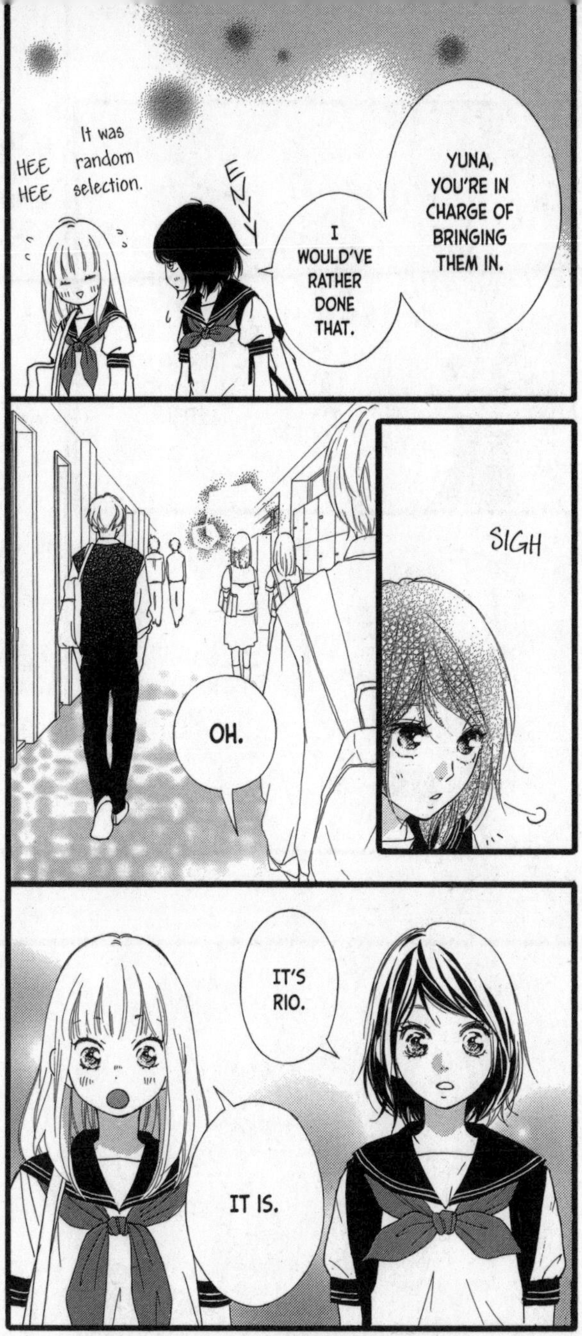
YUNA, YOU'RE IN CHARGE OF BRINGING THEM IN.
I WOULD'VE RATHER DONE THAT.
ENVY
It was random selection.
HEE HEE
SIGH
OH.
IT'S RIO.
IT IS.

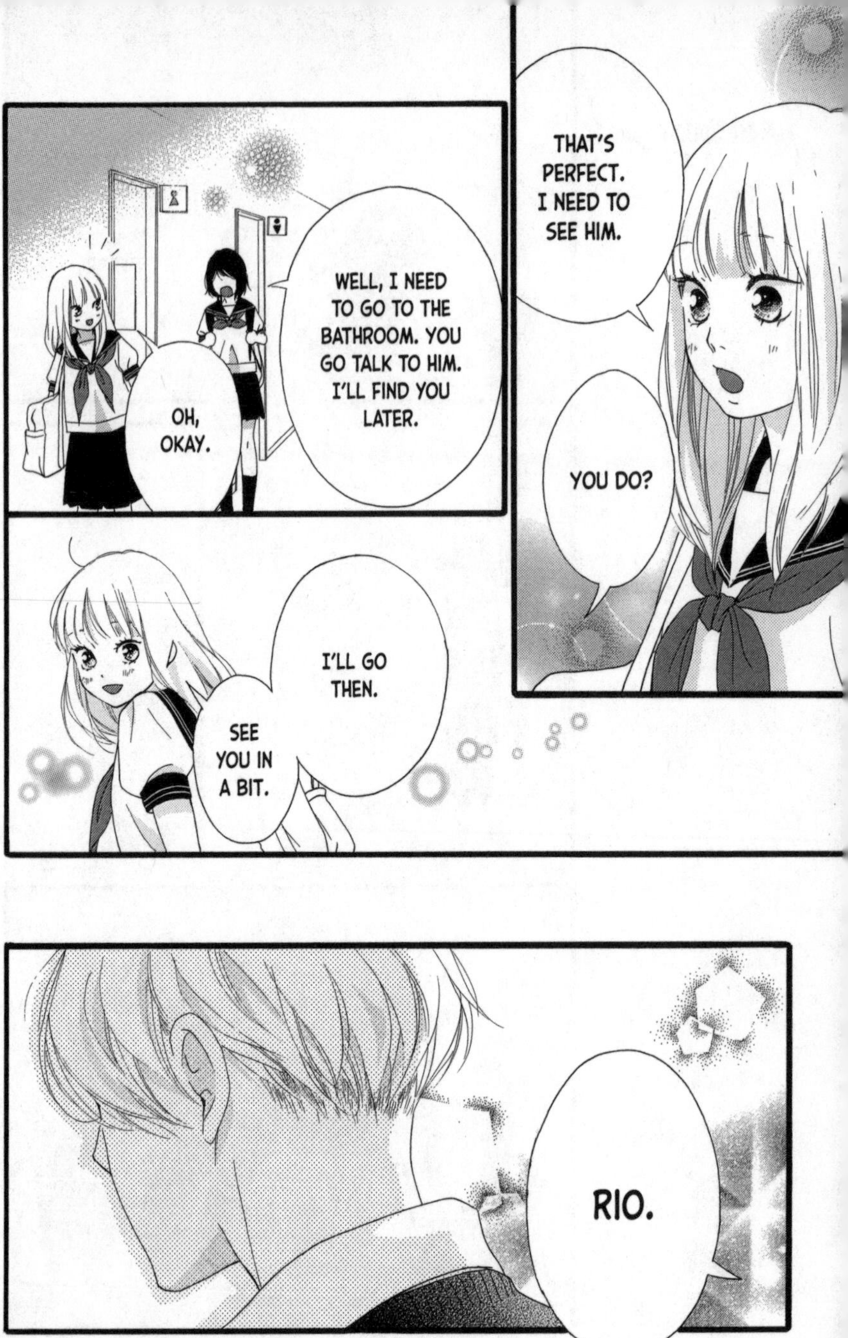
THAT'S PERFECT. I NEED TO SEE HIM.
YOU DO?
WELL, I NEED TO GO TO THE BATHROOM. YOU GO TALK TO HIM. I'LL FIND YOU LATER.
OH, OKAY.
I'LL GO THEN.
SEE YOU IN A BIT.
RIO.

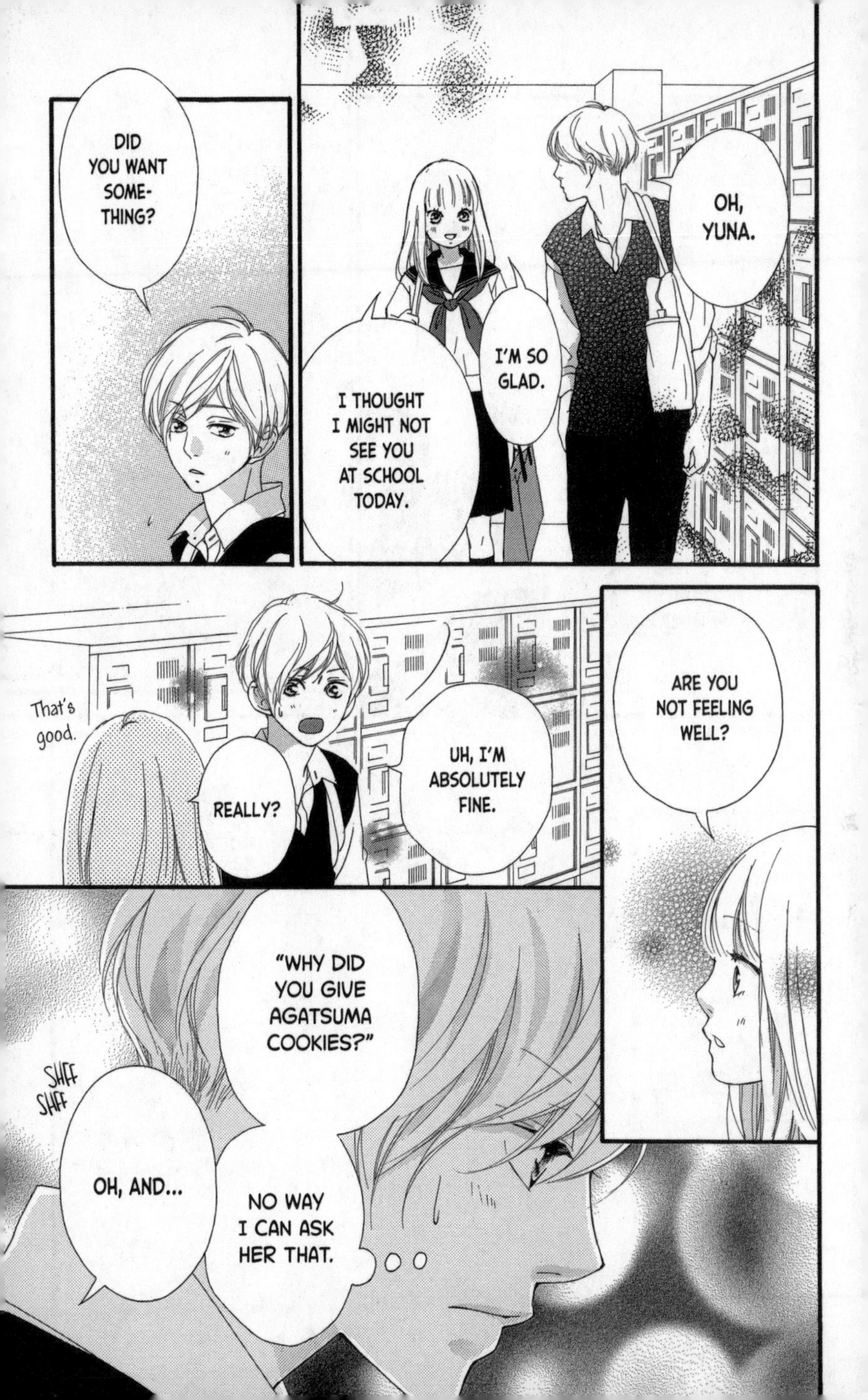
OH, YUNA.
I'M SO GLAD.
I THOUGHT I MIGHT NOT SEE YOU AT SCHOOL TODAY.
DID YOU WANT SOME-THING?
ARE YOU NOT FEELING WELL?
UH, I'M ABSOLUTELY FINE.
REALLY?
That's good.
"WHY DID YOU GIVE AGATSUMA COOKIES?"
NO WAY I CAN ASK HER THAT.
OH, AND...
SHFF SHFF

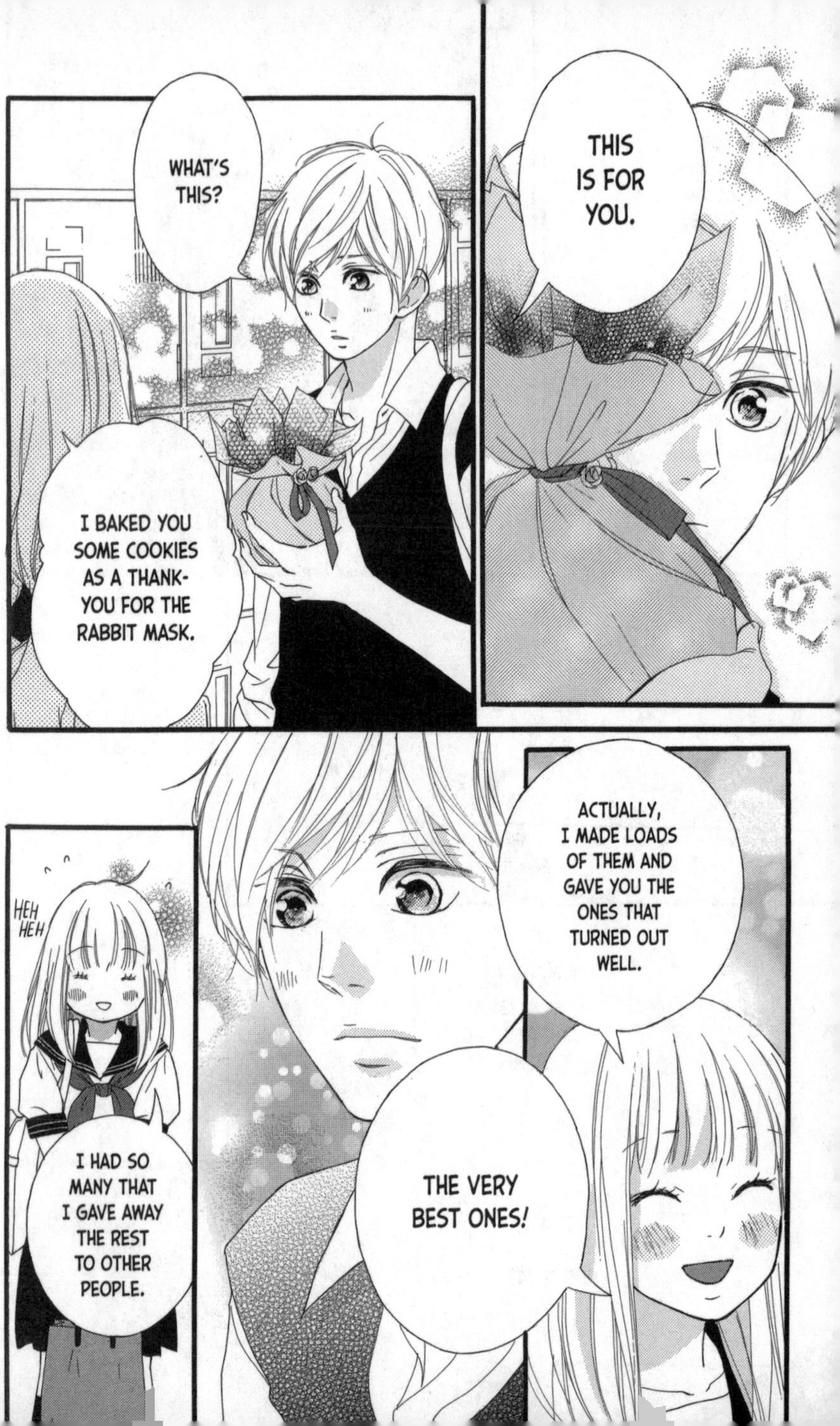
THIS IS FOR YOU.
WHAT'S THIS?
I BAKED YOU SOME COOKIES AS A THANK-YOU FOR THE RABBIT MASK.
ACTUALLY, I MADE LOADS OF THEM AND GAVE YOU THE ONES THAT TURNED OUT WELL.
THE VERY BEST ONES!
HEH HEH
I HAD SO MANY THAT I GAVE AWAY THE REST TO OTHER PEOPLE.

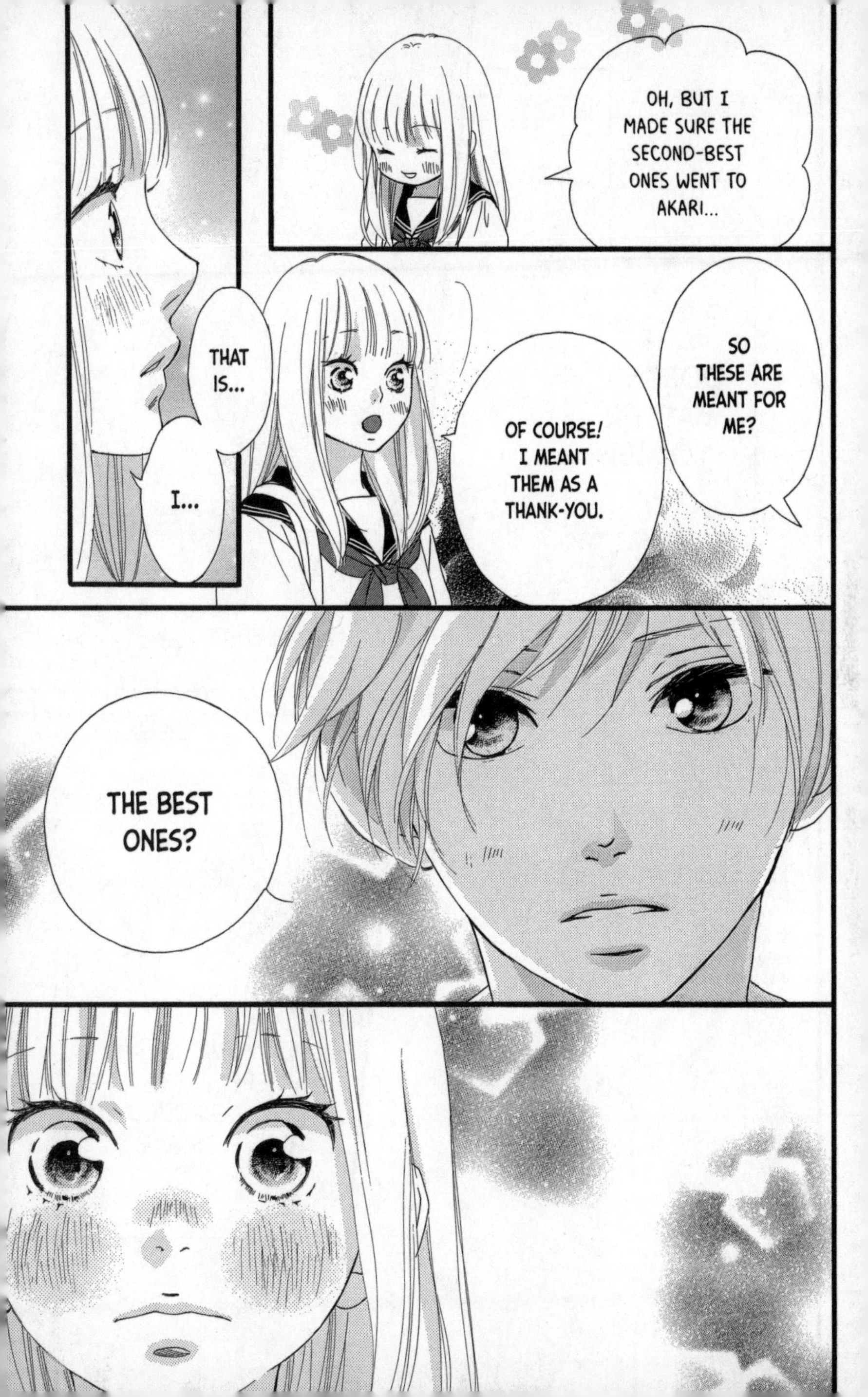
OH, BUT I MADE SURE THE SECOND-BEST ONES WENT TO AKARI...
SO THESE ARE MEANT FOR ME?
OF COURSE! I MEANT THEM AS A THANK-YOU.
THAT IS...
I...
THE BEST ONES?

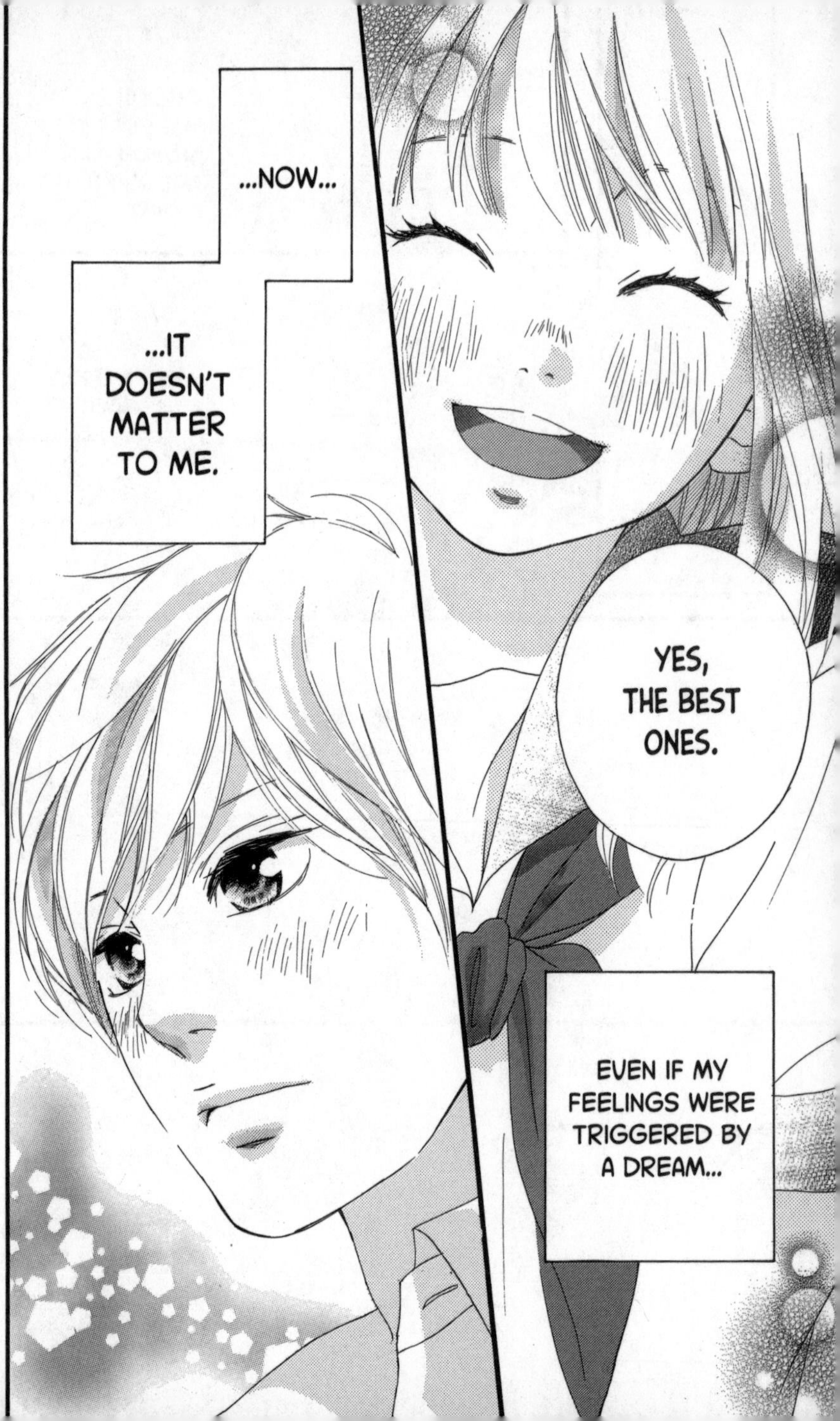
YES, THE BEST ONES.
EVEN IF MY FEELINGS WERE TRIGGERED BY A DREAM...
...NOW...
...IT DOESN'T MATTER TO ME.

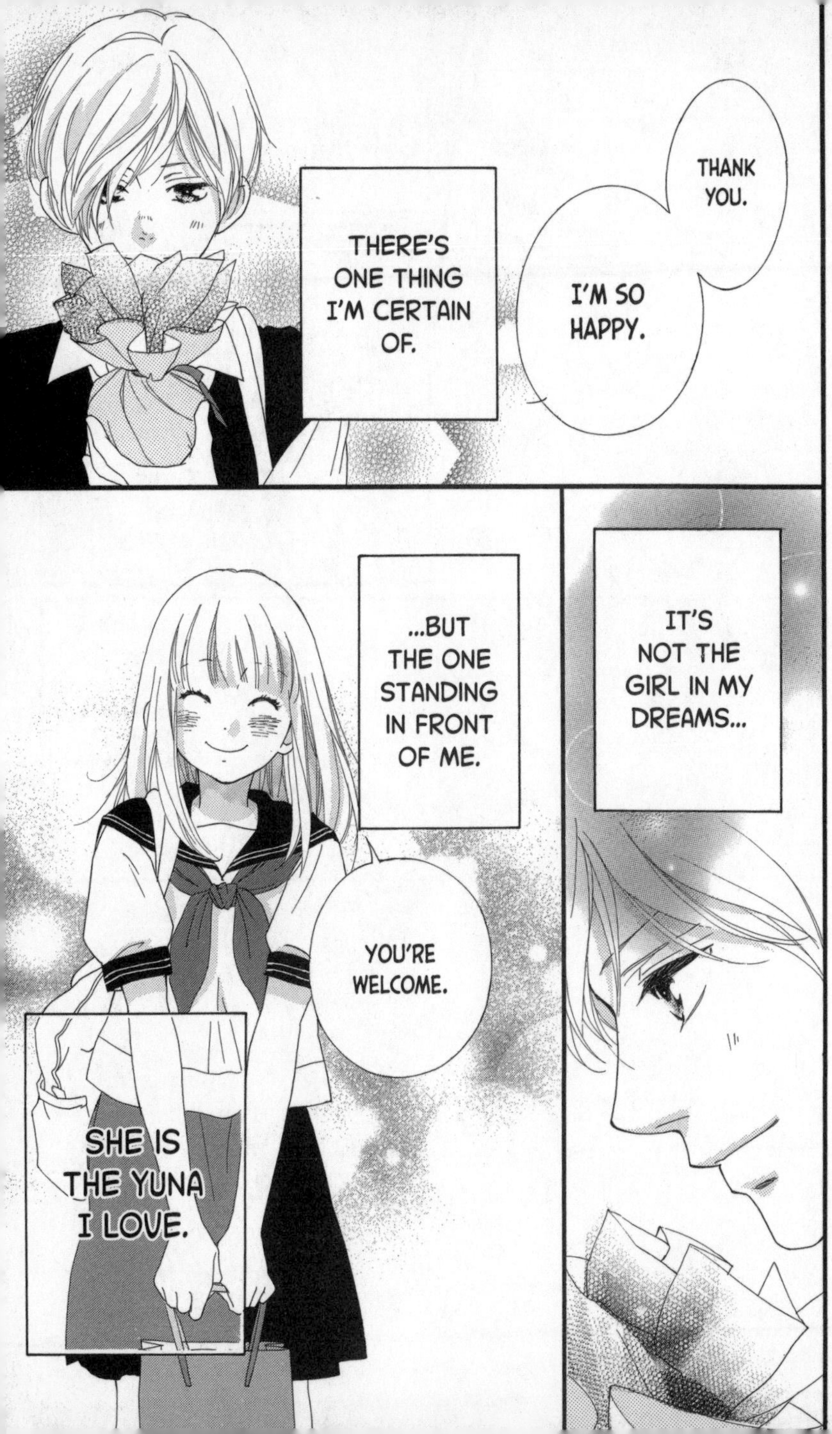
THANK YOU.
I'M SO HAPPY.
THERE'S ONE THING I'M CERTAIN OF.
IT'S NOT THE GIRL IN MY DREAMS...
...BUT THE ONE STANDING IN FRONT OF ME.
YOU'RE WELCOME.
SHE IS THE YUNA I LOVE.

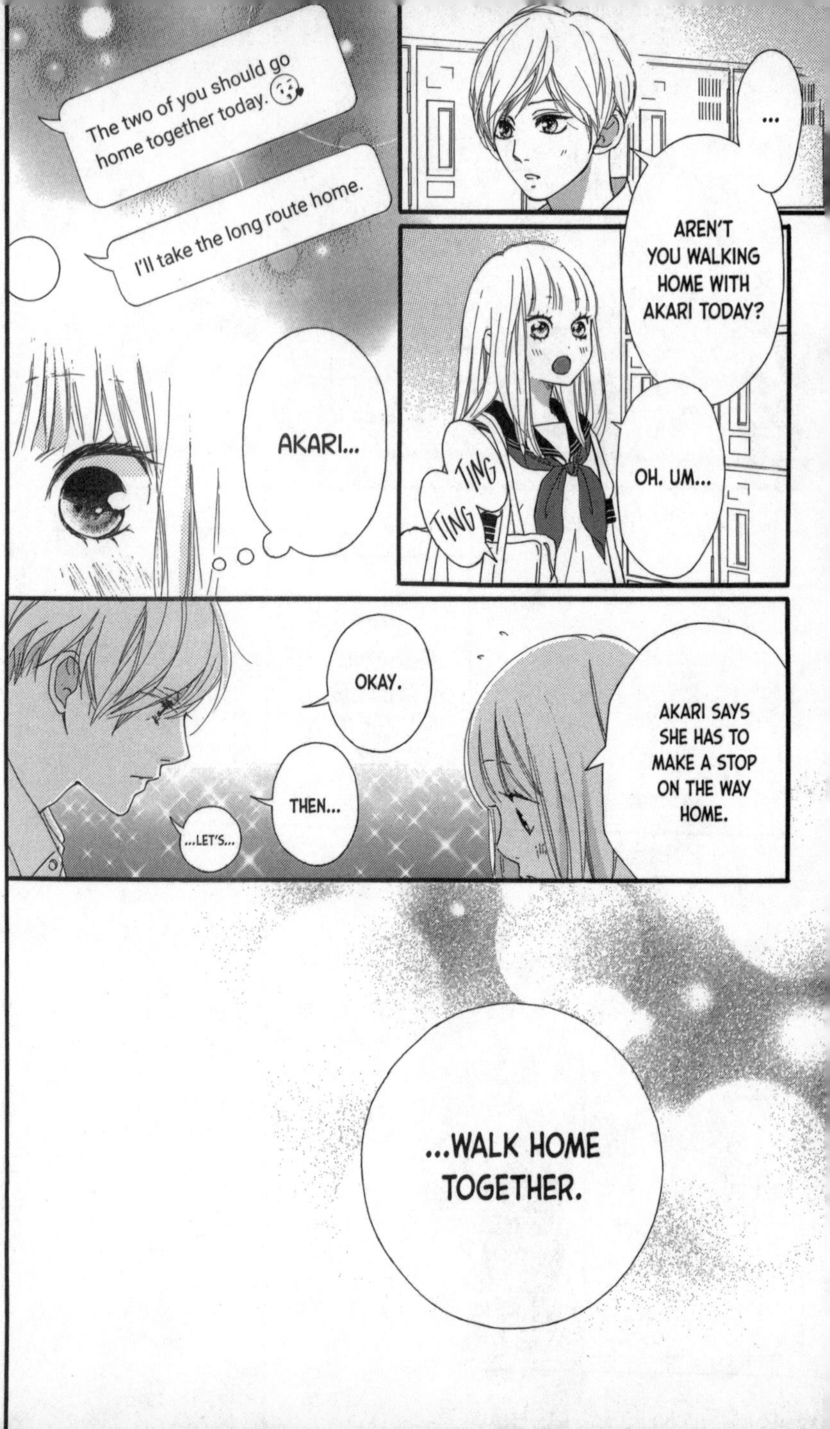
...
AREN'T YOU WALKING HOME WITH AKARI TODAY?
OH. UM...
TING TING
The two of you should go home together today.
I'll take the long route home.
AKARI...
AKARI SAYS SHE HAS TO MAKE A STOP ON THE WAY HOME.
OKAY.
THEN...
...LET'S...
...WALK HOME TOGETHER.

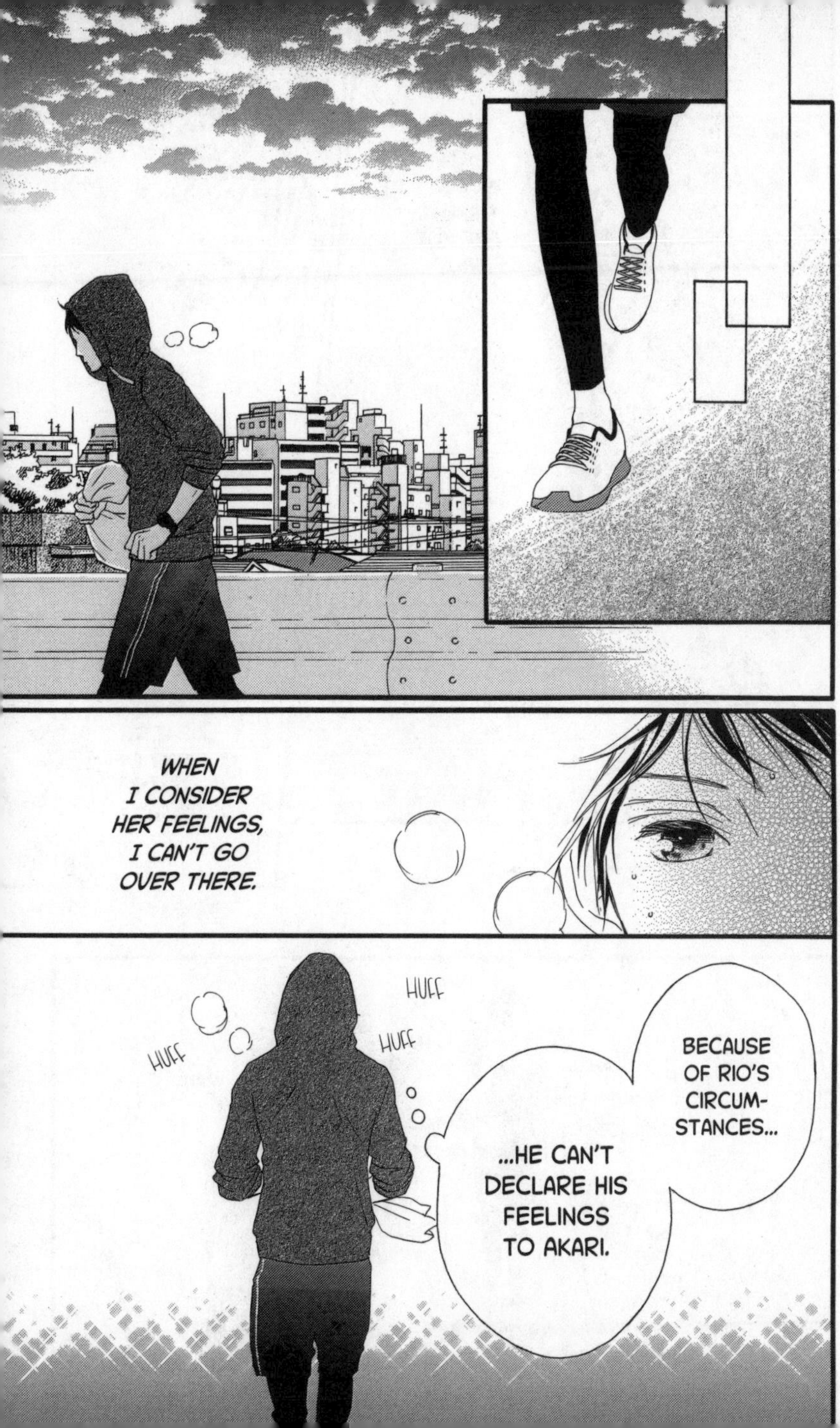
WHEN I CONSIDER HER FEELINGS, I CAN'T GO OVER THERE.
HUFF
HUFF
HUFF
BECAUSE OF RIO'S CIRCUM-STANCES...
...HE CAN'T DECLARE HIS FEELINGS TO AKARI.

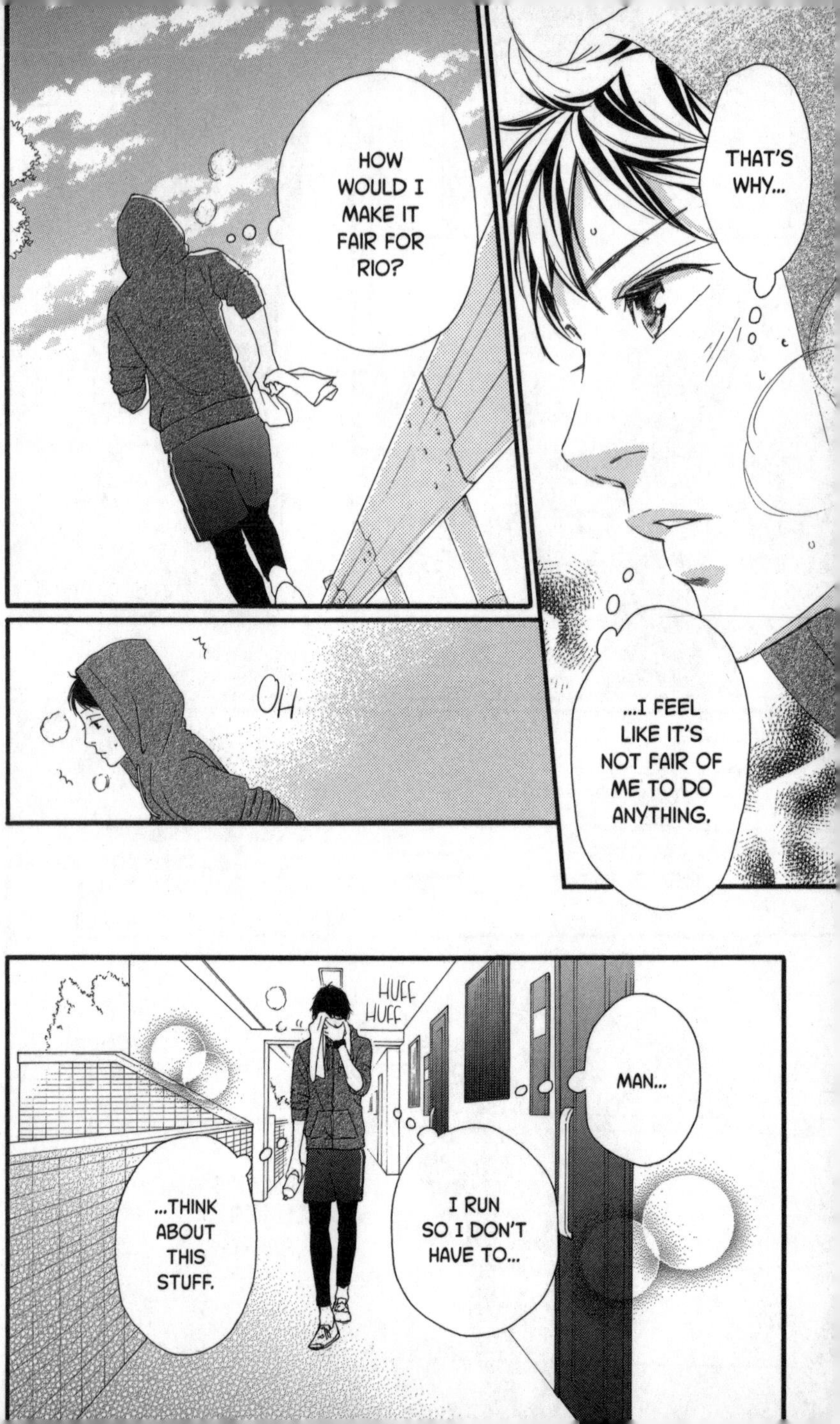
THAT'S WHY...
...I FEEL LIKE IT'S NOT FAIR OF ME TO DO ANYTHING.
HOW WOULD I MAKE IT FAIR FOR RIO?
OH
HUFF HUFF
MAN...
I RUN SO I DON'T HAVE TO...
...THINK ABOUT THIS STUFF.

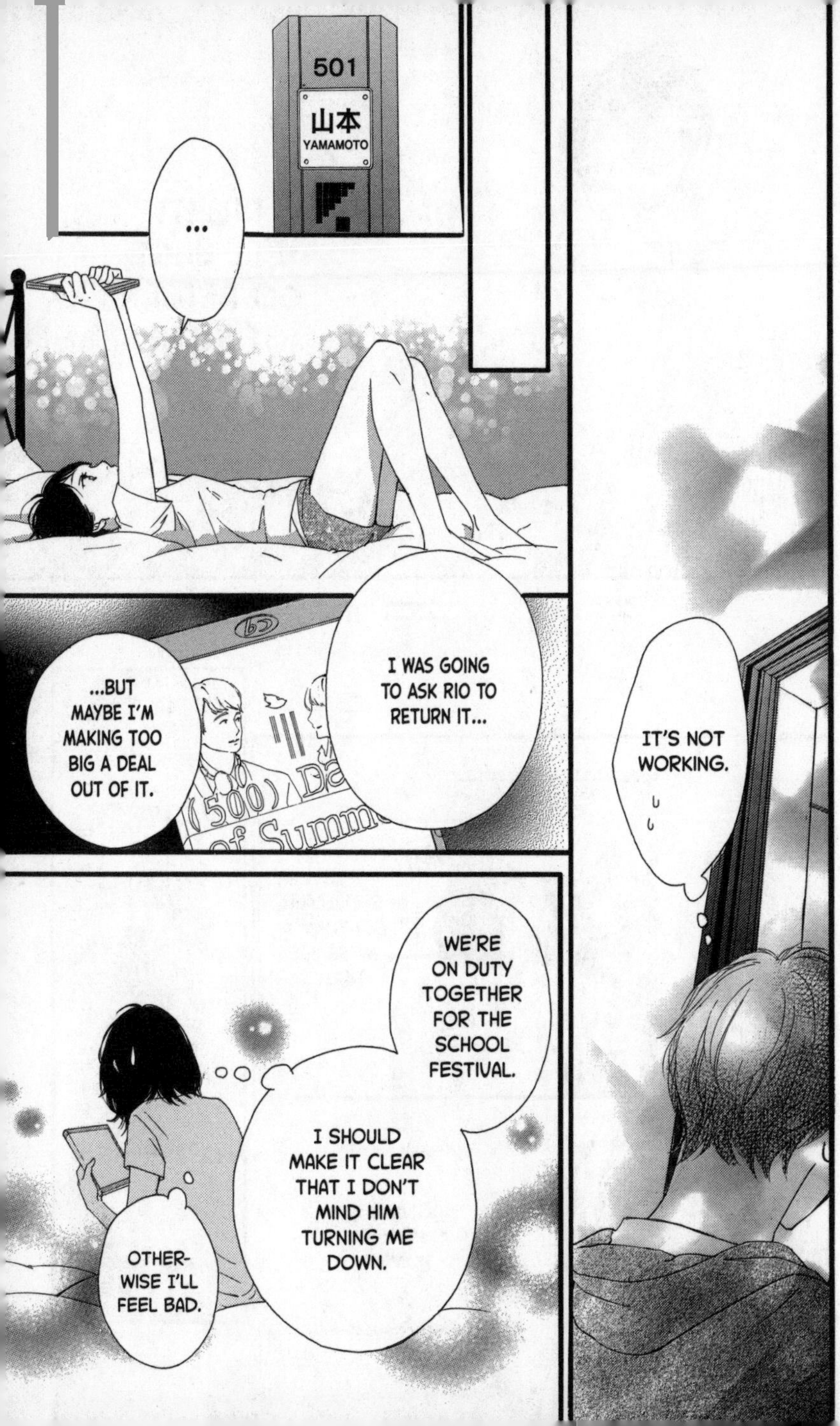
IT'S NOT WORKING.
501
山本
YAMAMOTO
...
I WAS GOING TO ASK RIO TO RETURN IT...
...BUT MAYBE I'M MAKING TOO BIG A DEAL OUT OF IT.
WE'RE ON DUTY TOGETHER FOR THE SCHOOL FESTIVAL.
I SHOULD MAKE IT CLEAR THAT I DON'T MIND HIM TURNING ME DOWN.
OTHER-WISE I'LL FEEL BAD.

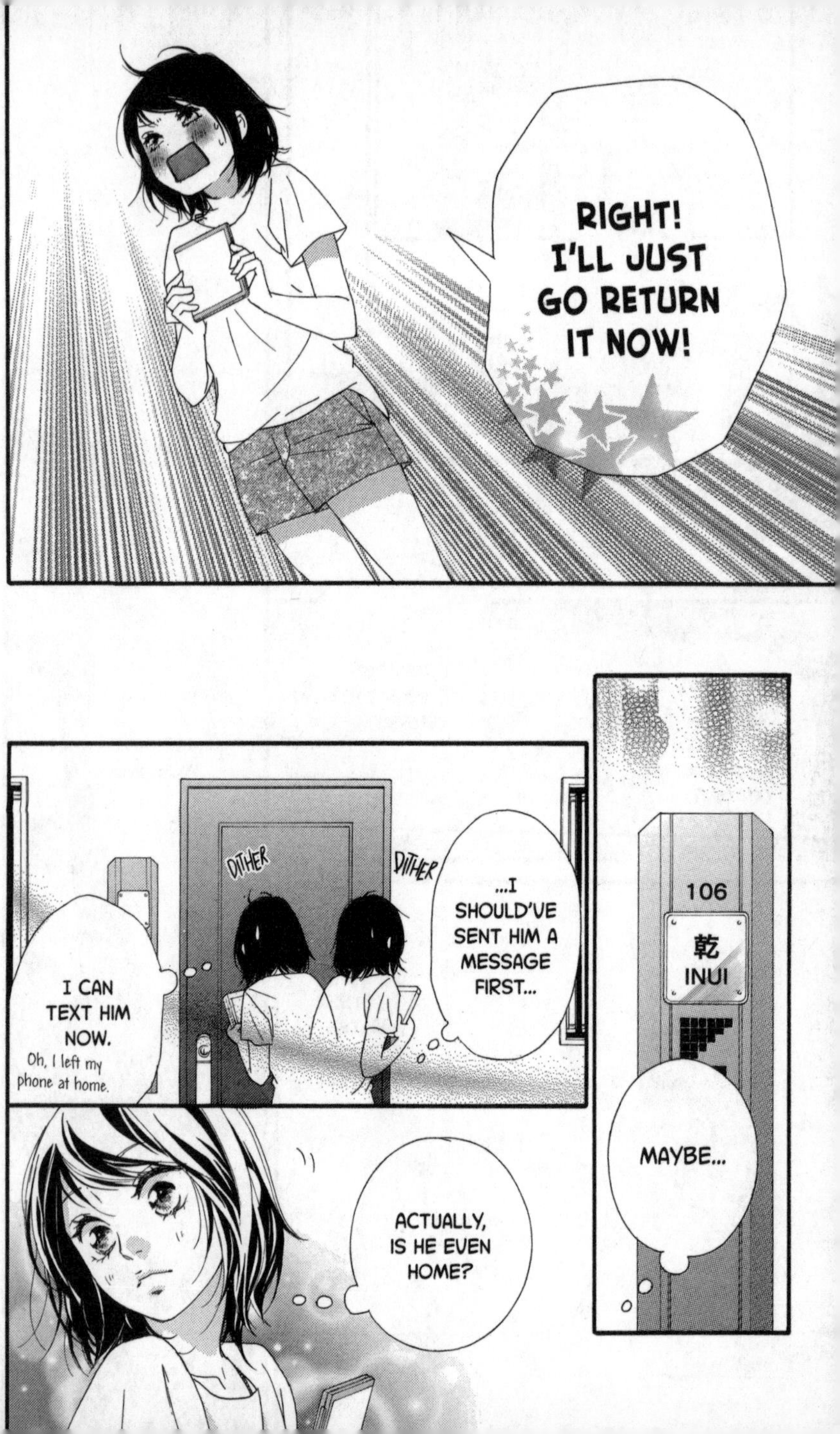
RIGHT! I'LL JUST GO RETURN IT NOW!
106
乾
INUI
MAYBE...
DITHER
DITHER
...I SHOULD'VE SENT HIM A MESSAGE FIRST...
I CAN TEXT HIM NOW.
Oh, I left my phone at home.
ACTUALLY, IS HE EVEN HOME?

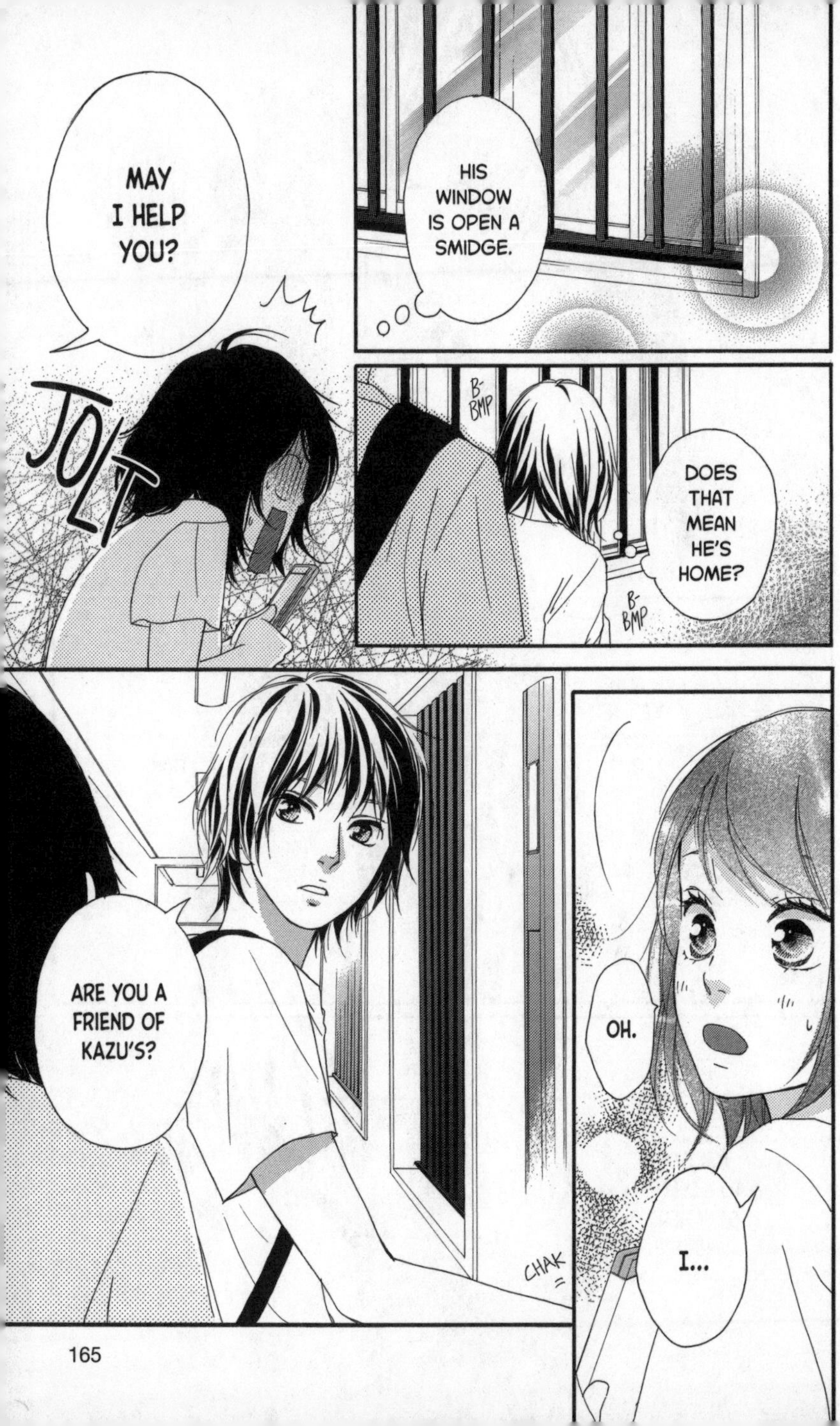
HIS WINDOW IS OPEN A SMIDGE.
B-BMP
DOES THAT MEAN HE'S HOME?
B-BMP
MAY I HELP YOU?
JOLT
OH.
I...
ARE YOU A FRIEND OF KAZU'S?
CHAK

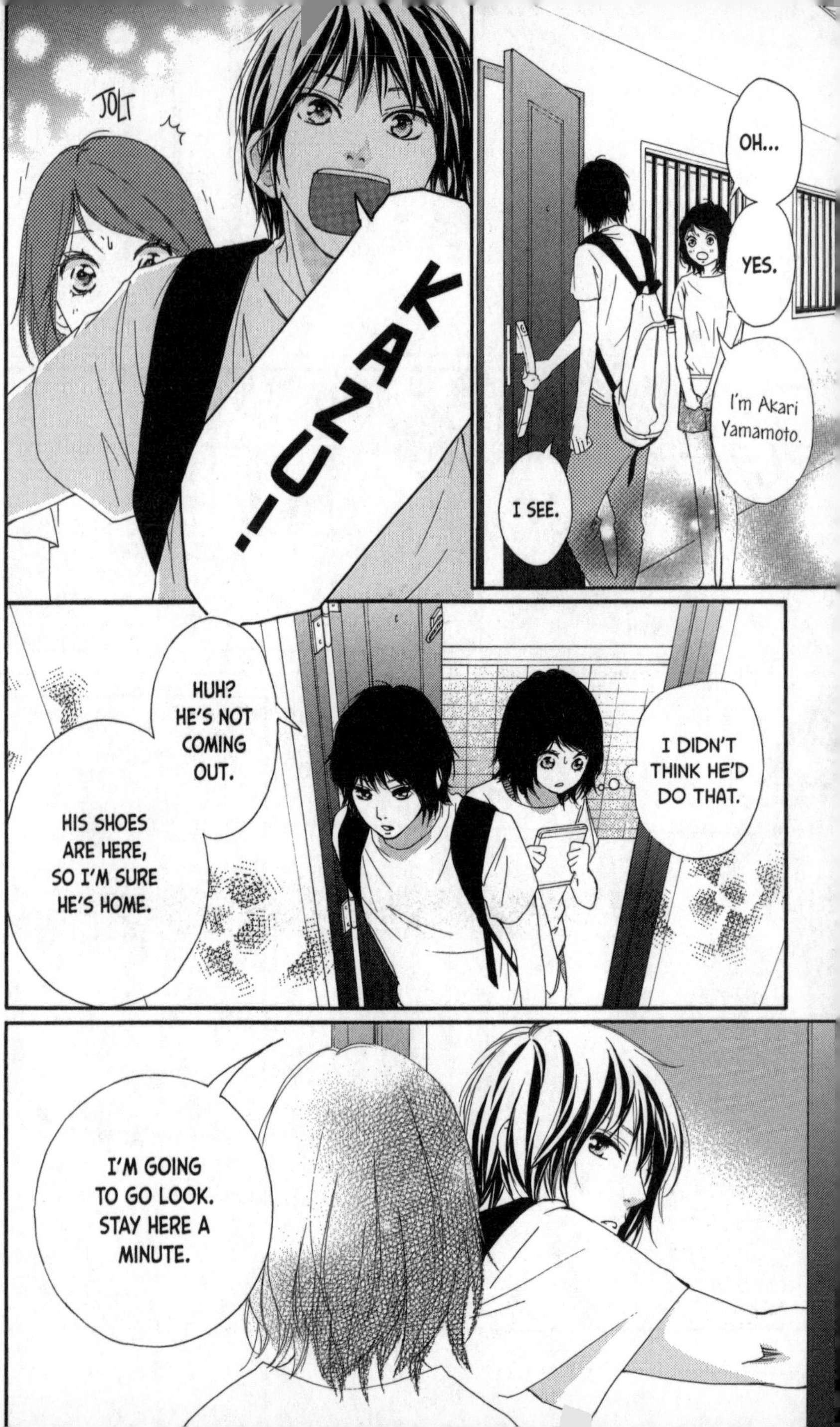
OH...
YES.
I'm Akari Yamamoto.
I SEE.
JOLT
KAZU—!
I DIDN'T THINK HE'D DO THAT.
HUH? HE'S NOT COMING OUT.
HIS SHOES ARE HERE, SO I'M SURE HE'S HOME.
I'M GOING TO GO LOOK. STAY HERE A MINUTE.

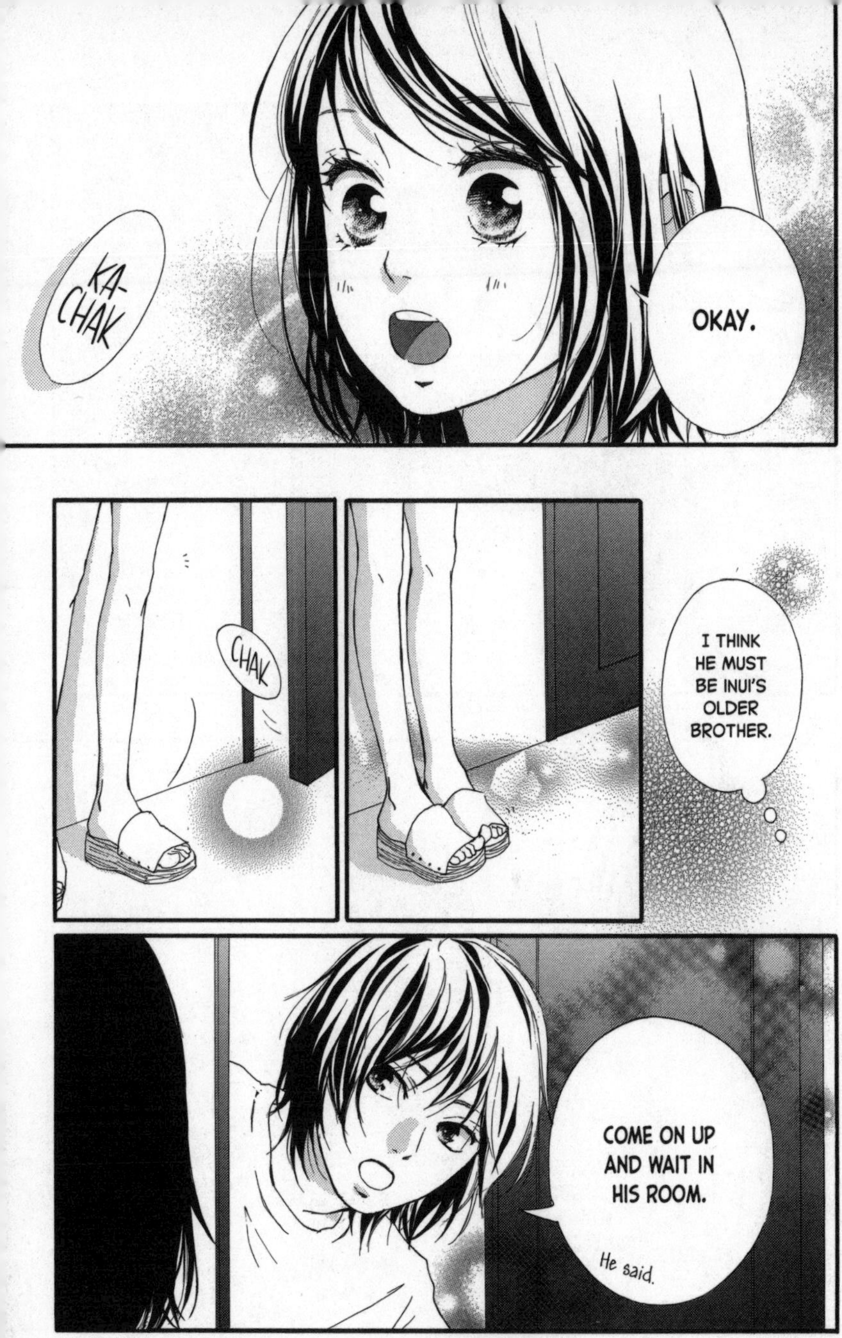
OKAY.
KA-CHAK
I THINK HE MUST BE INUI'S OLDER BROTHER.
CHAK
COME ON UP AND WAIT IN HIS ROOM.
He said.

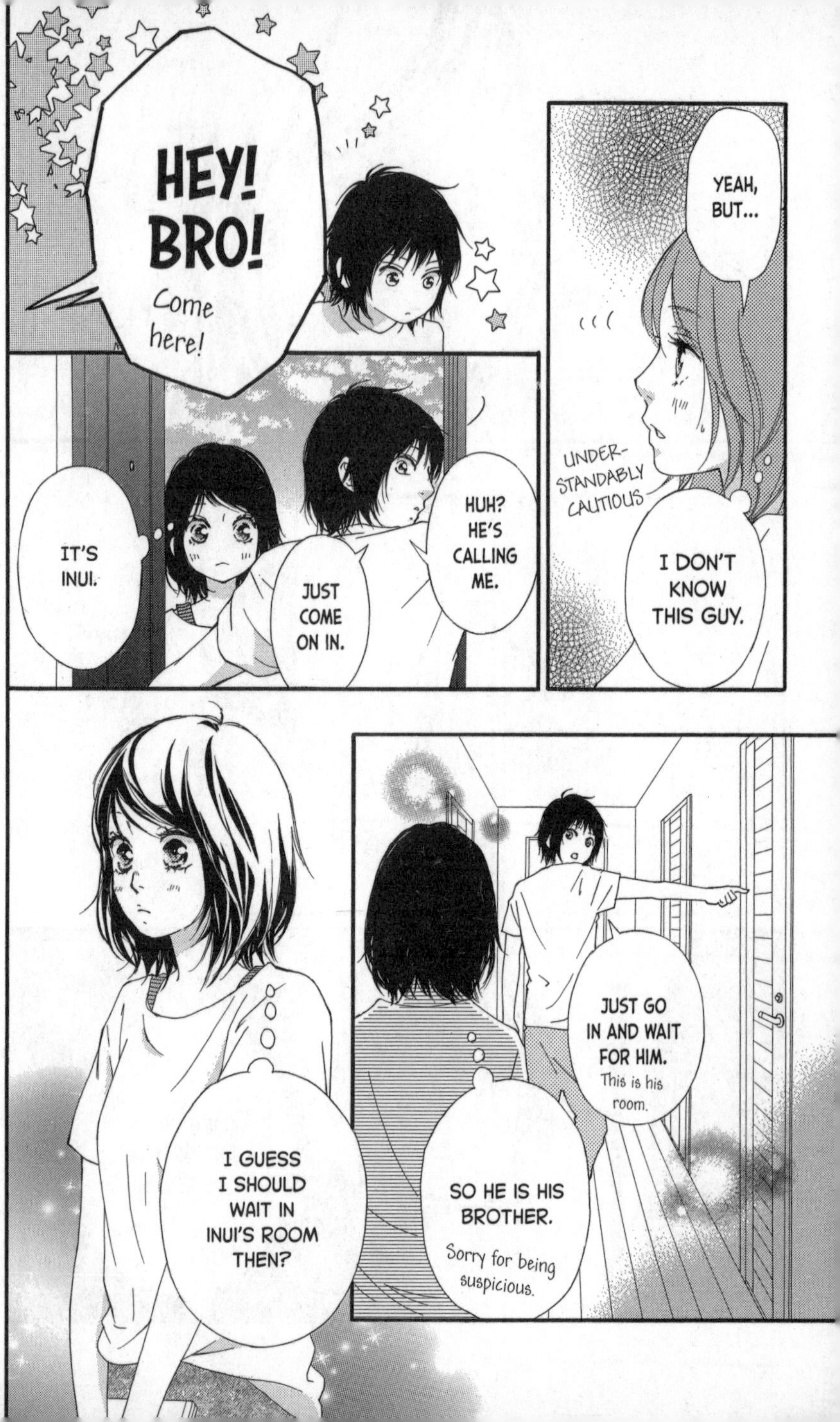
YEAH, BUT...
UNDER-STANDABLY CAUTIOUS
I DON'T KNOW THIS GUY.
HEY! BRO! Come here!
HUH? HE'S CALLING ME.
JUST COME ON IN.
IT'S INUI.
JUST GO IN AND WAIT FOR HIM.
This is his room.
SO HE IS HIS BROTHER.
Sorry for being suspicious.
I GUESS I SHOULD WAIT IN INUI'S ROOM THEN?

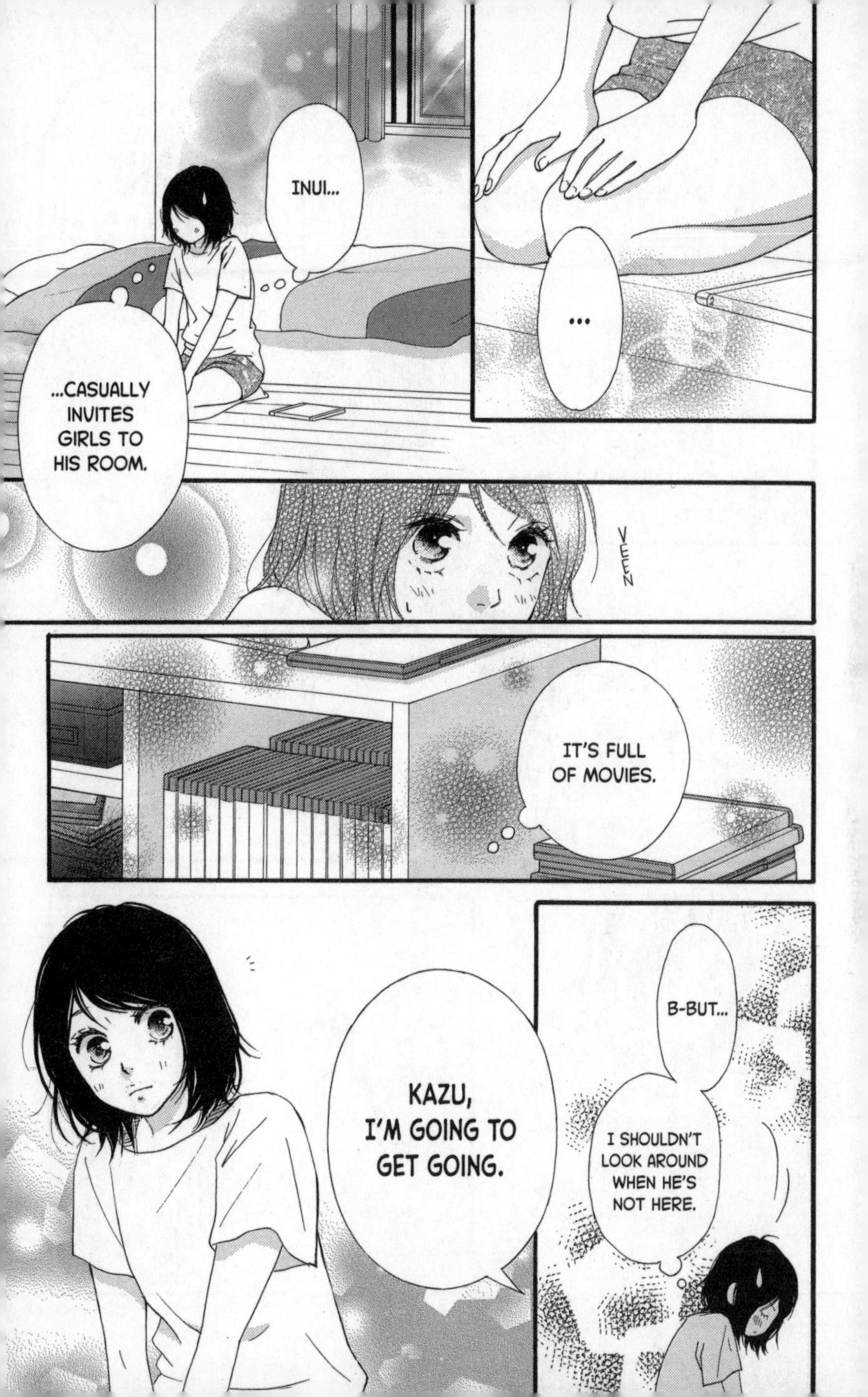
...
INUI...
...CASUALLY INVITES GIRLS TO HIS ROOM.
VEEN
IT'S FULL OF MOVIES.
B-BUT...
I SHOULDN'T LOOK AROUND WHEN HE'S NOT HERE.
KAZU, I'M GOING TO GET GOING.

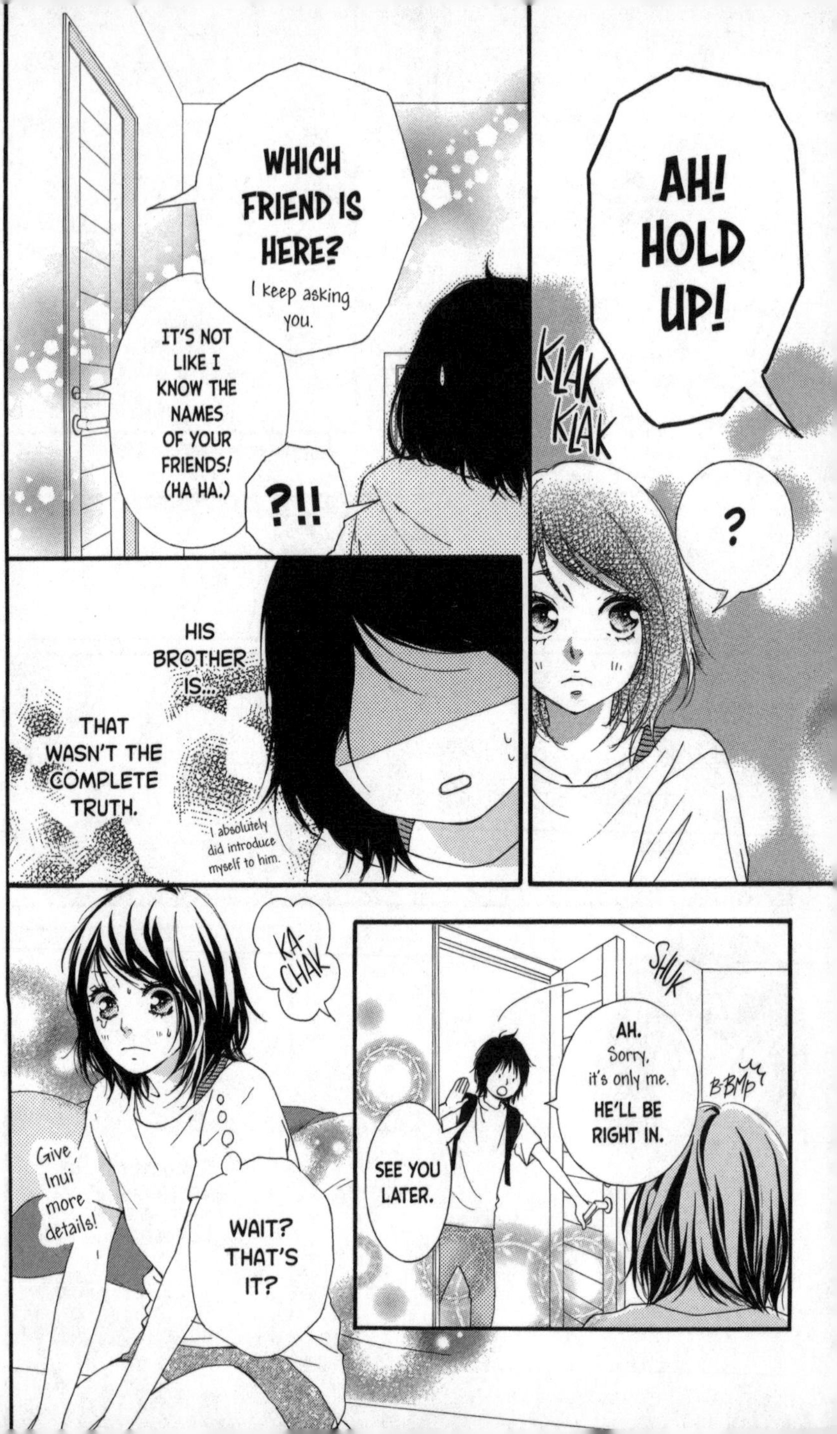
AH! HOLD UP!
KLAK KLAK
?
WHICH FRIEND IS HERE?
I keep asking you.
IT'S NOT LIKE I KNOW THE NAMES OF YOUR FRIENDS! (HA HA.)
?!!
HIS BROTHER IS...
THAT WASN'T THE COMPLETE TRUTH.
I absolutely did introduce myself to him.
SHUK
AH. Sorry, it's only me. HE'LL BE RIGHT IN.
B-BMP
SEE YOU LATER.
KA-CHAK
Give Inui more details!
WAIT? THAT'S IT?

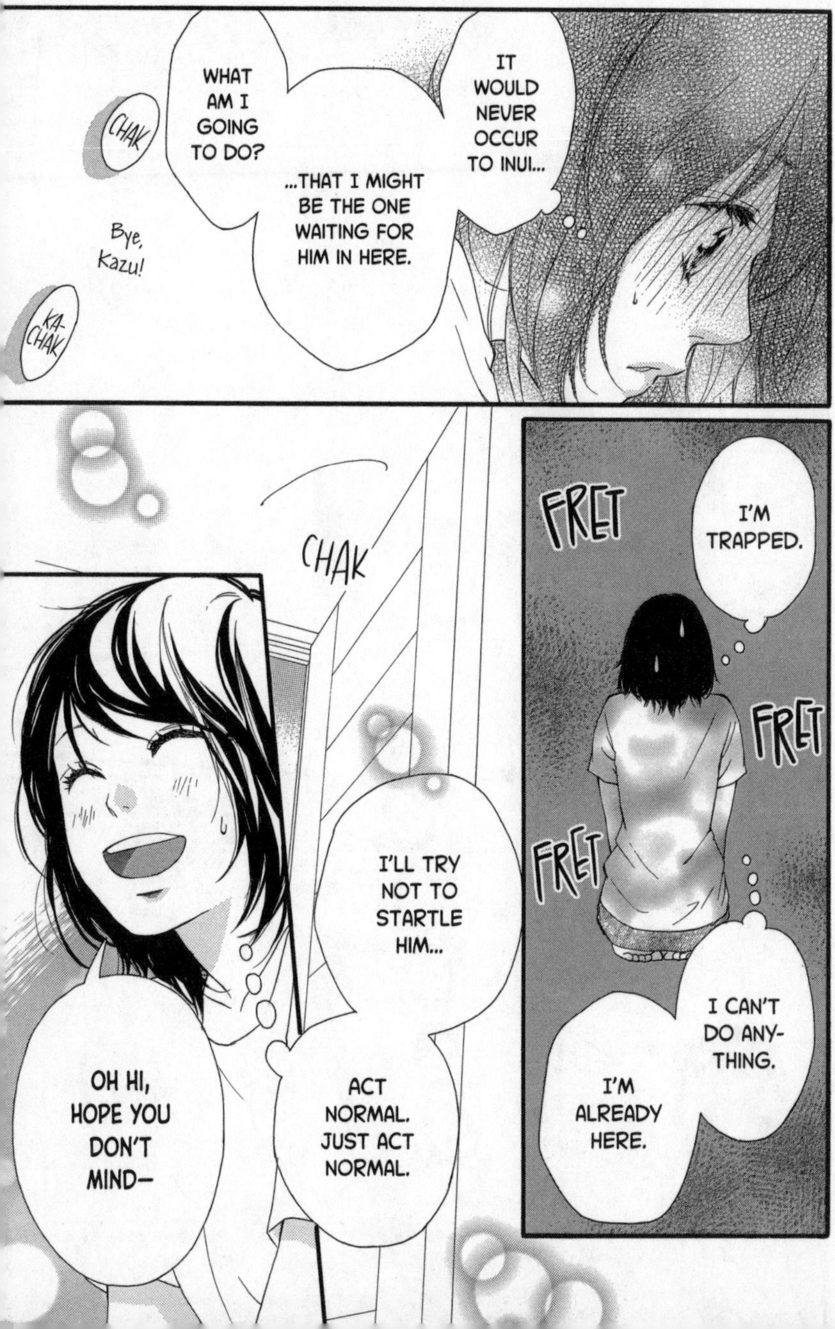
IT WOULD NEVER OCCUR TO INUI...
...THAT I MIGHT BE THE ONE WAITING FOR HIM IN HERE.
WHAT AM I GOING TO DO?
CHAK
Bye, Kazu!
KA-CHAK
I'M TRAPPED.
FRET
FRET
FRET
I CAN'T DO ANYTHING.
I'M ALREADY HERE.
CHAK
I'LL TRY NOT TO STARTLE HIM...
ACT NORMAL. JUST ACT NORMAL.
OH HI, HOPE YOU DON'T MIND—

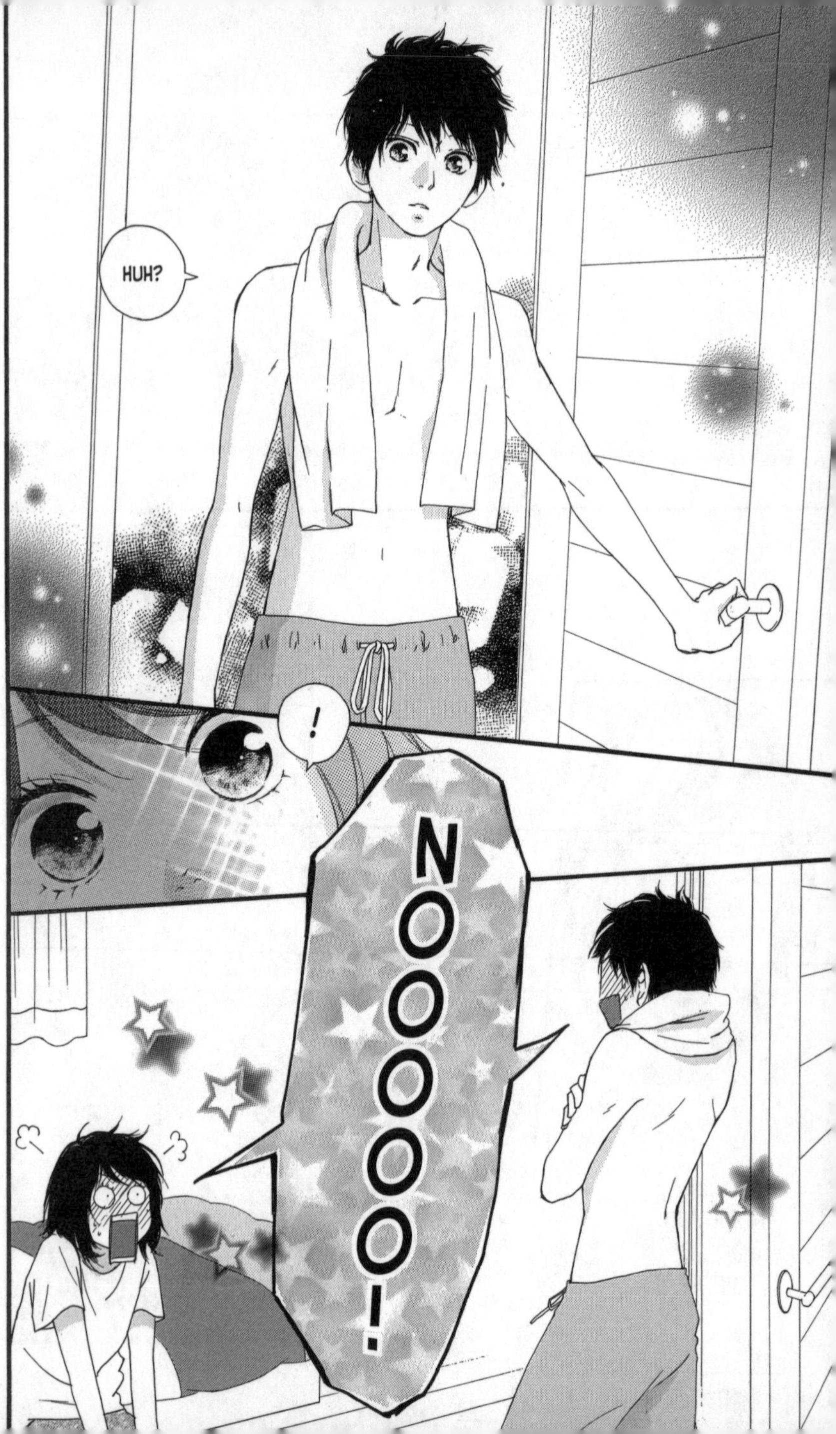
HUH?
!
NOOOOOO!

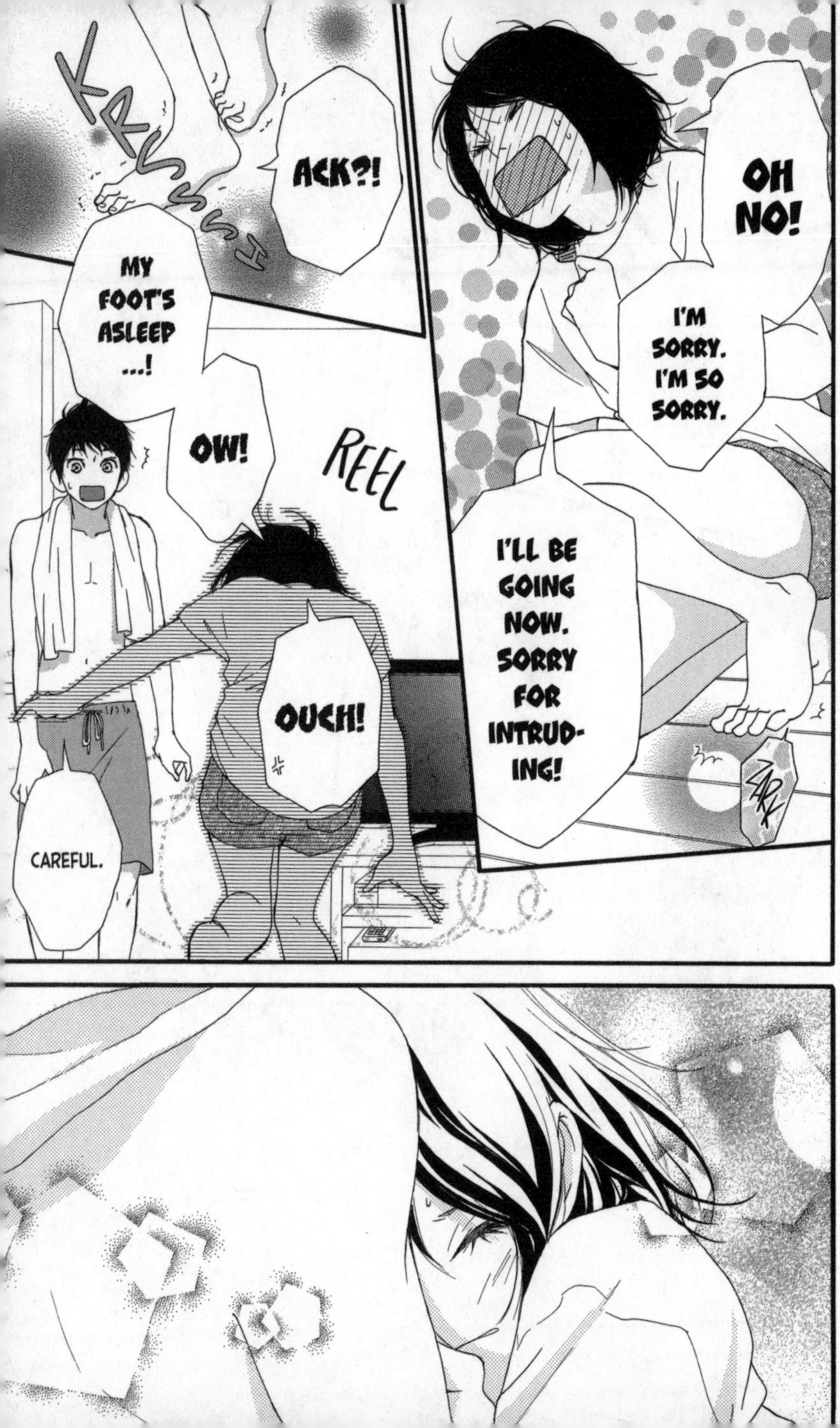
OH NO!
I'M SORRY. I'M SO SORRY.
I'LL BE GOING NOW. SORRY FOR INTRUD-ING!
ZARK
ACK?!
KRUNCH
MY FOOT'S ASLEEP ...!
OW!
REEL
OUCH!
CAREFUL.

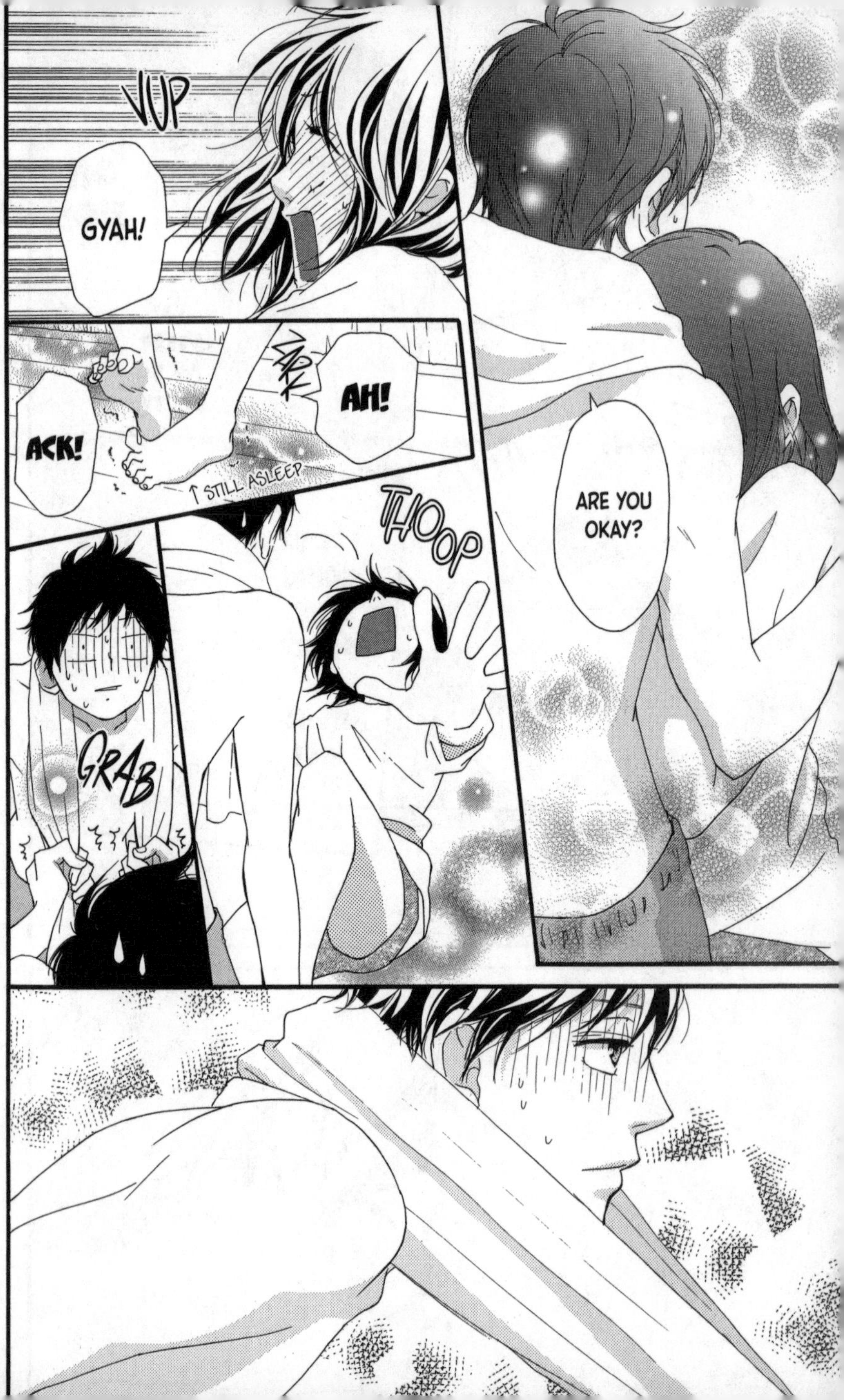
ARE YOU OKAY?
VUP
GYAH!
ZARK
AH!
ACK!
↑ STILL ASLEEP
THOOP
GRAB

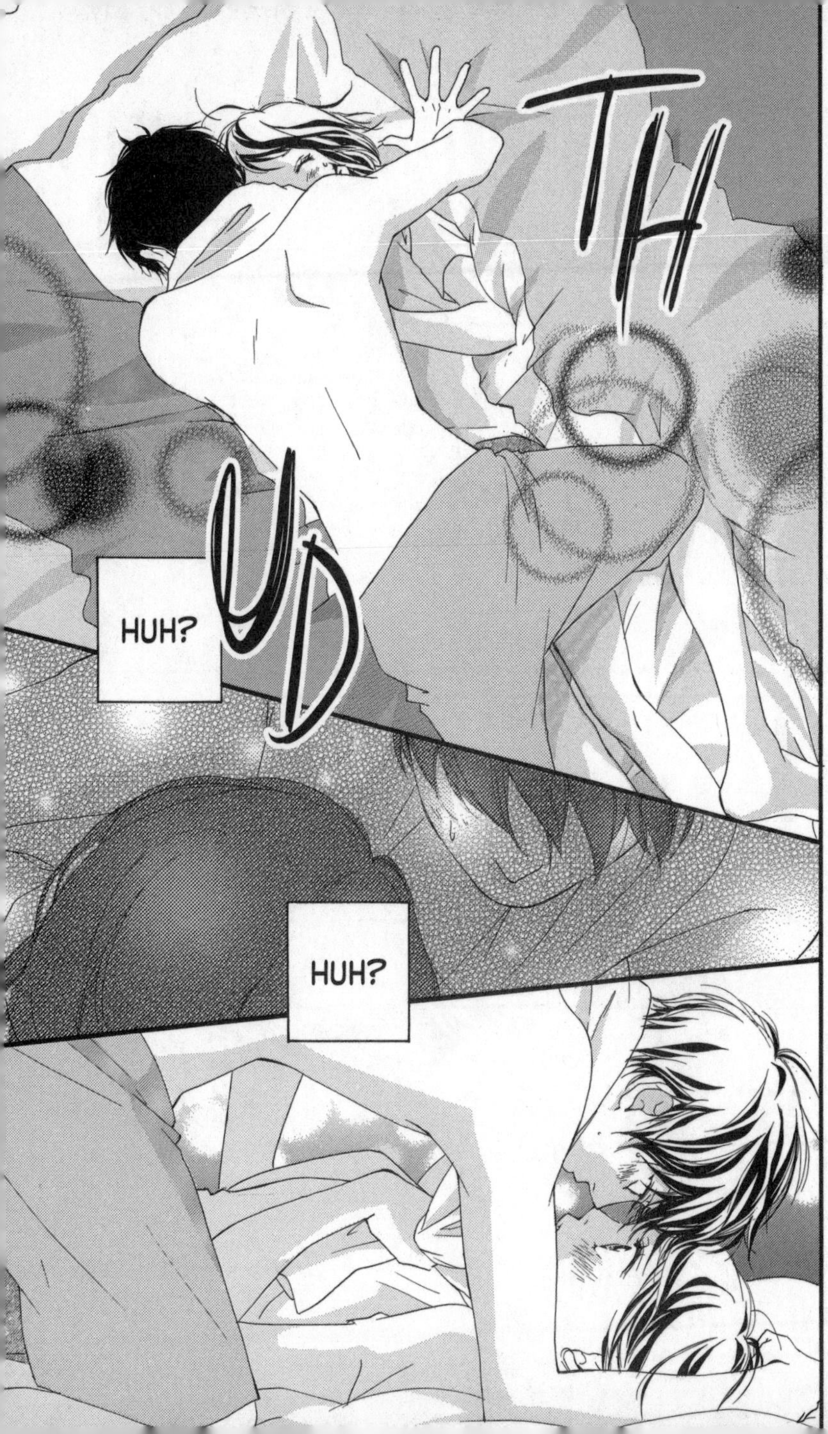
THUD
HUH?
HUH?

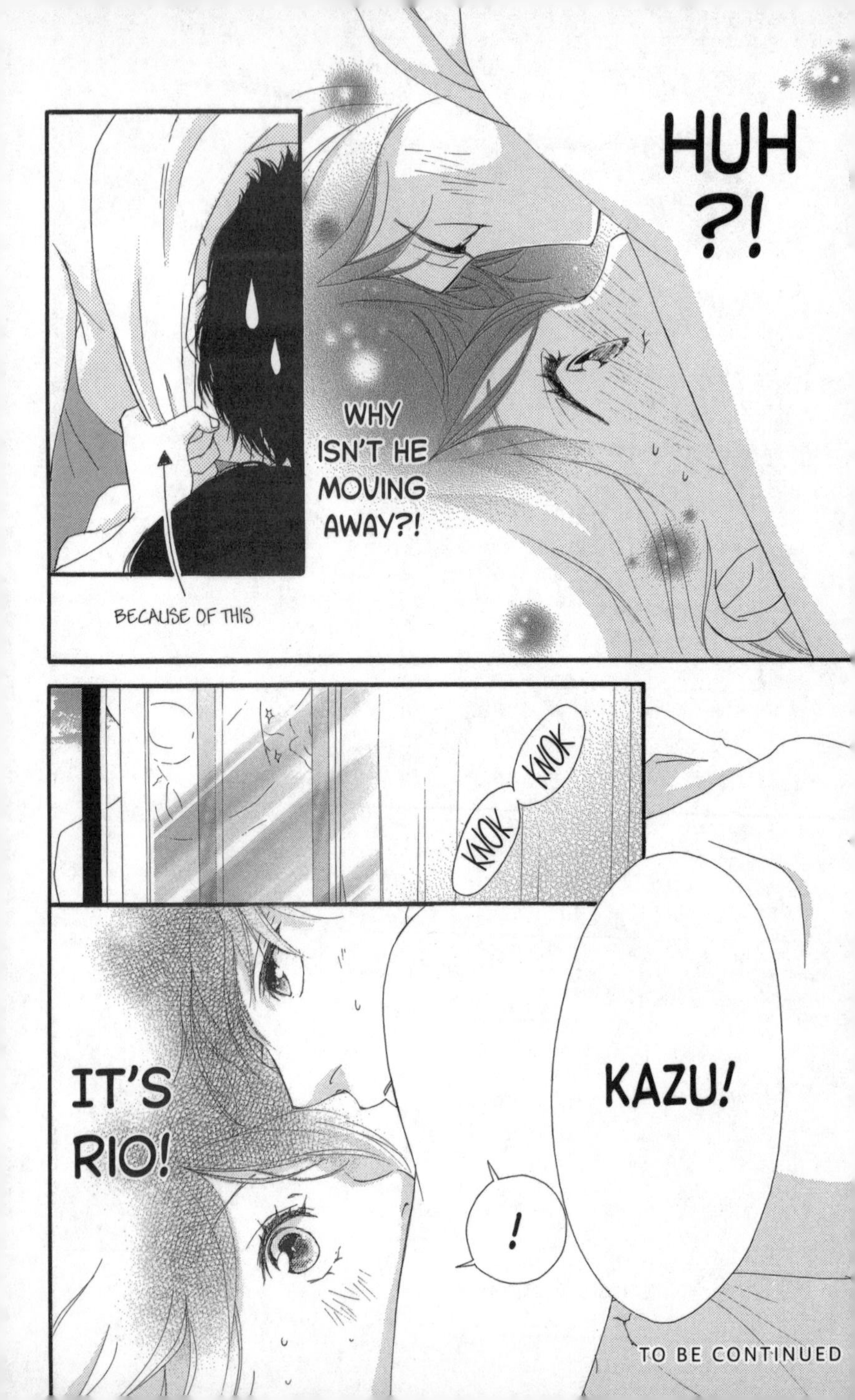
HUH ?!
WHY ISN'T HE MOVING AWAY?!
BECAUSE OF THIS
KNOK KNOK
KAZU!
!
IT'S RIO!
TO BE CONTINUED

AFTERWORD

Thank you very much for reading this through to the end!

In this volume, Kazuomi, who had been highly unaware most of the time, is now more complex and manly, shall we say. He must be going through a lot of turmoil because of this, and I'm having so much fun drawing him this way. I'm sure I can go on to show you all different sides of Kazuomi in his awakening.

Not just with Kazuomi, but when any character undergoes a transformation, I get very excited depicting that moment of change. (It's too much fun.) At the same time, in order to show that moment, I am very careful to draw all the events that lead up to it. Akari, Yuna, Rio and Kazuomi are all still growing. There will be many more moments that I will need to draw. I'll try hard to convey them to you so that I'm not the only one enjoying it. I'm hoping you'll join me in feeling all fluttery about those moments. And if you anticipate who is going to make the next move, I'll be very happy. Will it be this character? Or will this character make the first move? Or maybe...?

See you in the next volume!

Io Sakisaka

I brought back some sweets from my trip to share with my assistants. I regret my immaturity in opening the packages before my assistants arrived. On the other hand, I recognize my high level of self-knowledge in that I made sure to buy extra...

Io Sakisaka

Born on June 8, Io Sakisaka made her debut as a manga creator with *Sakura, Chiru*. Her series *Strobe Edge* and *Ao Haru Ride* are published by VIZ Media's Shojo Beat imprint. *Ao Haru Ride* was adapted into an anime series in 2014, and *Love Me, Love Me Not* will be an animated feature film. In her spare time, Sakisaka likes to paint things and sleep.

Love Me, Love Me Not

Vol. 5
Shojo Beat Edition

STORY AND ART BY
Io Sakisaka

Adaptation/Nancy Thistlethwaite
Translation/JN Productions
Touch-Up Art & Lettering/Sara Linsley
Design/Yukiko Whitley
Editor/Nancy Thistlethwaite

OMOI, OMOWARE, FURI, FURARE © 2015 by Io Sakisaka
All rights reserved.
First published in Japan in 2015 by SHUEISHA Inc., Tokyo.
English translation rights arranged by SHUEISHA Inc.

Printed in the U.S.A.

Published by VIZ Media, LLC
P.O. Box 77010
San Francisco, CA 94107

10 9 8 7 6 5 4 3 2 1
First printing, November 2020

PARENTAL ADVISORY
LOVE ME, LOVE ME NOT is rated T for Teen and
is recommended for ages 13 and up. This story
centers around teenage relationships.

 MEDIA

viz.com   shojobeat.com

Ao Haru Ride

STORY AND ART BY
IO SAKISAKA

Futaba Yoshioka thought all boys were loud and obnoxious until she met Kou Tanaka in junior high. But as soon as she realized she really liked him, he had already moved away because of family issues. Now, in high school, Kou has reappeared, but is he still the same boy she fell in love with?

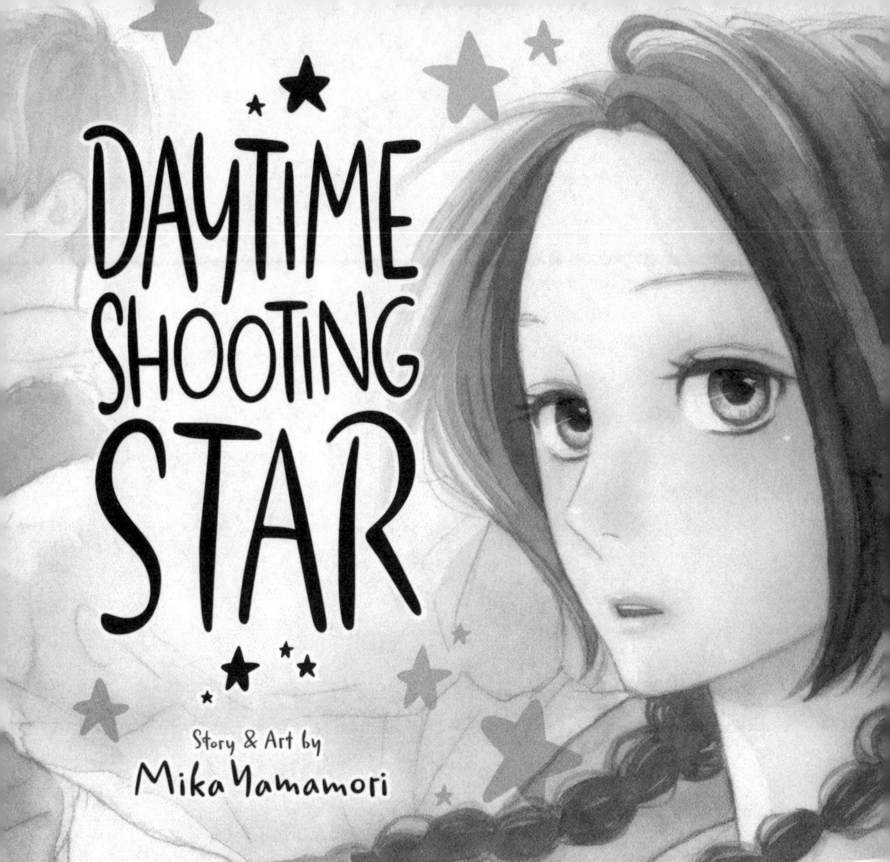

DAYTIME SHOOTING STAR

Story & Art by
Mika Yamamori

Small town girl Suzume moves to Tokyo and finds her heart caught between two men!

After arriving in Tokyo to live with her uncle, Suzume collapses in a nearby park when she remembers once seeing a shooting star during the day. A handsome stranger brings her to her new home and tells her they'll meet again. Suzume starts her first day at her new high school sitting next to a boy who blushes furiously at her touch. And her homeroom teacher is none other than the handsome stranger!

VIZ

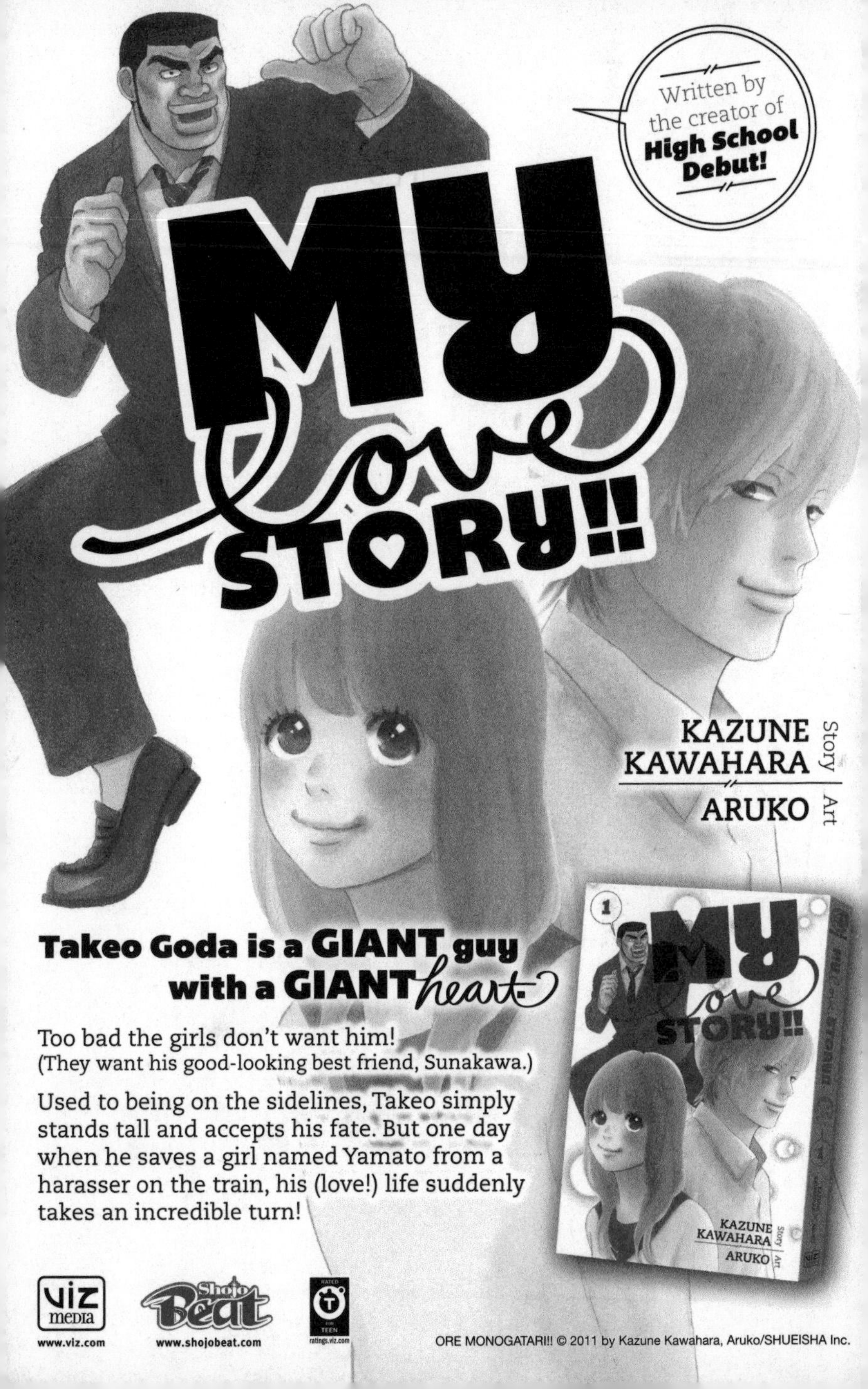

Written by the creator of High School Debut!
MY love STORY!!
KAZUNE KAWAHARA Story
ARUKO Art
Takeo Goda is a GIANT guy with a GIANT heart.
Too bad the girls don't want him! (They want his good-looking best friend, Sunakawa.)
Used to being on the sidelines, Takeo simply stands tall and accepts his fate. But one day when he saves a girl named Yamato from a harasser on the train, his (love!) life suddenly takes an incredible turn!
1
MY love STORY!!
KAZUNE KAWAHARA Story
ARUKO Art
viz media
www.viz.com
Shojo Beat
www.shojobeat.com
RATED T TEEN
ratings.viz.com
ORE MONOGATARI!! © 2011 by Kazune Kawahara, Aruko/SHUEISHA Inc.

Stop!

You may be reading the wrong way.

In keeping with the original Japanese comic format, this book reads from right to left—so action, sound effects and word balloons are completely reversed to preserve the orientation of the original artwork. Check out the diagram shown here to get the hang of things, and then turn to the other side of the book to get started!

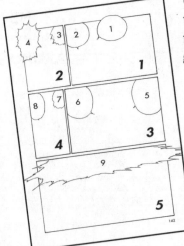